Bobbi

SELLING OUT

Selling Out

Academic Freedom
and the Corporate Market

HOWARD WOODHOUSE

Kinderdine

To Robbilee

Best wishes

Howard

McGill-Queen's University Press

Montreal & Kingston · London · Ithaca

© McGill-Queen's University Press 2009
ISBN-978-0-7735-3580-0

Legal deposit third quarter 2009
Bibliothèque nationale du Québec

Printed in Canada on acid-free paper that is 100% ancient forest free (100% post-consumer recycled), processed chlorine free.

This book has been published with the help of a grant from the Canadian Federation for the Humanities and Social Sciences, through the Aid to Scholarly Publications Programme, using funds provided by the Social Sciences and Humanities Research Council of Canada.

McGill-Queen's University Press acknowledges the support of the Canada Council for the Arts for our publishing program. We also acknowledge the financial support of the Government of Canada through the Book Publishing Industry Development Program (BPIDP) for our publishing activities.

Permission to publish extracts from the following articles and chapters has been obtained:
    In chapter 1, sections of my article "The Market Model of Education and the Threat to Canadian Universities," *Encounters on Education* 2 (2001): 105–22. (Permission of the editor.) In chapter 5, sections of my chapter "Evaluating University Teaching and Learning: Taking a Whiteheadian Turn," in *Alfred North Whitehead on Learning and Education*, ed. Frank G. Riffert, 385–402 (Newcastle: Cambridge Scholars Press, 2005). (Permission of Cambridge Scholars Press.) In chapter 7, sections of my article "A Process Approach to Community-Based Education: The People's Free University of Saskatchewan," *Interchange* 36, 1–2 (2005): 121–38. (Permission of Springer, the publishers.)

National Library of Canada Cataloguing in Publication
Woodhouse, Howard Robert, 1947–
    Selling out : academic freedom and the corporate market / Howard Woodhouse.
Includes bibliographical references and index.
ISBN 978-0-7735-3580-0
    1. Academic freedom – Canada. 2. University autonomy – Canada. 3. Business and education – Canada. 4. Higher education and state – Canada. I. Title.

LB2329.8.C2W66 2009   378.1'2130971   C2009-901280-4

Typeset in Sabon 10.5/13
by Infoscan Collette, Quebec City

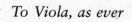

To Viola, as ever

Contents

Acknowledgments

The University of Saskatchewan has provided support for my work in various ways. The University Sabbatical Appeals Committee recommended a sabbatical leave during which I completed a substantial portion of the book. The College of Education awarded me a McIntosh Release Stipend and the University Publications Committee a manuscript preparation grant. The Department of Educational Foundations has provided a convivial intellectual home in which faculty and students have challenged and constantly refined my views.

For more than fifteen years, the co-directors of the University of Saskatchewan Process Philosophy Research Unit – Professors Mark Flynn, Bob Regnier, Ed Thompson, and Adam Scarfe – have enabled me to pose questions otherwise considered unspeakable. Professors Don Cochrane, Len Findlay, Ivan Kelly, Rhonda Love, Dianne Miller, Bill Notz, Jack Priestley, Peter Purdue, and John Valleau all passed on material that shed light on the erosion of academic freedom and university autonomy, while Henry Kloppenburg shared a steady stream of information on legal and medical matters, and Jacques Pauwels forwarded books and articles pertinent to the project. Stuart Bevan; Michael Collins, professor emeritus of the University of Saskatchewan; Allen Gunderson; Professor Claire Polster of the University of Regina; Professor Murray Scharf, former dean of education of the University of Saskatchewan; and Professor Jennifer Sumner of the Ontario Institute for Studies in Education at the University of Toronto all read parts of the manuscript and made numerous suggestions for improvement. Gerry Klein of the *Saskatoon StarPhoenix* was supportive of the project during his tenure as university editor, and Philip Jackman, editor at the *Globe and Mail*, published two articles of mine in the late 1980s when the threat to academic freedom was largely ignored. Eileen Herteis, director of the Teaching and Learning Centre at Mount Allison University, provided guidance in drawing up the open-ended interviews, Ginny Brown typed a good deal of the manuscript, and Mara Kumarian did the index.

More than thirty faculty, staff, and students at different universities graciously gave their time to be interviewed, providing insights that would otherwise have remained obscure. University administrators across the country declined to be interviewed, refused to sign the release form, or questioned the validity of the consent form that had been approved by the University of Saskatchewan Behavioural Research Ethics Board.

I am grateful to the two readers for McGill-Queen's University Press who provided valuable suggestions for improving the manuscript and to the following journals for publishing articles that prepared the ground for this book: *Canadian and International Education*, *Compare*, *Encounters on Education*, *European Education*, *Inquiry*, *Interchange*, and *Process Papers*.

I would also to thank the dedicated staff at McGill-Queen's University Press, who have provided strong support in many ways. Senior editor Dr Don Akenson first showed interest in the potential of the book and maintained his belief in its importance throughout. Deputy editor Kyla Madden provided insights about how to improve the manuscript, all of which proved invaluable. Coordinating editor Joan McGilvray gave solid advice in the book's final states, and copyeditor Joanne Richardson was patient and precise in her exacting work.

Professor Ian Winchester of the University of Calgary has provided constant support in all sorts of ways throughout the years. I am also grateful to Andrew Mason of Scott, Phelps, and Mason, who read the entire manuscript, as did Robert Martin, Professor Emeritus of Law of the University of Western Ontario.

John McMurtry, university professor emeritus at the University of Guelph, has been a continuing source of inspiration both for the theoretical framework of the book and for his careful reading and commentary on significant parts of the manuscript.

Viola, my wife, has sustained my enthusiasm throughout the long process of writing, acting as loving mentor when I needed the encouragement to continue with the work. Without her love and support, the book would not have seen the light of day.

SELLING OUT

Do not fear to be eccentric in opinion, because every opinion once eccentric is now accepted.

Bertrand Russell

Introduction

The whole tendency of modern prose is away from concreteness.

George Orwell[1]

In the mid-1980s I lost my job at the University of Western Ontario. As coordinator of an office whose mission was the improvement of teaching and learning on campus, I criticized a faculty member known for his support for apartheid in South Africa in a letter to the university newspaper. He threatened to sue the paper. Having received a warning for this offence, I was later summarily dismissed for a report I had written about the future plans of the educational development office, which university administrators considered to be inadequate. Without the protection of tenure or academic freedom, I sued the university for wrongful dismissal, a process which took three years. The case was finally settled in my favour at the Ontario Human Rights Commission. These events accentuated my interest in academic freedom, and eventually I began to write about faculty whose jobs were similarly threatened.

I wrote *Selling Out: Academic Freedom and the Corporate Market* in order to understand and critically assess the influence of the corporate market on universities in Canada. Having published on this topic for two decades, I wanted to know more about the details of the process transforming higher education. My scholarship had been long on generalization and short on specifics, and I set out to make it more concrete.

This book is distinctive in several ways. First, it tells the story of some of those who have opposed the influence of the market on teaching and research at Canadian universities.[2] Their stories demonstrate the courage needed to resist the market model of education and the personal cost that such opposition can exact. At the same time, the case studies show that it is possible to redirect the wave sweeping over the academy and to dispel the myth that corporate control is inevitable. The market model is often portrayed as though it were the only way forward: a position encapsulated in the TINA syndrome, an acronym for Margaret Thatcher's phrase "there is no alternative." This determinist position contradicts rational and critical debate as well as the idea of universities as seats of learning, leaving little room for the articulation of alternative ways of understanding the world.[3]

Second, the book proposes a theoretical framework that makes sense of the details of each story, showing how they conform to the principles of the market model of education. I believe this critical framework enables both reader and author to understand not only what is happening in each case study but also how and why it is happening. Indeed, it raises the question of whether or not public universities *should* be run as private corporations. It does so by showing how the goals, motivations, methods, and standards of excellence of education are undermined by corporate market demands. Too often, this process goes unnoticed by university administrators and even faculty and students. The mechanistic discourse of corporate culture has expunged the language of education: subject-based disciplines and the professors who teach them have become "resource units"; students are no more than "educational consumers" or "revenue units"; curricula have become "program packages"; graduates are now "products"; and "competing in the global economy" has replaced the search for truth.[4] *Selling Out* provides a picture of the threat that the market model poses both to academic freedom and to university autonomy. It explicates the link between theory and practice, showing how each case is related to an underlying pattern of market-based logic, and it suggests how universities can free themselves from this stranglehold by engaging in liberating kinds of education and research.

The book also shows that academic freedom and institutional autonomy are internally related: any change in one results in a change in the other. The intellectual independence of the individual scholar is linked to the freedom of the entire community of which s/he is a part. Their collective autonomy requires strong institutional forms that enable universities to limit corporate market demands by ensuring that knowledge remains a public good rather than a private good. This means that governments have a responsibility to fund universities fully as the only places in society where the critical search for knowledge takes place. Unfortunately, governments and private corporations are united in their belief that the goal of university education and research is to increase corporate profit margins. There is a kind of pincer movement at work in which these two powerful external sources of funding have combined in order to change universities into instruments to enhance private wealth. And university administrations have done little to resist this move.

Furthermore, the use of case studies is consistent with the concept of "generalization" operant in the work of Alfred North Whitehead. In contrast to schooling, where the student should "painfully rise from the particular towards glimpses at general ideas," Whitehead believed that, "at the University he [sic] should start from general ideas and study their applications to concrete cases."[5] The overall rhythm of education enables the student to understand the relationship between the particular/concrete and the general/abstract. Similarly, the goal of *Selling Out* is to reveal the workings of the market model by relating its abstract principles to the concrete experience of those faculty members whose academic freedom has been violated. The book's methodology alternates between the concrete and the abstract, providing, at both the personal and institutional levels, insights that are denied to other modes of inquiry. I apply a critical understanding gained from the study of general ideas, but I am not content with abstract generalizations about the corporatization of universities; always, I connect such generalizations to the concrete facts that illuminate this process. The case studies are, in the words of David Kirp, "tales that signify beyond their particulars, to make sense of this new world."[6] My hope is that the tales I describe and analyze will resonate with the experience of the readers, be they professors, students, staff members, or general citizens living in a world where privatization has become the norm.

The case studies serve as a window opening onto the corporate domination of universities, which is subordinating their educational vocation to service functions for the market and the private sector. This, indeed, is another distinguishing feature of *Selling Out*. Rather than simply confronting the corporate market as a threat to the freedom of individual faculty members, it examines the underlying principles of the market model of education to show that they entail the repression or abandonment of the very basis of university life. No less than the power to subvert the entire system of university education and research is at stake. In concentrating on the increasing institutional suppression of, and selection against, academic freedom, my aim is to alert faculty and other readers to the danger of over-looking the sea change taking place in universities. This rapid process of change has become so much a part of the strategic restructuring of university life that we are in danger of succumbing to its anti-educational undertow, which is getting to be beyond our power either to question or to challenge.[7] And if knowledge disseminated by universities is not impartial, how will citizens learn to distinguish between reality and "the shadows on the corporate media cave"?[8]

Chapter 1 begins with a description of the key features of the corporate market, including the subordination of the critical search for knowledge to the maximization of stockholder value, and the replacement of the core educational function of universities with training for private market functions. A detailed critique of the market model then follows, based on a theoretical framework articulated by Canadian philosopher John McMurtry and bolstered by insights from other historians and social scientists. I explain the contradictions between the goals, motivations, methods, and standards of excellence of education and the market, and I provide examples of statements by prominent university administrators, economists, and business people that illustrate the depth of the refusal to recognize these opposing logics of value. The chapter concludes with an analysis of the Canadian Association of University Teachers' "Model Clause on Academic Freedom," which emphasizes the critical search for knowledge as a public good and enshrines it as a basic value in research and teaching.

The case studies in this book include two accounts of the experiences of faculty members at the University of Manitoba and the University of Toronto, respectively, whose academic freedom was truncated because they expressed views that were critical of agents in the corporate market. While the details of each case are quite different, they both involve faculty who spoke out in a scholarly way against the actions of a business corporation that was about to give substantial amounts of money to their respective universities. Rather than defending their academic freedom, university administrators proceeded to punish them for their views. More concerned with obtaining money from the corporate sector than with preserving academic freedom, deans and others disregarded the value of critically pursuing knowledge in favour of the market principle of monetary gain.

The first case study, which is presented in chapter 2, concerns Dr Vedanand, a professor of marketing at the University of Manitoba (U of M), who was punished for questioning the claims of a Xerox sales representative, having intervened in his presentation at a company-sponsored seminar on campus. When the issue went to arbitration, it was Dr Vedanand who was found to have "exceeded the acceptable limits of academic freedom" because "his conduct comprised a breach of etiquette."[9] Dr Vedanand's freedom to teach and engage in scholarly work was truncated and his position in the Faculty of Management seriously compromised. Nevertheless, opposition to the dean, a former vice-president of the Bank of Nova Scotia, strengthened among professors who disagreed with his policies to restructure the faculty and to accommodate corporate market demands. The result was the non-renewal of the dean's seven-year term. The case is not well known outside U of M, but it illustrates quite clearly how, twenty years ago, the market model was already undermining universities.

By contrast, the second case study, which is presented in chapter 3, is widely known. It concerns Dr Nancy Olivieri, director of the Heminoglobinopathy Program at the Hospital for Sick Children and professor of medicine at the University of Toronto, whose clinical trials revealed that Deferiprone (L1), a drug prescribed for the blood disorder thalassemia, could cause liver and heart damage in her patients. Despite threats of litigation from the drug's manufacturers, Apotex Inc, the research team of which Dr Olivieri was principal investigator proceeded to publish an article analyzing its findings in the *New England Journal of Medicine*. The hospital then relieved Dr Olivieri of her position as director of the Heminoglobinopathy Program, only reinstating her when considerable pressure was mounted on both the university and hospital by, among others, clinical experts from Oxford and Harvard. The issue, however, is still not resolved.[10]

Both cases suggest the need for a broad institutional analysis in which the influence of the market is viewed as a problem pervading the various functions of universities. Two other cases in this study are concerned directly with the broader question of the threat to university autonomy posed by the encroachment of the corporate market and its underlying logic. The first case, presented in chapter 4, concerns the growing commercialization at the University of Saskatchewan (U of S), where the presence of the Canadian Light

Source synchrotron as the country's most expensive scientific facility in a generation requires governments and the university to fund its capital and operating costs.[11] As a wholly owned facility of the U of S, large subventions of this kind endanger other areas of scholarship and research that is perceived to be of little immediate utility for generating private monetary wealth. The synchrotron's connection with the corporate market is made clear in its mission statement: "To operate an industry friendly, not-for-profit facility, such that continuous investments and developments anticipate customer requirements and ensure international competitiveness."[12] The need for Canada to compete in global markets drives the operations of the Canadian Light Source (CLS). The not-for-profit facility *must* achieve this overriding goal through public funding and development that satisfies the demands of corporate customers, anticipating their wants and adding value to their products through "innovation." The stated goals of the CLS ensure that costs and risks are socialized and monetary profits privatized. In order to channel funds towards those "high priority areas" of synchrotron-based research, the university administration has devised internal control mechanisms whose effect is to undermine institutional autonomy and limit academic freedom. The case exemplifies the same pattern as the previous ones: the goal of universities is no longer the critical pursuit of knowledge but, rather, the maximization of stockholder value.

Nor is this pattern confined to university research. Student evaluations of teaching (SETs) that indicate "customer satisfaction" rather than the extent to which learning has taken place are an inaccurate measure of the quality of a faculty member's teaching. The systemic inaccuracy of these evaluations stems from their market orientation. Patricia Marchak underlines this point in the following terms: "Customers are not evaluated. The point is to sell them something and make them want it and like it so that they or their sisters will return for more. Customers are always right, and they cannot be failed."[13] Yet, such questionnaires continue to be used at most Canadian universities despite the fact that they may well hinder the critical questioning of one's presuppositions, which is what characterizes learning. The case study presented in chapter 5 examines the views of faculty and students interviewed at the U of S about SETs, placing them in the wider context of the literature about these evaluations. Almost all of those interviewed questioned their validity as a guide to the quality of teaching and learning and considered them a threat to the goals of education. As James Coté and Anton Allahar show, "evaluations can prevent professors from challenging students to work harder and think about issues in transformative ways that will help them grow intellectually in self-understanding and understanding about the world."[14] Faculty are then cast in the role of "customer service representatives"[15] whose goal is to sell a product to their customers. In order to facilitate challenging intellectual work and transformative growth among students, a different kind of evaluation procedure could easily be introduced – one that assesses learning before, during, and after classes. This would enable what students have actually learned, rather than their "customer satisfaction,[16] to emerge as the main criterion for determining the quality of teaching. This case study provides insights into an alternative method of evaluating teaching – one that overcomes the anti-educational bias of the market model.

Chapter 6 addresses a question raised in the first chapter: Why do certain university administrators refuse to acknowledge the opposing logics of value characterizing education and the market, respectively? Echoing statements in a World Bank report, several university presidents show how they subscribe to the market's closed value system, whose "assumed structure of worth rules out thought beyond it."[17] Any system that challenges the narrow assumptions of this particular value program is ruled out a priori. Fortunately, some university presidents do not subscribe to this view, questioning the sagacity of the federal government's "Innovation Agenda" and reasserting their belief in the importance of undergraduate education and its goal of developing critical thought. The market value program's hostility towards education is also apparent in a case study that deals with York University, where the freedom of expression of students was denied because they protested against corporate influence. The outcry from students and faculty over "police brutality"[18] during the protest led to a condemnation of the university's policies, which limited freedom of assembly, and a review of the "brand strategy" employed by York.[19] The chapter concludes with an analysis of private for-profit universities in Canada and the United States, viewing them as the apotheosis of the value program of the corporate market.

The importance of relating utopian thought to educational practice is brought home in the final case study in chapter 7. The Peoples Free University of Saskatchewan (PFU) was an attempt to step beyond the market and to establish a community-based form of higher education in which anyone could participate free of charge. Hundreds of students attended classes taught by professors, graduate students, and community members on a wide variety of topics. The slogan "Anyone can teach, anyone can learn" built on a Saskatchewan tradition of popular participation in education and civic affairs and reflected a belief in the creative potential of all human beings. The capacity of the imagination to build communities of learners and to envisage possibilities for change typified the praxis of the PFU. And its entire raison d'être was grounded in what McMurtry calls the life-code of value and its "instituted bearer," the "civil commons," which sustained its activities in a manner consistent with a Whiteheadian conception of life.[20]

When taken together, the case studies comprise a cumulative argument showing that academic freedom and university autonomy are currently threatened by private corporations and governments in Canada. A cumulative argument of this kind, as David Ray Griffin points out, "is a general argument consisting of several particular arguments that are independent from each other ... Rather than being like a chain, a cumulative argument is more like a cable composed of many strands. Each strand strengthens the cable. But if there are many strands, the cable can still hold a weight even if some of them unravel."[21] Each case study is a strand that provides support for the general argument, which holds weight by virtue of the several strands that make up the cable. Should the evidence supporting any of the individual strands not hold, the cable does not break but continues to hold weight. Those who are sceptical of the general thesis of *Selling Out* may focus on particular aspects in the case studies in order to discredit it, but the argument that academic freedom is under threat still stands. Alternatively, critics may take issue with the theoretical framework used to interpret the cases. However, given the evidence presented in these case studies, the question becomes: How else can one make sense of the evidence other than by concluding that education and the corporate market have opposing logics of value?

Each case serves as an example of the concrete manner in which academic freedom is threatened by the encroachment of the market into the life of the university. Taken together, they suggest that this process is now taking place in two ways. First, individual faculty members are at risk when speaking out against institutional links with big business. Whether in the fields of medicine or marketing, microbiology or macro-economics, professors who publicly object to reducing knowledge to a private good for sale in the corporate market will be shunned, persecuted, and possibly dismissed, just as were Dr Olivieri and Dr Vedanand. Second, and more important, the university's ability to engage in the critical pursuit of knowledge is being undermined by the manner in which teaching, learning, scholarship, and research are being reduced to market activities. Both the individual and institutional aspects of this process clearly show how, by virtue of its defining principles, the market model of education systematically selects against academic freedom and university autonomy. Only by identifying the ways in which market principles are being substituted for academic principles, on both these levels, can a successful defence of academic freedom be mounted. As the CAUT "Model Clause on Academic Freedom" makes clear, "the common good of society [which] depends upon the search for knowledge and its free exposition"[22] is currently endangered by corporate market demands on Canadian universities.

There are, of course, other threats to academic freedom. These include political correctness (often referred to as PC), which functions in ways similar to the market model. PC is an ambiguous concept, which the media have interpreted as consisting of the undue influence of subversive ideas that have been exerted on students by left-wing professors. Even though evidence for this claim is exaggerated it has been used in Canada and the United States, especially since 9/11, to attack faculty members who are critical of American foreign policy.[23]

A rather different notion of PC is attributed to members of oppressed and marginalized groups (women, Aboriginal peoples, blacks, gays, lesbians, and the disabled) who are engaged in an effort to ensure that they are no longer excluded from participation in university life by forms of speech that ignore or demean their experience and identity. On this view, academic freedom is, or should be, an integral part of an *inclusive* university.[24] This view promises a more equitable relationship between universities (which can only benefit from a diversity of worldviews) and groups whose presence is compatible, at least partially, with the demands of social justice.[25]

There have been several accusations of racism and/or sexism against faculty in Canadian universities.[26] Jeanne Cannizzo, professor of archeology at the University of Toronto's Scarborough College, was curator of an exhibit entitled "Out of Africa," which was on display at the Royal Ontario Museum in 1989–90. In addition to showing the beauty of African artefacts, the exhibit aimed to expose the racism of the nineteenth-century missionaries and army officers who colonized the continent. Some members of the black communities in Ontario interpreted it as a further example of colonialism and condemned it as "racist in effect if not intent."[27] Professor Cannizzo's classes were interrupted by hecklers, and, although she was given strong support by both the university's governing council and faculty association as well as the Canadian Association of University Teachers, the course was cancelled when she was forced to go on medical leave.[28]

This case raises an important question: Should the effects of words or cultural artefacts upon those who have been marginalized be what determines their meaning and intent? The implication is that not only would faculty members have to meet the reasonable demand of respecting the values of their students but also, and more important, they would have to avoid expressing views that might offend them. And this raises a further question: Is being offended by a professor's views adequate grounds for a student, or any member of the community, to object to the free expression of those views? Only, it would seem, if causing them to feel offended is itself an offence.[29] What matters in this view is not whether the student or community member's claim is true but, rather, whether they dislike what they hear in class, feel affronted by what they read, or object to what they see in an exhibit. Academic freedom is then weakened and becomes a matter of negotiation among the conflicting claims of different parties. The competing interests of students, community groups, university administrators, and business corporations now have to be met lest any one of them is offended by faculty engaged in teaching, scholarship, research, or artistic work that questions commonly held assumptions.[30] This process selects against any form of academic freedom that enables the expression of critical and unpopular views, however justified they may be.[31]

1

The Market Model of Education
and the Threat to Academic Freedom

The learned and imaginative life is a way of living, and is not an article
of commerce.

Alfred North Whitehead[1]

AN ENCOUNTER WITH THE MARKET MODEL

During the early 1990s, I attended a conference in Toronto, the theme
of which was "the university and democracy." Among those present
were university presidents, distinguished faculty from around the
world, graduate students, government officials, and several Canadian
businesspeople. The declared purpose of the conference was to
encourage dialogue among these different groups regarding the
importance of the university in a democratic society. What actually
transpired was rather different. The dominant view that emerged was
that the university should be tied more closely to the market principle
of monetary gain in order to serve the needs and interests of business
corporations. While this view was articulated by members of each
of the constituent groups, not surprisingly, it was the businesspeople
who were its strongest advocates.

One paper, in particular, stood out as a clear example of this
orientation. It was presented by the then president of the Edmonton
Research Park, a private consortium of companies "more interested
in the practical aspects of technology development than in underlying
philosophy or basic principles." He argued that, as universities
become less dependent on government funding, they would enter a
new phase of development in which closer "relationships with industry and business" would be necessary to meet the needs of "multinational technology-based companies [which] have a critical need

for skilled human resources and relevant research."[2] While such relationships certainly strengthen the ability of corporations to compete in the global market, they were alleged to benefit universities by increasing research activity and placing a greater emphasis on vocational training.

For this to happen, however, universities would be required to accept the following kinds of links with business as a baseline for their continuing operation: a dependency on "technology transfer [and] innovation centres," whose primary purpose is to serve business corporations; growth in the number of "research consortia" and "research parks" designed to make their work readily available to the market; more "joint professorships" conducting "contract research" for corporations within universities; and a greater emphasis on vocational training programs feeding directly into the private sector.[3]

In order to ensure that vocational training performed this market function efficiently, Glenn Mitchell insisted that universities give up their "monopolistic control" over "the world's most strategic resource: educated manpower [sic]" to business. As long as the freedom to plan, implement, and evaluate the education of students rested in the hands of universities, corporations could not be sure that the training required for extracting monetized wealth from "the world's most strategic resource" had been put into place. Academic criteria consistent with the standards of excellence required for university teaching and learning, and determined by faculty on the basis of scholarly norms and the search for critical understanding, were, he argued, to be replaced by the overriding corporate goal of "adding value" to their products. Students, that is, must learn that the goal of education is to reduce the costs of business and to increase its revenues. "Relevance" to the market, in turn, was to be measured in terms of both the "volume output" of students as "manpower" and "skilled human resources" and "the critical need for ... relevant research."[4]

Indeed, research was far too important to be left in the hands of professors unaware of how to discipline their discoveries to the production and sale of marketable products: this is where the expertise of Mitchell and others in bringing products to market could be facilitated by the kinds of institutional links between universities and business that he advocated. Only with "business methods" could education realize its proper value and function, and "technology development" and prosperity occur.

At the University of British Columbia, for example, the University-Industry Liaison Program was already specializing in pairing up scientific researchers with corporate clients, and its Intellectual-Property Office claimed to issue about one commercial licence per month for technologies originating in university laboratories. The university also allowed a representative from the private sector to occupy its reserved seat on the provincial government's granting committee as a kind of quid pro quo for their continuing relationship.[5] In other words, the university had enabled big business to replace it on a government committee that makes important decisions about how funding is to be awarded to higher education – a kind of "restructuring" that ensured the university was made accountable to the "real world" of the market.

Nor was the economic dependency of universities to end there, according to Mitchell. The issue of who owned the patents to the various products discovered in their laboratories was far from resolved. While some might accrue to universities or be shared among the faculty responsible for such research, most intellectual property and other "Deliverables" should pass into the hands of "corporate clients" who have the money to develop the technology in question. Indeed, the Corporate Higher Education Forum, a lobby group comprising seventy chief executive officers from Canadian-based multinationals as well as presidents of Canadian universities, was at the time recommending that all such Deliverables become the property of corporate clients.[6] This, they claimed, was the most desirable way for universities to do business. The result would be twofold: (1) universities would find themselves dependent on corporate clients in control of their intellectual property, and (2) this corporate control would ensure that vocational training and applied research replaced the critical search for knowledge as the major goal of universities.

On one level, Mitchell acknowledged that corporate control of this kind would mean "a loss of traditional autonomy." But he thought this would only happen where universities refused to change their research and education functions to meet the needs of business corporations (since governments operating in compliance with the market model would not offer them public funding). As he put it: "A university that does not spend more of its energies and resources at the critical interface between university, industry, and government for the public good may soon find itself with reduced freedom of action and

control over its own affairs."⁷ The same edict to comply with the
corporate market was later issued by the World Bank at a UNESCO
conference in Paris: "Public universities [that] resist radical change ...
are not immune to the loss of increasingly scarce public revenues."⁸

Like the World Bank, Mitchell was advocating nothing less than
"a paradigm shift in the concept of the university as we know it."
All of his proposed reforms were "instruments and ... possible
barometers of a fundamental change in the modern university" aimed
at overcoming any lingering "university lethargy" towards full integration with the market. The motivation behind this shift, Mitchell
claimed, was "clearly self-interest, and it is the self-interest of the
university, the state, and private enterprise in combination which is
creating the pressures that are bringing about a change in the role
and function of the university." The self-interest motivating market
agents was now the driving force behind universities and the state,
and their goals were to be no different from those of the corporate
sector. Once each of these institutions acted out of self-interest the
result would be monetary wealth in the public interest: "the critical
interface between university, industry, and government [acts] for the
public good."⁹ The "invisible hand" of the market would, Mitchell
believed, mysteriously create the public good out of the self-interest
motivating private corporations, universities, and government.¹⁰

At this point it is worth taking note of the following features of
Mitchell's market model of universities as they are integral to the
corporate program currently transforming universities into what
have been called "private revenue-generating machines."¹¹ I analyze
each one in greater depth in the second section of this chapter. Now,
however, I wish to underline their importance as fundamental
assumptions of the market model of education:

1 The "Prime Functions" of universities are to meet the "critical
  need for skilled human resources and relevant research" capable
  of producing "Prime Outputs" for the corporate market.
2 Vocational training is to become the core educational function of
  universities. "Prime Outputs" now consist of "Key manpower [sic]"
  capable of "adding value" to corporate revenues "through the
  application of sophisticated scientific and market knowledge."
3 In order for research to be geared to the market and its findings
  made into products through the process of "technology development," the kind of expertise offered by "research and science

parks" is required. Patents for such products increasingly and exclusively accrue to business corporations because they have the money resources to turn such research into more money or "value added."

4 Entering into numerous business "partnerships" in this way ensures that universities remain instruments of monetized economic growth and receive the funds from government they require to continue fulfilling this role lest they "find themselves increasingly out of step with events around them."

5 The institutional autonomy and academic freedom, which have enabled universities and faculty to advance learning and disseminate knowledge as a public good in itself, is correspondingly selected against and abolished. As Mitchell put it: "Many university people continue to believe and to assume that they are the masters of their own destiny and that they can continue to chart their own directions much the same way as they have in the past. *I would submit that there is more fiction than fact in this point of view.*"[12]

As I listened to his polemic, it seemed to me that Mitchell showed little understanding of just how devastating his market reforms would be for universities. The critical search for knowledge would no longer be the goal of university education and research. Both activities were subordinated to the purpose of helping business corporations to maximize their monetary profits. Research and understanding as values in themselves, which lie at the base and forefront of teaching, were not mentioned. The academic freedom that makes such inquiry possible was excluded. The possibilities for dialogue and community with students and colleagues engaged in the pursuit of knowledge were instrumentalized and made subservient to the overriding demand to maximize stockholder value, which was presented as the true goal of learning. The importance of universities in educating citizens for democracy was extinguished and replaced by the need for them to outperform others in the global market. The idea that universities should serve the common good was expunged and replaced with the idea that they should pursue private monetary wealth. Like agents in the corporate market, universities were to be motivated exclusively by self-interest. This reduction of universities (and governments) to machines for maximizing corporate revenues ruled out any possibility of knowledge being presented as integral to the common good, advanced through a public process of critique and understanding. Indeed, it reduced "knowledge" to digitized "bytes" of "information" to be moved instantaneously in "the highly competitive information-based society"[13] so as to facilitate corporate investment in foreign markets around the world.

Business methods like this ruled out as "inefficient" the very practices in which I had been engaged as a student and faculty member for more than twenty-five years, and which are heirs to a tradition of reason that is over 2,500 years old. The pursuit of impartial and critical knowledge, normally considered the central goal of universities, was to be banished and replaced by market principles and practices whose goal was to maximize the monetary profits of private corporations.

It is striking that advocates of "the corporate market," like Mitchell, misleadingly refer to it as "the free market." In reality, however, the two are quite different. There are few "real free markets" remaining in the industrialized world, but they serve to illustrate this point quite graphically. The food sold by organic farmers at local markets, for example, is the product of the skill-intensive work of the owners themselves, who also act as vendors, often in conjunction with their families. The medium of exchange among such producers is cash or the promise thereof, whereas in modern "supermarkets," which typify the corporate system of food distribution, credit card and bill payment are the norm. Vendors here are certainly not producers; rather, they purchase the labour of others in order to sell any commodity at all – food, clothing, home appliances, pharmaceutical goods, film equipment, and so on. Whereas organic farmer/vendors establish face-to-face relationships with local individuals who buy their produce, "supermarkets" rarely establish any relationship with their "clients" as their commodities are designed for a global mass market. While any surplus value created by organic farmers is kept primarily by them, in the corporate system it accrues to stockholders who produce nothing.[14]

In the years since the Toronto conference, the kinds of changes advocated by Mitchell have increasingly become the daily reality of universities in Canada. Government underfunding continues to accompany growing corporatization. This pincer movement ensures that universities move ever faster to subordinate the pursuit of knowledge to the overriding market principle of monetary gain for stockholders. Universities compliant with this principle place at risk not only the freedom that makes the pursuit of knowledge possible but also the very process of understanding itself. Rather than enabling an inclusive understanding of reality on the part of faculty and students engaged in an uncensored exploration of ideas, monetary principles subordinate the pursuit of knowledge to the exclusive goal of private monetary gain.

This model is advanced uncritically not only by business corporations but also, and increasingly, by governments, senior university administrators, and even certain faculty and students. Those of us who oppose it must reaffirm the distinguishing features of the vocation of higher education that make possible the independent and critical search for knowledge – in particular, the traditions of academic freedom and university autonomy. Resistance to the market's systematic disregard for these principles is rooted in what Professor Janice Newson refers to as a "shared commitment to the university as an institution that should exist to serve the public good rather than to produce privately owned goods."[15] Only if such resistance is successful will universities be able to overcome being both "dumbed down" and subjugated to a model of training designed to serve corporate functions rather than educational aims. Should we fail in this task, what will be left of public university education?

A CRITIQUE OF THE MARKET MODEL OF EDUCATION

In the preceding section I show how the market model of education undermines academic freedom and the institutional autonomy of universities. Now it is necessary to offer a more systematic analysis of the market model and the reasons for its growing influence. I argue that it is by overriding the fundamental differences between the distinctive goals, motivations, methods, and standards of excellence of education that the market threatens the autonomy of universities. I use the analytic framework articulated by Professor John McMurtry to consider the opposing characteristics of universities and the market.[16]

I also follow the research lead of Professor Janice Newson and Professor Michiel Horn, whose lucid analyses of the ways in which Canadian academic freedom and university autonomy are under attack from the corporate market complement my own. Important questions about this process are also raised by Professor Conrad

Russell, whose work on the loss of academic freedom in Britain suggests strong similarities between universities both there and in Canada. I begin by contextualizing the marketization of Canadian universities within broader international terms.

The Market Model and British Universities

Prior to his death a few years ago, Professor Russell was an outspoken critic of the policies of the British government that have reduced universities to institutions based exclusively on market principles. As the Liberal Party's official critic of higher education in the House of Lords, son of the philosopher Bertrand Russell, and professor of history at King's College, London, he was particularly well placed to engage in such a critique. Russell showed how the critical pursuit of knowledge, which is at the core of university research and teaching, is systematically devalued by the intrusion of market principles like "efficiency" (as "the reduction of unit costs") into all the distinctive activities of these institutions. This results in "targeted" and "contract" research being undertaken simply as a means of making money, thereby reducing the researcher to "a sort of 'hired gun' at the disposal of ... [her/his] employer." Wherever a "contractor," whether from the private or the public sector, can control the "output of an academic" because it is equated with "services available for the contractor to buy," academic freedom is clearly at risk. Such control can take the form of "prohibiting publication" of research, either because the contractor owns the intellectual property rights or because the "consent of the Secretary of State [of Education]" is required, wherever government contracts are undertaken. In either case, control over academic research has passed into the hands of "contractors" who now "own" it. The process of sharing research with one's peers is systematically blocked, and the possibility of gaining knowledge through exposure to the critical thought of others is undermined. When this occurs, the distinctive value of knowledge-seeking is destroyed since "it is ... a fundamental academic value, and one in necessary conflict with commercial values, that ideas and findings must be shared with fellow scholars, and become part of our professional stock-in-trade."[17]

As Russell makes clear, knowledge is a shared good that can only be realized where a community of scholars engaged in critical thought determines the adequacy of its claims. This process of critical inquiry can only succeed where claims and refutations are made public, which implies that knowledge is itself a public good whose value is realized through its being shared. This "fundamental academic value" is "in necessary conflict with [the] commercial values" of the market since the value of goods sold in the corporate market is determined simply by their price. Unlike knowledge, they are "ready-made products" that require nothing else to realize their value. And universities that produce these products are simply, in the words of Peter Mandelson, Britain's former secretary of state for trade and industry, "engines of economic growth."[18] Even elite universities like Oxford and Cambridge cannot escape this market imperative. In 2005, the vice-chancellor of Oxford University proposed to establish a small board of trustees, composed of alumni with strong corporate links, that would effectively run the university. This prompted open dissent from faculty (known as dons).[19]

Here we find a central theme of this study. The value of critical understanding, which lies at the core of university life, is fundamentally opposed to the corporate practices of maximizing private monetary profits. As Russell has shown, to the extent that the value of research is equated with priced goods for sale in the corporate market, academic freedom and the critical search for knowledge are likely to disappear. Any such attempt to reduce knowledge to its market price neglects the fact that the logic of education is fundamentally opposed to that of the corporate market.

Russell's use of the phrase "necessary conflict" suggests a logical tension between the values of university research and education, on the one hand, and the commercial values of the market, on the other. It is not a question of the two conflicting with one another as a matter of fact, from time to time, or in specific circumstances; it is a matter of their being in fundamental opposition to one another. The logic of education and research upholds such values as sharing one's ideas with others, while the logic of the market upholds such values as the maximization of stockholder profit. It is only by understanding the ways in which the logic of these respective activities are in fundamental conflict with one another that we can recognize the threat that the market poses to university autonomy and academic freedom. More specifically, in the course of my analysis I suggest answers to the following questions: How does the public process of sharing knowledge and understanding conflict with the process of selling goods for private monetary profits in the corporate market?

And in what ways is the value of teaching, learning, scholarship, and research debased when these activities become private goods for sale in such a market?

Opposing Goals

One way of interpreting the opposition between the logic of education and the logic of the market is to recognize that "the aims and processes of education and the market are not only distinct, but contradictory."[20] The contradiction is between education's goal of publicly sharing knowledge among those seeking it and the market's goal of making ever more money for private individuals and companies. Put differently, the goals of pursuing knowledge and maximizing private profit contradict one another because sharing knowledge with others is incompatible with accumulating money for oneself. Newson explains this incompatibility in the following terms: "The principles that benefit markets undermine the objectives of education and conversely, education that achieves its intended purposes cannot serve well as a marketable commodity."[21]

More specifically, the goals of education and the goals of the market are based on "wholly distinct and often opposed logics of value":[22] one enables deeper and broader understanding of reality, while the other maximizes corporate stockholder value. Sharing knowledge with others is a valuable activity in the context of an institution that enables professors and students to engage freely, and without fear of censure, in the public process of sharing critical understanding. Rather than excluding others, the logic of this process includes their desire for knowledge, which "is maximized the more its accumulation is shared by others, and the more others have access to every step of its development."[23]

Advocates of the market model make a fundamental error when they identify the goals of education with those of the market, where "private profit is acquired by a structure of acquisition that excludes others from its appropriation."[24] The more that private monetary profits are accumulated by individuals or business corporations, the less access others have to the use of such money or to gaining control over it. The logic of the market excludes all those who lack the money to pay for access to its goods. In contrast, the inclusive logic of education enables all who seek knowledge to share in its accumulation.

As I show, this basic opposition between these two logics is not recognized by advocates of the market model.

The initial report of the Corporate Higher Education Forum provides an early example of this refusal to acknowledge these opposing value systems. The Forum, comprising corporate chief executive officers and university presidents, commissioned two private-sector economists to assess the possibilities for increasing "cooperation" between universities and business in order to make the Canadian economy internationally competitive. Judith Maxwell and Stephanie Currie produced *Partnership for Growth* in 1984, anticipating many developments, like "business partnerships," "research parks," "targeted research," and "research consortia," that have since engulfed Canadian universities. Their goal was to determine how best to attune "the research effort and the university curriculum ... more closely to the needs of the marketplace."[25] This, they claimed, would produce the following kinds of "excellence": "Excellence in research, ensuring that Canadians are generating new technology for use in Canadian industry; Excellence in education, ensuring that new graduates and those who return for further training are acquiring the best possible skills for the post-industrial era; and finally, effective technology transfer, ensuring that Canadian firms have access to leading edge technology."[26] According to them, the goal of university research should be (1) to serve the corporate market by generating technology for use in Canadian industry and (2) to ensure that effective technology transfer occurs by making leading-edge technology available to private corporations based in Canada. Similarly, all education should be reduced to receiving training in the best possible skills for the postindustrial era; namely, those skill sets capable, in Mitchell's words, of "adding value ... through the application of sophisticated scientific and market knowledge."[27] In both cases, educational excellence should be subordinated to the overriding need to produce "value added" for industry.

In achieving these goals, the values or "cultural differences" distinctive of universities would quickly dissolve into those of the market. Maxwell and Currie see these cultural differences as a major stumbling block to greater cooperation between universities and business since they reflect "the different values, expectations, and mode of operation of the two types of institutions." This barrier must be overcome, and it is universities that must adapt to the corporate market, not vice versa. According to Maxwell and Currie, the commitment to "the extension and transmission of knowledge ... freedom of communication and publication ... [and] creative and self-paced ... selection and management of ... research" is at odds with the "profitability" and "efficiency" of delivering products or services that determine value in the market. For them, "research is oriented towards the development and commercialization of new and improved products [and] deadlines ... and proprietary rights are closely guarded [so as] to obtain a competitive edge in the market-place." Lest there be any uncertainty about which set of values should dominate, Maxwell and Currie write that "the nature and scope of corporate-academic collaboration will be *determined by the needs of the corporation* and by the areas of expertise that a university can offer."[28] Since the needs of business corporations are driven by the market, where profitability and efficiency are dominant values, universities wishing to "collaborate" must abide by the same set of market values. This means discarding their outmoded goal of advancing and disseminating shared knowledge in favour of pursuing private monetary profits. Indeed, this new goal will determine the areas of expertise in which they will provide private goods and services consistent with "the needs of the corporation." In order to make this regime of externally determined, market-oriented research and teaching work smoothly, universities must also discard academic freedom, whose creative and self-paced approach no longer has a place in the "new reality." The reduction of universities' values to those of the market will be hastened since, in the words of Michiel Horn, "one set of values trumps the other, and ... the corporations hold the high cards."[29]

Among influential individuals who subscribe to this view is Dr Tom Brzustowski, who, as Ontario's deputy minister of colleges and universities, made the following statement: "I contend that the one global object of education in Ontario must necessarily be a greater capability of the people of Ontario to create wealth ... [to] export products in which our knowledge and skills provide the value added ... to develop new services which we can offer in trade on the world market."[30] Brzustowski not only advocates the creation of wealth as the one global object of education but also apparently considers it to be the only conceivable goal of university education and research. The phrase "must necessarily be ... to create wealth" indicates that – as a matter of necessity – there can be no other goal. This market-based logic does not recognize the sharing of knowledge as having any part to play in the goal of university education. There is no room here for the dissemination of shared knowledge. Brzustowski, by identifying the goals of universities with those of the market, reduces the former to machines for generating private wealth. And he does so as a public representative of public education and a former vice-president academic of the University of Waterloo.

As president of the Natural Sciences and Engineering Research Council of Canada, Dr Brzustowski, who was trained as an engineer, continued to promote this view of education. His participation on the Expert Panel on the Commercialization of University Research resulted in a report for the Prime Minister's Advisory Council on Science and Technology that called for "innovation" to become the fourth mission of universities, in addition to teaching, research, and community service. The report, which was tabled in May 1999, defines "innovation" in exclusively commercial terms as "the process of bringing new goods and services to the market, or the result of that process"[31] – a view consistent with Brzustowski's identification of the goals of universities with those of the market. Two-thirds of the expert panel were presidents or vice-presidents of banks and business corporations, and their advocacy of "innovation" meant that it was seriously considered in terms of forming part of the mission of universities.

The same kind of flawed reasoning pervades the *Employability Skills Profile* published by the Corporate Council on Education of the Conference Board of Canada, a powerful lobby group consisting of some twenty-three corporate members engaged in market-based educational reform in universities, colleges, and schools. The profile articulates "the critical skills required of the Canadian workforce" to "ensure Canada is competitive and successful in the global economy," and it was widely circulated as a kind of corporate manifesto for marketizing all levels of education. Indeed, without any justification, the goals of education are identified with those of the corporate market, while the skills enumerated are all designed to satisfy "Canadian employers [who] need a person who can get, keep and progress on a job and ... get the best results." The goal of "academic skills," in particular, is to "provide the basic foundation to get, keep and progress on a job and to get the best results" by "adding value" to a company's products. The "basic foundation" of academic work is thereby reduced to those skills that maximize private monetary profits. The profile makes no mention of "understanding" but, rather, regards all learning as a matter of acquiring skills in isolation from the academic disciplines in which they can be used. The goal of learning to "think critically and act logically," for example, is "to evaluate situations, solve problems and make decisions" in ways that are useful to future employers but that do little to enhance the critical thought of students. Problem-solving of this kind is a matter of acquiring skills, which are seen as "discrete and repeatable exercises that can be improved by practice," not as constituents of a broader understanding rooted in various disciplines of thought.[32] Students trained in this way cannot ask critical questions either of the knowledge claims made in various academic disciplines or of their own social reality because, quite simply, they lack the understanding that would enable them to do so.

Indeed, "academic skills," decoupled from any disciplinary base, are really no different from "personal management skills," which enable "a person ... to get, keep and progress on a job and to get the best results." The only significant difference is that personal management skills achieve this goal by training individuals to adopt the correct "attitudes and behaviours" – those that will "contribute to the organization's goals" of maximizing stockholder value.[33] The goal of university education is to train students to be loyal to this overriding value. Once again, no reasons are given for this. The Conference Board simply presupposes that the only goal of university education is to transmit skills that will enable future employees to provide "value added" to the companies for which they work. Their refusal to acknowledge that the goal of education could be different from that of the market is a prime example of what McMurtry calls an "unexamined value system," or "value program" – an "overall structure of thinking" connecting "goods that are affirmed and bads that are repudiated," that blocks any understanding of "the incoherence of these assumptions." The Conference Board's value program rejects any alternative account of education "because its nature is to be closed to any possibility that it could be wrong." It is as though there is "a herd-pattern operating beneath consciousness."[34]

The Corporate Higher Education Forum, Brzustowski, and the Conference Board all ignore the fact that the goal of universities is opposed to the goal of the market. Knowledge acquisition, as I argue more fully in the next section, enables those engaged in the search for critical understanding to have access to knowledge as a shared good. By reducing education to the production of knowledge and skills that give value added to the goods and services sold by business corporations, advocates of the market model liquidate the opposing values of education. They are blind to the fact that these two systems seek quite different goods. One strives for the material possession of uniform artefacts, while the other strives for the attainment of knowledge that will enhance the distinctive mental capacities of those who seek it. Material goods can be owned, and this limits them because, once owned, they can no longer be used by others. Mental or intellectual goods cannot be "owned" in this way because their possession actually enhances the understanding of others through teaching, scholarship, and research.[35] The market model of education cannot accommodate this deep structural aspect of education because its doctrine depends on the presupposition that the goal of all enterprises is to maximize monetary profits for private stockholders. This systematic disregard for counter-evidence is integral to the closed nature of the value program of the market model, which expunges any position that values knowledge as a shared good.

Opposing Motivations and "The Spirit of the Age"

The determining motivation of education is to satisfy a person's desire for knowledge regardless of whether or not s/he has the money to pay for it. Knowledge as a shared good is accessible to everyone who desires it provided they are willing to pursue it. In contrast, the determining motivation of the market is to satisfy the wants of anyone who has the money to purchase them. All those who sell goods in the market proclaim its ability to "satisfy the wants of customers" as a universal criterion of its efficiency.[36] When the same criterion is applied to education, however, it wreaks havoc with the distinctive activities of, in particular, university teaching and learning.

William A. Cochrane, former president and chief executive officer of Connaught Laboratories Limited in Toronto, provides a good example of why the determining motivation of the market cannot apply to education. In suggesting that universities must satisfy the wants of their customers, who comprise "the general public, the business or industrial sector and government," Cochrane fails to recognize the opposing logics of value that are at work in these very different spheres of human activity. He regards the determining motivation of the market, which is to satisfy the wants of customers, as a fundamental principle that "should be at the forefront of any activity of universities or institutions of higher learning." The principle is a simple one: "stay near the customer." And he believes that this would enable universities, like buyers and sellers in the market, to "determine the customer's short- and long-term wants." This principle presupposes that want-satisfaction should be the overriding motivation for universities, just as it is for the market. Yet, no evidence is offered in support of this claim. Cochrane simply begs the question by assuming that the dominant motivation of university education is to satisfy the wants of those who have the money to buy it. If, however, universities were to "stay near the customer," they would have to ignore the distinctive goods of knowledge and understanding that are to be shared with all those who seek them.[37]

Cochrane's position is at odds with an entire tradition that is based on satisfying anyone's desire for knowledge insofar as s/he is willing to pursue it. Satisfying the wants of the customer in purely market terms is not only different from, but actually opposed to, developing the kind of understanding that typifies university education. Their desire to buy or consume the latest product often prevents students from gaining an understanding of the subject matter they are studying. It diverts their attention away from the self-discipline required for intellectual growth towards a fascination with "commercial television, rock records or mall wandering."[38] The danger here is that, by satisfying customers' wants, the market may well sap their ability to develop a comprehensive understanding of the disciplines they study or, indeed, of reality itself. Where want-satisfaction becomes a fundamental principle of education in the manner suggested by Cochrane, universities are in danger of becoming mere "shopping malls of the mind." Rather than enhancing intellectual growth, they try to satisfy those "customer" wants that stimulate further market activity, regardless of any understanding that the "customer/student" may develop.

Where this happens, the basic motivation of education is violated in at least two ways: first, the overriding motivation of the market does not recognize students' desire for knowledge as having any real import in the process of learning and, therefore, replaces it with determining how to satisfy their wants as customers; second, the beneficiaries of this process include only those who have the money to pay for such services. When the determining motivation of the market, which requires customers to pay for the private goods they buy, is applied to universities, significant increases in tuition fees are one obvious way that this principle is put into practice. Indeed, since 1999, as university education has come to be regarded as a private rather than a public good, and government financing has shrunk accordingly, tuition fees for Canadian students have more than doubled.[39]

In Britain, where tuition fees have risen even more dramatically than they have in Canada, some universities welcome this development as a market opportunity. In the late 1990s, Sir Geoffrey Holland, then vice-chancellor of the University of Exeter, established a "complaints procedure" for better serving the wants of "customers" attending his institution: "This," he wrote, "is very much *in the spirit of the age* as tuition fees have clearly completed the process of making students our 'customers,' 'paying guests' as we should think of them."[40] True to the overriding motivation of the market, Holland regards those customers who can afford to pay for the market good of education as being entitled to a complaints procedure that ensures the satisfaction of their wants. He considers this procedure as an embodiment of "the spirit of the age" because it reveals a deeper purpose at work in the commercialization of his campus. Acknowledging that high "tuition fees have clearly completed the process of making our students our customers," he suggests that they now be regarded as "paying guests," presumably because they are able to pay for private accommodation in or around the university. Their growing status is a direct result of the increase in their market activity and, as their wants for private goods grow, the university responds by establishing a mechanism to ensure their satisfaction. Nowhere does Holland allow that the desire for knowledge, regardless of a student's ability to pay, should be a criterion for determining access to the complaints procedure. More important, he rules out in principle the possibility of establishing an evaluation process for determining the quality of teaching on the basis of (1) what students actually know and (2) how well their capacity for critical thought has grown. This would require him to recognize that the desire for knowledge and its satisfaction in the form of the growing capacity for independent thought are the basis for teaching and learning, not some externally imposed requirement such as the ability to pay. In "the spirit of the age," Holland hastens the market domination of universities by disregarding their distinctive overriding motivation in favour of a mechanism that furthers the want-satisfaction of his paying guests.

The flawed approach advocated by Cochrane and Holland is silent about the need for universities to satisfy students' desire for knowledge regardless of their ability to pay, focusing instead on their wants for private market goods for which they must be able to pay. Failure to recognize the opposing logics of value embedded in these distinct activities is the result of an adherence to presuppositions that exclude anything that does not conform to market doctrine. This refusal to consider whether university education might conceivably be based on a motivation that differs from that of the market is reminiscent of the way in which Brzustowski, the Corporate Higher Education Forum, and the Conference Board expunged any counter-evidence to their views regarding the goal of universities. In both cases, reasoned argument is replaced by a faith in the market's "invisible hand," which functions to liquidate any remaining differences that might set universities apart from the "new reality." The underlying value program shared by advocates of the market model simply erases any possibility that education might embody a motivation or goal different from that of generating monetary wealth for private stockholders.

Opposing Methods

The method of the market is to buy or sell ready-made products at whatever price one can get. This means that everything in the market is obtained through the money paid for it. In contrast, the method of education is not to buy or sell its good to anyone but, rather, to require of all those who would have it that they fulfill its requirements autonomously. As a result, "nothing that is learned in education is gotten by the money paid for it" because knowledge can only be earned through learning to exercise one's mental capacities for oneself. This is not a requirement in the market, whose goods need not be earned autonomously or on the basis of one's own work. Ironically, the market's capacity to provide ready-made products and services to those who can pay for them often deprives consumers of the ability to think and act for themselves. This is evident among the very rich, who, being dependent on others for everything they want, continue to demand the products they supply. The overwhelming desire to satiate their wants results in a kind of "infantile stage" in which any "responsibility for the production, preparation, delivery, and service of any" of these private goods is absent.[41]

An education that can be bought on the market, however, is "a fraud," while purchasing someone else's performance to replace one's own work is, in McMurtry's words, "an expulsionable cheat" precisely because the method of achievement in education "rules out the method of the market as its most essential violation." Attempts to buy and sell education as a ready-made product for whatever price one can get are opposed to the autonomous intellectual activity comprising the method of education. Furthermore, ready-made goods produced for the market depreciate in value as they are used, eventually wearing out. In contrast, the goods created by education do not wear out for "the more and longer an education is put to work, the better and more durable it grows."[42] As students' capacity for independent thought develops, they learn to use knowledge in new and creative ways, enhancing the scope of their understanding. Advocates of the market model ignore this opposing logic of value and reduce the method of education to that of the market.

Dr Michael R. Bloom, senior research associate for the National Business and Education Centre of the Conference Board of Canada, is prominent among those who identify the method of education with the method of the market. Not surprisingly, his views mimic those of the Conference Board's "Employability Skills Profile," but his own emphasis is on the competition that allegedly unifies education and the market. "The real issue," he claims, "is that our education system is competing with the education systems of other countries just as Canadian businesses are competing with their international rivals."[43] Clearly, the source of this alleged identification is the fact that Canadian education and business are both competing with their international rivals. Nor is this meant simply as an analogy since "our education system" is competing with other systems in just the same way as ("just as") Canadian businesses are competing with other businesses in the global market. Competition between Canadian universities and their international rivals is, on this view, no different from the competition of companies involved in the corporate market: the two are identical. A claim of identity such as this can be represented as "P is the same as Q," which, in this case, becomes: "competition in education is the same as competition in the market." This can be further simplified by striking the terms "competition in" from either side of "is the same as," giving the following: "education is the same as the market." In trying to justify this claim, Bloom draws exclusively on evidence from the market, expunging all evidence that might oppose his goal of reducing education to a market activity; notably, the distinctive method of university education, which insists that all those engaged in the search for knowledge achieve it themselves rather than receive it "problem free" as consumers or clients. For Bloom, competition defines both Canadian universities and the corporate market, and it provides the means for subordinating education to this "new reality."

"The real concern of business," he continues, is to help restore "our relative educational advantage[, which] is slipping [in comparison with] the education systems of other countries ... with [whose] businesses ... we are competing in world markets."[44] Upon closer examination, improving "relative educational advantage" amounts to the university's ability to provide "comparative advantage" to Canadian-based business corporations. It requires universities to reduce business costs by "adding value" to the products and services they provide. This ensures that what holds is the market principle of comparative advantage, whereby societies "produce those goods and services in which they have lower resource input cost than other countries." In this way, Canada's continuing specialization in such products as forestry, oil and gas, wheat, genetically modified canola, computer software, and executive jets is secured by keeping their input costs down. The function of universities is to facilitate this process, so that "producers and sellers in the market are impelled to invest" in Canada, where these "costs are relatively low."[45]

What, one wonders, are the likely benefits to universities of this increase in market-based competition? Will they be required to perform an exclusively service function to business by competing more effectively with their "international rivals" in order to receive government funding? Is Bloom prescribing greater dependency on the market for universities or promoting the autonomous intellectual activity that their distinctive method requires? Since both the universities and the market allegedly share an identical method of competing with others in the buying and selling of ready-made products for whatever price they can get, there is no question in his mind that the former must serve the latter. Yet, Bloom's whole argument rests on the presupposition that competition as the method of the market is identical to competition as the method of education.

How well does this claim hold up in light of the counter-evidence that he dismisses?

The brute fact is that Canadian universities are already competing internationally in just this way. They successfully manage to reduce the price of products and services, affording comparative advantage to business corporations. Dr Marc Renaud, when he was president of the Social Sciences and Humanities Research Council of Canada, was among those who acknowledged this growing trend. "In reality," he wrote, "universities are now active in the market square, making alliances (so-called partnerships) and deals, exchanging goods and services in exchange for monetary and symbolic rewards, commercializing research results, scouting and selling talents, providing policy and organizational advice for government and industry, and so on."[46] Universities, then, are making the very "partnerships" with business favoured by Bloom. They are commercializing their research results by making goods and services available to companies in return for "monetary and symbolic rewards," and they are advising government and industry on both policy and strategy for use in world markets. Bloom obliterates such evidence in order to assert that the "relative educational advantage" of "our education system" is "slipping." The reason for this is simple: he wants universities to produce even more value added goods and services to Canadian business corporations in order to provide them with an even greater comparative advantage.

In contrast, Renaud does recognize that the commercialization of universities threatens the critical search for knowledge that has been their main function. This search can only take place where there exists freedom of a distinctively academic kind – namely, "freedom to disagree, freedom to challenge taken-for-granted assumptions, freedom to create from scratch."[47] Among advocates of the market model, Renaud is unusual in his recognition both of the value of academic freedom and of how it is opposed to the method of buying and selling products in the market. Posing critical questions of presuppositions, on the basis of evidence and reasoned argument, is a crucial activity, and it is one in which universities must continue to engage.

There is, however, a second kind of competition pursued by Canadian universities, and neither Bloom nor Renaud recognizes it. This distinctive kind of educational competition creates value that is independent of any comparative advantage in the market. Universities consistently offer excellence in their programs and facilities, in the quality of teaching and scholarship they make available to students, and in the research they conduct in a wide variety of disciplines, all of which contributes to the public good. They compete for a relative advantage in all these areas with other universities in Canada and, increasingly, abroad. To take but one example, when faculty publish articles in refereed journals, as is a requirement of their employment, they are competing successfully with other faculty from around the world who are striving to do the same. Their work is reviewed by peers and is judged to be of sufficient quality to merit publication in an international "marketplace of ideas" in which the goods exchanged are theories, evidence, arguments, and critical questioning of all stated knowledge claims. Such international competition, which is at the core of university life, goes largely unrecognized because it is opposed to the method of the market, in which the buying and selling of ready-made products for whatever price one can get is the regulatory norm. The method of education nurtures growth and the autonomous use of one's mental capacities, which, in the case of publication, broadens and deepens the understanding of an international readership. This method cannot be considered identical to the method of the market without irreparably undermining the educational vocation of universities.

Opposing Standards of Excellence

Competition among universities, then, secures a distinctive kind of educational excellence that is opposed to the market. Teaching, scholarship, and research that broaden the understanding of students, researchers, and international scholars must meet the standards of educational excellence. Scholars do this by ruling out both any "one-sided presentation" of relevant evidence and engaging in any "manipulative conditioning" of their audience in an attempt to get it to agree with their findings. Any university program that did engage in either of these activities would be a failure because all its knowledge claims would be partial. Yet, the very devices deplored by educators are embraced by market agents and are used to sell their ready-made products. "One-sided sales pitches" that use "operant conditioning" to impel customers to buy products are common since one measure of excellence in the market is how well a product is made to sell. Successful advertising campaigns do not generally make "rigorous demands on people's reason," preferring to utilize want-satisfaction on an unconscious level in order to increase the demand for private goods. University programs that achieve excellence, however, do so by ruling out "biased appeals to unconscious desires"[48] precisely because they stunt the development of an inclusive understanding among students and faculty.

A second standard of excellence indicates just how different the logic of value for education is from the logic of value for the corporate market. The "best product on the market" is one that is, and remains, "problem free for its buyer" – delivered "ready-made" for "instant easy use" with a "guaranteed replacement" if it does not work and that is "repaired cost-free" whenever it needs maintenance. The opposite holds true of quality education: it cannot be "produced or delivered by another" since this would negate the autonomous process of growth required to develop one's intellectual capacities. For the same reason, education can never be ready-made or instant, nor can a guaranteed cost-free replacement be offered if it is not working. The better the education, the harder students need to work, especially when overcoming any "failures" on the road to knowledge. This is because knowledge is very far from being "immediate in [its] yield," and an education worthy of the name can never be "problem-free" because it "poses ever deeper and wider problems the higher the level of excellence it achieves."[49]

These opposing criteria of evaluation are not recognized by Cochrane, who, having reduced the overriding motivation of education to that of the market, does the same with its standards of excellence. Impatient with the "natural inertia of universities," which "makes them too insular and ... not interested in the needs of business," he prescribes what "business wants"; namely, to "increase their responsiveness to issues identified by business as important."[50] To demonstrate their responsiveness to business, universities must employ different standards of excellence drawn exclusively from the market, and these standards must cover all their activities, including research. These market-based standards will rule out any "costly research that is unrelated to practical problems," replacing it with "sound basic research" that has "specific objectives, responsible time frames, and adequate evaluation," all determined by business. Most important of all, the results of basic research will increase "the transfer of discoveries into industrial reality." For even basic research is to be evaluated in terms of the amount of "technology transfer" it provides to the market. Excellence in research and scholarship is no longer a matter of posing problems that broaden and deepen our understanding of reality – an approach quite "unrelated to practical problems" of concern to business corporations. "Adequate evaluation" is to be based on one criterion alone: how well any research enables the transfer of discoveries into industrial reality so that business corporations can maximize their private monetary profits.[51]

Cochrane expunges the standards of excellence that are distinctive of education – impartial understanding and the ability to pose ever deeper problems of reality – in one fell swoop. He replaces them with two criteria: how well a product sells (in this case, how well research enables business to sell their products) and how problem-free such research is (namely, how easily it can be transferred into products for "industrial reality"). These market-imposed standards of excellence mean that only research transferable into ready-made products for business corporations has any value. Research that poses questions regarding reality so as to broaden and deepen our understanding is a remnant of universities past, and they should "decide to discontinue" it, along with other "inadequate products or programs" that fail to meet the standards imposed by industrial reality. Canadian universities must raise an "aggressive, constructive and unified voice" that is in tune with what "business wants" if they wish to survive in this "new reality," where servicing ready-made products for the market is the only standard of excellence.[52]

This theme is reiterated by William Thorsell, former editor-in-chief of the *Globe and Mail*, who declares that "universities are moving into an entrepreneurial culture in which ... excellence can be promised in a world of market accountability."[53] Thorsell spends little time explaining the meaning of market accountability even though, like Cochrane, he believes it is the basis of the one standard of excellence to which universities must conform in carrying out their research and teaching. He prefers to trade on the ambiguity of the term "excellence" in the hope that his readership will identify with it, even though its implementation may destroy universities as institutions in which impartial, disinterested, and critical thought takes place. After all, who could possibly be opposed to excellence? As Horn points out, "Thorsell's use of [such persuasive techniques] belongs in the Newspeak world of marketing [which] is what the market requires."[54]

Cochrane and Thorsell's refusal to acknowledge any standards of excellence other than "industrial reality" and "market accountability" is consistent with their acceptance of the value program of the market model of education. As a result, they are unable to recognize the incoherent assumptions at the base of their prescriptions.

Opposing Realities: Autonomy or Dependency

Universities in Canada currently face a stark choice. They can become institutions whose goal is to provide services for business corporations or they can assert their autonomy and determine for themselves which goals, motivations, methods, and standards of excellence they wish to embody. Typically, their distinctive logic of value has enabled universities to educate individuals, pursue scholarship, conduct research, and govern themselves in a relatively autonomous fashion. The core purpose of universities is to enable those in search of knowledge to develop their intellectual capacities for their own use. This constitutes both their goal and their standard of excellence. The better the education they offer, the more those who acquire it learn to think and act independently. This can only happen where the freedom to pursue knowledge critically is sustained by an institutional autonomy guaranteeing the university's independence from powerful social forces, including governments and the market.

The influence of the corporate market already permeates universities in multiple ways: through the actions of chief executive officers like Cochrane and Mitchell; through organizations such as the Corporate Higher Education Forum and the Conference Board of Canada; through government officials like Brzustowski; economists like Maxwell, Currie, and Bloom; journalists like Thorsell; senior university administrators like Holland; and faculty who are wedded to the market model of education. The logic of value peculiar to the market is only successful where buyers are dependent on the ready-made goods it produces. The more buyers remain independent of its products in both thought and action, the less market value is achieved. From the "brand-identification" reinforced by advertising,[55] to the one-sided sales pitches extolling the "quality" of any given product, to the internet's abundance of corporate "messages," the market's logic of value is achieved only where customers are dependent on the goods and services, and the ways of thinking and acting, that it offers. To imagine that academic freedom and institutional autonomy

would survive in universities regulated by market principles is to fail
to understand how the value system of the university is opposed to
the value system of the market. Unless their distinctive logic of value
is protected, universities will become "engines of economic growth,"
producing ready-made products and standardized ideas for the
corporate market.

Throughout this section I have drawn attention to the fact that
advocates of the market model of education tend to expunge all
counter-evidence that does not accord with the overriding need to
limit the scope of universities to "what business wants." This style
of "argument" rules out opposition by closing itself off from any
other points of view. The value program of the market model prevents
its advocates from recognizing that the goals, motivations, methods,
and standards of excellence of university education are opposed to
those of the corporate market. Among those whom I have considered,
only Marc Renaud acknowledges the importance of academic freedom to the process of critical understanding that sets universities
apart. The rest see such freedom as an encumbrance to the "increased
efficiency" demanded by "industrial reality" and as one of many
"inadequate products" to be eliminated from "aggressive" universities.[56] They regard the corporate market as a totalizing moment in
human affairs, a "regime of truth" to which every institution must
be subservient lest its global rule be disturbed.[57] I return to the question of the value program of the market and the totalizing tendency
of its advocates in chapter 6.

OPPOSING THE MARKET MODEL: ACADEMIC FREEDOM IN CANADIAN UNIVERSITIES

In direct contrast to the market model of education, I argue that
academic freedom is indispensable to the critical search for knowledge. Indeed, academic freedom is central to the life of universities.
Without it, the search for knowledge could not take place. Academic
freedom enables professors and students to espouse views and to
articulate theories that differ from those dominant in their discipline,
their university, and/or their society. Dissenting views can flourish
because they are protected. Such freedom is contingent upon both
the evidence that can be brought forward in support of these views
and a respect for the freedom of one's colleagues to advance contesting

theories of reality, truth, and value. Without academic freedom and the institutional autonomy of which it is a part, the purposes of university education, scholarship, and research cannot be achieved. Together they make possible a critical reflection upon the foundations of all knowledge, which is something that universities alone are capable of pursuing. Such critical thought enhances the growth of knowledge by subjecting every stated knowledge claim to radical scrutiny and by posing questions regarding its adequacy.

A long and illustrious tradition conceives of academic freedom in precisely these terms.. Critical thought and academic freedom are commonly recognized as necessary conditions for the vitality of universities and their distinctive activity of advancing and disseminating shared knowledge. Leading theorists from different countries agree that, where these characteristics are threatened, universities are in danger of becoming training centres for government, business, or both.[58]

Several Canadian organizations strongly support academic freedom and recognize the need for universities to be independent of strong external forces. Among these is the Canadian Association of University Teachers (CAUT), whose "Model Clause on Academic Freedom" has been the basis of most collective agreements between faculty and their respective university administrations since 1979. The model clause was updated recently by the Policy Statement on Academic Freedom approved by CAUT Council in November 2005. However, I scrutinize the former because it furnishes a full understanding of the centrality of academic freedom not only to universities and the work of faculty but also to "the common good of society." The common good is strengthened by "the teaching function of the university as well as ... its scholarship and research," whose purpose is "the search for knowledge and its free exposition." By relating the free and open pursuit of knowledge to the common good of society, the clause emphasizes the importance of all faculty "exercising their legal rights as citizens" in the performance of their teaching, scholarship, and research. "Any member of the academic community" is entitled to such rights because their critical search for knowledge engages a variety of publics – graduate and undergraduate students, faculty, and the general public itself – and thereby contributes to the public interest.[59]

This stands in stark contrast to the market model of education, whose ruling out of academic freedom as a value is matched by a disregard for reason and knowledge as constitutive of the public good. In the academic conception of knowledge, the critical search for knowledge is connected with the overall well-being of society both by setting an example of free and open debate about the adequacy of contesting ideas and by contributing to the general stock of knowledge of civil society; in the market conception, knowledge is simply a means for private business corporations to maximize their monetary profits. These two conceptions of knowledge, which are currently being contested at Canadian universities, profoundly affect both academic freedom and university autonomy.

The CAUT clause makes clear that faculty must be free to carry out research, publish their results, teach, and engage in free discussion "regardless of prescribed doctrine." In other words, this distinctive freedom enables faculty to pursue knowledge in a critical fashion, whether or not their findings are in keeping with the dominant beliefs of their discipline, their department, their colleagues, their university, or society as a whole. Without this freedom, the pursuit of knowledge will stagnate as faculty become fearful of posing questions critical of the presuppositions in their discipline(s). Academic freedom enables faculty to pose critical questions of presuppositions, subjecting every stated knowledge claim to radical scrutiny without external interference, whether from business, government, the university administration, or the faculty association itself. For this reason, faculty have the freedom "to criticize the university and the faculty association" without "institutional censorship," for only with such protection can they speak out in the name of the common good. Where the freedom to explore knowledge is "hindered ... impeded ... infringed ... [or] abridged" the good of all those with whom such knowledge might have been shared is also undermined – a point to which I return shortly.[60]

The CAUT clause asserts that, far from requiring "neutrality on the part of the individual ... academic freedom makes commitment possible." An open exchange of ideas can only take place where faculty are free to express their beliefs so that they, too, are subjected to the critical scrutiny of all members of the academic community. Such a commitment serves to keep ideas alive in the classroom, in the laboratory, and in research publications as it encourages debate over key concepts and their presuppositions. At the same time, due to the very nature of the process of critical inquiry, there is a limit to what can be taught or published by faculty as "academic freedom carries with it the duty to use that freedom in a manner consistent with the scholarly obligation to base research and teaching on an honest search for knowledge."[61] The ethical concepts of duty and scholarly obligation imply that faculty have a keen responsibility to base their teaching and research on a critical search for knowledge rather than on prejudice or dogma. Blind commitment to a belief in the power of the market, or the state, to solve all of humanity's problems, untempered by exposure to counter-arguments, results in research that is deeply flawed and unworthy of the title of knowledge. Similarly, a faculty member who blindly advocated the former Soviet Union as the ideal and just society in his/her lectures, and entertained no counter-argument, would be engaged in indoctrination rather than education. In both cases, "an honest search for knowledge" is sacrificed because it does not accord with one's set presuppositions. This is why critical thought, which seeks out the unexamined assumptions of any position or discipline, is central to the search for knowledge. Without it, faculty cannot meet their scholarly obligation to create and disseminate knowledge in an open-minded and honest way.

The CAUT clause also indicates that knowledge claims that are not based on critical inquiry are deficient and lie beyond the pale of academic freedom. The freedom to teach, discuss, and publish what they choose is relative to faculty members' scholarly obligation to search for knowledge in an honest and open manner. This suggests the need for making a distinction between knowledge claims that are adequate and those that are not. By critically examining the evidence supporting each claim, openly discussing it with others, and honestly trying to evaluate its worth, faculty may reach a judgment as to its adequacy. Where the evidence is inconclusive, as is often the case, the reasonable course of action is for faculty to teach or write about such claims in ways that leave open the question of their adequacy. However, where knowledge claims do not acknowledge existing evidence, both their adequacy and their right to be protected by academic freedom can be challenged. To return to the examples mentioned above, any knowledge claim about the power of the market to solve humanity's problems that is made without being exposed to counter-arguments is inadequate, as is any similar claim concerning the justice of Soviet society. Teaching, scholarship, and/or research advocating these and other claims in this sort of one-sided manner amount to indoctrination rather than an honest search for knowledge, and they are not entitled to the protection afforded by academic freedom. While this may seem too stringent a condition, it follows from the conception of knowledge and freedom articulated in the CAUT clause.[62]

The CAUT clause, like other statements on academic freedom, reflects enlightenment conceptions of liberty in which individual freedom is paramount. At the same time, however, it provides a deeply important connection between two goods: the freedom to pursue knowledge critically and the common good of society. The link between these two goods lies, as I have pointed out, in the distinctive nature of knowledge, which requires public critique from scholars, researchers, students, and others. This makes academic freedom a distinctive kind of liberty, one in which individuals are related to a variety of publics by virtue of their teaching, scholarship, and research. Suppression of the academic freedom of one individual undermines the freedom of all members of these publics since it threatens their ability to pursue knowledge in a critical manner. This, in turn, suggests an important difference between academic freedom and individual liberty. The academic freedom of one faculty member contributes to the freedom of others and is, itself, enhanced by the freedom of this community of scholars to engage in the same critical process. In the context of the critical search for knowledge, the freedom of the individual and the freedom of the group are mutually supportive, enabling both to appeal to a wider community whenever institutional threats to academic freedom occur, as is currently the case with the imposition of the standards of the corporate market.[63]

Institutional safeguards strengthening academic freedom must recognize its full-blooded character if universities are to resist the threat to their autonomy posed by the market. As Horn points out, "three ancient desires" rooted in the deep structure of universities provide the basis for a systematic defence of their distinctive logic of value; namely, the desire "for intellectual independence, collective autonomy, and the time and financial security needed to carry on scholarly and scientific work."[64] The intellectual independence of the individual scholar is, as I have argued, linked to the freedom of the entire community of which s/he is a part. Only where knowledge is advanced, disseminated, and sustained as a public good can researchers share it with their various publics. Their collective autonomy requires strong institutional forms that enable universities to limit the power of the market by ensuring that knowledge remains a public, not a private, good. This, in turn, requires governments to fund universities fully as the one place in society where the honest search for knowledge takes place, whether it results in value-added, ready-made products or not.

None of this is meant to imply that Canadian universities have always been havens of critical inquiry. Nostalgia for an ideal age in which autonomous institutions engaged primarily in curiosity-based research and teaching and learning for their own sake is misplaced. Threats to academic freedom in which dissenting faculty voices were silenced, or nearly silenced, have been commonplace. The cases of professors Frank Underhill at the University of Toronto, Harry Crowe at United College (now the University of Winnipeg), and George Grant at York University are among the better known instances of faculty who resisted threats to the free expression of their ideas.[65] In the mid-1970s, Dr Walter Worth, provincial deputy minister of advanced education, exerted ongoing pressure on the universities of Alberta and Calgary to comply with the need for "directed task-oriented research," with little regard for the academic freedom of faculty.[66]

These examples show just how important the principle of academic freedom is for maintaining those "traditions of learning that are themselves kept under critical review." As Chris Arthur argues: "Universities afford spaces where thoughts can be voiced freely, opinions formulated without fear of unfounded censure, where ideas can be tested, where people are taught to think for themselves."[67] Without the distinctive liberty that enables one faculty member to contribute to the freedom of others in their search for knowledge and that is, itself, sustained by their freedom when engaged in critical thought, the process of inquiry cannot take place. Professor Ramsay Cook recognized this fact when writing to Crowe after his reinstatement by the board of regents of United College: "Whatever else happens, this must seem an important day for academic freedom in Canada."[68] A victory for one member of the scholarly community was indeed a victory for all.

THE CASE STUDY METHOD

Before concluding the chapter it is important to explain why I use the case study method to investigate the workings of the market model of education. I suggest in the introduction that case studies are an application of the Whiteheadian concept of "generalization," a process of learning and researching in which one "should start from general ideas and study their applications to concrete cases." This approach implies that "the wide sweep of generality" is best achieved through a balanced understanding of "the abstract" and of "concrete fact," whereby "concrete fact should be studied as illustrating the scope of general ideas."[69] For Whitehead, the overall rhythm distinguishing university research enables an understanding of the relationship between the particular (i.e., the concrete) and the general (i.e., the abstract). An alternating gaze on the concrete and the abstract provides insights at both the personal and institutional levels that are often denied to other modes of inquiry. The goal is to understand the experience of faculty members whose academic freedom has been violated by the abstract principles of the market. The interplay between the concrete experience of individuals and the abstract principles of the market proceeds from "a vehement and passionate interest in the relation of general principles to irreducible and stubborn facts."[70] The process of generalization embodied in the case studies is a powerful tool in this regard. In this book I apply critical thought gained from the study of general ideas, but I am not content with abstract generalizations about the corporatization of universities; rather, I choose always to connect to the concrete facts that illuminate that process.

Dialogue characterizes the investigative approach used in the case studies. Participants willingly shared the rich complexities of their experience and their insights. My role as researcher was to pose questions and to pay close attention to the replies, interpreting the meaning of what people said in an open-minded but critical fashion.[71] At times, this meant asking follow-up questions and probing for clarification during our prolonged conversations. Faculty, students, and staff talked about university life, expressing their ideals and concerns for the institution in ways that would not have been possible on the basis of the "thin slice of reality" revealed by the "superficial questions" used in large-scale survey research.[72]

Another advantage of case studies is their flexibility. By investigating events pertaining to specific cases, I was able to incorporate the views of a wide range of participants at different universities and to contextualize them in a discursive manner. A systematic focus on the experience of participants coupled with a critical examination of their presuppositions, as well as my own, guided my inquiry throughout and led to constructive and imaginative proposals that question present-day reality. Through the use of multiple textual sources, I constantly cross-checked information from participants, evaluating what was said in light of what had been written on the subject at hand.[73] While the goal of this process of "triangulation" was to minimize possible distortions, conflicting interpretations of events were also a source of contested knowledge. The entire process flows from Whitehead's injunction to avoid "the merest hint of dogmatic certainty as to finality of statement[, which] is an exhibition of folly."[74] Failure to reject such dogmatism would have resulted in my adopting a value program that was incapable of thinking beyond its own assumptions.

CONCLUSION

There is an urgent need for universities in Canada to ensure their independence from the market so that they remain capable of sustaining academic freedom and the critical search for knowledge. In order to prevent the liquidation of these defining characteristics, universities must move beyond the narrow assumptions of the market model and rejuvenate their own distinctive goals, motivations, methods, and standards of excellence. A tradition of individual and collective autonomy linked to the common good of society lies at the heart of this revival. And this, in turn, requires a new vision. Professor Ian Angus refers to this vision as "the possibility of a democratic university ... rooted in the respectful give-and-take of cooperative learning ... [which] cannot be kept alive without raising basic questions about the meaning and function of the university in a corporate environment and pressing for the greatest possible cooperative autonomy that will sustain criticism of that environment. Nothing less befits the institutions of thought."[75] By advancing and disseminating ideas cooperatively, faculty and students can share their knowledge and raise critical questions about the limitations of thought placed on them by the corporate market. The struggle between the market model of education and the vision of a cooperative and democratic university is evident in the case studies presented in the following chapters.

2

A Marketing Professor Meets the Market

Public education is a $150 billion a year business ... Business will have to set the new agenda ... a complete restructure [sic] driven by competition and market discipline, unfamiliar ground for educators.

David Kearns[1]

On the afternoon of 28 September 1988, Dr Vedanand made his way to the University of Manitoba Faculty Club. As one of several faculty members invited to a seminar by Xerox, he felt a certain responsibility to attend the event, the purpose of which was to enable the company "to make a brief presentation to our department and heads of other departments regarding the employment prospects of Xerox Canada for our students."[2] A memorandum to this effect had been circulated by the head of the department of marketing and, since one of his areas of specialization was the marketing strategies of Japanese corporations, Vedanand was interested in what might be said about Xerox's ability to compete in the global marketplace. He could not have imagined just how much the events of that afternoon would affect his future life.

The seminar was given by William Morrissey, a major account sales manager and former student in the Faculty of Management, who spoke of Xerox's track record for photocopier sales worldwide. He claimed, among other things, that the company had "regained its position as top seller in the market" after having lost this place "to other companies in recent years." Sceptical of the veracity of this claim, Vedanand intervened, pointing out that Canon "remained the leader in the home copier field." This, he said, was largely because of "a superior marketing strategy which the US had not been able to match" in such fields as automobiles and electronics. And, he went on to say, many American "companies far bigger than Xerox" had lost their market share to Japanese corporations. According to Vedanand, Canon's competitive edge in photocopy machines had been secured by "a low end entry strategy with a low and high priced product which leads the market" in photocopy machines. Canon had done this by creating a new market segment for personal, small business, and home photocopiers ("a low end entry strategy") in which both their low- and high-priced machines "led the market." Morrissey's "factual error" seemed to indicate Xerox's refusal to acknowledge that their loss of market share to Canon was the result of distinctive marketing techniques with which they had been unable to compete (AA, 4, 62).

At this point, James Lovie, Morrissey's superior, stepped in, saying that Xerox was "not in the small copier market." Vedanand replied that the company had failed to make use of an opportunity "to attack its competitors" in this field. Had they done so, they too might have been selling home copiers – a view to which David Kearns, chairman of Xerox US, apparently subscribed in acknowledging that the company "had misjudged things [through] complacency in managerial ranks when Japanese companies were nibbling at market shares." In any case, Vedanand concluded, "if you look at Canon, it had become Number One and it still is Number One in the small paper copy market" (AA, 5).

This exchange between Vedanand, Morrissey, and Lovie lasted several minutes, after which Morrissey completed his presentation. There was no question of the talk's being abandoned as Vedanand's intervention throughout was scholarly and polite. Indeed, the discussion between the three men continued once the seminar was over, when Lovie even mentioned "the possibility of his taking part in a seminar at a later date in Dr. Vedanand's class." There was also talk of Vedanand's being "invited … to make a presentation to Xerox," a point that Lovie and Morrissey later denied, just as they "denied walking up to Dr. Vedanand" to make the invitation. Lovie, however, did remember "Dr. Vedanand offering to give a seminar," saying that, even though "he had no interest in Dr. Vedanand's doing it, [he] would take it under advisement" from his superiors. Significantly, relations between the Xerox sales representatives and Vedanand were cordial enough for such invitations to be exchanged in a serious fashion, despite the latter's interruption of Morrissey's presentation (AA, 7).

No one who was present, including Vedanand's colleagues, his department head, and the associate dean, took him to task for his conduct during the reception. Nothing was said to him in the days following the seminar. Nevertheless, his criticism of Xerox's marketing strategies had called into question the corporation's competitiveness in the global market, thereby casting doubt on its desirability as an employer for graduates of the Faculty of Management. The incident could have been laid to rest at this point: a faculty member had simply used his knowledge of the field of marketing to question the claims of a couple of Xerox salespeople who disagreed with him. Opposing views had been shared and an invitation extended by each party to further the conversation. But Vedanand had questioned the plans of the new dean to privatize the Faculty of Management, and this could not go unpunished (AA, 4, 7).

THE BANKER AS DEAN

Robert Mackness had been appointed dean of the Faculty of Management a few months prior to this seminar. His appointment was a controversial one because, before his arrival at the University of Manitoba (U of M), he had been senior vice-president at the Bank of Nova Scotia: "In the eyes of some members of the university community, he had been imposed on the Faculty by the business community in order that business interests, not the university and its academic staff, would control the Faculty of Management."[3] His appointment was a symbol of just how far business interests had come to dominate the university and the Faculty of Management. And the process of recruitment used to hire Mackness had compromised the university's established hiring practices.

It was "the Associates program," a group of "the heads of most of Winnipeg's major businesses," that was instrumental in ensuring that Mackness was appointed as dean. The Associates, who provide "an active link between the business community and the faculty [of management], and bring the school advisory, counseling, and fundraising support,"[4] had selected two chief executive officers of transnational corporations to represent them on the hiring committee. Jack Fraser (who was to become chairman of Air Canada) and Arni Thornsteinson, chief executive officer of Cargill (who was eventually appointed president of Petro Canada Limited by the government of Brian Mulroney),[5] used their influence to persuade the vice-president academic to suspend the usual hiring process in order to attract prominent candidates from the business community. This required the foregoing of any public presentations to the faculty, the successful candidate's being introduced only when the decision had been made, and general secrecy throughout lest candidates' names became publicly known. The vice-president academic, together with one of the Associates on the committee, met with the Faculty of Management Council, which agreed to the Associates' plan. Associate Dean Jerry Gray subsequently referred to the Associates as "professional people ... neither malicious nor threatening in their motives [but simply] wanting to pay $1,000 per year for an investment in our place."[6]

The actions of the vice-president academic in allowing the Associates to suspend university policy were consistent with the central administration's increasing dependence upon the business community. Since the mid-1980s, U of M had been actively seeking corporate "donations" for "a major fund-raising program to finance construction at the University" – construction that, in the past, had been largely paid for by governments. In the context of the "new reality" of debt reduction and cost cutting, however, administrators had turned to the corporate sector as an alternative source of funding. As a corporate agent, Mackness was well positioned to attract business funding and to ensure that Xerox's "donation" of $75,000 to the Faculty of Management would be maintained with annual installments of $15,000. One of his responsibilities as dean was to ensure that "corporate contributions" such as this would be secured not only from Xerox but also from other members of the business community that had secured his appointment (AA, 14).

This ability to attract outside funds was matched by Mackness's determination to bring business interests to bear on the Faculty of Management itself. Having been appointed to the Board of Governors of Federal Industries and Great West Company soon after his arrival as dean,[7] Mackness rapidly formulated a "development plan," the first draft of which he presented to the faculty in January 1989. The goal of the plan was to ensure that the faculty's teaching programs and research directly served the corporate market. Moreover, "the Plan itself limited Faculty participation to either accepting or rejecting the Dean's plans,"[8] and those faculty members who disagreed were ignored. Many faculty members believed that Mackness had been hired to ensure that "business interests" rather than educational goals and values "would control the Faculty of Management."[9] The

Faculty would then be in a position to "'restructure itself' to fit 'the needs of the economy.'"[10]

As evidence of the dean's determination, "considerable savings" were to be made in the form of greater "efficiency."[11] The process of "market-based efficiency" involved "simply the reduction of unit costs"[12] by ratcheting down expenditures on those aspects of teaching, learning, and research that did not deliver monetized value, and channeling the savings into areas better positioned to meet the demands of private corporations. They would reap the benefits of Mackness's plan when the could hire "products" capable of lowering "the ratio between the cost inputs for a firm and its priced outputs." The development plan superseded the university's own distinctive form of efficiency, which sought to extend a deeper and wider understanding "to a more comprehensive range."[13] The value of this kind of understanding is not reducible to the narrow calculations of market-based "efficiency."

Mackness, "a man imbued with his mission," claimed that his "faculty development plan [would] place the faculty of management in the ranks of leading Canadian schools by the mid-1990s."[14] This goal, which proved to be unrealistic, was to be achieved by procuring an additional $2.5 million in annual funding over a period of five years from various "partners" to the faculty. As he put it, "We'll move fairly rapidly to a situation where you'll have about a third of the costs covered by tuition, a third covered by alumni and 'friends of the university' and a third covered by government or the public sector."[15] The "friends of the university" to whom Mackness referred were members of the Associates Program who "unanimously approved its fund-raising target of $500,000 per year by 1994." This amounted to only 20 percent of the funding required for the plan, not one-third as had been claimed. Students, meanwhile, agreed to an increase in tuition fees, which amounted to another "20 percent share of the burden,"[16] and were encouraged to think of themselves as consumers making decisions about "a better product" rather than as learners seeking shared knowledge. Government would still provide most of the funding, but its role would be curtailed because, in Mackness's words, "it tends to affect the standards" of education by demanding academic excellence in place of the "skill levels that make them [i.e., student-consumers] fully competitive internationally" in the corporate market.[17] This "much healthier balance" among the various "stakeholders" would, he claimed, have a refreshing impact on the standards of vocational training by making it "more accountable" to the needs of business.[18]

THE DEAN'S DEVELOPMENT PLAN

The goal of the development plan was to hasten the privatization of the Faculty of Management by limiting the role of government in the setting of educational standards. At the same time, corporate influence on vocational training and research was to be maximized. The public education of managers was to be replaced by skills training in which greater "efficiency" would be produced by a market discipline that conceived of the reduction of unit costs as the sole standard of educational value. While the plan still depended upon government funding for success, Mackness's strategy was to minimize public control over the teaching and research functions of the faculty. This was because, in his own words, "governments insist on forcibly extracting wealth from the productive elements of society"[19] by preventing universities from opening up as markets in which private companies control the sale of educational goods and services.

A closer examination of the plan shows that privatization was to be achieved in the following ways:

1 *A transfer of "resources," however "scarce," into the "high-demand mainline business disciplines – Finance, Marketing, Management and Accounting."* The goal was to improve "the depth and capacity of the Faculty" in these disciplines, ensuring that vocational training for the corporate market was paramount.

2 *An "elimination of low-demand courses and patterns ... [that] serve the specialized academic or research interests of senior faculty."* The aim was to expunge from the curriculum those courses that reflected the research interests of established researchers and scholars whose commitment to the advancement and dissemination of knowledge did not serve Mackness's plan. This would then free up resources for the "high-demand mainline business disciplines."

3 *An active search for additional funding for the four mainline business disciplines and their vocational training programs.* Funds were to be gleaned from the sources mentioned above:
   a. *"Special grants from the government,"* which was increasingly interested in the short-term benefits of vocational training in business. This strategy was designed for the provincial

government's spring budget in 1989 and required rapid
approval of the development plan's final draft in order to meet
the deadline.

b. *"A tuition fee surcharge to be paid for by the students in the
faculty."*[20] The surcharge amounted to $93 in 1990, increasing
to $355 in 1994. When this was added to the regular fee struc-
ture of about $1,400 in 1989, the effect was to establish a "cost
recovery program" for the faculty's undergraduate program.[21]
The surcharge did actually raise one-third of the money required
for implementation of the development plan, amounting to
$500,000 over five years.

c. *"Donations from the business community,"* particularly from
the Associates Program and corporations like Xerox, whose
"contributions" and "donations" to the faculty were to be
tapped in a systematic way.[22]

In order to ensure that the last strategy of the development plan
would work, the need "to cultivate positive relationships with the
business community" became an overriding goal. Educational values
that might block the plan's implementation were seen as "wasteful."
The significance of this value-set cannot be over-emphasized for it
enables one to understand Mackness's actions as dean. It is best
summarized in the following statement from the *Arbitration Award
between University of Manitoba Faculty Association and University
of Manitoba*: "There is a relationship between the Faculty of Management at the University of Manitoba and segments of the business
community of Manitoba. Graduates of the Faculty of Management
have assumed responsible positions in the business community and
the business community retains contact with the Faculty of Management for a variety of reasons which include a desire to have access
to, and an opportunity to hire, promising graduates of the Faculty"
(AA, 14).

The statement suggests that the goals of the Faculty of Management
and those of the corporate market were closely aligned. Graduates
of the faculty had "assumed responsible positions" within the corporate segment of the business community and maintained contact
with the Faculty of Management for a variety of reasons, including
"a desire to have access to ... promising graduates of the Faculty"
and "an opportunity to hire" those same graduates. Business

corporations could screen those students whom they found promising (through personal contact, summer employment, and work/study programs) and hire them once they graduated in order to provide "value-added" to their products (AA, 9).

The overriding goal of strengthening the relationship between the Faculty of Management and corporate "segments of the business community" enabled companies to assess the skilled resources ("promising graduates") produced by the former and hire those best equipped to ensure the maximization of stockholder value. Corporate "donations" were to be targeted towards strengthening vocational training and research in the "four high-demand mainline business disciplines" of finance, marketing, management, and accounting. These strategies could not work, however, if the demand for "promising graduates" was not met. On the basis of his educated understanding of the company's marketing strategies, Vedanand had questioned the market reputation of Xerox at the seminar, thus damaging its reputation. His remarks might have persuaded those students who were present to question the company's desirability as an employer. As a result, he was seen as a threat not only to Xerox's relationship with the Faculty of Management but to the dean's development plan (AA, 5).

Mackness's plan to provide extra resources to four high-demand mainline business disciplines was designed to achieve the following goals:

1 Subordinate the Faculty of Management to the overriding goal of cultivating "positive relationships with the business community" and ensure an ongoing flow of skilled graduates capable of generating value-added products for the corporate world.
2 Transfer funds into the disciplines of finance, marketing, management, and accounting.
3 Facilitate the search for government and corporate funding for vocational training and research in these areas.
4 Liquidate courses in other disciplines that reflect the research and scholarly interests of faculty who are antithetical to the plan's corporate bias.
5 Exact a "surcharge" in tuition fees for undergraduate programs.
6 Use market-based "efficiency" so as to effect "the reduction of unit costs" of teaching and research in all but the "high-demand mainline business disciplines."

It was in the context of this process of privatization that Mackness responded to Vedanand's questioning of the Xerox sales representatives.

THE DEAN PUNISHES DISSENT

A day or two after the reception, Jerry Gray, the associate dean, "expressed to Dean Mackness the view that Dr Vedanand had embarrassed the Faculty and everyone at the reception," suggesting that his behaviour was "rude" and out of keeping with the informality of the gathering. Gray, who had hosted the seminar on behalf of the dean, "did not think that it was the time or place for Dr Vedanand to conduct himself in this manner" for his "tone" had been "challenging." Following this conversation, Mackness spoke to the head of the Department of Marketing, Dr Marvin Beckman, who described Vedanand's "interjection" as "aggressive" and "quite a confrontation" and his "tone" as "quite unpleasant." After consultations with one or two other faculty members, who spoke of conversations among colleagues (many of whom were not present at the seminar) "overheard" in the halls, Mackness decided to act (AA, 6–8).

He asked Beckman, as head of Vedanand's department and someone with "first hand knowledge of the event," to draft a memorandum disapproving of what Vedanand had done. Beckman did so on 13 October 1988, "but for some reason it lay on his desk and was not forwarded to Dean Mackness" until the dean requested the proposed memo almost three weeks later. Before sending it Mackness consulted with Gray because "he wanted to go out of his way to make sure that he would not offend" (AA, 8).

The "confidential" memo from Mackness to Vedanand, which was finally sent on 4 November with a copy to Beckman, read as follows: "I have been disturbed at several reports of your comments to the Xerox people at the September 28 reception. The tone of your challenge concerning their report on share of market was unpleasant, and your 'grilling' of sales representatives on company strategy inappropriate. The Faculty is working very hard to cultivate positive relationships with the business community and your remarks were counterproductive" (AA, 9). Vedanand later said he was "shocked" at receiving the memorandum, which "had a chilling effect on him, [because it] almost seemed to be a reprimand" from the dean, who had sent the memo "without the facts being checked." He "was not grilling the sales representative" nor was he "trying to embarrass anyone [but was simply] trying to put the facts in perspective [with] the Xerox people." Moreover, "his tone was not unpleasant" but, rather, was "very casual." Indeed, "the two presenters would not have walked up to him and agreed to come to his class and invite him to give a seminar had he misconducted himself." The memorandum was "inaccurate" and a distortion of what had taken place at the seminar, which Mackness now referred to as a "reception" (AA, 5, 8–10).

Vedanand also felt a strong "chilling effect" from Mackness's memo with regard to his teaching. In the words of the chair of the subsequent arbitration hearing, "it caused him concern about what he [would] do as a professor in his classroom" because he could not express his views freely for fear of incurring the dean's wrath. In order to teach students about theories of marketing and their practical applications, Vedanand needed to engage in open discussion of a wide variety of views. Academic freedom, as encoded in the CAUT Model Clause, enables the expression of dissenting views in teaching "regardless of prescribed doctrine."[23] In the context of the Faculty of Management, the prescribed doctrine had become one of cultivating "positive relationships with the business community" – an overriding goal or "orthodoxy line" to be followed without question.[24] The expression of opposing views, even those grounded in research and scholarship, made Vedanand persona non grata. The fact that Mackness's memo "relate[d] to Xerox in the classroom" meant that it threatened Vedanand's freedom to teach. Indeed, it showed that his views were "not welcome" in a faculty in which the educational principles of the university were being superseded by the values of the market (AA, 39).

Mackness, in contrast, claimed that the memo "was not meant as a form of discipline," was never kept in "a personnel or discipline file," and was intended simply "to inform Vedanand of the view of his peers." Nevertheless, the content of the memo was seen as a threat to the academic freedom of a faculty member whose criticism of Xerox was based on considerable expertise in the field of marketing. Professor Kenneth Westhues of the University of Waterloo has likened the actions of administrators in cases such as this to those of "the chief eliminator, [who acts as] the symbolic embodiment of the academic unit, of the values it celebrates and the purposes it serves," thereby depriving faculty like Vedanand "of the sense of self-worth required to walk across campus, stand in front of a class, and teach."[25] Even if this were not the dean's "avowed purpose," the memo had the effect of undermining the free expression of ideas in Vedanand's classroom. Vedanand had allegedly offended the Xerox salesperson on the basis of market practice, according to which "the accepted way in which to gain market favour [is] to offend no one and no vested interest."[26] Xerox, as an important customer of the Faculty of Management, was not to be offended since the company had a vested interest in receiving an ongoing supply of graduates capable of creating value-added products (AA, 4, 9).

THE THREAT TO ACADEMIC FREEDOM AND UNIVERSITY AUTONOMY

Mackness's memorandum made two basic claims: the first concerned the unpleasant tone of Vedanand's challenge to the two Xerox sales-people, which amounted to a "grilling" about company strategy and was "inappropriate"; the second suggested that Vedanand's remarks were "counterproductive" because they threatened the "positive relationships with the business community [that] the Faculty is working very hard to cultivate" (AA, 9).

The first allegation only makes sense in light of the second. Vedanand's remarks were considered rude in the context of the over-riding goal of cultivating "positive relationships with the business community." This goal provided the motivation for Mackness's development plan, and Vedanand's questions to "the Xerox people" put that plan at risk. Xerox's "donation" and their policy of hiring graduates from the Faculty of Management were just the kind of corporate connections that the dean had been hired to cultivate. Vedanand's dissenting ideas, which conflicted with the plan, had to be suppressed (AA, 7, 9).

As former senior vice-president of the Bank of Nova Scotia, Dean Mackness considered the goal of university education to be no different from that of the market – namely, the maximization of private monetary profits. In the words of CAUT's subsequent Committee of Inquiry, "Dean Mackness appeared to disregard or misunderstand university traditions and procedures"[27] to such an extent that basic principles of academic freedom and university autonomy were at risk. Neil Tudiver, professor of social work at U of M, put it this way: "For a dean with strong corporate ties, free critical expression seemed as unacceptable in the university as in the banking system."[28] It was this refusal to acknowledge the distinctive values of the university, in which academic freedom enables "free critical expression," that made Mackness's actions so damaging. While the immediate threat was to Vedanand's academic freedom, the freedom of other faculty members who did not subscribe to the opposing values of the market was also at risk. The well-orchestrated campaign to establish strong links between the Faculty of Management and the corporate market was supported by some powerful allies.

The U of M's central administration regarded Mackness's development plan as a welcome blueprint for change based on the discipline of the market. The market, after all, was a place where "everybody doesn't win," and, in the dean's own words, it could "dish out some very stern discipline to those who aren't meeting the market."[29] President Arnold Naimark himself would later develop "professional ties to Apotex" Inc, a pharmaceutical company that would fund medical research at U of M, brokering a number of "donor agreements" with the same company.[30] Moreover, the dean's development plan had already attracted favourable attention from the provincial government. The main reason for pushing ahead with the approval of the plan was to ensure its inclusion for discussion at a cabinet meeting on 5 April 1989. Indeed, the final draft was distributed to members of the Faculty of Management Council on 23 March for their approval before that meeting. The culmination of this exercise was the following declaration in the throne speech delivered to the Manitoba Legislature on 18 May: "My Ministers will also provide additional support for the growing capabilities of the Faculty of Management at the University of Manitoba."[31] This clear reference to Mackness's development plan shows that funding was secured from the provincial government, which, ironically, would have a greater role than before in shaping the training of future corporate managers.

It was left to faculty members to raise questions about the ways in which university autonomy was compromised, democratic decision-making disregarded, and their own jobs threatened by the introduction of the development plan. Indeed, opposition to Mackness's policies grew and resulted in the establishment of a CAUT Committee of Inquiry in October 1990 to determine "the reasons for the obvious discontent of the faculty at the University of Manitoba with the conduct of the Dean of Management."[32] Mackness refused to testify. President Naimark appeared before the committee in the spring of 1991, defending both the dean's development plan and the "autocratic manner" in which it had been "imposed" on the faculty. He did, however, express concern about a letter Mackness had written on 30 January 1989, which many condemned.[33] I return to this issue later in the chapter.

Vedanand understood the threat posed to his academic freedom only too clearly. He found the last sentence of Mackness's memo "very disturbing" and subsequently made the following statement: "Professors have a moral responsibility as scholars to present correct information and not to be subservient to the needs of the business community" (AA, 9–10). He had, after all, used his knowledge of the academic discipline of marketing to question the claims made by Xerox salespeople about their company's market share. Where such knowledge claims were mistaken, Vedanand had every right to point this out and to engage in debate with those who advocated them. If this meant challenging the views of members of the business community, then academic freedom entitled him to do so. Indeed, he believed that his moral responsibility as a scholar required him to interrogate all such information to determine its adequacy and accuracy. Rather than being "subservient to the needs of the business community," a scholar should critically examine all knowledge claims on the basis of the available evidence. Recognizing the incompatibility between his responsibility as a scholar and the restrictions placed on it by the dean's memo, Vedanand consulted with the University of Manitoba Faculty Association (UMFA) (AA, 13).

THE FACULTY ASSOCIATION'S GRIEVANCE AND MACKNESS'S STRATEGY

In early December 1988, UMFA filed an association grievance stating: "The Dean of Management has issued a letter ... which violates the fundamental right of academic freedom ... [and] attempts to prevent a faculty member from discussing his subject in a manner consistent with his scholarly obligations ... [Moreover,] this letter is one of institutional censure against the faculty member's right to discuss his subject" (AA, 10). Mackness had violated Vedanand's academic freedom and used his authority as dean to censor further expression of Vedanand's scholarly views. These two claims were central to

Vedanand's case, and, in order to deflect attention away from them, Mackness adopted a strategy that would trivialize both.

UMFA proposed the following constructive solution as a means to resolve the grievance: "Immediate retraction of the letter of November 4 ... [and] a declaration by the Dean and the President that the Collective Agreement has been violated [together with] any other remedy just and reasonable in the circumstances" (AA, 11). The grievance elicited a meeting between UMFA, Dean Mackness, and Vice-President (Administration) Falconer in early January 1989, which resulted in a subsequent letter from Falconer stating that it was clear that Mackness's "perception" of the effect of his memo on Vedanand's academic freedom "differed from that of the Faculty Association."

The extent of the difference in these perceptions became clear in a second "confidential memo" from Mackness to Vedanand, dated 17 January 1990. He reiterated the charge that Vedanand's "remarks were unpleasant, rude and offensive," constituting a "'grilling' of our guests" from Xerox, and he added the following: "I wish to make it clear that my communication to you was not in any way meant to have any bearing on your academic freedom ... These observations are a matter of politeness and have absolutely nothing to do with academic freedom" (AA, 11). Mackness was reiterating the claim that the goal of his first memorandum was simply to underline how rude Vedanand had been. He now begged the question of academic freedom by substituting "a matter of politeness" for established fact and reasoned response. By dismissing academic freedom as irrelevant, he expunged the core of Vedanand's grievance. Any reference to the overriding goal of cultivating "positive relationships with the business community," which had comprised the basis of his first memo, was also omitted. This strategy disguised the dean's attack on Vedanand's academic freedom as a mere slap on the wrist for his "unpleasant, rude and offensive" behaviour. Once the overriding goal, or "orthodoxy line," of Mackness's development plan to cultivate positive relationships with private business corporations was no longer considered relevant, Vedanand's scholarly criticism of Xerox appeared to lack substance (AA, 11, 9, 50).

As if to prove the point, Dean Mackness described the whole episode as "trivial" during the meeting with UMFA on 9 January. Once thought important enough to deserve a punitive memo, the incident became trivial once UMFA invoked the principle of academic freedom in Vedanand's defence. If Mackness could succeed in presenting the episode as trivial, then the charges that the principle of academic freedom had been violated and institutional censure invoked could also be trivialized. This would leave politeness as the only pertinent issue. Mackness's approach turned out to be far from trivial in its effect on subsequent events (AA, 13).

THE FACULTY ASSOCIATION'S REPLY

Not surprisingly, UMFA refused to accept Mackness's second memorandum as a resolution to the grievance. The president of UMFA, Professor Kenneth Osborne, made this clear in a letter sent on 26 January 1990 to Vice-President Falconer, in which he stated that the original memo had "not been removed from Dr. Vedanand's file, as stipulated in the grievance, [and] there are now two unacceptable memoranda on record." The second memo did nothing to correct the false accusations of the first. Rather than personally investigating "the facts concerning the incident of which he complains," Mackness supported "the testimony of a small number of others, with no attempt to contact the parties directly concerned" – all of which were elements of a design to override fact. Even though both memoranda relied on hearsay evidence, UMFA took the accusations they made "very seriously" (AA, 12–13).

The main thrust of UMFA's letter focused on the very concepts that Mackness tried to expunge: his first memorandum "still is a manifestation of institutional censure," and its impact "must be such as to make a faculty member wonder whether, if he or she says something that gives offence to a Dean, there might not be repercussions in the future." It was the fear of such repercussions that constituted institutional censure of Vedanand's free critical expression. A faculty member in receipt of such a memo would be unlikely "to speak his or her mind" for fear that the dean would "take umbrage" at the honest expression of any views, however scholarly they might be. Mackness's denial that he had wanted "to limit academic freedom" ignored the fact that "the memorandum must inevitably have such an effect" (AA, 12–13). "Quoting the historian Frank Underhill,[34] Osborne demonstrated the importance of academic freedom to 'the role and effective functioning of the University': To seek new knowledge and new understanding about nature and society, to keep asking questions, often very embarrassing ones, about established beliefs and conventional wisdom" (AA, 12). It is this process of questioning established beliefs that lies at the core of the search for knowledge, and it is this that Mackness had described as "rude." The letter from UMFA pointed out that there was no evidence that "the business representatives were in fact troubled" by Vedanand's questioning as businesspeople "are, in fact, quite able to defend themselves."[35] If the administrators present at the Xerox seminar were embarrassed, this was because they too failed to understand that "the pursuit of knowledge can involve the asking of tough questions," which some might think of as a grilling, even if the process formed an integral part of the search for knowledge. Moreover, grilling was a "loaded word" used to smear both the process of critically questioning knowledge claims and the integrity of the person engaged in it. Without knowing precisely in what the grilling consisted, "it is impossible to know whether it was inappropriate" (AA, 12–13).

The letter concluded that the only course of action left was "to proceed with the grievance, which now presumably moves to arbitration." The possibility of "some other resolution" was still open and, before proceeding, UMFA's President Osborne awaited Falconer's response. On 3 March 1989, he replied, recognizing the association's position to be "that Dean Mackness' first memorandum violates the right of academic freedom, notwithstanding his second memorandum and notwithstanding whatever Professor Vedanand may or may not have done at the reception." Despite this accurate interpretation of the grievance, Falconer concluded "that the collective agreement has not been violated ... [and that] the grievance and the remedy sought therein are therefore denied." The stage was now set for an arbitration hearing (AA, 14–15).

THE BATTLE BEGINS

The hearing, which lasted nine full days during the period between 16 May and 24 December 1990, began with the following statement from the lawyer for U of M: "The University unequivocally stipulates that the memorandum referred to in the grievance was non-disciplinary, was a non-disciplinary communication" (AA, 16). This stipulative definition of the non-disciplinary nature of Mackness's first memo suggests that it was not an attempt to limit Vedanand's academic freedom. The statement continued in the same vein: "The University categorically affirms that the Dean's letter will not be used in any subsequent action against Dr Vedanand or [sic] will Dr. Vedanand be prejudiced by it in respect to any future proceedings of a disciplinary nature" (AA, 12).

The university itself now joined the campaign of operation to rule out fact *as* fact. Its reaffirmation that Mackness's letter would not be used in any subsequent disciplinary action also undercut UMFA's argument that it had been a form of institutional censure as it assured the hearing that that incident would have no further repercussions on Vedanand's career. While the university's statement did nothing to mitigate the chilling effect of the dean's memo or the threat to Verdanand's academic freedom at the time, it gave the impression that the problem had somehow disappeared – a point reaffirmed by Mackness later in the hearing: "I give Dr Vedanand my absolute and unqualified assurance that he has no cause for fear in any dealing he will have with me" (AA, 16).

Here we find the inner logic of this epistemology: to deny any reason or factual basis for Vedanand's fear of the dean's punitive authority even though it had already had a chilling effect on his academic freedom. These past events were now seen as having little or no bearing upon the hearing and were to be expunged from memory. Mackness's assurance, together with that of the university, convinced the chair of the arbitration hearing that Vedanand's academic freedom was not in danger.

Both assurances damaged UMFA's case as they excluded from further consideration the very principles of academic freedom and institutional censure that were at the core of the grievance – principles that were virtually expunged by simple strokes of the pen. This left UMFA with the difficult task of trying to redirect the focus of the hearing onto these matters of principle. Mackness's strategy, in contrast, was to bring the issue of Vedanand's "rudeness" to the fore, lest the dean's overriding goal of cultivating positive relationships with the business community became an object of critical scrutiny at the hearing. Perry W. Schulman, QC, made the following statement: "As the events developed which led to this proceeding, Xerox did not complain to the University about Dr Vedanand's conduct and Xerox was not involved in the writing of Exhibit 2 [Mackness's first memo]" (AA, 16). As chair of the hearing, Schulman may have had reason to suppose this claim to be true, but he provided no evidence to support it. The statement suggests that Xerox exerted no "invisible hand" on the internal affairs of the university;

that the university proceeded independently in its handling of Vedanand; and that any "non-disciplinary" action taken against him emanated from Mackness alone. In other words, the university was now performing the function of an autonomous police force on behalf of private corporate interests. The statement itself did nothing to dispel the fact that Mackness's development plan tied the faculty more closely to both the provincial government and corporate segments of the business community; and that Mackness had stemmed Vedanand's academic freedom because of the "embarrassing" questions he had posed of the two Xerox salespeople. Mackness was systematically overriding the distinctive value system of the university, replacing it with that of the corporate market. And, in so doing, he was undermining not only the academic freedom of faculty but also the autonomy of the institution itself. In order to mask this fact the strategy to trivialize Vedanand's grievance would now be brought to the fore.

THE COCKTAIL PARTY

A key aspect of the Dean's strategy was to focus on the "rude" and "offensive" nature of Vedanand's questioning. This meant concentrating on the "tone" of the questioner rather than on the content of his remarks. Mackness himself said, when he sent him the memoranda, that he "was not aware of the substance of Dr Vedanand's remarks" but, rather, was simply concerned with "the tone of his remarks." This is odd, since the first memo stated quite clearly that "the remarks were counterproductive ... [and undermined] the positive relationships with the business community." By focusing on the tone of Vedanand's comments, the dean was now making an accusation that eluded rational rebuttal. Beckman, as author of the memo, took up the chant when he stated that "his intention was to refer only to tone [sic] of the remarks."

The only dissenting voice was that of Professor Keith Wilson, a colleague who had also been present at the Xerox seminar. In a sworn affidavit Wilson stated that "none of Dr Vedanand's comments were unpleasant in tone, nor were the remarks unpleasant, rude or offensive, and the remarks did not constitute a 'grilling' of any of the employees of Xerox" (AA, 6). This simple statement contradicted the testimony of the other witnesses. By dispelling any impression that Vedanand had been rude, Wilson's evidence challenged

Mackness's strategy at its core. It cast doubt upon the dean's claim that he was not aware of the substance of Dr Vedanand's remarks when writing the first memo. Wilson's testimony made it possible for the hearing to refocus on this underlying, and now disguised, goal and to examine it in a critical manner. In order for this to happen, however, Wilson's evidence would have to be allowed to stand on its own merits. Yet Schulman, as chair of the hearing, treated it as "information" to be noted, not as evidence having the same weight as that of other witnesses. Wilson's views were sidelined because he was too ill to undergo the process of cross-examination and, hence, unable to testify in person (AA, 36, 50).

Several of U of M's expert witnesses repeated Mackness's mantra that the grievance was "trivial." Why, one wonders, did the university call four expert witnesses if the case against Vedanand was so trivial? Could it be that his questions had struck at the heart of the dean's plans to privatize the Faculty of Management, a strategy that the central administration supported? Foremost among those who trivialized Vedanand's position was John Crispo, professor of management at the University of Toronto, who stated that "the academic freedom which tenure ensures is too important to make a mockery of it by pursuing frivolous cases. Yet that is what I think this case amounts to. It's ridiculous ... A cocktail party to cultivate relations between a faculty and a prospective employer of its graduates is hardly the place to display one's academic freedom especially when it is done offensively" (AA, 51, 41).

Crispo dismissed the entire case as frivolous and ridiculous because it took place at "a cocktail party," whose goal was polite chit-chat about how to cultivate relations between a faculty and a prospective employer. His denial that academic freedom applied to this occasion, which marked relations between the university and a business "partner," meant that Vedanand had no right to question the Xerox salespeople about the truth of their sales figures. Crispo's apparent goal was to erase any discussion of academic freedom from both the cocktail party and the arbitration hearing, ensuring, by emphasizing Vedanand's rudeness, that the "trivial" nature of the grievance came to the fore. The vagueness of the language he used to describe what had taken place made his task a lot easier: "frivolous cases" like Vedanand's were "ridiculous" and made "a mockery" of academic freedom when pursued at a "cocktail party," which "is hardly the place to display" one's freedom, especially when this is "done offensively." His words were vacuous, lacking any referent other than their intent to attack and malign. What had once been a seminar-type gathering given by Xerox to discuss the employment prospects of graduates had become a cocktail party at which only "polite" conversation was allowed.

Another of the university's expert witnesses took up the chant of "politeness" and, like Crispo, trivialized Vedanand's case by using vague language. Dr Thomas J. Collins, provost and vice-president (academic) of the University of Western Ontario, stated: "It is my view that cases such as this trivialize and demean the nature and the principle of academic freedom" (AA, 51). He gave no indication as to why this was so, but he found "the circumstances ... trifling" and, like Crispo, thought a cocktail party was not the place where it was possible for a violation of academic freedom to occur. Collins went further, asserting that, "if the grievance were to succeed, the principle of academic freedom would be unduly diluted," and the "trivializing potential" of the case would have succeeded in demeaning a principle that should not "concern itself with trifles." Even if Vedanand had used his expertise in questioning the salespeople's claims about Xerox's market share, the occasion was "trifling" and did not merit the protection of academic freedom. Like Crispo, Collins used language whose goal was simply to attack Vedanand's credibility. No reason was given for excluding the principle of academic freedom from the "cocktail party" other than the "trifling" nature of the occasion, which would allegedly have resulted in its becoming "unduly diluted" (AA, 61–2).

This attempt by Crispo and Collins to render the Xerox seminar a trifling affair unworthy of the protection of academic freedom was an integral part of the strategy, initiated by Mackness, to trivialize the grievance. However, even if the occasion had been a cocktail party or a reception, significant questions were raised in opposition to the claims made by Xerox. Why should Vedanand's critique of these claims not be protected by academic freedom? After all, he had used his own scholarship and research in the field of marketing to justify his knowledge claims. Was this not an exemplary case of the use of one's academic freedom? And was "the search for knowledge and its free exposition"[36] not evident in the line of questioning he had pursued? Collins and Crispo begged these questions by belittling the importance of the occasion. And, by denying the relevance of academic freedom to Vedanand's knowledgeable critique of Xerox, they were attacking the principle itself. Because they were implying that, at other occasions marking "partnerships" with business corporations, academic freedom would not protect the expression of dissenting views, they were effectively silencing any free critical expression on the part of faculty sceptical of such relationships. Mackness's strategy, so eagerly supported by Crispo and Collins, had ramifications not only for U of M but also for other universities. If allowed to succeed, not only would Vedanand be censured but the principle of academic freedom itself would be "unduly diluted." Free critical expression would no longer be protected at the very occasions when the independence of universities from the corporate market was being celebrated in a concrete way (AA, 14, 62).

This strategy exemplifies the tendency, already noted in the previous chapter, that advocates of the market model of education tend to expunge all counter-evidence that does not accord with their overriding goal of maximizing monetary profits. This style of "argument" rules out opposition such as Vedanand's by obliterating whatever does not conform to its own narrow presuppositions. These are drawn exclusively from the market, but in this case they were hidden from view by the constant repetition of such words as "rude," "offensive," and "politeness," which disguised the basis of the marketeers' case behind a veneer of corporate "etiquette." In their view, universities must become mere instruments for "what business wants," purged of the kind of critical thought capable of opposing the market's rule.

WHAT IS REASONABLE?

While the Mackness mantra regarding the rude tone of Vedanand's remarks was reiterated by the chorus of expert witnesses called by the university, under cross-examination they all admitted "the possibility" that the word "remarks" might indeed refer to the content of the questions he had posed. This, in turn, implied that "Dr Vedanand could reasonably interpret the word 'remarks' to refer to the content" of what he had said. Wishing to press home the point, Mel Myers, QC, UMFA's lawyer, argued that confusion over the meaning of the word "remarks" was the result of Mackness's second memo. Its omission of any reference to the overriding goal of cultivating "positive relationships with the business community" decontextualized

Vedanand's remarks in order to focus attention on their allegedly rude tone. Schulman, however, pointed out that, while "it is not unreasonable for Dr. Vedanand to be in doubt on the subject and to believe that the content of his remarks may be the subject of the [first] memorandum," Mackness's second memo should have convinced him that "he could still not think that the content of the remarks are referred to ... [since] there is no specific reference" to the "counterproductive" nature of what he had said. In other words, Vedanand was being "unreasonable" for believing that the overriding goal, or "orthodoxy line," of the Faculty of Management rendered his views on Xerox unspeakable because it simply wasn't true that an "attack on business is not acceptable at the University" (AA, 9, 36–7, 50, 53–4).

Indeed, Vedanand's own reasonableness came under attack from several witnesses, who claimed he had overreacted. If he had gone straight to see the dean when he first received the memo, the problem could have been resolved in a "reasonable" manner. Jerry Gray, for example, would have "go[ne] to the Dean and talk about it,"[37] while Beckman "would have gone to see the Dean" to give him his own "version of what had transpired," but "it would not have entered his mind that there was a question of academic freedom involved" since such an idea was quite "unreasonable." This point was taken up by Crispo, who "did not consider ... [that the memo] comprised a threat to academic freedom and tenure." It was simply a question of "how confident you are in yourself and how well you know your stuff." Unlike Vedanand, Crispo "would have gone to the Dean and argued with him" because he had both the knowledge and self-confidence to do so.[38] Yet Vedanand, who had posed knowledgeable questions to the Xerox salespeople in the presence of both his associate dean and head of Department, was hardly lacking in knowledge and self-confidence. This fact was systematically overlooked by the university's witnesses, who preferred to attack his credibility by using language that had no grounding in reality. Beckman, for example, revealed nothing about the nature of Mackness's memo when he claimed that "it would not have entered his mind" that academic freedom was at stake; rather, he was refusing to recognize that the dean's actions threatened free critical expression (AA, 39–40).

Just as important, Crispo had committed the informal fallacy known as the argumentum ad hominem (abusive) in order to besmirch

Vedanand's character. Literally translated as "argument directed to the person," this fallacy is described by Irving M. Copi as follows: "[This fallacy occurs] when, instead of trying to disprove the truth of what is asserted, one attacks the person who made the assertion ... This argument is fallacious, because the personal character of a person is logically irrelevant to the truth or falsehood of what that person says or the correctness or incorrectness of that person's argument."[39] Instead of trying to determine the truth or falsehood of Vedanand's statements about the violation of his academic freedom, Crispo attacked him personally as lacking confidence and not knowing his "stuff." These personal characteristics were logically irrelevant to the truth-value of what Vedanand had said as well as to the validity of his argument that Mackness's memo had censored his free critical expression. The apparent goal in smearing Vedanand's character was to exclude the content of his critique of Xerox from rational discussion. Further appeal to fallacious abuse is one of several strategies commonly used to modify people's "perceptions" of the corporate market.[40]

Ironically, Schulman elevated this logical error to the level of principle. He used Crispo's notion of "how confident you are in yourself" as the basis for defining a "reasonable man [sic]" as someone "free both from over-apprehension and from over-confidence." As chair of the arbitration hearing, Schulman then proposed that Vedanand was "unduly timorous" in thinking that Mackness was threatening his academic freedom as a university teacher. His fear that "adverse comments about Xerox [would] not be tolerated in the classroom" was, he claimed, exaggerated, for Mackness's memo was not intended to limit his free critical expression when teaching. Indeed, Vedanand's "unduly timorous nature" led him to entertain all sorts of "concerns on this point [that] exceeded the concerns which would properly be described as reasonable" (AA, 67, 39–40).

Schulman ignored the conception of "the reasonable person" articulated in the precedent-setting Canadian case on informed consent. Had he not done so, he might have reached a different conclusion. Former chief justice Bora Laskin stated in 1980 that "[the] objective standard would have to be geared to what the average prudent person, the reasonable person in the patient's particular position, would agree to or not agree to, if all material and special risks of going ahead with the surgery or foregoing it were made known to him (or her)."[41] How, then, does the criterion of the reasonable person apply to Vedanand? Mutatis mutandis, as a prudent person in his particular position – namely, a professor of management attending the Xerox seminar – had he acted reasonably in questioning the salespeople's claims about market share? He was well aware of the risks involved but believed that his responsibility as an authority in the field should guide his actions. As a senior member of the professoriate, he had every right to assume that academic freedom applied to a meeting taking place on campus at which there was disagreement about issues that fell within his own area of expertise. All of this evidence suggests that he was indeed a reasonable person.

Schulman, however, placed his trust elsewhere: "I prefer the evidence of the experts called on behalf of the University" (AA, 55). This is a simple statement of faith in the evidence provided by the experts called by the university. No matter that Crispo had used a fallacious argument to criticize Vedanand's character. Schulman admired Crispo's "overconfidence," seeing it as a character trait that reflected "a person who has had an occasion to test and consider the bounds of academic freedom." In his evaluation of the two, Schulman found Crispo, the "expert," to be "reasonable" in a way that Vedanand, the "timorous" professor, was not. He disregarded the use of reason as a method of examining all knowledge claims on the basis of the available evidence. For Schulman, when it came to successful character traits, "overconfidence" was preferable to "over-apprehension." By valorizing personal characteristics, Schulman failed to distinguish between fallacious reasoning and abuse, on the one hand, and valid argument, on the other (AA, 54–5, 18).[42]

Earlier in the arbitration hearing Schulman had stated that he favoured the evidence of "others who were present" at the Xerox seminar to the testimony given by Vedanand. This was because they were "in a better position to give [him] a picture of *the appearance of what took place.*" In other words, the appearance of being rude held more weight than what had actually taken place at the Xerox seminar. At issue was not the market's encroachment on the university, or the threat it posed to academic freedom, but the appearance of Vedanand's lack of "politeness."[43] This is because money, not knowledge, was at issue when Xerox was invited on campus, and "etiquette" was of prime importance if the company were to have ongoing access to promising graduates as a condition for maintaining its "donation" to the Faculty of Management (AA, 4, 14).

FROM BREACH OF ETIQUETTE TO VIOLATION
OF ACADEMIC FREEDOM

As chair of the arbitration hearing, Schulman's initial sympathy for
Vedanand ("I can understand why Dr Vedanand ... should correct
the error [of the sales representative] in these circumstances") shifted
to outright condemnation ("he could have waited until the presentation was over and asked to be allowed to ask a question or make a
correction"). According to him, Vedanand "chose to interrupt the
presentation and correct the error," and he even "sidetracked the
presentation for several minutes as he engaged in a presentation" of
his own on Canon's "relative marketing technique." Schulman then
repeated the mantra at the core of the trivialization strategy: "a significant number of faculty members present at the event disapproved
of Dr. Vedanand's conduct, [because it was] unpleasant ... unacceptable and rude [and constituted a] 'grilling' of the business' spokesman"
(AA, 62–3).

Schulman's claim that such conduct constituted rude and unpleasant
behaviour was based on two allegations. First, Vedanand should
have "asked to be allowed to ask a question or make a correction."
Permission to speak was the prerogative of the Xerox salespeople,
and then only at the end of their talk. Respect for their authority
was required lest questions challenged their presentation in unfore-
seen ways. Second, instead of keeping quiet, Vedanand had "engaged
in a presentation" on the "relative [i.e., superior] ... marketing
technique" of Canon. Vedanand cast Xerox's desirability as "a prospective employer of ... graduates" into doubt due to his authority
as a scholar in the discipline of marketing. By correcting their sales
figures, he had directly challenged the authority of the company – an
act that violated generic politeness: "Dr Vedanand's conduct was
unreasonable in relation to time, place, subject matter and tone. I
find that he exceeded the acceptable limits of academic freedom. His
conduct comprised a breach of etiquette which entitled Dean
Mackness to make some comment. Exhibit 2, a confidential memo
with a very limited circulation was not an act of institutional
censorship. (AA, 63–4).

Schulman's allegations are so numerous that it is important to
keep track of them: Vedanand's conduct was unreasonable given the
time and place of the reception and the "subject matter and tone"
of his remarks; he went beyond the acceptable limits of academic

freedom, primarily because his conduct "comprised a breach of etiquette"; Mackness's confidential memo was "not an act of institutional censorship" because it had "a very limited circulation." For Schulman, it was now Vedanand who had exceeded the acceptable limits of academic freedom, while Mackness was innocent of having censured him (AA, 41, 62–3).

Trivialization had now reached a new level, having been made into a strategy of "doublespeak." Not only had Vedanand's "rudeness" caused offence, but, in naming the outrage as a violation of his own academic freedom, he was being trivial in the extreme. On this view, Vedanand's initial offence was compounded by a trivial insistence on the relevance of academic freedom to what had taken place. The doublespeak strategy brought into the open the alleged link between Vedanand's "breach of etiquette" and his having "exceeded the acceptable limits of academic freedom." For the first time in the hearing, the hidden premise of Mackness's strategy emerged – namely, that being rude was a sufficient condition for not being protected by academic freedom. It was, after all, the "social and community limits to academic freedom" that were to override the free and open expression of ideas in the name of what was considered acceptable. "Decorum" was the main criterion for determining whether these limits had been exceeded, and even though "the Xerox speaker was not prevented from speaking," Vedanand had somehow transgressed "the acceptable limits of academic freedom" (AA, 7, 44, 63).

The doublespeak strategy gained support from the views of Pierre-Yves Boucher on the social limits to academic freedom. As executive vice-president of the Association of Universities and Colleges of Canada, he was called as the third expert witness by the university and, in Schulman's words, "gave the most balanced presentation" of all those "who gave expert evidence at the hearing." Boucher, it seems, had looked at some forty-eight collective agreements from Canadian universities and found that, in almost half of them, there was "a corresponding obligation" to use academic freedom responsibly by affirming "the right of others to hold different points of view." In those agreements where this obligation was not explicit, academic freedom was "related to the expression of opinion or dissemination of knowledge which flows from the research and the pursuit of knowledge." Strikingly, Vedanand's process of questioning at the Xerox seminar met both these criteria.

Boucher, however, believed that universities had the right to punish
faculty members when their "conduct ... [was] not conducive to the
normal social interchange of the academic community and the community that surrounds it." Yet, Vedanand had furthered the exchange
of ideas between the university and the business community by
engaging in debate with the Xerox salespeople, even going so far as
to invite one of them to his class. This did not deter Boucher, who
interpreted the norms of social interchange to mean only what was
acceptable to those colleagues who found Vedanand's behaviour rude
and offensive. Boucher regarded this as sufficient proof that Vedanand
had transgressed the norms of the academic community, despite the
fact that they were based primarily on hearsay claims, as the counter-
evidence in the testimony given by Professor Wilson showed (AA, 19,
22–3, 58, 7, 14).

Boucher's presentation prompted Schulman to make the claim that
"in some circumstances, rudeness, short of shutting down a presentation can exceed the bounds and would not satisfy the obligation
which is imposed on faculty members in Article 19.2.2" (AA, 58–9).
Put differently, rudeness can exceed the bounds of the obligation
imposed on faculty members to respect the views of others, even if
they allow a speaker to complete a presentation that they have interrupted. This was allegedly the case with Vedanand, whose rudeness
exceeded the bounds of academic freedom. Yet, upon examination,
Article 19.2.2 from the collective agreement of the University of
Manitoba does not support this interpretation. It states that "faculty
members shall act reasonably, fairly and in good faith in dealing
with others and the University shall have the same obligation in
dealing with faculty members" (AA, 70). There is nothing here for-
bidding faculty from interrupting visiting speakers or questioning
corporate salespeople. Nor is any mention made of rudeness as a
violation of the "conduct conducive to the normal social interchange
of the academic community." On the contrary, the article suggests
that Vedanand had fulfilled his obligation by posing questions "fairly
and in good faith," and in proposing a "reasonable" explanation
for Canon's market share. Moreover, the obligation is reciprocal,
requiring the university to act reasonably, fairly, and in good faith
in dealing with faculty members (AA, 14, 23, 64).

Boucher's further inculcation of "the community that surrounds
it [the university]" is a clear reference to the norms of the business
community. Vedanand's behaviour is considered offensive because

it was not conducive to "the normal social interchange" between the university and Xerox, which might reconsider its connections with the Faculty of Management and undermine Mackness's development plan. In circumstances such as these, where rudeness upsets the relationship between the two "partners," Boucher claimed that "academic freedom ... does not protect against impolite or boorish attitudes in expressing those results of research that are protected by academic freedom." The term "boorish" is misplaced for it suggests someone who is "clumsy or ill-bred," possessing the character of a "peasant."[44] Boucher's false allegation heaped further abuse on Vedanand's character by attacking him with language that bore no relationship to reality (AA, 14, 23, 19).

Even if it were true that Vedanand had exhibited impolite and boorish attitudes in posing questions to the Xerox salespeople, would this have justified the truncation of his academic freedom? Boucher's affirmative response presupposed acceptance of the value system of the corporate market as definitive of the university. He refused to acknowledge what Professor Michiel Horn considers as definitive of academic freedom; namely, that, "although civility is important, academics owe a loyalty to something more important yet; they must commit themselves to the search for knowledge and truth *as they see it*."[45] If the social values of civility, decorum, or etiquette are allowed to override academic work, faculty can no longer pursue the university's distinctive goal of advancing and disseminating shared knowledge. And without academic freedom, this goal cannot be achieved. Yet, private corporations are always likely to find faculty who question their own knowledge claims "rude," "impolite," and "boorish" if such questioning poses a threat to the overriding goal of maximizing monetary profits. Their value system stifles "the scholar's right to say what she or he has said," which Boucher acknowledges as important but which he then disregards in favour of the need to be polite. In reality, his "balanced presentation" is an attack on the academic freedom of any faculty member like Vedanand who criticizes the corporate market on the basis of their research (AA, 14, 23, 19).

BUSINESS AS USUAL

Dr George Connell, a chemist and former president of both the University of Toronto and the University of Western Ontario, was the fourth witness called by the university. He was convinced that strong links between universities and business made good financial sense and did not endanger academic freedom. "Universities," he stated, "would be much the poorer if they were not able to draw upon corporate resources for support in a multitude of ways. This dependence should not, and in my experience has not, led to any constraint upon faculty members in designing their research programs, nor in publishing the results of their research" (AA, 49). Connell ignored the fact that a "donation" like Xerox's often had strings attached, and that, "even where no strings are visible, they may operate in hidden form."[46] His characterization of the relationship between universities and private corporations as one of "dependence" indicates a willingness to sacrifice university autonomy for closer links with the corporate market.

The dangers of dependency upon business corporations at the University of Toronto have become evident since Connell stepped down as president. "Donations" from the corporate sector have resulted in critical questions being raised by faculty and students regarding the constraints placed upon faculty members in designing their research programs and in publishing the results of their research – constraints that Connell denied. These questions are be considered in detail in the following chapter, which addresses the case of Dr Nancy Olivieri.

Nevertheless, Connell managed to convince Schulman that close relationships between universities and business corporations posed no threat to university autonomy and academic freedom: "I accept Dr Connell's evidence that enterprise jointly undertaken by university and business does not normally constitute a threat to a university's independence" (AA, 61). Connell's experience as president of two universities carried the day. After all, if schemes jointly undertaken with private corporations did not threaten a university's independence, how could they possibly undermine the academic freedom of faculty? Schulman accepted Connell's testimony on the basis of his authority as a former president, one who denied any evidence that dependence on big business threatened the advancement and dissemination of shared knowledge.

Following Crispo and Collins's flawed arguments that the "cocktail party" was no place to exercise critical judgment about Xerox's competitiveness, Schulman found that "Dr Vedanand's conduct was unreasonable in relation to time, place, subject matter and tone ... [and that he had] exceeded the acceptable limits of academic freedom ... [because] his conduct comprised a breach of etiquette" (AA, 63). The value of not being rude was, as Boucher had falsely claimed, greater than that of pursuing knowledge. As such, etiquette should have overridden Vedanand's desire to pose critical questions of the knowledge claims made by the two Xerox salespeople. And, since Connell had falsely claimed that the independence of the university was in no way threatened by strong ties with the market, the issue of Vedanand's academic freedom was indeed "trivial." Schulman concluded the arbitration award on 11 February 1991 as follows: "The Association has failed to prove on a balance of probabilities that the writing of Exhibit 2 [Mackness's first memo] comprised a breach of Dr. Vedanand's right of academic freedom. The grievance is therefore dismissed" (AA, 63–4).

VALUE SYSTEMS IN CONFLICT

The striking differences in character, value, and principle between Dr Vedanand and Dean Mackness are reflected in their contrasting views of the relationship between U of M and the corporate market. Vedanand saw university autonomy and academic freedom as cornerstones of the critical search for knowledge; Mackness saw the university as an instrument for achieving the goal of the corporate market – namely, the maximization of private monetary profits. These two conceptions of the university embody two "wholly distinct and often opposed logics of value,"[47] and they can be characterized in the following two ways:

By questioning the salespeople from Xerox,
Vedanand was actually serving the goal of university education,
which is to advance and disseminate shared knowledge.

Although the Xerox seminar was considered to be the wrong "time [and] place" for a faculty member to pose critical questions of the company's sales in the global market, Vedanand's reason for breaking this new and repressive code was simply stated: "Professors have a moral responsibility as scholars to present correct information and to not be subservient to the needs of the business community." He dared to challenge the view that occasions celebrating corporate "partnerships" constitute a kind of protected free trade zone that lie beyond the criticism of faculty (AA, 50, 44, 9–10).

Once his academic freedom had been truncated following the Xerox "reception," Vedanand's ability to pose critical questions of market orthodoxy in his teaching and research was also under threat. The long shadow of the market, personified by Mackness, hung over all Vedanand's academic activities, preventing him from carrying them out in a manner consistent with the advancement and dissemination of shared knowledge. The memorandum prevented the free expression of Vedanand's ideas, whether in the classroom, in conversation with colleagues and students, or in his research because he feared further punishment from a dean who was intolerant of dissenting ideas. This strategy is part of the "ritual blaming," which Professor Ian Angus refers to as "finger-pointing at 'troublemakers' who 'do not play by the rules' [something that] is essential to the administrative diktat of corporate rule."[48]

Without the opportunity to make "honest judgment" or "independent criticism," Vedanand could not pursue activities distinctive of a university professor. It was Mackness's refusal to distinguish between the value system of the university and that of the market that violated the notion of "the university ... as a place where people have to have the right to speak the unspeakable and think the unthinkable and challenge the unchallengeable."[49] Mackness mistakenly believed that the unspeakable must be silenced if it challenged the inviolable principles of the market (AA, 13).

Mackness embodied the values of the corporate market
by ensuring that the Faculty of Management served
the goal of maximizing private monetary profits.

Mackness did not acknowledge any distinction between the value system of the university and that of the corporate market. His overriding goal, "to cultivate positive relationships with the business community," could best be achieved by privatizing the Faculty of Management. As former senior vice-president of the Bank of Nova Scotia, he was now in charge of a "firm" with that name. In contrast to the university, where "self-direction, critical assessment, or alternative viewpoint" is integral to the process of advancing and disseminating knowledge, these activities only have value in the corporate market if each "promotes an overriding end" – namely, "the employer's special interest of commercial advantage." Anything that does not promote this commercial goal "will almost certainly be dismissed 'in the interests of the firm.'" Vedanand's exercise of academic freedom threatened Mackness's own "special interest" as an "employer" and deserved punishment according to "the market's accepted principles of employer-employee relations."[50] Fortunately, Vedanand could not be fired under existing university regulations because he was tenured, but Mackness did enough to undermine his academic freedom in the classroom as well as his research. And, as a market agent, Mackness carried out precisely what he had advocated in "dish[ing] out some stern discipline to those who aren't meeting the market."[51]

Mackness saw university autonomy as a hindrance because it presupposed that faculty members, acting in a collegial manner, knew best how to determine and implement the distinctive goals, methods, and standards of excellence of their own institution. Values other than the maximization of stockholder value had priority in determining the kinds of teaching, learning, scholarship, and research that took place, given U of M's overriding goal of advancing and disseminating shared knowledge. This value system, in which academic freedom was fundamental, endangered Mackness's goal of cultivating strong relationships with corporate "segments" of "the business community," and it had to be subverted.

Mackness was explicit about why this shift in values was necessary. In an Open Letter to Faculty, dated 14 October 1993, he asserted that "the collegial system has not worked well" in the Faculty of Management and should be replaced by "executive" decisions made by the dean. Acting as chief executive officer, Mackness could then enforce "a tough programme of internal rationalization [through] tough administrative decisions" on such academic matters as the following:

1 "The teaching competence of a small number of long-term faculty members ... [who were] simply removed from the classroom, as was my right and responsibility."
2 "The denial of tenure or promotion to weak candidates."
3 [The] "elimination of low-enrolment, low demand courses ... [which, while] controversial ... [was] absolutely necessary."
4 [The] "redirection of resources from low to high demand areas [i.e. from the Department of Public Policy and Actuarial and

Management Sciences to the departments of Finance, Marketing, Management, and Accounting]."

5 [These decisions] "did not lend themselves to proper resolution by the collegial process ... [because their goal was] to improve our efficiency and cost effectiveness."[52]

The reduction of unit costs in the manner of the corporate market was to override established university policy on teaching, tenure, and course offerings. Collegial decision making was replaced by executive action, whose goal was narrow economic "efficiency." While Mackness did invoke "higher standards and accountability" as principles of his regime, their use raises the following questions: who would set the standards, and to whom was the faculty to be accountable? The higher standards he referred to were those of the market, as embodied in his development plan, which transferred resources to "the four high-demand mainline business disciplines." Accountability was not to the academic community, the public, or even the students or central administration; rather, it was to those who had put up the money for "the large discretionary increase in resources that has been made available" to the Faculty of Management. By this Mackness meant the provincial government and, more especially, the Associates, those market agents who had ensured his deanship. On the basis of "new accountabilities"[53] to the Associates, Mackness was building an even greater dependence on the corporate market.

WAS BIAS A FACTOR?

Earlier I drew attention to those aspects of Mackness's development plan that were criticized by faculty members in management, by UMFA, and, eventually, by a committee of inquiry appointed by CAUT. I also suggested a possible connection between discriminatory statements in the first draft of the plan, including the alleged "reliance of the Faculty of Management on foreign trained and non-business trained faculty," and Mackness's suppression of Vedanand's academic freedom. (In the final version of the plan, the passage was changed to "weakness in faculty composition.") Is it possible that his freedom was truncated, at least partially, because he was from the subcontinent of India, where he had received two university degrees (with a PhD from Michigan State University)? Was Mackness motivated by a desire to replace foreign-trained faculty like Vedanand with "Canadian-born business scholars" in order to meet the overriding goal of his development plan to cultivate positive relationships with the business community? If so, is it also possible that the suppression of Vedanand's academic freedom was just one step in a process of sweeping the Faculty of Management clean of its "foreign-trained faculty" so that it would resemble "other Canadian business schools?"[54] In light of further evidence that emerged during Vedanand's arbitration hearing, these issues are worthy of consideration (AA, 14).

During his cross-examination of Mackness, Mel Myers presented a letter written by the dean that suggested that "an improper motive" had prompted the sending of his first memo. This took the form of a "bias of Dean Mackness against Dr. Vedanand." The document in question was "Exhibit 32, a letter dated January 30, 1989 from Dean Mackness to his predecessor enclosing a copy of the development plan, stating '... if we don't do something soon, we will all retire together and leave the place to Third World mathematicians'" (AA, 38). The letter, sent to Professor R.G. Grandpré, former dean of the Faculty of Management, together "with a copy of [Mackness's] Development Plan," contained an assurance that "the time [was] ripe" for its implementation. The force of the letter was "directed specifically at" members of the Department of Actuarial and Management Sciences and Public Policy (AA, 37).

The department was no longer considered among the "high-demand mainline business disciplines" that fed directly into the market, and Mackness's development plan "did not consider [them] to be central to the direction that the Faculty of Management should be taking." Indeed, his assessment of the discipline of actuarial and management sciences was closely connected to his attack on "Third World mathematicians." On several occasions, the head of the department, Professor Yash Gupta, had tried, to no avail, to explain the value of his colleagues' work: "He [Mackness] repeatedly told me that Professors Bector and Bhatt did not belong in the Faculty of Management since they were, according to him, mathematicians. I corrected him each time and advised him that operations research is a very important and integral part of management education."[55] Mackness's denigration of operations research and the entire discipline of actuarial and management sciences eventually led Gupta to resign – an action prompted when "Dean Mackness denied his request for a two-year leave of absence to accept an endowed chair

at an American university." This decision, coupled with his refusal
to replace Gupta, led to a growing scepticism among faculty about
the dean's reasons for denying him leave, which were "perceived as
insincere or untrue, particularly given his later attempts to dissolve
the department."[56] Mackness finally achieved this goal, establishing
a division of actuarial science that had no autonomy and that was
under his direct control as dean.[57] Staffed by "Third World mathematicians," its role in cultivating positive relationships with the business
community could only be assured once he established executive
control over its members (AA, 37).

It was not only faculty members in the Department of Actuarial
and Management Sciences who felt under attack from the contents
of Mackness's letter but also "minority group members" in every
faculty. The CAUT Committee of Inquiry Report had also found his
comments "objectionable, repulsive and inexcusable."[58] Once
Mackness's letter became public knowledge, following his cross-
examination at the arbitration hearing in late August 1990, there
was growing pressure on the dean to retract his statement. UMFA
"passed a motion expressing its concern about the letter," which it
found to be "entirely unacceptable behaviour on the part of a dean
of the University of Manitoba." Two days earlier, President Naimark
had formally acknowledged the letter "and indicated that he would
deal with the matter after the arbitration was complete." In the
meantime, he wrote to the dean and stated unequivocally: "I regard
it as essential that you convene at the earliest opportunity, a meeting
of the Faculty of Management Council in order to explain your
position."[59]

On 6 September 1990, Mackness invited faculty members in
management to a meeting "so that he could make a statement and
answer any questions" about reports in the press concerning his
letter. This was not a formal Faculty Council meeting: there was no
agenda, no opportunity for motions to be made or voted on, and
no formal minutes requiring an "independent record of what transpired at the meeting" were taken. Mackness flaunted the president's
formal request to hold a council meeting. Rather than apologizing
for the statement in his letter and recognizing its harmful effects on
faculty members from the developing world, Mackness simply
described his words as "ill advised" and "poor." Moreover, he provided faculty members with only twenty-four hours notice to attend
the session. At no point in the meeting did he explain the basis of

his ideas or suggest how they could have been expressed in non-racial terms. Even in his subsequent letter of apology to the faculty, Mackness maintained his view that "Third World mathematicians" were inferior: "Lack of success in hiring business scholars forces an increasing reliance on non-business scholars and sessional lecturers. It was this financially-induced reliance on non-business scholars that I was referring to in my comment '... and leave the place to Third World mathematicians.'"[60] In other words, competitive market forces, specifically the very tight market for recruiting business scholars, had led the dean to express his views. There was no question of any moral responsibility on his part and, hence, no need for an apology to those who were offended by his remarks. He had simply obeyed the laws of the market, which required that the Faculty of Management resolve its "financially-induced reliance on non-business scholars."

Following the meeting on 6 September, Mackness published his own account of it in *The Manitoban*, the university newspaper. The article read like formal minutes of the meeting, but its accuracy was "disputed by some of those who were present."[61] For example, Mackness claimed that Professor Earl Rosenbloom, a well-known critic of his "Third World mathematicians" letter, had "acknowledged that there was no racist or malevolent intent in the phrase in question."[62] In fact, Rosenbloom "emphatically denie[d] he['d] ever made such a statement."[63] Moreover, when, in the *Winnipeg Free Press*, a letter describing his statement about "Third World mathematicians" as "jocular" appeared, Mackness circulated it to faculty members in management, describing it as a "thoughtful letter offering an outside perspective of recent events."[64] His view was disputed by a faculty member in the Department of Mathematics and Astronomy, who pointed out that "a senior administrator responsible for making academic decisions should at least be aware that mathematicians are hired, not for their geographical origins, but rather for their mathematical abilities, especially in the areas of teaching and research."[65] According to Professor Padmanabhan, Mackness's refusal to acknowledge the competence of faculty in mathematics and other areas to teach and carry out research posed a threat to "academic freedom and excellence."[66]

When, following the meeting on 6 September 1990, nineteen faculty members in management wrote to President Naimark and the Board of Governors asking that "Dean Mackness ... be dismissed," there was no response. Moreover, "other members of the university community who had also written to the President and Board" claimed that they never received a reply, even though Naimark later assured the CAUT Committee of Inquiry "that he had replied to all the letters he had received."[67] There was a growing tension on campus, a mistrust of the central administration's handling of the situation, a subsequent call from the faculties of arts and social work for Mackness's removal,[68] and a request by UMFA for CAUT to conduct a committee of inquiry into Mackness's actions as dean of management.

In a special President's Letter dated 7 September 1990, Naimark reiterated his view that an evaluation of the situation would be carried out later because Mackness's letter was being used as evidence in the ongoing arbitration with Vedanand. This statement was later "affirmed by the Board of Governors" as policy, even though it was regarded by a growing number of faculty as "inadequate." Naimark's letter expressed the position of the university as follows: "The University regards the expression used by Dean Mackness ... [as] offensive and unacceptable; and the University repudiates, without reservation or qualification, any implication whatsoever that the University will tolerate discrimination on the basis of age, sex, race, creed, colour or disability."[69] Despite his condemnation of Mackness's letter, Naimark's refusal to take disciplinary action suggested to many faculty members continuing support for the dean.

An executive committee of CAUT was duly struck in December 1990 to determine the reasons for "the obvious discontent of the faculty of the University of Manitoba with the conduct of the Dean of the Faculty of Management."[70] The CAUT Committee of Inquiry found no evidence of "discriminatory action" on the part of the dean towards "colleagues who were members of visible minorities." "We cannot conclude," the report states, "that racism played any role in his actions ... [because] the Dean was in conflict with many of his colleagues," not just with "members of visible minorities" like Vedanand.[71] Mackness, it would seem, took issue with anybody who disagreed with his overriding goal of cultivating positive relationships with the business community.[72] The report warrants this conclusion, providing evidence that Mackness discriminated against anyone opposed to his development plan, including "Third World mathematicians."

BREAKING THE UNDERLYING PATTERN

The events surrounding the Vedanand case show quite clearly how the logic of university education is being subordinated to the logic of the market. As a former market agent, Mackness did not acknowledge that such subordination could only destroy a value system in which the worth of knowledge is independent of any ability to make money. Apparently unable to conceive of knowledge other than as an instrument for increasing the market value of business corporations,[73] he set the Faculty of Management firmly on course to produce graduates and research that did just this. The views of faculty members like Vedanand simply had no place in this program, and so they were to be expunged.

The loss of Vedanand's academic freedom, however, spawned a growing opposition to the dean's imposition of the market's value program on the Faculty of Management. Many of the faculty members who publicly criticized the statement concerning "Third World mathematicians" now organized stiff opposition to Mackness's rule. Vedanand had shown how important it was to oppose a market agent willing to trample on the university's distinctive value system. The story of how his colleagues broke the underlying pattern of the corporate market by divesting U of M of its dean of management provides a worthy conclusion to this chapter.

In September 1993, a core group of about twenty faculty members in the Faculty of Management served the following notice of motion at a special meeting of the Faculty Council: "Be it resolved that the Faculty of Management censure Dean William Mackness and express no confidence in his management of the Faculty." They took this action because Mackness's "management style" was based on decisions that "impede collegial governance of the Faculty, divide rather than unify the Faculty, result in unjust treatment of Faculty members, and reduce the reliability of information communicated from the Faculty administration."[74]

Among the dean's actions that angered faculty are several I have already analyzed: the imposition of his development plan; the letter about "Third World mathematicians" first revealed during Vedanand's arbitration hearing; the disbandment of the Department of Actuarial and Management Sciences and its subsequent replacement by a division "under the direct control of the Dean."[75] Faculty also pointed to Mackness's refusal to provide an annual report about "the Associates Program ... [especially its] membership and funds to the Faculty" as well as the departure of twenty-six professors during his tenure, most of whom had been replaced by junior faculty or term appointments.[76] In both cases, faculty had been kept in the dark about "the income and expenses" of the Faculty of Management. This contrasted sharply both with the practice of the previous dean, R.G. Grandpré, who had provided faculty with annual financial reports and with Mackness's declared commitment to accountability. In fact, faculty members had no way of knowing whether his claims about the Associates' providing $250,000 per year to the Faculty of Management were true or not. Nor could they determine "how Development Fund monies have been used" since "the outflow of people is nearly equal to the inflow [in terms of raw numbers],"[77] making it impossible to evaluate the alleged success of the development plan.

In October, the Executive Committee of the Board of Governors ruled the Faculty of Management Council's non-confidence motion out of order. It was "strongly of the view that Faculty and School Councils do not have the power to recommend censure and non-confidence" in deans or other administrators. Indeed, the Executive Committee reminded the chair of the Faculty of Management Council that it was "incumbent on the President to investigate any statement by members of an academic unit that its administration is unsuccessful and to take appropriate action."[78] Undeterred by this setback, faculty members organized a closed meeting at which they passed a second motion, by thirty-four votes to seventeen, stating that Mackness should not be renewed as dean once his term expired on 30 June 1995.

While Mackness had escaped censure, the Board of Governors and the president had been alerted for a second time of the level of opposition within the Faculty of Management to his anti-collegial form of governance. Mackness insisted that "real changes" to the faculty had increased funding for "20 new staff positions provided by the [development] plan" as well as "Library acquisitions for the Ph.D. programme, research grants for new faculty members, the graduate student computer facility,"[79] and countless other benefits. None of this could be challenged by faculty members, who were denied access to the relevant financial information. Naimark, however, was in a position to know that the dean's claims regarding the funding for these changes were untrue. In time, he would take appropriate action.

Mackness's reputation was now sufficiently tarnished that the Presidential Advisory Committee for the Appointment of the Dean of Management, having interviewed him, did not recommend renewal of his contract. The committee's deliberations lasted ten months, but, despite pressure from the two Associates on the committee to reappoint Mackness, the members were unable to find a suitable candidate. The committee finally decided, in February 1995, that Dean Mackness was "not an acceptable candidate."[80] This resulted in a systematic campaign on the part of the corporate segment of the business community to pressure the university to overthrow its decision.

The Past Presidents' Group of the Associates, comprising six corporate executives, wrote to the Board of Governors asking for a meeting to correct this "unreasonable judgement ... that appears unfair and without merit." The group claimed that the advisory committee's decision "denied fair play" to Mackness and ignored his "outstanding record of strengthening the Faculty, raising standards and increasing accountability."[81] Following a meeting of the Associates' Board, President Lawrie Pollard wrote to the chair of the Board of Governors urging "an open and frank hearing by your Board and final determination of this matter" so that "Dean Mackness should be allowed to continue the mandate to which we are all committed."[82] On the same day, Del Crewson, "past chairman [sic]" of the Associates Board, wrote to his membership that the board had passed a unanimous motion expressing both "full confidence in Dean William Mackness and ... the highest regard for his accomplishments." The advisory committee's decision "to exclude Dean Mackness from consideration," Crewson continued, was "unfair and unreasonable ... [and] reflects very poorly on the University where respect for achievement should rank ahead of particular interest."[83] Despite the Associates' own particular interest in supporting Mackness, their partiality was disguised as a concern for the well-being of the university as a whole.

This strategy did not go unnoticed. William Notz, professor of business administration, wrote to the chair of the Board of Governors that he was "saddened to read Del Crewson's recent letter demanding that the University's appointment process be overthrown and Mr. Mackness reappointed immediately ... [for] should the Board of Governors accede to this direct intervention in the University's processes, I fear that the destruction of the University as a respectable institution for higher learning will inevitably follow."[84] At stake was nothing less than the university's independence from a corporate lobby group whose direct intervention in its appointment procedures would, the letter stated, destroy its credibility as an institution of higher learning. Mindful of the fact that these same market agents had persuaded the university to suspend its established procedures when Mackness was first appointed, Notz urged the board to respect the decision of the Presidential Advisory Committee. When Mackness declared that he was going to meet with the Board of Governors "to discuss procedural problems with the search process," Professor Rosenbloom of the Department of Actuarial and Management Sciences pointed to the "disturbing precedent" this would set and "the very dangerous journey" on which the board was embarking by agreeing to such a meeting. "The intensive lobbying efforts of the Board of Associates," he continued, "to affect the appointment of either a Dean or an interim Dean for the Faculty of Management ... [is based on the alien] concept of external groups lobbying for particular appointments [and] turns university procedures into political contests ... If ... successful ... the results will be chaotic."[85] By pressuring the university to reinstate Mackness, the Associates Board was undermining established hiring procedures, which reflected the institution's distinctive educational values, and was attempting to replace them with market values, which favoured their own corporate candidate. If they were to succeed in their goal, the effect on the university would be "chaotic."

Mackness himself appealed the Presidential Advisory Committee's decision to the Board of Governors. He then sent out letters on university letterhead to all alumni of the Faculty of Management informing them that the decision was "unfair and unreasonable"[86] – the very phrase used by Crewson. Mackness included with the letter "the confidential list of the search committee [and] a list of the Board of Governors" together with "their addresses and phone numbers"[87] so that they could be easily contacted by alumni supportive of his reappointment. He then conveyed his overall strategy to pursue "all possible steps open to him to make his circumstances known"[88] to President Naimark. Buoyed by the level of corporate support from the Associates, and believing that alumni could bring the Board of Governors to its knees, Mackness was positioned to overturn the committee's decision and disband established hiring procedures. He could then reassume the mantle of dean of a faculty operating as a private business corporation. It was in this context that President Naimark finally acted to reestablish control on the part of the university.

THE PRESIDENT SPEAKS TO THE FACULTY

On 24 March 1995, Naimark addressed a packed auditorium of faculty and students in the Faculty of Management. In attendance were Dean Mackness and Associate Dean Gray. The president's goal was "to correct some of the erroneous figures" that had been circulated regarding "the contribution of the Development Plan to the ongoing budgetary resources of the Faculty."[89] He referred explicitly to the $3 million alleged by Mackness to have been provided as a "major permanent increase in annual funding" as well as to his claim that "twenty baseline-funded, continuing academic positions"[90] had been secured on the basis of the development plan. Naimark disproved these figures by showing that it was the university that had funded the plan, not the government or the Associates. In 1994–95, for example, "new money" from government together with differential tuition fees from students amounted to only 8 percent of the total funding of the Faculty of Management – a tiny fraction of its $11.1 million budget. Even within the development plan's component of the budget, 65 percent of ongoing funding ($1.56 million) came "directly or indirectly from the University." These figures "do not include current funding provided directly by the Associates" for the simple reason that their five-year commitment to the plan had ceased in 1994. Similarly, the government, which was supposed to replace the Associates' funding, "did not in fact do so."[91] Their promise to provide $1,139,000 per year in new money after the initial five-year period failed to materialize; instead, the government reduced the university's general operating grant by almost $800,000, cutting its contribution to the development plan to $349,000 – once again, a fraction of its initial commitment to Mackness's scheme.

Under critical scrutiny from Naimark, none of Mackness's claims about increased funding from government or the Associates stood up. It was the university that was subsidizing the dean's development plan through funds from its operating budget. The main reason that twenty faculty positions had been retained in management was that the university had made a commitment to do so – an example that, in Naimark's words, typified the entire situation, in which "a very significant part of the ongoing funding attributable to the Development Plan has come out of the hide of the University."[92]

Naimark then underlined the real threat to university autonomy posed by Mackness's relationship with the Associates. This had come to supersede the dean's "contractual relationship" with both the Faculty and the University. As the main communication link between the faculty and the Associates, Mackness saw himself as accountable first and foremost to the latter. "In such circumstances," Naimark warned that "it is easy for the role of the Dean to be seen as that of the chief executive officer of a virtual corporation one might call the University of Management with the Associates as its Board of Directors."[93] As chief executive officer of this "virtual corporation," known as "the University of Management," Mackness considered himself accountable to the Associates as its only legitimate Board of Directors. They, after all, had demonstrated "loyal support" both for his reappointment and his plans to establish "a private business school existing as an independent corporation with its own board"[94] – one that would draw on the university's name and infrastructure but that would be loyal to the Associates.

Naimark had shown what many suspected – that Mackness's goal throughout had been to establish a private business school answerable to the Associates as its Board of Governors. He could then run the Faculty of Management as a private corporation without need of the "inefficient" values of the university. Naimark warned that this attempt at privatization "[would] in the end fail, [but that] much damage [would] be done in the process." Not only was Mackness undermining "the formal rules and procedures" of the university but also, and more important, its distinctive "values," among which "academic freedom, the tolerance of dissenting views and the importance of peer relationships, including peer evaluation,"[95] were fundamental. It was these values that Mackness had first denied to Vedanand almost seven years earlier, and, by calling attention to them, Naimark was reminding those present that the dean had undermined university norms from the very beginning of his appointment. Mackness had consistently refused to recognize the value of "both collegial and executive processes" as aspects of "sound, productive and effective governance," preferring to override the former with his own executive decisions on academic matters such as tenure. This, according to Naimark, led to "dysfunctional" governance where "the inappropriate exercise of executive authority [was allowed] to subvert legitimate collegial processes in pursuit of personal agendas."[96] Mackness's own agenda to privatize the Faculty of Management had so undermined the university's value system that the corporate sector's pressure on the Board of Governors to have him reinstated was now creating a "climate rife with intimidation and pressure tactics." The Associates' attempt to "replace reasoned debate with the rhetoric of tribal conflict" was making any rational process to select the dean impossible. As a result, Naimark had decided to disband the Presidential Advisory Committee and, at a later date, would recommend to the Board of Governors an "interim administration of the Faculty of Management beginning July 1, 1995."[97] Even when this appointment was announced the Associates wanted "Mackness [reinstated] for three years." They quickly voiced their opposition to an interim dean whose selection was "a denial of the fundamental principle of the Associates ... to elevate the degree of excellence of the students coming out of the Faculty,"[98] an excellence that translated into value-added being created for private corporations.

FACULTY RESISTANCE TO THE LOSS OF AUTONOMY

Naimark's defence of the distinctive educational values of academic freedom, tolerance for dissenting views, and the collegiality inherent in peer evaluation indicated just how far the Faculty of Management had drifted down the road towards corporate control. However, at no point in his speech did Naimark refer to the independence of the university being at risk. Yet Mackness's actions as "CEO of the virtual University of Management" posed a real threat to the institution's autonomy, a fact to which the president alluded but that he spent little time analyzing. Was this out of deference to the Associates – "I sincerely hope that in time, when the fever of the moment has cooled, there will be a rapprochement between the academy and the Associates of the Faculty"?[99] It is hard to know. In any case, Naimark refused to reach the logical conclusion of his own discourse; namely, that the university's independence had been seriously compromised by the actions of a dean who, acting in conjunction with powerful market agents, had treated the Faculty of Management as a private business corporation.

It was faculty members who experienced this loss of autonomy through their ongoing subjugation to the rules of the corporate market. They endured a seven-year regime in which collegial decision making had been systematically disbanded in favour of executive decisions taken by Mackness as chief executive officer. This had led the Faculty Council of the Faculty of Management to pass a vote of no-confidence in the dean, a motion that the Board of Governors had promptly ruled out of order. Three years earlier, faculty from across the university had recommended Mackness's dismissal for his remarks about colleagues in the Department of Actuarial and Management Sciences.[100]

Mackness's remarks had first come to light during the arbitration hearing for Dr Vedanand. It was he who signalled the dangers to academic freedom and university autonomy of the dean's executive decision making following the Xerox seminar at which he had dared to question two of the company's salespeople. Vedanand's academic freedom had been trivialized by "expert witnesses" at the arbitration hearing, who then vilified him for being "rude" and, in the words of the chair, for having "exceeded the acceptable limits of academic freedom." This was the first of several incidents that warned faculty of the threat Mackness posed to the value system of the university. Their concrete experience of his market-based rule coupled with the central administration's support for his deanship until late in the day resulted in faculty members taking the lead in organizing a sustained opposition. Through their teaching, scholarship, research, and ongoing dialogue with one another, faculty showed the importance of a value system in which knowledge is shared with others, not used for private profit. Inspired by "the university's mission[,which is] inextricably connected with democracy," it was they who upheld the idea of an institution "as a 'fortress' for freedom of speech, inquiry, and criticism of established truths."[101]

3

Taking on Big Pharma

The issue is not about whether their inconvenient findings were correct.
It is about individual conscience in conflict with corporate greed. It is
about the elementary right of doctors to express unbought medical
opinions, and their duty to acquaint patients with the risks they believe
to be inherent in the treatments they prescribe.

John le Carré[1]

A WELL-KNOWN CASE

The case of Dr Nancy Olivieri has become a cause célèbre. Different
authors have described it as "the greatest academic scandal of our
era," "so important to the public interest that it has attracted
national and international attention," because it "raise[s] questions
about how willing medical schools and their affiliated hospitals are
to resist pressure from corporate donors," and "whether and how
the pursuit of scientific truth and of profit can be reconciled with
one another" given "the increasing dependence of universities on
corporate funding of research."[2]

Unlike the previous case of Dr Vedanand, known mainly to faculty
at the University of Manitoba, Dr Olivieri's dispute with the generic
drug manufacturer Apotex Inc, the Hospital for Sick Children, and
the University of Toronto has been in the public domain for several
years. Scrutiny from ethicists, historians, legal theorists, research
scientists, the media, and two committees of inquiry has resulted in
the case being widely publicized. Almost everyone is concerned about
the questions raised about the future of medical research because
they touch on basic issues of life and death and the freedom of doctors to communicate the results of their research to patients and
other scientists.

I begin with a narrative of the main events of the Olivieri case and a summary illustrating its key aspects. My focus in the rest of the chapter is fourfold. First, I analyze the fiduciary nature of the doctor-patient relationship, showing how it is different from contractual relationships in the market. I argue that Dr Olivieri understood this difference and recognized that the right to informed consent, which applies to the doctor-patient relationship in general, is crucial in the context of research. Second, I show how important academic freedom is to researchers conducting clinical trials, and I explain the ways in which it was violated when Dr Olivieri communicated the results of her findings to patients and other scientists. Administrators at the Hospital for Sick Children (HSC) and the University of Toronto (U of T) did little, if anything, to defend her academic freedom. Third, I consider the structural problem of universities' and hospitals' dependency on corporate "donations," which is a direct result of government underfunding. An analysis of Apotex's influence on university research and its flawed claims regarding the safety of deferiprone (L1) follows. This, I argue, is but one of the ways in which university governance at U of T was undermined by different "donor agreements." Fourth, I analyze several proposals for reform of "partnerships" between pharmaceutical companies and university hospitals. I argue that greater regulation and control of such "partnerships" is inadequate. There is a need to move beyond partnerships and to ensure a fair share of profit for university-originated discoveries. And, in order to fully serve the public interest, socialized medical research and the removal of patents should be considered since the latter limit the epistemic possibilities of research.

The lessons to be learned from the Olivieri "scandal" illustrate quite graphically the ways in which the corporate market threatens university research in science and medicine, and how such influence can be resisted.[3] The familiar pattern of the conflict between the goals of university research and education to advance and disseminate shared knowledge, on the one hand, and the market's overriding goal to maximize stockholder value, on the other, is played out in this drama. The clash between the opposing logics of value highlights the importance of Dr Olivieri's actions in protecting the health of her patients and communicating her findings to other research scientists. As Arthur Schafer, professor of philosophy and director of the Centre for Professional and Applied Ethics at the University of

Manitoba, puts it: "Despite the apparent complexity of the facts and circumstances surrounding the scandal, the Canadian public almost immediately understood the gist of the underlying ethical issues. With seeming indifference to the campaign of vilification against Olivieri – a campaign which questioned her scientific competence, her ethics, her personality, and even her sanity – both the scientific community and the general public appeared intuitively to understand that when Olivieri spoke out publicly against perceived dangers to her patients, she was acting in a manner consistent with the highest traditions of her profession."[4]

A NARRATIVE OF LIFE AND DEATH

The Doctor, the Drug, and the Contracts

Dr Olivieri is a specialist in the treatment of hereditary blood disorders. During the early 1990s, she and Dr Gary Brittenham (also a hematologist, now of Columbia University) carried out a pilot study on the drug deferiprone (L1), which appeared to reduce dangerous levels of iron in a group of children suffering from the genetic blood disorder thalassemia, common to people of Mediterranean, African, Southeast Asian, and Chinese descent. Its victims produce insufficient amounts of hemoglobin, the substance in the blood that carries oxygen. Children born with the most severe form, thalassemia major, have stunted growth and enlarged spleens, and eventually the disorder can lead to heart failure and other fatal complications. Red blood-cell transfusions, which are rich in iron and antibiotics, have improved the survival rate, but regular transfusions cause iron to build up in the body, and this can severely damage the heart, liver, and other organs. In order to prevent this from happening, the chemical purging of excess iron from the body, known as chelation therapy, is required. The standard procedure for chelation therapy involves a painful under-the-skin-infusion of the drug deferoxamine that is effective for only nine to twelve hours and is difficult for patients to maintain.[5] The attraction of L1 was that it was a pill that could be easily ingested.

Dr Olivieri's pilot study on L1 initially showed promise and was supported by an operating grant from the Medical Research Council of Canada (MRC) and conducted at HSC, an affiliated teaching hospital with U of T. Dr Olivieri held appointments at both institutions and was at the time director of the Hemoglobinopathy Program at the hospital. Her publication record is impressive, her clinical and research programs are respected by leading international specialists, and her status in the field was recognized by Dr Arnold Aberman, dean of medicine at U of T in 1997: "I consider Nancy Olivieri an outstanding clinical investigator and an authority of international stature on hemoglobinopathies."[6]

In order to continue with research on L1, Dr Olivieri and the team at HSC, of which she was principal investigator, needed corporate funding for a randomized control trial. In 1993, together with Dr Gideon Koren, a clinical pharmacologist, she signed a contract with Apotex, the pharmaceutical manufacturer of L1 (the contract was referred to as LA-01). It contained a confidentiality clause that gave Apotex the right to control communication and publication of the data for one year after termination of the trial, a provision consistent with existing U of T policy on contract research. The MRC provided matching funds under its university-industry program. Dr Olivieri has since been advised that the confidentiality clause may have been illegal under Canadian law.[7]

Meanwhile, the pilot study on L1 continued as a long-term trial, but there was no confidentiality clause in the contract (LA-03) signed in 1995. Dr Olivieri and Dr Brittenham had also agreed to act as consultants on a short-term safety trial at various international sites. Although this contract (LA-02) had a three-year post-termination confidentiality clause, it was "supplanted," or overridden, by the 1995 agreement.[8]

Apotex's interest in partially funding the research was based on the assumption that it would commercialize L1, provided that the findings were favourable. The randomized trial (LA-01) was designed as the pivotal study and safety trial for licensing the drug and, together with the pilot study (LA-03), formed the basis for assessing its efficacy in reducing toxic effects, especially chronic levels of iron capable of endangering the liver and other vital organs.

Problems Emerge with the Drug

After publishing a paper favourable to the drug in the *New England Journal of Medicine* in 1995 with other members of the research team, Dr Olivieri identified an unexpected medical risk; namely, that there was a loss of sustained efficacy of L1 for patients in the clinical trial (LA-01). Having informed Apotex of the risk, which it disputed, she sought direction from the chair of HSC's Research Ethics Board (REB), who concurred that her primary responsibility was to inform her patients. "A no brainer" was how Dr Stanley Zlotkin later described the "self-evident decision."[9] However, as soon as Dr Olivieri took action to inform both her patients and the authorities, Apotex terminated both trials in May 1996 and threatened her with legal action.

In February 1997, Dr Olivieri identified a second, potentially more serious risk: L1 might cause progressive liver fibrosis. Once again she took steps to inform her patients, despite further legal warnings from Apotex, arranging for them to transfer back to the standard treatment, a complex process that took several weeks because the treatment using deferoxamine required the ongoing testing of each patient. This procedure did not threaten their health, however, as the newly identified risk was not acute.

Two challenges were then issued to Dr Olivieri's professional judgment. Dr Hugh O'Brodovich, HSC's pediatrician-in-chief, claimed that the most recent risk to patients was acute toxicity and should be reported to the hospital's REB. His judgment was not based on expertise in haematology and was made following discussions with both Apotex and Dr Koren. The College of Physicians and Surgeons of Ontario later refuted the claim, exonerating Dr Olivieri on this and all other matters.[10]

The pressure mounted by Apotex to show that L1 was safe and to discredit Dr Olivieri then intensified, as the Canadian Association of University Teachers' independent inquiry shows:

> At the same time Apotex began efforts to persuade medical administrators and patients in Toronto, as well as regulatory agencies and the scientific community that L1 was effective and safe and should be in wider use. Apotex proposed a new treatment for Toronto thalassemia patients in which annual liver biopsy, the test that had led to the identification of both of the unexpected risks of L1, would not be an integral part of the safety monitoring for all patients. Apotex's proposal was not accepted by Dr Olivieri, who had phased out use of L1 in the clinics she directed. She had the support of hematologist Dr Michael Baker, Physician-in-Chief of The Toronto General

Hospital, where adult thalassemia patients received their care under her supervision.[11]

The support of Dr Michael Baker for Dr Olivieri's program of research would prove significant in her ongoing struggle to refute the claims of Apotex. It is also important to note that, by February 1997, Dr Olivieri had already stopped using L1 with her patients because of the drug's attendant risks.

Ethical Questions about Apotex's Funding of Research

It appears that Dr Koren continued to receive substantial research funding from Apotex after the company had terminated the clinical trials (LA-01 and LA-03). Unbeknownst to Dr Olivieri, he used the data from the terminated trials, reanalyzed them, and, in 1999, published findings that "the drug was effective and safe."[12] However, the following facts are not clarified:

> The article does not disclose that Apotex funded the work of the three co-authors. The article does not acknowledge the contributions of Drs Olivieri, Brittenham, Jacob, and others to generating the data reported in it. The article does not mention the risk of progression of liver fibrosis identified by Dr Olivieri in data of the same cohort of patients, even though Dr Olivieri had fully appraised Dr Koren of this finding in early February 1997 and she had published the finding in 1997 abstracts and in a 1998 article in the *New England Journal of Medicine*.[13]

Dr Koren's alleged violation of accepted standards of conduct in scientific publication and the relevant policies of the University of Toronto was eventually dismissed.[14]

Dr Koren's findings were then used by Apotex "in communications with Health Canada to counter Dr Olivieri's adverse findings on its drug." His research enabled the company to defend the efficacy of L1 by stating that there was a "scientific disagreement" between them and to claim "that Dr Olivieri was wrong about the science." This assertion ignored the fact that Dr Koren's "article does not mention the risk of progression of liver fibrosis identified by Dr Olivieri in data of the same cohort of patients."[15]

Lack of Support by the Hospital to Combat Corporate Influence

From May 1996 onwards, Apotex issued a series of legal warnings to Dr Olivieri not to communicate the risks she had identified with regard to L1 and its effect on her patients. Neither HSC nor U of T provided her with legal assistance. The hospital claims to have made behind-the-scenes efforts to dissuade Apotex from suing her.[16] The Canadian Medical Protective Association did give Dr Olivieri legal support for the first two years of the dispute, but its mandate was limited to minimizing her legal exposure as an individual client rather than defending the public interest challenged by the case.[17]

Since the early 1990s, ongoing discussions had been taking place between the hospital, the university, and Apotex, which was considering a multi-million-dollar donation for a new biomedical research centre. By 1998, an agreement in principle had been reached that included matching funds from other sources. Talks were suspended when the controversy between Apotex and Dr Olivieri became public later that year, but they were resumed in 1999 when the company asked the university for assistance in lobbying the Government of Canada against proposed changes in drug patent regulations that would have cut into its profits.[18] The president of U of T, Robert Prichard, duly wrote a letter to several federal ministers, including Prime Minister Jean Chretien, stating that "the proposed new legislation might make [it] financially impossible for Apotex to fulfill its $20 million donation toward the University's new Centre for Cellular and Biomolecular Research."[19] The total of Apotex's donation was at that time $55 million, the largest-ever corporate investment in a Canadian university. Prichard later apologized to the executive committee of the university, admitting that his actions had been wrong. His lobbying efforts on behalf of the company proved unsuccessful, and Apotex withdrew from the agreement.[20] In 2000, however, the company made a smaller multi-million dollar investment to U of T.

The Naimark Report

During 1997 and 1998 a growing number of medical scientists expressed concern about the lack of effective action from HSC and the university in assisting Dr Olivieri in her legal disputes with

Apotex. Several colleagues formally requested the hospital to support her, but neither institution took up the case and their inaction resulted in calls for an independent inquiry. The case eventually became public in August 1998, two years after it had begun, following the publication of Dr Olivieri's critical article in the *New England Journal of Medicine*.[21]

The following month HSC established a review of the controversy without consulting any of the other parties. Dr Arnold Naimark was named as the only reviewer. It is worth remembering that several years earlier, as president of the University of Manitoba, Dr Naimark had done little to support the academic freedom of Dr Vedanand in his dispute with Xerox Canada Inc. He intervened in the non-renewal of the dean who had censured Vedanand only when faculty members in the Faculty of Management were enraged by their treatment by the former banker.

Naimark's appointment as reviewer at HSC was controversial because he was seen to be biased: "Dr Naimark had raised money from Apotex while President of the University of Manitoba, and was a member on the Board of Directors of the Canadian Imperial Bank of Commerce (CIBC). The Chair of the CIBC Board, Mr A.L. Flood was a member of the Board of the HSC Foundation and the CIBC was active in raising funds for Hospital projects."[22] As Dr Olivieri put it, "Dr Naimark had close relationships with those he was allegedly to 'review'! This is, in my view, [a] serious conflict of interest."[23] The Naimark Review Panel have since claimed that "any donations from Apotex to the University [of Manitoba] were made without his involvement."[24] Nevertheless, Schafer has suggested that the choice of Dr Naimark as "the sole reviewer" was problematical given his "commercial ties to a member of the Board of Trustees and professional ties to Apotex" and has questioned the board's "disrespect for the principle of an impartial investigation by a disinterested investigator."[25]

Dr Olivieri and her colleagues refused to participate in the review process because they were opposed to the unilateral manner in which Naimark was selected. They also felt that important documents and "material information" were missing and that they would not have the opportunity to express opinions in an independent manner.[26] Two months after he had begun working on the report, Dr Naimark invited two colleagues to become associate reviewers. Absent for most of the interviews conducted with administrators and medical staff, their participation was limited to providing critiques of several drafts of the final report.[27]

The report claimed that it was "not prescriptive" in that it was the first part of a larger process that was to make explicit policy changes to HSC. Nevertheless, it pointed to the "weak policy infrastructure" of the hospital that required "a clean slate rather than ... simply tinkering with the present policies." In particular, hospital and university policies regarding research should be harmonized, explicit REB rules for modifying or discontinuing clinical trials enacted, greater guidance given to the chair of the REB about his/her powers to act in special circumstances, proper grievance procedures established for scientific and medical staff, and provisions for legal support from the hospital made clear.[28] Most of Naimark's prescriptions were later implemented by HSC's Policy Review Implementation Committee.[29]

Nevertheless, "critical omissions" in the documentation coupled with "incorrect or false information" meant that "the Review was compromised in two material ways."[30] These flaws are documented exhaustively in the CAUT independent inquiry entitled *The Olivieri Report*, and it is not necessary to review all of them here. But one of the main conclusions reached by the Naimark Review Panel illustrates the problem quite clearly: the repeated allegation that Dr Olivieri had failed to report the toxicity of L1 to the REB.[31]

One of the many documents not considered by the Naimark Review Panel consisted of a chapter written by Dr Koren in a 1993 book on research ethics – a book that he edited. Koren made reference to several studies at HSC that do not require REB approval, including what was later called Health Canada's Emergency Drug Release Program (EDR), under which L1 continued to be administered to some patients after the termination of both trials (LA-01 and LA-03). According to the authors of *The Olivieri Report*, "this information confirms that, under HSC policy, Dr Olivieri was not required to obtain REB approval to treat patients under EDR, and that she was not required to obtain REB approval to publish data obtained from chart review."[32] The Naimark Review Panel's failure to consider this piece of evidence had serious consequences. It was on this basis that HSC referred the matter to its Medical Advisory Committee and thence to the College of Physicians and Surgeons of Ontario "concerning Dr Olivieri's failure to report her concern about liver toxicity to the Research Ethics Board, which is well documented in the [Naimark] review."[33]

Dr Koren also made two contradictory statements to the Naimark Review Panel. In a letter reproduced in full, bearing the date 8 February 1997, he allegedly wrote to Dr Olivieri to say that he was "shocked and dismayed to receive [her] analysis of liver toxicity." Later in the report, however, we find the following statement based on Dr Koren's testimony: "No information was provided by Dr Olivieri to ... Dr Koren or the REB about this serious adverse reaction until inquiries were made of her in the latter part of February 1997."[34] The report identifies this later date as 19 February of the same year. Had the Naimark Review Panel investigated this discrepancy, its members might have questioned the reliability of Dr Koren's testimony.[35] Independent evidence from another report by HSC's own investigator, Ms Barbara Humphrey, shows that Dr Koren had received Dr Olivieri's report on the newly identified risk of L1 on or before 8 February 1997.[36] While the *Humphrey Report* was released one year after the *Naimark Report*, the panel could have acknowledged the significance of its findings in its *Commentary on the CAUT Inquiry*, which was published in December 2001. Instead, it continued to defend its interpretation of the "purported discrepancies between statements made by Dr Koren," claiming that the "review Panel ha[d] not been provided with a copy of the transcript of [the] Humphrey Report and therefore cannot comment on its findings."[37] Two years had elapsed since the following statement appeared in print: "Dr Koren acknowledged that he had received a copy of the letter from Dr Olivieri's [Canadian Medical Protective Association (CMPA)] counsel at McCarthy Tetrault in early February 1997, together with a bound book of documents relevant to the liver toxicity issue."[38]

The conclusive evidence from the *Humphrey Report* showed that Dr Koren had indeed been informed by Dr Olivieri, through her counsel, of the risk of liver toxicity associated with L1 on 8 February. The Naimark Review Panel overlooked this fact in its most recent commentary on the Olivieri case.

Fallout from the Naimark Report: A Mediated Settlement

Released to the public on 9 December 1998, the Naimark Report denied there had been any moves towards "constructive dismissal" of Dr Olivieri from her post as director of the hemoglobinopathy program.[39] But on 6 January 1999, HSC summarily removed her from this position. The reasons given varied from alleged failures to perform administrative duties to her "personal" opposition to the decentralization to regional hospitals of the sickle cell disease (SCD) program formerly under her direction.[40] HSC also issued "directives" to Dr Olivieri and her colleagues, Drs Helen Chan, Peter Durie, and Brenda Gallie, not to discuss publicly their concerns about what had taken place.[41]

A wide range of individuals and groups then coalesced in their opposition to HSC's actions. On 7 January, CAUT and the University of Toronto Faculty Association (UTFA) held a press conference denouncing Dr Olivieri's dismissal. Without full responsibility for the patients in her program, she would be unable to continue with her clinical research. Both associations called for her immediate reinstatement and an independent inquiry into the events at HSC. Letters from physicians around the world poured in to U of T demanding Dr Olivieri's reinstatement. They included letters from Dr Sir David Weatherall of Oxford University and Dr David G. Nathan of Harvard University, both experts in thalassemia and SCD. There was also a phone call to President Prichard from Derek Bok, former president of Harvard University. Among the groups who wrote to U of T were the Association for Public Accountability, the Urban Alliance on Race Relations, and the American Association for the Advancement of Science.[42]

The university remained unmoved. But in a letter from the Provost, dated 12 January, UTFA learned that President Prichard had warned HSC that, unless Dr Olivieri were given the opportunity to respond to the allegations that led to her dismissal, "the University could not support the Hospital's decision." Under continuing pressure, the provost requested UTFA and CAUT to arrange a meeting on 20 January at which Dr Olivieri gave testimony to the administration about why her dismissal prevented her from continuing with her research. The three-hour meeting proved inconclusive because the administration dallied on the issue of who should conduct a scientific review of her work: the international experts or HSC administrators.[43]

Several days after the meeting, Drs Weatherall and Nathan arrived in Toronto at the invitation of CAUT, together with Dr John Porter of University College London and Dr Alan Schechter of Bethesda, Maryland, experts in clinical trials and hemoglinopathies. It was at this point that the university decided to act. "To their credit," said UTFA/CAUT president Bill Graham, "the University, in the end, did the right thing."[44] President Prichard mediated an agreement signed on 25 January 1999 by HSC and Dr Olivieri, resolving some of the issues between them. Drs Weatherall and Nathan were instrumental in helping to achieve this goal.[45]

The terms of the agreement enabled Dr Olivieri to relocate her office to the Toronto General Hospital, where she would remain as director of the hemoglopinothy program and report to Dr Baker. This meant that she could continue with her clinical research and maintain control over her patients at both hospitals as she retained her appointment at HSC. The latter hospital agreed to cover any costs if Apotex were to sue her for events that had transpired since 1996, and it paid for any legal expenses already incurred by Dr Olivieri to a maximum of $150,000. HSC stated that the letter of 6 January 1999, which dismissed her as director of the hemoglobin-opathy program, had "no continuing force or effect." The hospital also lifted the directives (or "gag orders") that had been placed on Drs Olivieri, Gallie, Durie, and Chan – a tacit acknowledgement that their academic freedom had been expunged. Other clauses in the agreement, carefully worded by lawyers representing all sides of the disagreement, provided Dr Olivieri with a "mini-sabbatical" and a twelve-month sabbatical with full pay at a later date.[46]

Missing from the agreement was any commitment on the part of HSC or U of T to conduct a fully independent inquiry into "the scandal." As a result, a central issue remained unresolved; namely, "how to protect researchers in an era when the largest portion of research funding comes from the pharmaceutical industry, whose commercial aspirations depend on that research."[47] The problem was exacerbated by the fact that the affiliation agreement between HSC and U of T had elapsed at the end of 1998. UTFA wanted to tie the renewal of the agreement to Dr Olivieri's reinstatement and to improvements in hospital regulations affecting all professors. But the university refused, renewing the affiliation in January 1999 for a period of one year only.[48]

Another agreement between the parties, mediated by President Prichard and Dr David Naylor, dean of the Faculty of Medicine from July 1999, was not enacted until much later. The November 2002 settlement allowed Dr Olivieri to focus on her research without having any other hospital responsibilities. The university and UTFA set up a combined working group, whose goal was to make recom-mendations on U of T's conflict of interest policy and limits on publishing the results of research. The rest of the agreement was confidential. However, monetary compensation for the legal expenses of the four doctors who were Dr Olivieri's principal supporters – Drs Gallie, Durie, Chan, and Dick – was one of the elements, as was support for their research programs and for the work environment, in which they should no longer feel under threat for the collegial stance they had taken. As Dr Olivieri put it, "I think this sends a message to scientists, particularly clinical scientists, that academic freedom is worth fighting for."[49]

The Medical Advisory Committee Reports

Meanwhile, upon receipt of the Naimark Report in December 1998, HSC had initiated an inquiry by its Medical Advisory Committee (MAC) into Dr Olivieri's conduct. The MAC has the power to advise the hospital's Board of Directors on disciplinary action against staff physicians, and it was directed to consider her "failure" to report the risk of liver toxicity to the REB. This central finding of the Naimark Report was based on misinformation garnered from Dr Koren, to which I have already drawn attention. Nevertheless, it could still be found on HSC's website as recently as January 2008.[50]

During the course of the inquiry, new allegations were made by Drs O'Brodovich and Koren concerning Dr Olivieri's use of "dangerous" liver biopsies on some of her patients during the period after Apotex had terminated the LA-01 trials in 1996. Yet, "had MAC members diligently reviewed Dr Olivieri's submission and reviewed the medical literature cited in it, or consulted independent experts, they would have discovered that liver biopsy is a safe procedure that is necessary for proper management of the care of transfusion-dependent thalassemia patients ... regardless of whether or not they are in a research trial."[51] Drs O'Brodovich and Koren also claimed that Dr Olivieri had carried out the biopsies for purposes of research and not for clinical reasons, even though she had not been conducting any research on L1 since the first risk was discovered in May 1996. MAC's own ad hoc committee report supported her point of view, stating that "no reference was made to an ongoing research project"[52] in the charts of those patients undergoing liver biopsies that they had examined. This evidence, together with Dr Olivieri's own submission to the MAC, was ignored. The inquiry also denied her due process, sending a series of questions without any information

about the evidence brought against her or giving her the opportunity
to correct the mistakes contained therein.[53]

On 27 April 2000, the hospital's board and the MAC announced
they were referring the allegations against Dr Olivieri for investigation by the College of Physicians and Surgeons of Ontario (CPSO)
and U of T. Dr Laurence Becker, the MAC chair, wrote to the CPSO
and the university on 2 May about the "concerns" of the committee
regarding both her "patient care" and "research."[54] The concerns
were threefold: Dr Olivieri's continuing administration of L1 to
patients after her discovery of the risk of liver toxicity; her use of
liver biopsies for research rather than the clinical needs of patients;
and her "failure" to advise her department chief and co-workers
about the risks of L1. The Complaints Committee of CPSO rejected
all three allegations on 19 December 2001. First, the committee
found that "Dr Olivieri ceased to administer L1 in a timely and
expedient way, and in a manner which was in the best interests of
her patients." Second, they concluded that "Dr Olivieri's judgement
in advising patients to undergo biopsies was not only reasonable,
but commendable in the circumstances." Third, the committee concurred that "Dr Olivieri communicated diligently with those who
required information about her concerns."[55] As a result, the CPSO
took no further action against her, exonerating her on all counts.
The U of T then reached the same conclusion. Dean Naylor stated
in a letter of 7 January 2002 to Dr Olivieri that he was dismissing
the allegation that she "should have reported her conclusions with
respect to L1 toxicity to the Research Ethics Board," and he concluded that "the University will not be proceeding further with this
matter, and the allegations are hereby dismissed."[56]

Apotex's Relationship with Dr Koren

During the entire controversy over L1, the long-standing relationship
between Dr Michael Spino and Dr Koren remained unchanged.
Dr Spino had been a faculty member in the Faculty of Pharmacy at
U of T since 1975; however, following a leave of absence that he
spent with Apotex in the early 1990s, he became the company's
vice-president of Scientific Affairs. From 1992 onwards, he had a
"status only" professorship at the university and maintained a laboratory and office space at HSC, engaging in collaborative research
with Dr Koren both before the L1 clinical trials began and once they

were over. Spino claimed that Apotex had invested $1 million in thalassemia research at HSC. And, according to *The Olivieri Report*, "of this total, approximately one-quarter was transferred into Dr Koren's research accounts *after* the clinical trials were terminated. Dr Koren did not disclose that Apotex was the source of a $250,000 grant made to him around the time the trials were terminated, when receipt of the grant is documented through the University's Department of Pediatrics."[57]

As Apotex's principal representative, Spino had terminated the L1 trials in May 1996 after Dr Olivieri had identified the first risk associated with the drug. Together with the company's lawyer, he repeatedly issued legal warnings to dissuade her from informing her patients of the risk. Similar warnings to deter her from presenting and publishing the findings about L1 comprised a violation of Dr Olivieri's academic freedom, a point to which I return later in the chapter.[58]

As early as March 1997, Spino had tried unsuccessfully to persuade Dr Brittenham not to present an abstract on the risk of progressive liver fibrosis at an international conference. During this correspondence, Spino described liver biopsy as "a needless, invasive procedure with its attendant risks and costs."[59] In January 1998, Apotex Research Inc included the following statement as part of its regulatory submission for L1: "because of its invasiveness, the assessment of body iron in liver biopsy samples is not generally accepted ... in the clinical setting, although it does have limited application in clinical trials."[60] In May of the same year, Spino wrote to Dr O'Brodovich, claiming that Dr Olivieri's reference to data from the monitoring of patients in clinical settings, which she made when presenting a paper to an international conference, constituted unauthorized research. He based his allegation on the following: that the patients had not "received notification that they were in a new trial ... [requiring] authorization from the Ethics Committee."[61] Spino emphasized the same point in a letter to Dr Naimark dated 24 November 1998. Referring explicitly to the liver biopsies conducted on patients in early 1997, he alleged that Dr Olivieri had continued to administer L1 "in order to collect more hepatic biopsy data"[62] as part of her research. But the Naimark Report made no mention of the liver biopsies and did not consider them to be an issue.

It was not until Dr Koren made allegations of a strikingly similar nature that they were taken seriously by the MAC. His judgment as a physician added considerable weight to the claims of Dr Spino, who was not a medical doctor but, rather, held a doctorate in pharmacy. In a letter to the MAC in December 1998, Dr Koren reiterated the claim that liver biopsies conducted in 1997 were for the purposes of research and required permission from the REB. He went even further than Apotex Research in claiming that the risks of liver biopsy comprised "a potentially life threatening procedure."[63] Bear in mind that it was annual liver biopsy procedures that had revealed both of the risks associated with L1.

Dr Koren's Anonymous Letters Result in Disciplinary Action

Both the Naimark and MAC reports had relied heavily on the evidence of Dr Koren in order to reach their conclusions about Dr Olivieri's conduct. The Naimark Report alluded in passing to "a growing estrangement between two highly-talented scientists and collaborators" and suggested that this had occurred because Dr Olivieri "did not share her findings suggesting liver toxicity of L1 with Dr Koren."[64] But Dr Olivieri *did* share her findings with him, as both the CPSO and U of T judgments make clear. So it is reasonable to infer that the cause of the problem lay elsewhere.

Dr Koren, an expert on the effect of drugs on children, was the holder of Canada's first chair in child health research, the result of a $2 million gift from CIBC to HSC, entitled the CIBC-Wood Gundy Children's Miracle Foundation Chair in Child Health Research. Even though Dr Olivieri was listed as the principal investigator on the 1993 MRC application, Dr Koren had played a leading role in negotiations with Apotex both before and during the time the clinical trials for L1 were run and, as we have seen, continued to collaborate with Dr Spino once they were terminated.[65]

Between October 1998 and May 1999, a series of anonymous letters was sent to various parties, some of them faxed to the press, attacking the personal and professional integrity of Drs Olivieri, Durie, Chan, and Gallie. On the basis of evidence compiled by a private detective and analyzed by forensic experts, the four professors lodged a formal complaint in May identifying Dr Koren as the author. He denied any involvement. HSC then hired its own investigator, Ms Humphrey, whose work continued for several months, partially because it was "frustrated" and "obstructed" by a number of "lies"[66] told to her by Dr Koren.

In December 1999, Dr Olivieri and her colleagues obtained further forensic evidence, in the form of DNA samples that matched with those found in a hand-written letter sent by Dr Koren, that he was the author of the anonymous letters. They were advised by HSC's chair of the Board of Trustees to say nothing and to wait for publication of Ms Humphrey's report lest they damage the reputation of a colleague. Dr Koren was informed of the new DNA evidence identifying him as the author on 10 December, and a week later he admitted responsibility. On 20 December, HSC president Michael Strofolino informed the press that the author of the anonymous letters had been identified, and the next day the Toronto papers carried articles identifying him. On 21 December, Ms Humphrey's report was released to the press. She concluded, by comparing the use of language in both the letters and in the various articles he had published, that Dr Koren was the culprit.[67]

Dr Koren was then suspended from both hospital and university duties with pay, pending a disciplinary hearing. He admitted in the pages of the *Globe and Mail* that his actions were "inappropriate and unbecoming" but claimed "the only way I could express myself was in those [anonymous] letters [because] we were told [by the hospital] not to talk to the media ever which I religiously regarded … but when you are attacked savagely by five people over three years, you may do these things."[68]

In its *Commentary on the CAUT Report*, the Naimark Review Panel raised the question of its reliance on "Dr Koren's trustworthiness" in its earlier report. Not surprisingly, it concluded that, "when the references to information provided by Dr Koren for which he was the sole source are removed from the HSC Report, the main conclusions and recommendations of the Report remain unimpaired."[69] Yet I have pointed to one instance in which Dr Koren's testimony did mislead the Naimark Review; namely, the date on which Dr Olivieri informed him of the risk of liver toxicity related to L1. This is significant since it was the basis of the erroneous complaint against Dr Olivieri to both the CPSO and U of T. Furthermore, the Naimark Panel was now aware of the letter proving that Dr Olivieri had told Dr Koren of the risk earlier than he had claimed.[70] But it did not revise its initial judgment on the basis of this evidence.

Dr Koren was given due process in a hearing that lasted four months, and on 11 April 2000 disciplinary action was imposed on him. A letter from Presidents Prichard and Strofolino cited three types of misconduct: "disseminating anonymous harassing correspondence"; denial of involvement to the hospital, the university, and Ms Humphrey; and "late admission of responsibility." The letter noted: "you have provided no acceptable explanation for your misconduct" and "your actions constitute gross misconduct and provide sufficient grounds for dismissal." However, the two presidents did not dismiss Dr Koren for several "mitigating reasons," which included his accomplishments as a researcher, particularly his "recent MRC Senior Scientist Award." Nevertheless, they extended his suspension until 1 June 2000, removed him from the CIBC-Wood Gundy Chair in Child Health Research as well as from a university administrative position, and imposed a $35,000 fine "as partial restitution" for the cost of Ms Humphrey's investigation.[71]

The presidents restricted their disciplinary action to conduct to which Dr Koren had admitted. While their letter mentioned "the allegation of misconduct that you deny ... that you prepared 'two false letters for submission to Dr Naimark,'" they did not proceed any further on the issue. Expressing concern about "whether the letters had been prepared on the dates shown [especially since] in throwing away the computer on which you typed these letters, you might have destroyed the evidence that could have proved or disproved this action," they concluded that "the case on this allegation is not closed."[72]

Presidents Prichard and Strofolino did, however, deplore Dr Koren's "complete disregard for colleagues and for the values which the Hospital and the University seek to foster." They emphasized the need for physicians and clinical faculty to "cooperate and be truthful [since] academic freedom cannot flourish in an environment in which unwarranted attacks are made on colleagues' personal and professional integrity."[73] This is a clear acknowledgment that the academic freedom of Drs Chan, Dick, Durie, Gallie, and Olivieri was violated by Dr Koren's series of letters. Until that point, neither HSC nor U of T had acknowledged the relationship of academic freedom to the controversy over L1, preferring to refer to it as "a scientific dispute." The commitment of the hospital to the values it proclaimed remained ambiguous, however. Just two weeks after disciplinary action was taken against Dr Koren, HSC initiated its complaint against Dr Olivieri to CPSO and U of T, an action that not only threatened her academic freedom but that could have permanently damaged her career had not both institutions exonerated her on all counts.

Summary

According to Professor Margaret Somerville, director of the McGill Centre for Medicine, Ethics, and Law, "the Olivieri case reads like a horror story on the involvement of corporations in university-based research."[74] The salient points illustrating the truth of this statement are as follows:

1 The contract signed by Drs Olivieri and Koren with Apotex in 1993 (LA-01) to conduct a randomized trial on L1 contained a confidentiality clause that prevented disclosure of scientific findings for one year without permission of the company.

2 Nevertheless, Dr Olivieri informed her patients and the authorities in 1996 when she identified a risk of loss of sustained efficacy of L1. Apotex then threatened her with legal action and curtailed the clinical trials in May. Despite further threats of legal action, Dr Olivieri promptly informed her patients and the authorities in 1997 when she identified a second, more serious risk that L1 might cause liver fibrosis.

3 Apotex tried to persuade the medical community that L1 was safe and that the procedure of annual liver biopsy, which had revealed both risks of the drug, was unnecessary for monitoring patient health. The medical evidence available at the time suggested that "liver biopsy is a safe procedure that is necessary for proper management of the care of transfusion-dependent thalassemia patients."[75]

4 Since the early 1990s, U of T had been negotiating with Apotex to donate as much as $55 million for a new biomedical centre. President Prichard tried unsuccessfully to pressure the federal government to drop proposed changes in drug patent regulations that would have reduced Apotex's private profits. He later admitted his actions were wrong.

5 HSC established a review chaired by Dr Naimark who, it was claimed, had raised money for Apotex and who sat on the board of CIBC. His report, released in December 1998, was incomplete in its documentation, relied upon incorrect testimony from

Dr Koren, and concluded falsely that Dr Olivieri had not properly reported the toxicity of L1.

6 Dr Olivieri was then removed from her position as director of the hemoglobinopathy program at HSC, preventing her from continuing with clinical research. As a result of mounting pressure from UTFA and CAUT, President Prichard mediated a settlement between HSC and Dr Olivieri in January 1999 with the help of two internationally renowned hematologists, moving her position to the Toronto General Hospital, where she could continue with her research.

7 An inquiry conducted by the MAC at HSC denied Dr Olivieri due process and reiterated the Naimark Report's claim that she had not reported the risk of toxicity of L1 to the hospital's REB (even though this was not required). The report also claimed falsely that the procedure of liver biopsy she had conducted was unsafe and was conducted for research purposes rather than for clinical reasons.

8 It was Apotex's vice-president for Scientific Affairs, Dr Spino, who claimed that Dr Olivieri had used the procedure of liver biopsy for unauthorized research. These allegations were also made to the MAC inquiry by Dr Koren, who continued to receive substantial funding from Apotex for his research after the clinical trials for L1 were terminated. Dr Koren had used data from the trials without the permission of Dr Olivieri and had co-published an article with two employees of Apotex claiming that L1 was safe and effective.

9 In December 1999, Dr Koren was identified on the basis of forensic evidence as the author of a series of anonymous letters, which had attacked the personal and professional integrity of Dr Olivieri and her principal supporters. Following a disciplinary hearing, Dr Koren was stripped of his CIBC-Wood Gundy Chair and fined for having obstructed HSC's own inquiry.

10 Two weeks later, in May 2000, MAC chair Dr Becker referred the main allegations from the MAC Report concerning Dr Olivieri's use of the procedure of liver biopsy and her "failure" to adequately report the toxicity of L1 to the Complaints Committee of the CPSO and to U of T. Both the CPSO and U of T exonerated her on all counts.

11 Another settlement mediated by the dean of Medicine, Dr Naylor, eventually gave compensation to Dr Olivieri's major supporters,

Drs Chan, Dick, Durie, and Gallie, for their legal costs as well as for their research and for the abuse they suffered for their collegiality. The legal battles between Apotex and Dr Olivieri are still not over.[76]

THE DOCTOR-PATIENT RELATIONSHIP

The Olivieri case has captured the public's imagination because it raises important questions about the relationship between doctor and patient. What responsibilities, for example, does a medical doctor have to inform her patients of the risks of a certain intervention or drug? What rights does the patient have to be informed and how are these rights guaranteed? The issue is complicated by the fact that Dr Olivieri was engaged in clinical trials for the purposes of both research and therapeutic care. It is important, nevertheless, to understand the nature of the doctor-patient relationship in general terms. One can then appreciate the additional questions involved when a doctor, who is engaged in research, identifies a risk associated with a drug and, breaking confidentiality, decides both to inform her patients and to communicate the results to others.

A Fiduciary Relationship

The relationship between doctor and patient is fiduciary in nature. It is based on trust that the doctor, who is in a position of authority by virtue of her knowledge, will act in ways that sustain and promote the health and interests of the other. The etymological root – the Latin *fiducia* – means trust, or confidence, and a fiduciary relation is defined as "the relation existing when one person justifiably reposes confidence, faith, and reliance in another whose aid, advice or protection is sought in some matter." It is "good conscience [that] requires" the person in authority "to act at all times for the sole benefit and interests of another with loyalty to those interests."[77] When providing aid to her patient, the doctor justifies the confidence placed in her on the basis of an ethical awareness enabling her to act in ways that promote the patient's health. The needs and interests of the patient to lead a healthy life are her primary concern at all times.

The fiduciary relationship is quite different from relationships associated with contracts drawn up in the market. The goal of the owner of an automobile, like all those who sell goods in the market, is to satisfy the wants of the customer (in this case for a working vehicle with the status s/he is seeking). The profits achieved from the sale are, in turn, enjoyed or invested by the owner in whatever way s/he wants because the automobile is his/her private property. In the case of both owner and customer, "want-satisfaction is ... the overriding motivation ... and the primary justification of the market as an organizing principle of social exchange."[78] But this is not the case in the relationship between doctor and patient. Whereas the owner of the automobile has no responsibility to teach the customer how to drive, the fiduciary relationship implies that the physician has a *duty* to act in ways that continue to meet the health needs of her patients. The relationship is an ongoing one in which the doctor's responsibility towards patients operates throughout the course of a disease. In order for patients to understand the treatment being offered, the doctor must take the time to explain the risks involved and must do so in language they understand.[79]

Whereas the market can only satisfy the wants of those with the money to buy the private goods it sells, the doctor-patient relationship presupposes that health care is a public good accessible to all. Unless there is universal access to the health system the doctor cannot fulfill her obligations to patients, who may be unable to pay the price for the treatment they receive. The fiduciary relationship is based on what David Roy, John Williams, and Bernard Dickens call "covenantal ethics[, which] implies a readiness to serve that reaches beyond the borders of calculated self-interest ... a commitment not to abandon patients, especially when professional skill and the terms of a contract have reached their limits."[80] Unlike market contracts, in which want-satisfaction is the overriding principle, the doctor's responsibility is based on a covenant to uphold the health of her patients, a service of which all persons are in need at some time during their lives. Health care is an integral part of the "civil commons," that web of institutions that sustains and promotes life by providing free, universal, and accessible services in the form of unpriced goods.[81] The Canada Health Act recognizes this fact by enshrining the key values of the health system as universality, comprehensiveness, portability, equality, and public administration.[82] Moreover, the 2002 Royal Commission on the Future of Health Care (known as the Romanow Commission) reaffirmed these basic principles because "it is a far greater perversion of Canadian values to accept a system where money, rather than need, determines who gets access to care."[83]

Dr Olivieri's actions demonstrate a commitment to both the fiduciary relationship and the public nature of the health care she was providing. Her prompt action in informing patients of the risks associated with L1, her move to transfer some patients back to the standard treatment using deferoxamine, and her continuing use of the procedure of liver biopsy for those who decided to remain with L1 provide clear evidence of this commitment. As she put it: "Because I considered the health of my patients to be my primary responsibility, I told them of the toxic effects of deferiprone [L1] even though the original contract with Apotex forbade such disclosure on my part."[84] The duty to uphold the health needs of her patients outweighed any contractual responsibility to Apotex. As a doctor, her primary responsibility was to their health, and she ensured that it was not compromised by the risk of liver fibrosis as, "if safety is in doubt, we should err on the side of caution."[85] The lives of her patients were more important than the development of L1 as a commercial product capable of making money for the company and furthering her own career.

The logic of Dr Olivieri's decision making is explained by Schafer as follows: "Once Dr Olivieri came to believe, based on scientifically credible preliminary evidence, that the experimental treatment she was administering might cause unanticipated harm to some of her patients/research subjects, she was duty bound to disclose those risks."[86] Her commitment to the ethics of the fiduciary relationship coupled with an understanding of the need to disclose full material risks on the basis of a dispassionate consideration of all the available evidence overrode any temptation to capitulate to the want-satisfaction of the market. And this despite ongoing threats of legal action from Apotex. Dr Olivieri's resolve to "maintain a reasonable standard of care" was, in the words of the College of Physicians and Surgeons of Ontario, "commendable in the circumstances."[87]

Informed Consent

Dr Olivieri also based her actions on the principle of informed consent, which is an integral part of the fiduciary relationship. In the therapeutic context, informed consent means that a doctor has "a *duty* to explain to patients what is proposed in a way of treatment and, if the explanations are understood, then patients are aware of the risks involved and will make an informed choice."[88] In order for the doctor to obtain a legally valid informed consent, she must not only disclose the risks involved but she must also do so in a way her patients understand. The Supreme Court of Canada laid down the following conditions in the groundbreaking legal case of *Reibl v. Hughes* (1980): the appropriate standard of disclosure for informed consent is not simply what "the ordinary reasonable person would want to know, but what an objective reasonable person *in the patient's particular position* would want to know."[89] Similarly, any information regarding the risks involved in the treatment must be given at a level that the particular patient can understand. The twin standards of disclosure and comprehension require a doctor to accommodate what a reasonable person, given her/his particular situation, needs to know about the risks of any proposed treatment at her/his specific level of understanding.[90]

The duty to inform participants in clinical trials of any changes or risks identified during the course of research is even greater than it is in a therapeutic context. Newly identified risks may affect the participants' consent and result in their refusal to continue in the research process. The legal case of *Halushka v. University of Saskatchewan et al.* (1965) states quite clearly that "the duty imposed upon those engaged in medical research … is at least as great, if not greater than, the duty owed by the ordinary physician or surgeon to his patient." The reason for this is that "there can be no exceptions to the ordinary requirements of disclosure in the case of research [unlike those instances] in ordinary medical practice," when the doctor uses her professional judgment to withhold information from a patient in order to prevent greater harm (e.g., the patient may experience greater harm than good if s/he knows that s/he has to undergo treatment for a terminal disease). Such exceptions have no place in clinical trials because, as *Halushka v. University of Saskatchewan et al.* explains, "the example of risks being properly hidden from a patient when it is important that he should not worry can have no application in the field of research." The main goal of research is to advance medical knowledge, and the researcher does not have to balance the probable effect of lack of treatment against the risk of the treatment itself. As a result, participants in "medical experimentation [are] entitled to a full and frank disclosure of all the facts, probabilities, and opinions which a reasonable man [sic] might be expected to consider before giving his consent."[91] In order to enable a reasonable person to give her/his consent freely, a doctor engaged in research must disclose any risks involved and as much of the related evidence as the patient understands.[92]

Since many of the patients suffering from thalassemia are children, it is worth asking if they have the same right to informed consent as adults. Canadian law presumes that children are competent to consent to treatment unless this presumption is removed either by provincial legislation, judicial orders, or court order.[93] In legal terms, children are regarded as capable of making rational choices about the treatment they receive, whether for therapeutic or research purposes. The ethical dimensions of informed consent involve basic value questions about the capacity of children to make such important decisions. The purpose of research guidelines in Canada is to enable doctors and other health professionals to make ethical decisions in support of the free and informed consent of all participants in the research process. The MRC *Guidelines for Research Involving Human Subjects* (1987) and the *Tri-Council Policy Statement: Ethical Conduct for Research Involving Humans* (1998) may lack legal authority, but they both contain clauses advocating the involvement of children in decisions about research. For example, the latter document includes "those whose competence is in the process of development, such as children whose capacity for judgment and self-direction is maturing."[94] In cases where a child has both linguistic ability and a growing decision-making capacity, there seems little reason to exclude him/her from full involvement in the consent process.[95]

Two particular aspects of informed consent bear upon the case of Dr Olivieri. First, there was a potential conflict between the responsibilities she had as researcher and those she had as caregiver. Her decision to disclose the risks of L1 to her research participants and patients was based upon the ancient command embedded in the Hippocratic oath, *"primum non nocere* – above all, do no harm."* Dr Olivieri interpreted this principle as overriding any other consideration, including the confidentiality clause in the research contract with Apotex. She was supported in her professional judgment by the chair of the REB, Dr Zlotkin. Both of them agreed with Schafer's observation that "when there is uncertainty about the possibility of harm to research subjects, should the prevailing ethic not be the precautionary principle that requires physicians (and drug companies) to warn patients about possible risks?"[96] Second, by disclosing the risks of L1, Dr Olivieri recognized "the need for renewed authorization for research conducted over a long period of time."[97] Even though all her subjects had given their consent when first enrolling in the clinical trials, either directly or through their parents, the situation had now changed, and she saw the need to inform them of the risks and ask if they wished to continue as participants in her research.

The professional judgment exercised by Dr Olivieri was consistent with the principle of informed consent as it applies to research in general and to research on children, in particular. Daniel A. Soberman, emeritus professor of law at Queen's University, provided support for her position in a letter to the CAUT Inquiry dated 21 March 2000. After quoting from a section on informed consent in a book entitled *The Law and Business Administration*, of which he was co-author, Professor Soberman stated: "I believe it is clear from the above discussion that a physician is under a legal duty to disclose 'material' or 'significant' risks, and that failure to do so may well amount to the tort of negligence. The main issue of a physician's liability may be whether the risk has any reasonable basis ... if the researcher has a reasonable basis for her belief ... then failure to disclose is a breach of her legal duty to that patient and committing tort."[98]

Dr Olivieri's belief in the risk of liver fibrosis and the decline in efficacy of L1 was based on findings that were confirmed by several independent pathologists.[99] She was also in a position to infer that the risks in question were likely to materialize and were statistically significant. Under these circumstances, failure to report them would have broken any duty she had to both her patients and research subjects, and it would have amounted to committing a tort.

Dr Olivieri clearly understood what Somerville describes as "the ethical and legal obligations of the researcher to disclose risks, if there are reasonable grounds to believe that they are present."[100] She recognized the need to protect the public interest as a doctor whose obligations to the health and safety of her research subjects overrode those towards Apotex, which had partially funded the clinical trials. The Naimark Report agreed – at least in principle – that where research is "supported by external sponsors ...the overarching objective must be the protection of the rights of the subjects involved [and] in achieving those objectives, the principle of full disclosure should be pre-eminent."[101] But the Naimark Review Panel ignored a good deal of the scientific evidence supporting Dr Olivieri's judgment that the health of research subjects was endangered by L1.

ACADEMIC FREEDOM UNDER FIRE

The narrative I have recounted suggests a pattern in which the academic freedom of Dr Olivieri was violated in a variety of ways. Institutional constraints, threats of legal action against her by Apotex, removal from her clinical position, a flawed hospital report, "gag orders" not to discuss her situation in public, denial of due process, the unauthorized use of research data, false allegations about her clinical practice, and an anonymous letter campaign attacking her integrity as well as that of her main supporters all undermined her capacity to conduct scientific research and disseminate her findings to other scientists. In this section, I concentrate on some of the main ways in which Dr Olivieri's academic freedom was curtailed by the influence of the corporate market.

Academic Freedom in the Clinical Context

During the first two years of the dispute between Dr Olivieri and Apotex, the question of her academic freedom was never raised. This is a striking omission. Nothing less than her independence as a researcher to communicate adverse findings about L1 to both her patients and the scientific community was at stake. It was not until the interventions of UTFA and CAUT in November 1998 that the principle of academic freedom was invoked.[102]

This lacuna underlines a general problem relating to clinical research professors working in university-affiliated hospitals in Canada. Many of them "have not fully benefited from advances in procedural protection for fundamental rights enjoyed by their colleagues in other faculties,"[103] and their academic freedom has not been well protected. Clinical researchers have been largely unaware of the CAUT's Model Clause, which states that "academic staff shall not be hindered or impeded in any way by the university or the faculty association from exercising their legal rights as citizens, nor shall they suffer any penalties because of the exercise of such legal rights."[104] The right to express critical views about the risks of the drugs they are testing is crucial precisely because their research is concerned with public health, and the communication of any adverse results supports the common good of society. The dissemination of such knowledge to colleagues in the scientific community in the form of conference papers or journal articles is important both for its own sake and as a means to promoting the health and well-being of others.

Far from being a luxury for an elite few, academic freedom is, as Somerville states, a principle that benefits the public in general: "Contrary to popular belief, values such as academic freedom are not meant primarily to benefit the academics who claim them. These values are intended to benefit the public, to promote the common good: it is in the public interest that academics such as Dr Olivieri are not harmed or punished for speaking out when it is required in order to protect individuals or the common good."[105] Without robust protection of their academic freedom, clinical researchers may be reluctant to publicize their findings on the adverse effects of the drugs they are testing, thereby endangering both their patients/research subjects and the public interest.

I have already suggested that this was the main problem with the mediated settlement between HSC and Dr Olivieri: it did not preserve the academic freedom of professors and clinical staff in general or protect the rights of children in clinical trials, as she herself points out.[106] Moreover, an earlier clause on academic freedom was removed from the 2001 agreement between HSC and U of T, according to a report published four years later by Dr Philip Welch and associates, with "the University agreeing to no longer being a signatory – diminishing its ability to offer protection for clinical faculty."[107] The U of T's refusal to offer the protection of academic freedom for clinical research professors is part of a larger systemic problem besetting university-affiliated hospitals that enter into "partnerships" with pharmaceutical companies. According to Marcia Angell, former editor of the *New England Journal of Medicine*, "academic medical centres [in the United States] have become supplicants to drug companies, deferring to them in ways that were unheard of just a few short years ago."[108] As a result, the opposing goals of medicine and the market are "often deliberately obscured" in the following ways:

Academic medical centres are charged with educating the next generation of doctors, conducting scientifically important research, and taking care of the sickest and neediest patients. In contrast, investor-owned businesses are charged with increasing the value of their shareholders' stock ... In the case of drug companies, the point is to sell profitable drugs, not necessarily important ones; and they sponsor clinical research as a means to that end. Further, drug companies are not in the education business, except as a means to the primary end of selling drugs.[109]

Once medical research and education are subordinated to the goal of maximizing stockholder value, academic freedom as a necessary condition for the advancement and dissemination of knowledge is likely to become a casualty of the market's logic of value.

Academic Freedom and the Market

The opposing goals of university research (to advance and disseminate shared knowledge) and of the corporate market (to maximize stock-holder value) are based upon two contradictory logics of value. The value of knowledge depends upon its being freely shared with others who have access to every step of its development.[110] Knowledge seeking is a public process in which every aspect is open to critical scrutiny – from one's methods of inquiry through the data accumulated to the conclusions reached. This is quite unlike the corporate market, where, as McMurtry points out, *the private patent and copyright control* of every piece of knowledge and information that corporate market agents can legally monopolize ... is required by their fiduciary trust to their stockholders."[111]

Academic freedom makes possible the critical questioning and dialogue without which knowledge cannot advance. It does not guarantee that knowledge and truth will be achieved, but it provides the climate in which the growth of knowledge may be maximized through a process of trial and error. On the basis of the available evidence from the clinical trials she conducted, Dr Olivieri identified the probability of the risks of L1 as "heart and liver disease, endo-crine dysfunction, and premature death in children and young adults."[112] She was not required to be absolutely certain of her con-clusions in order to communicate them to the scientific community, but they had to be based on what the CAUT Model Clause calls "an honest search for truth."[113]

As soon as Dr Olivieri acted in this way, her academic freedom was truncated. Her communication to other scientists of the risks of L1 contradicted Apotex's goal of commercializing the drug. The private profit that the company was seeking from L1 was based on a structure of acquisition that excluded others from its appropriation.[114] Access to the scientific data was denied to others by means of a strict confidentiality clause, which prevented the dissemination of information about any risks associated with the drug for the period of one year. It is for this reason that a growing number of researchers, ethicists, and faculty associations have called for the disbandment of confidentiality clauses in research contracts.[115]

Once Dr Olivieri broke the confidentiality clause, she received a series of letters from Apotex warning of legal action. It is worth considering the content of these letters for the logic of value they exhibit. The letters from Spino or Apotex's counsel were written between May 1996 and May 1997 at a rate of approximately one per month. In a letter to Dr Olivieri dated 12 August 1996, Spino wrote: "Your unfounded allegations may have ramifications on the commercial viability of this product and, if that proves to be the case, Apotex would be compelled to take appropriate action."[116] The logic of the letter is striking. Dr Spino criticized Dr Olivieri's communication of the risks of L1 as "unfounded allegations," which might prevent L1 from being marketed and result in Apotex's being "compelled" to take the "appropriate action." An earlier letter, dated 24 May, is more explicit about the nature of such action: any "information" from the clinical trials must "be and remain secret and confidential … [or] Apotex will … pursue all legal remedies in the event that there is a breach of these obligations."[117] Another letter from Apotex's counsel to Dr Olivieri's counsel on 3 April 1997 threatens legal action if she were to publish abstracts for an international conference: "Apotex Inc has stated on many occasions that Dr Olivieri is not entitled to publish any such information without its consent … please note that Apotex will hold Dr Olivieri liable for damages caused by unfounded statements about deferiprone at this [Malta] conference."[118] The various statements made by both Dr Spino and Apotex's counsel are consistent with the logic of the market. They contested the validity of Dr Olivieri's research because the dissemination of knowledge about the risks of L1 shared "secret and confidential" information and would thereby diminish the drug's profitability.

When it came to providing evidence to the Naimark Review, however, Apotex denied having issued any threats of legal action to Dr Olivieri. In a letter dated 24 November 1998, Spino wrote to the Naimark Review as follows: "It is evident … that there was no threat to Dr Olivieri relating to the presentation of information on hepatic fibrosis … Apotex did not threaten Dr Olivieri, and did not advise her not to tell patients or the REB about her alleged findings on deferiprone-exacerbated hepatic fibrosis."[119] This statement contradicts those already cited, in which Dr Olivieri was warned that "appropriate action" in the form of "all legal remedies" would be taken against her if "information" did not "remain secret and confidential." The more restrained approach was reiterated by Dr Barry Sherman, CEO and chair of the Board of Apotex Inc, on CBS's program *60 Minutes* on 19 December 1999: "At no time was she [Dr Olivieri] told by anyone not to say whatever she thought was appropriate to any patient." The program then provided excerpts from Spino's telephone message recorded on Dr Olivieri's voice-mail on 24 May 1996, during which he said, "if you in any way attempt to convey it [information that L1 was working in only a minority of patients] you will be subject to legal action."[120]

The discrepancy between the established documentary record and Apotex's denials of having issued legal threats against Dr Olivieri is striking. Contained in the same message left by Spino on Dr Olivieri's voice-mail was the following: "we have every intention of bringing it [L1] to market as soon as possible."[121] This statement provides a clue as to why Apotex later denied having warned Dr Olivieri not to inform her patients (and eventually other researchers) of the risks of L1. The truth-seeking that characterizes the advancement of knowledge has no meaning in the context of the market. "Knowledge," "information," and "truth" are all overridden by the goal of maximizing private profit. What follows logically from this is that "any knowledge or information that does not contribute to this goal has no right to existence."[122] Apotex's goal of making money from L1 was threatened not only by Dr Olivieri's statements about the drug's risks but also by its own subsequent threats of legal action against her. Once the Naimark Review was established, even this information had no right to existence because it might undermine the company's image, thereby minimizing the profitability of L1.

Who Was Defending Academic Freedom?

Dr Olivieri's duty to inform her patients when she found evidence of the "unanticipated harm" that L1 might cause them was matched by a duty on the part of HSC and U of T to protect her academic freedom as a research scientist. In Schafer's words, "Olivieri's university and her hospital had a corollary duty to support her request for assistance in this exercise of academic freedom and in the performance of her obligations as a physician and a researcher."[123] Yet *The Olivieri Report* found no evidence that administrators at either institution acted "robustly to protect academic freedom." Nor were they particularly forthcoming in "bringing to bear the full weight of their resources in cases [such as this] where large private corporations attempt to infringe academic freedom."[124] Their lack of action leads one to wonder if, indeed, university-affiliated hospitals like HSC have become, in Angell's words, "supplicants to drug companies."

Following the first letter of warning from Spino, Dr Arnold Aberman, dean of medicine, set up an informal meeting with Apotex president Jack Kay in June 1996, at which he informed him that "Apotexy [sic] should stop threatening legal action against Nancy and should not proceed with legal action ... Mr Kay said that he would considr [sic] my request."[125] The meeting had no apparent effect. Four more letters of warning were issued to Dr Olivieri and copied to the dean by the end of November. Once again, *The Olivieri Report* found no evidence that Dr Aberman arranged a more formal meeting with Mr Kay or sought assistance from the university provost or president, even though, "as Dean, he had a responsibility to have taken more effective action."[126]

The letters of warning from Apotex continued into 1997. Eventually, Dr Olivieri, who was concerned about the status of her clinical research programs, met with Vice-President (Research) Dr Heather Munroe-Blum in September of that year. Dr Munroe-Blum undertook a review of "the important policy issue" and then referred her to the Provost, "to whom the Dean reports."[127] In October, Dr Olivieri met with the provost about her concerns as well as the findings of a Faculty of Medicine committee of investigation, which had rejected her complaint against a colleague whom, she believed, had used her research without permission and concluded that L1 was safe.[128] A month later, she was informed in writing that she could not appeal the committee's decision.[129]

Shortly before her article analyzing the connection between L1 and liver fibrosis appeared in the *New England Journal of Medicine*, Dr Olivieri sought administrative support from the university once again. On 1 August 1998, she wrote to Dr Munroe-Blum "with respect to the matter of Apotex and the disclosure of findings arising out of Apotex-supported trials of the iron chelator deferiprone conducted at the University of Toronto."[130] Dr Olivieri expressed the view that there was insufficient protection of scientific integrity and medical ethics at HSC. In light of growing support from both physicians and scientists, she called for an independent inquiry of the influence of Apotex on some of the research taking place at the hospital. She concluded that the refusal of Dr Buchwald (director of the HSC Research Institute), the HSC administration, and Dr Aberman to resolve the issue of L1 and Apotex placed "the protection of patients in clinical trials conducted in this Hospital and University at risk" and was "unacceptable."[131]

Dr Munroe-Blum replied in writing that HSC matters should be resolved within the hospital and that Dr Olivieri's complaint alleging inaction against Dr Aberman be brought to the provost.[132] Dr Olivieri wrote to Provost Sedra, enclosing a package of relevant materials, and on 12 August he replied that he had met with Dr Aberman, who was willing to meet with her "in resolving the matters in dispute."[133] On the same day, at an "Open Meeting," which took place at HSC to discuss a petition from medical staff asking for an independent inquiry of the Apotex affair, Dr Olivieri asked Dr Aberman for assistance. Following the publication of her article on 13 August, Dr Olivieri requested a full and impartial inquiry into both the L1 dispute and support for her clinical and research programs.[134] On 20 August Dr Aberman wrote, reiterating Dr Munroe-Blum, that the main issues involved HSC and that, "in these circumstances, in my judgment, it would be inappropriate for me as Dean, in the absence of any allegation of a breach of University policy, to launch an inquiry at this time … However, if any specific allegation of a breach of U of T policy is made … I will, as I have in the past in this matter, immediately institute appropriate proceedings."[135]

The Dean's judgment is inconsistent with a previous statement he made at a meeting with the president of Apotex in May 1996, when he said that the company "should stop threatening legal action against Nancy and should not proceed with legal action." There were, after all, policies in place at U of T regarding academic freedom relevant to the case. The university's definition of academic freedom specifically includes "freedom from institutional censorship" so that faculty have "freedom in pursuing research and scholarship and in publishing or making public the results thereof."[136] Even though none of Apotex's letters of warning resulted in legal action, they had the effect of curtailing Dr Olivieri's academic freedom. For example, two draft abstracts that she had prepared for the July 1996 meeting of the American Society of Hematology (ASH) on data from the clinical trials were sent to Apotex for consideration. The company responded with a legal warning on 12 August, which I have already quoted. However, she managed to persuade the CMPA to provide her with legal coverage because of strong support from Drs Weatherall and Nathan, who assured the association of the "reasons why publication is so important."[137] The CMPA then wrote to Apotex of "the overriding public interest" that would be served by publication of the data, which "must override any duty which Apotex claims Dr Olivieri owes it."[138] When Dr Olivieri sent the revised abstracts to Apotex, it issued another warning to deter her from submitting them to ASH, claiming she had manipulated the data.[139] Dr Olivieri replied on 23 August, explaining the scientific basis for the data.[140] On the same day, counsel for Apotex issued yet another legal warning.[141] Nevertheless, Dr Olivieri submitted the abstracts to ASH with CMPA legal support.

Dr Olivieri's freedom to publish and make public the results of her research was only protected by the intervention of renowned authorities in the field of haematology. On the basis of their expertise, the CMPA used "the overriding public interest" as a means to combat the repeated legal warnings of Apotex. Meanwhile, administrators at HSC and the U of T allowed Apotex to undermine Dr Olivieri's academic freedom without intervening. It was only later, in December 1998, when UTFA and CAUT had themselves intervened, that President Prichard declared: "The University's pre-eminent obligation is to ensure the academic freedom of all its members, wherever they work."[142] Earlier he had been lobbying the prime minister to keep corporate patent protection laws in place for Apotex so as to not "jeopardize the building of the university's proposed new medical sciences centre."[143] Prichard's actions are part of what McMurtry calls "a pattern of corporate corruption of the university which continues with legal impunity and lucrative promotions for the administrators involved."[144] Prichard's actions also fall foul of what Schafer refers to as "the dangers that can ensue from university reliance upon industry 'philanthropy.' When career success for university/hospital presidents and deans is measured in significant part by their ability to raise vast sums of money from corporate donors, such fundraising can easily become a dominating priority."[145]

THE PRICE OF CORPORATE DEPENDENCY

Repeated infringements upon the academic freedom of Dr Olivieri are symptoms of a deeper problem. Systematic underfunding from Canadian governments for programs in medicine and other disciplines has resulted in a turn towards private corporations as a means of filling the shortfall of university research and teaching.[146] Corporate funding of clinical trials has become common at affiliated teaching hospitals across Canada, and universities increasingly see themselves in competition with one another to gain access to these funds.[147] In 2002, worldwide sales of pharmaceuticals amounted to more than US$638 billion, making them second only to the armaments industry.[148] University teaching hospitals continue to provide the expertise and facilities that make this figure possible by running clinical trials for all the major pharmaceutical companies. Growing acceptance of the need to garner corporate support created a climate at HSC and U of T in which dissenting voices were treated as an embarrassment, as biting the hand that fed the system. In this section, I analyze the connections between Apotex and U of T and how they and other "partnerships" undermined institutional autonomy. But first I consider the company itself, including "donations" it has made to Canadian universities and claims with regard to the safety of L1 made on its website.

Apotex Inc

Apotex Inc was founded in 1974 and is now the largest Canadian-owned pharmaceutical company. According to its website, "Apotex produces more than 220 generic pharmaceuticals in approximately 3,000 dosages and formats which, in Canada, are used to fill over 55 million prescriptions a year." Apotex exports its products to

115 countries around the world. The company's founder, chairman, and CEO, Dr Sherman, states that, "as a free enterprise, we enjoy opportunities and value the rights which our society confers. However, to quote John D. Rockefeller Jr, ' ... every right implies a responsibility.'" The opportunity to maximize private profit is to be counterbalanced by Apotex's responsibility for "corporate giving to support our communities and our direct customers ... [because] when we strengthen our publics, we strengthen ourselves."[149] The company's mission of "corporate philanthropy" includes a statement by St Francis of Assisi – "For it is in giving that we receive" – which attempts to link the paradigm of Christian charity with Apotex's claim of being "a conscientious corporate citizen."[150]

Among the company's various "donations" to universities has been a $5 million investment in U of T's Faculty of Pharmacy for an Apotex Resource Centre and Apotex Multi-media Classroom, coupled with a further $2 million in 2004 for an atrium. According to the university's *Campaign Quarterly*, these "Gifts to the Heart" are part of a "20–year history of generosity towards the pharmacy faculty," which has included more than $6.4 million in support of the Doctor of Pharmacy program and the largest donation to the F. Norman Hughes Chair in Pharmacoeconomics.[151] More recently, The University of Manitoba announced that Apotex had pledged $3 million to create a new research facility in its Faculty of Pharmacy. President and Vice-Chancellor Emoke Szathmary was "delighted" in "the generosity shown by his [Mr Kay's] company[, which] will enhance the Faculty's ability to address the current and future demands placed on the health care system." The announcement on Apotex's website appears on university letterhead with the title "Cutting Edge Facility for Faculty of Pharmacy" and the comment that this facility will provide "advanced lecture theatres, an undergraduate teaching laboratory ... a manufacturing lab ... and comprehensive research facilities."[152]

The other side of Apotex's claim to be "a conscientious corporate citizen" is revealed by the money and effort the company spent to persuade the medical community that Dr Olivieri's research was invalid. Numerous press releases on the company's website chronicle its campaign to ensure the licensing of deferiprone (L1) by the Commission of the European Communities. Where there was a threat to the money it could make from bringing the drug to market, Apotex utilized its global research network in order to discredit Olivieri's findings. The company was ultimately successful in having L1 approved in Europe.[153] But it did not always reveal the close connections between the researchers and the source of their funding.

For example, on its website entitled *Executive Summary of Background Information Re: Nancy Fern Olivieri v. Commission of the European Communities* and dated 18 December 2003, Apotex refers to a number of articles favourable to its own position. The first of these was by Spino and Dr Fernando Tricta.[154] Dr Tricta was an Apotex employee who had been hired at about the time the clinical trials in Toronto were terminated by Spino. He had not been involved in either of the trials but, together with Dr Koren as senior author, published two abstracts for an international conference in Malta in April 1997. According to the findings of *The Olivieri Report*, "neither abstract acknowledged Dr Olivieri's contribution to generating the data reported … Neither disclosed the Apotex funding support received by the authors (except for giving Dr Tricta's Apotex address."[155] By October 2001, Dr Tricta had become medical director of Apotex Research Inc.[156]

The *Executive Summary* then makes the following claim: "1997–1998: Dr Olivieri claimed that deferiprone [L1] worsens or induces liver damage based on data that some would consider unacceptable. In response, six peer-reviewed studies have reported no drug-induced fibrosis."[157] What, then, is the evidence for this claim? One of the studies was conducted by Dr Victor Hoffbrand, who had presented findings at an ASH conference in December 1996 that showed a loss of sustained efficacy of L1 similar to those reported by Dr Olivieri.[158] Another article was published by Dr Piga, who had been an investigator on one of the LA-02 sights. A third study was conducted by Dr Francesco Callea of Brescia, Italy, who was hired by Apotex in February 1997 as a consultant to review the liver biopsy data used by Dr Olivieri in support of her conclusions.[159] At the time, Apotex was trying to persuade the medical community that the practice of liver biopsy was unnecessary for the monitoring of the safety of patients with thalassemia. On the basis of his analysis, Dr Callea asserted that "there was a [statistically] significant decline in hepatic fibrosis"[160] among those patients treated with L1. However, this is not the whole story. Liver pathologist Dr Ross Cameron was invited by Dr Olivieri to examine slides of biopsy data from nineteen patients who had participated in the LA-03 clinical trial, with the following results: "reaching the preliminary conclusion that L1 was the probable cause of liver fibrosis among some of the patients ... Dr Cameron felt he should re-check his analysis ... [and eventually his] first analysis was confirmed." It was on this basis that, in early February 1997, he "agreed to co-sign a report to the regulators [together with Drs Brittenham and Olivieri]. It was only then that Dr Olivieri could say that L1 did pose a risk of progression of fibrosis."[161]

The *Executive Summary* also appears to omit any evidence disconfirming Apotex's claim of the non-toxicity of L1. In June 1997, Dr Olivieri presented her results about the risks of liver fibrosis at a symposium at the Cooley's Anemia Foundation. She went ahead with her presentation, despite a legal warning from Apotex in May, because she had the support of the CMPA to attend the meeting and present her work. According to the testimony of Drs Dick and Nathan, both of whom were in attendance, "Apotex employees criticized her work and presented Dr Callea's opposing results on liver fibrosis on the issue of whether L1 caused progression of liver fibrosis."[162] Following the meeting, Dr Olivieri had the liver biopsy slides reviewed by three independent liver pathologists from England and the USA. All three confirmed Dr Cameron's finding that L1 was the probable cause of progression of liver fibrosis in some patients. Drs Olivieri, Brittenham, and the liver pathologists published their results in the *New England Journal of Medicine* in August 1998. It was this article that initiated widespread coverage of the L1 controversy in the popular press.[163] Another article published in the same journal in 1998 by a Swiss team of investigators reported that "Dr Olivieri's findings on the loss of sustained efficacy of L1 were confirmed in three of their nine patients on whom comparative HIC data was available."[164] (HIC data are from a liver biopsy or are the result of a complex method that, at the time, was available at only two places in the world.)

Readers of the company's *Executive Summary* are presented with partial information. This is a strategy consistent with the market's measure of excellence; namely, how well a product-line is made to sell. One-sided sales pitches are frequently used to impel customers into wanting to buy a product. In contrast, disinterested, impartial, and inclusive understanding rules out one-sided biases and the impulsiveness of appetite.[165]

Corporate Connections and University Autonomy

Apotex's $7 million investment in U of T's Faculty of Pharmacy was considerable; however, if the biomedical centre that had initially been proposed in the early 1990s had materialized, the company's stake in the medical sciences at the university would have been far greater. The centre was shelved when the controversy between the company and Dr Olivieri over L1 became public, but its estimated cost was $92 million and Apotex was considering a contribution of $55 million, the largest corporate donation to a Canadian university in history.[166] Since that time, Apotex has invested $627 million in a new research and development centre of its own as well as several major expansions of its facilities at different sites throughout the Toronto area.[167]

The threat to institutional autonomy, however, was not limited to the relationship between Apotex and U of T. A larger pattern developed during the 1990s, in which the university established partnerships with various corporations in order to secure funds for predominantly business-oriented programs. These agreements often ignored established policies on academic freedom and university governance. Open and democratic discussion was eroded as senior administrators used more secretive decision-making procedures.

In December 1996, for example, a donor agreement with the Joseph L. Rotman Charitable Foundation passed through several governing bodies and was only challenged at the Academic Board (the equivalent of the Senate) by individual faculty, including the dean of medicine, UTFA, and the student newspaper known as *The Varsity*.[168] The Rotman Foundation had pledged $15 million to the Faculty of Management with the goal of creating a "pre-eminent school of business in Canada and one of the most distinguished in the world." The plan was referred to as "the vision." In return, the university would contribute endowed adjustment funds taken from the employees' pension plan, which was in surplus. As Professor Bill Graham points out, "the vision" required "the unqualified support for and commitment to the principles and values underlying the vision by the members of the faculty of management as well as the central administration"[169] and was, therefore, in violation of the university's policy on academic freedom.

The implications of the Rotman agreement went further, however, challenging the independence of the university to make decisions about internal academic and financial matters. So anxious was U of T to obtain the $15 million that, in the words of the acting provost, "the University is prepared to make a number of undertakings that in a number of ways involve new commitments or variances from previously approved allocations or University policy." These undertakings allowed the Rotman foundation, if dissatisfied with the progress towards "the vision," to redirect to some other purpose not only their own investment but also the matching funds from the university. The variances from university policy called for the establishment of an advisory committee of external businesspeople to "be consulted by all search committees at any time in the future of faculty of management appointments." The autonomy of faculty members to determine who should be hired as their academic colleagues was undermined. Moreover, the same advisory committee of businesspeople had the authority to commit significant amounts of the university's future resources to the foundation's "vision designs," a right to which the university's own faculties and departments were not entitled.[170]

Another donor agreement between the university and Mr Peter Munk, together with his corporations, Horsham and Barrick Gold, was described by Graham as "even more scandalous in many ways."[171] The agreement was approved by the university's governing bodies without any consultation from the Academic Board, even though it created a "business-academic relationship." Munk agreed to invest $6.4 million over ten years in the Centre for International Studies, and, in return, U of T promised that the project would "rank with the University's highest priorities for the allocation of its other funding, including its own internal resources."[172] No mention was made of the established policies on academic freedom or the need to protect institutional autonomy. An advisory board was once again established, which included former prime minister Brian Mulroney who was, in turn, advised by former US President George Bush. The role of the advisory board was to "provide such assistance and resources as the board in its discretion considers appropriate, and the council (of the Centre) will be receptive thereof."[173] Munk himself could exert considerable leverage over the teaching and research activities of the centre since, like Rotman, he was entitled to withdraw funding at any time if dissatisfied with its progress. The independence of the university from the interests of Horsham and Barrick Gold was put into question.

A third donor agreement with Northern Telecom Ltd (Nortel), signed in January 1997, followed a similar pattern. The university agreed to set up the Nortel Institute for Telecommunications with $8 million coming from the company together with two matching-fund chairs and three junior faculty positions, all to be appointed "in consultation with Nortel." Yet again, there was no reference to established university policies and no commitment to the academic freedom for faculty members who were engaged in research. The agreement undermined university autonomy in at least two ways. First, it prescribed that Nortel technicians and a permanent Nortel representative, who would oversee the work of the institute, be appointed as members of staff. Second, it contained a secret section concerning intellectual property rights, which was not released.[174]

Clauses such as this, like the confidentiality agreement with Apotex, show how the public disclosure of knowledge at the base of scientific inquiry is compromised by partnerships with companies, especially when intellectual property rights are controlled by either party. The Association of University Technology Managers (AUTM), however, embraces the opportunity "for universities to utilize trade secrecy more as businesses do [in order to] protect software, hardware, databases, and new processes ... and other tangible results of research." AUTM believes that secrecy is necessary in order for universities to bring such research to market and that "the tenure track system – with its emphasis on publication – acts as a disincentive to the maintenance of information as a trade secret."[175] AUTM's desire to replace the open dissemination of knowledge as a touchstone of critical inquiry with an overriding trade secrecy about its "products" threatens the independence of the university. Its approach characterized the various "donor agreements" at U of T, undermining both academic freedom and university autonomy. Like the Olivieri "scandal," the agreements contributed to the subjugation of the university to "the global marketplace and its demands as [though they were] the ultimate framework of human freedom and value."[176]

WHAT IS TO BE DONE?

The Olivieri case has alerted universities and their affiliated hospitals both in Canada and elsewhere to the need for greater protection for clinical researchers and their patients. This is a step forward. There has been a growing awareness that Dr Olivieri's academic freedom was violated due to a climate in which links with multinationals like Apotex erode the autonomy of university hospitals and their host institutions. Steps have been taken to try to avoid the occurrence of another such scenario. There have been calls from some quarters for greater regulation and control of the relationships between pharmaceutical companies, individual researchers, and their home institutions. Others consider a move towards regulation as inadequate and ineffective. They believe that public universities and research hospitals should dispense with "partnerships" with pharmaceutical companies altogether and, with the help of changes in legislation, fund research in the public interest. In order to strengthen this proposal, some advocates call for the socialization of research so that alternative therapies could be dispassionately considered rather than ruled out on commercial grounds. I consider each of these positions in turn, arguing in favour of the disbandment of corporate partnerships and the socialization of medical research as the most plausible alternative.

Regulating Partnerships?

Recognizing the dangers to the public interest of cases like that of Dr Olivieri, some critics advocate "a coordinated national approach" to the corporate funding of university research. A set of rules regulating university-industry partnerships would, they argue, provide "a starting point" for more "prudent engagement ... designed principally to protect the university's most precious commodity: intellectual integrity." One example of this approach would be "a standard, Canada-wide contract governing university-industry relationships enshrining the right of the academic to disclose potentially harmful clinical effects immediately, and publish freely after a modest interval." Steven Lewis, a health consultant, and his co-authors from several universities and affiliated hospitals propose that the Association of Universities and Colleges of Canada act as "an institutional home" to oversee "ethical standards" requiring academics to exercise "due diligence to protect the essence of academic inquiry." The goal is to ensure that research scientists "dance carefully with the porcupine, and know in advance the price of intimacy." The pharmaceutical industry (the porcupine in question) would be asked to engage in

"voluntarily improved industry behaviour, with enlightened companies adopting honourable codes of conduct."[177]

One obvious weakness of these proposals is their voluntary nature.
How likely is it that private corporations would willingly adopt
"honourable" codes of conduct if the latter happened to conflict
with the goal of maximizing stockholder value? Lewis et al. acknowledge that, whereas "the duty of universities is to seek the truth. The
duty of pharmaceutical companies is to make money for their shareholders." And they provide two examples of Canadian medical
researchers whose work was suppressed through "intimidating tactics" from large pharmaceutical companies. Bristol-Myers-Squibb
brought a lawsuit against the Canadian Coordinating Office on
Health Technology Assessment in order "to suppress its statin report,"
and AstraZeneca threatened legal proceedings against McMaster
University researcher Anne Holbrook "for her review of medications
for stomach disorders." The "intended effects" of such "industry
harassment" is to create "unease"[178] among researchers with regard
to disseminating any findings that run counter to corporate interests.
But Lewis et al. still cling to the belief that dancing with the porcupine is acceptable provided a voluntary regulatory framework is in
place to govern the rules of the dance. And they make this claim
knowing that the goal of universities ("to seek the truth") and that
of pharmaceutical companies ("to make money for their shareholders")
are in conflict with one another.

Lewis et al. acknowledge that there are other cases, like that of
Dr David Healy, where "the financial clout of industry may influence
academic behaviour more subtly."[179] Healy was prevented from
taking up his position as professor of psychiatry in the Mood and
Anxiety Disorders Programme at the Centre for Addictions and
Mental Health (CAMH) at U of T following a conference presentation
there in November 2002. In his lecture, he "touched peripherally on
the central claims of … [his] book – that SSRIs [selective serotonin
reuptake inhibitors, like Prozac] can make people suicidal."[180] Eli
Lilly, the manufacturer of Prozac, had donated $1.55 million to
CAMH two years earlier. When Dr Healy delivered the same lecture
at Cornell University the following week, the dean of medicine
"made it clear that [he] had been fired" from CAMH. Upon his return
to the University of Wales, where he was awaiting a visa to take up
his position at U of T, Healy received an e-mail message from

Dr David Goldbloom, physician in chief at CAMH, that read: "Essentially, we believe that it is not a good fit between you and the role as leader of an academic program in mood and anxiety disorders at the Centre. While you are held in high regard as a scholar of the history of modern psychiatry, we do not feel your approach is compatible with the goals for development of the academic and clinical resource that we have. This view was solidified by your recent appearance at the Centre in the context of an academic lecture."[181]

Lewis et al. believe that "there is no evidence of direct involvement by Eli Lilly in this decision, [but the company] did withdraw corporate funding from the Hastings Center after its journal published a series of articles critical of antidepressant prescribing practices."[182] Schafer disagrees: "Since he [Healy] was unhired almost immediately after he gave his conference lecture at CAMH, the inference is inescapable that his contract for employment was cancelled because of the contents of his lecture that day."[183]

Dr Healy, who was the author of one of the articles in the *Hasting Center Report* to which Lewis et al. refer, has found no evidence that regulating pharmaceutical companies has worked in the past. "It is difficult," he writes, "to find any evidence in the psychotropic story that further regulation might be the answer. To date, regulation has all too often handed companies an easy means to show that they are playing by the rules while, in fact they buy the rulebook. Far from containing companies, regulations are likely to become a hazard to the consumers they are designed to protect."[184] According to Healy, further regulation actually compromises the public interest. This is because such regulation puts pharmaceutical companies in a better position to persuade "consumers" that they are acting in their best interests, while nothing changes with regard to the regulation of drugs since "it has become almost standard practice for advisers to the FDA [the US Government's Food and Drug Administration] to have a direct financial interest in the drug or topic they are asked to evaluate."[185] While Healy's evidence is drawn from the field of psychopharmacology, he refers to the same companies as do Lewis et al. The situation is much the same in this country, where, according to Dr Michelle Brill-Edwards, formerly Canada's senior physician responsible for the approval of prescription drugs, lax regulation at Health Canada "serves the pharmaceutical industry by allowing it a wide and long-lasting market."[186] Nevertheless, Lewis et al. maintain that a voluntary code of ethics would protect the autonomy of universities against "drug companies," whose "ultimate goal is sales," and enable them "to dance carefully with the porcupine."[187]

The manner in which Lewis et al. frame the problem of university-industry links is too narrow. By focusing exclusively on the need to regulate "partnerships," the authors ignore the many ways in which the structure of universities is deeply affected by such relationships. Professor Claire Polster argues that Lewis reduces the complexity of these relationships to "a series of narrow, discrete and technical problems" to be resolved by means of "a series of discrete and technical regulations."[188] The market forces at play in the Olivieri case had a systemic effect upon U of T and its affiliated hospitals, eating away at their autonomy, damaging their system of governance, undermining academic freedom, and compromising the integrity of scientific research. The corporate market threatened to transform both institutions into instruments of private wealth maximization in which knowledge was no longer a public good to be shared openly among the community of researchers. Academic freedom is not, as Lewis et al. suggest, an individual right to be protected through regulation; rather, it is a freedom accruing to faculty as members of a distinctive kind of community engaged in the advancement and dissemination of knowledge. In order for this community to function, and knowledge to serve the public interest, there is need for faculty to participate in university governance and to protect institutional autonomy through a process of "active and collective involvement [that shapes] the larger context or environment within which all our work is carried out."[189] To the extent that faculty members believe these goals can be achieved through regulation alone, academic freedom may actually be compromised.

The process of ensuring that universities maintain their independence from industry is not a matter of regulation alone. Mandatory disclosure of all agreements and contracts with industry, as well as registration of all clinical trials, may be an improvement over previous practices.[190] U of T's adoption of a policy requiring that research contracts worth more than $250,000 be made publicly available is a case in point.[191] But regulations such as these are unlikely to resolve the problem either in the short or the long term. Universities and their teaching hospitals' dependence on corporate dollars continues unabated: they received $161 million from industry in 2000 alone, and pharmaceutical companies' contribution to university research rose from 18 percent to 48 percent in the previous decade.[192] Dancing with the porcupine may turn out to be a dance of death.

Beyond Partnerships?

Schafer argues that governments need to develop "new mechanisms so that a fair share of the resulting profit [of university-originated discoveries] would be captured for the benefit of universities and hospitals." Where such research is commercialized either through patents, intellectual property rights, or spin-off companies, private profits should be ploughed back into universities and their affiliated hospitals. Governments that implemented a system that "recaptured ... a fair share of profits"[193] for the purpose of strengthening the common good could appeal to the principle of justice as fairness as their touchstone. Schafer's argument to this point differs from that of Lewis et al. only with respect to the mandatory nature of the regulations governing university-industry "partnerships." But his proposal to tax commercial research opens up the possibility for a quite different approach, which he refers to as "the sequestration thesis."[194]

For Schafer, universities can only serve the public interest if their research is supported by public tax dollars. The bulk of curiosity-based research "must be sequestered from the process of commercialization" through a process of "special taxation." The public interest would be better served "if drug research were publicly funded," for "there might actually be a net saving, because drug costs would be significantly lower." At present, pharmaceutical companies spend millions of dollars on advertising, on patenting, and on "ineffective or positively harmful treatments." Moreover, "the cost of lives lost" is significant.[195] According to the research conducted by Dr Healy and others, Prozac and other SSRIs (selective serotonin reuptake inhibitors), for example, can cause suicides.[196]

Schafer is not alone in arguing that changes in taxation are a necessary condition for the independence of university research. Professor Neil Tudiver argues for "special taxes on pharmaceutical companies" that would enable clinical trials to be "financed entirely by government." While private corporations still paid for the trials, there would be "no direct connection to the investigators" because, as in Schafer's proposal, they would be fully funded by the tax system. Ironically, drug companies might also benefit from this approach since "they need the moral authority of independent university-based researchers to ensure studies are free of contaminating influence" as a way of securing "public confidence in their products."[197] The public interest would then be served in two ways: university research would be freed from the taint of corporate influence and prescription drugs might be both safer and cheaper. Initially, this proposal might be more costly, but Schafer maintains that "there would actually be a net saving because drug costs would, in the absence of patents, be dramatically lower."[198]

Along with these proposals for tax reform Schafer advocates for the establishment of an independent institute responsible for the design and performance of all clinical trials. Pharmaceutical companies wishing to bring a drug to market would be required to provide the funding necessary for the trials. The institute would then determine which university and hospital researchers were best qualified to conduct the trials so that "the independence and objectivity of clinical research would thereby be protected."[199] The institute's mandate could be extended to the investigation of any hazardous events that took place after the drug was marketed. Once again the manufacturer of the drug in question would fund the research necessary to determine the seriousness of these developments. Where hospital and university researchers found persistent problems, they would recommend that the drug be withdrawn from the market. Alternatively, patient cooperatives could take over the design and management of clinical trials, placing control directly in the hands of the public who are exposed to the risks of SSRIs, for example. This is unlikely to happen in the United States, where "private IRBs [institutional research boards] have sprung up in recent years often run by the same companies who run the clinical trials for pharmaceutical companies." As a result, Dr Healy believes that "it may take a European country or Canada to safeguard the legal rights of American citizens."[200]

Successful monitoring of the effects of any drug requires pharmaceutical companies to make their data publicly available. In September 2004, eleven leading medical journals adopted a policy of only publishing studies registered in a public database "accessible to the public at no charge, electronically searchable, and managed by a not-for-profit organization." The International Committee of Editors published the editorial in the *New England Journal of Medicine*, the *Lancet*, the *Canadian Medical Association Journal*, and the *Journal of the American Medical Association*, among others, proposing that "each study must be described in detail, from its primary and secondary measures to its funding source, and be registered at or before patient enrollment."[201] The policy was designed to prevent pharmaceutical companies from hiding the kinds of unfavourable results identified by Drs Olivieri and Healy. "Honest reporting," the editors wrote, "begins with revealing the existence of all clinical studies, even those that reflect unfavourably on a research sponsor's product."[202]

Socialized Medical Research?

Professor Schafer's proposals are part of a comprehensive and systemic approach. Medical research at universities would be conducted free from corporate influence as a result of changes to the tax structure. The establishment of an independent institute responsible for both clinical trials and the monitoring of adverse effects of drugs once they were brought to market would increase patient and product safety. Dr Healy's suggestion that clinical trials be placed in the hands of patients' cooperatives would complement this process. Leading journals have already made a commitment to publish only those medical studies whose data are publicly available.

The public interest would be better served by such measures, but are they sufficient to ensure that private interests no longer prevail? Could medical research itself be socialized in order to emancipate it from corporate demands? Would this be a way to harmonize scientific inquiry with the system of socialized medicine operant in Canada and most other industrialized countries?

In a market system of medical research, even one that is highly regulated, there is no incentive to conduct research on medical solutions to health problems that cannot be patented. Pharmaceutical companies show little interest in developing herbal medicines that do not maximize private profit. This is especially true of medications commonly used in the developing world. Neither the crushed berry from the endod bush, which has been shown to be effective in treating schistomesis (bilharzia), nor the leaves from the quinquina tree, used as a traditional cure for malaria when made into tea, have received funding from pharmaceutical companies.[203] This, despite the fact that both diseases kill millions of people in the developing world each year. The market in these countries is limited because most people cannot afford patented medications manufactured in the West. As an article in the *Wall Street Journal* points out, when

Cipla Ltd of Bombay, India, brought a generic drug for AIDS to market in Ghana, a patent dispute arose with Glaxo Wellcome PLC.[204] In 2000, worldwide sales of Combivir (a combination of Glaxo's "blockbuster drugs" AZT and 3TC) were expected to top $1.1 billion.

The limitations of a market system of medical research are primarily epistemic, according to Professor James Brown. Where self-interest determines the research that is conducted, alternative approaches are excluded a priori. This limits the scope of human knowledge by making it impossible to compare the efficacy of patented pharmaceutical products with other drugs, therapies, herbal cures, or diet and exercise. He points out that, "without seriously funded rival approaches, we'll never know how good or bad particular patentable solutions really are." Scientific evaluation of the efficacy of patented products is impossible without publicly funded research being conducted on alternative therapies. The claims of multinational corporations like Apotex, Glaxo Wellcome, and Eli Lilly cannot be fully ascertained because there is virtually a null set of data with which they are presently compared. "It is," Brown states, "the crucial generation of a wide class of rival theories that is lacking in for-profit research."[205] And this is its Achilles' heel.

Brown, like Schafer, recommends increased public funding for medical research and also advocates for the elimination of patents. It is the patenting of the products of medical research that prevents their proper scientific evaluation. He challenges the claim that the removal of this external motivation for private profit would result in the decline of first class research since "the most brilliant work around, in mathematics, high energy physics, evolutionary biology is all patent free." In these fields, a love of the subject matter as well as "curiosity, good salaries, and peer recognition are motivation enough." Why, then, would this not be true of medical research? Blind testing, for example, was adopted as a methodological requirement of medical research once the bias of placebo effects was discovered, and it now operates as a kind of epistemic norm ("You *ought* to use blind tests"). Why, then, not view the current situation in a similar light, Brown asks?

"We have learned *empirically* that research sponsored by commercial interests leads to serious problems, so serious that the quality of that research is severely degraded. The switch to public funding solves many, if not all, of these epistemic problems. So, as an epistemic norm we advocate public funding for medical research."[206]

The similarity between the epistemic norms of blind testing and public funding of medical research is, "to put it simply, an epistemic discovery." In each case, the norm is necessary in order for scientific work to advance. The science underlying medical research is, according to Brown, degraded by its intimate connections with private corporate interests. The socialization of medical research overcomes this epistemic problem by enabling medical researchers to compare and evaluate *all* rival claims made about different therapies.

Far from encouraging the development of innovative compounds for drugs, "patenting in practice leads all companies to produce similar compounds at the same time" so that the marketplace gets flooded with "blockbuster drugs" like Calcium Channel Blockers, ACE inhibitors, and SSRIs. Instead of greater choice, the consumer is offered a series of drugs that make more money for their manufacturers. Indeed, Dr Healy argues that "the current patent system produces great profits not great innovation."[207] By way of contrast, an economic system in which patents no longer operated would overcome this restraint, freeing up the market for greater competition among companies both large and small. A system of socialized medical research in which drugs were not patented and private corporations no longer controlled their development would serve the public health needs of Canadians well.

Professor Brown does not underestimate the difficulties in establishing socialized medical research as an epistemic norm and believes that "a long hard fight" will be needed to overcome them. But he is "optimistic about the long haul, since good medical research is in the interest of far too many people" to be overridden by private corporations, however powerful. This is why "philosophical argument in the public domain is essential,"[208] because without it debates about public policy are far too limited. Socialized medical research based on the epistemic norm ("You *ought* to pursue inquiry wherever the search for knowledge takes you") illustrates the opposition between the logics of value of education and the market quite clearly.[209] The goal of advancing and disseminating shared knowledge about the risks of certain drug therapies is threatened by pharmaceutical companies' goal to maximize private profit. The motivation to satisfy the wants of corporate customers, which have the money to purchase the research they want, undermines the desire for knowledge regardless of the ability to pay. The rational and disinterested process of evaluating all alternative therapies is impossible as long as scientific inquiry is limited to the products of these same companies. Until the goal of health research becomes that of sharing knowledge freely about *all* available therapies, the common good will not be served.

CONCLUSION

The Olivieri case has far-reaching implications for both medical research and the relationship between Canadian universities, their hospitals, and the pharmaceutical industry. Dr Olivieri's fiduciary duty to inform her patients participating in clinical trials of the risks of L1 was threatened by continuing legal threats from Apotex, thereby placing their health at risk. Her own academic freedom to alert the medical community of these risks was consistently violated by the same company, and she received little or no support from the institutions in which she worked. Corporate sponsorship of clinical trials; university-industry grants from the federal government; stiff competition among hospitals, universities, and researchers for dwindling public funds; and administrators concerned with securing and managing "partnerships" with business all created a climate in which Dr Olivieri's dissenting views about the efficacy and safety of L1 were severely punished. As Professor Jon Thompson, chair of the Independent Committee of Inquiry into the Olivieri/Apotex case commissioned by CAUT has warned: "This case is not isolated, and exemplifies what can happen in a context where universities, teaching hospitals, and researchers have come under increasing pressures to seek industrial sponsorship for research projects and facilities."[210]

My own focus in this chapter is on the fiduciary nature of the doctor-patient relationship and the right to informed consent both in general and, more especially, in the context of medical research; on the need for greater protection of the academic freedom of clinical researchers; on the close relationships between private corporations like Apotex and the University of Toronto that threaten institutional autonomy; and on several proposals for radical reform, including changes to the tax system, the establishment of an independent institute responsible for clinical trials and so on, and a system of socialized medical research, where drugs are not patented and private corporations no longer control their development. Only by means of such systemic measures are the public health needs of Canadians likely to be served.

4

Commercializing Research
and Losing Autonomy

And of course, the Canadian Light Source will pump 10.6 million dollars into the Saskatchewan economy annually for the next five years just due to the CLS Major Facilities Access grant. This is in addition to the value of direct construction benefits and the provincial sales tax revenue on construction and services, local spinoffs from visiting researchers, increased funding from the federal Indirect Costs program ... the list goes on.

Peter MacKinnon[1]

SUBSIDIZING APPLIED RESEARCH
FOR BUSINESS

During the mid-1990s, I came across a newspaper article claiming that costs "as high as $15 million a year"[2] were being transferred from the University of Saskatchewan's operating budget to subsidize applied research for business. Tucked away on the inside pages of Saskatoon's *StarPhoenix*, the article implied that the University of Saskatchewan (U of S) was actively servicing the market needs of private corporations.

At that time, U of S, like all universities in Canada, had endured two decades of government underfunding, exacerbated by cuts to transfer payments by the federal government in the mid-1990s. This latest round of cuts to U of S resulted in tuition fees almost doubling, the loss of faculty and staff worth $19 million, and a severe reduction to the library budget of more than $2 million.[3] Access to "the people's university" was now driven by students' ability to pay rather than their academic excellence; cuts to faculty were resulting in overcrowded classrooms and heavier work loads; fewer staff meant that the quality of services to both students and faculty was being reduced;[4] and fewer books, journals, and library support made teaching, scholarship, and research more difficult. The university's educational vocation was being selected against at the very time that almost 10 percent of its budget was channelled into applied research for business corporations.[5] Indeed, its mission to educate students in a climate that encouraged critical and creative thought was being systematically undermined.

The associate vice-president of research claimed that it was "the indirect costs incurred"[6] by U of S, in the form of heating, lighting, maintenance, and other such overheads, that constituted the subsidy for applied research with business. According to Dr Dennis Johnson, the university had never subsidized the direct costs of conducting such research; namely, laboratory equipment, computer time, the salaries of faculty and graduate students, and so on. This issue had been addressed at University Council, the governing academic body of U of S, when a motion from the chair of the Research Committee to charge private companies "a specific minimum rate of the total cost of all research contracts as a standard overhead/indirect cost" was defeated. The motion suggested the charge should be 30 percent but allowed the Office of Research Services the authority to determine the amount "based on the recuperation of the University's true overhead costs."[7]

The chair of the Research Committee, Professor Gordon Hill, a chemical engineer previously employed by SaskOil, made clear his reasons for wanting to change university policy: "It's not ethical to take tax dollars to apply research for a private company to be successful in its objectives. That is taking money out of the area of students and academics. If those outside agencies don't cover overhead costs, university facilities are used at the expense of other resources."[8] Hill recognized that subsidies for corporate research were unethical if they involved taking money from programs designed to educate students. Tax dollars would then be used by private companies to maximize stockholder value, and the university's publicly funded facilities would become a conduit for private profit.

Two years later, Dr Johnson claimed that all of the costs were now covered by "an overhead charge ... applied to the indirect costs of conducting research."[9] This suggested that the university had changed its policy with regard to subsidizing applied research for business. University Council had in fact defeated the original motion to charge companies a minimum overhead rate of 30 percent. In its place, council "approve[d] the recommendation" brought forward by Hill that U of S "adopt a more definitive policy on overhead/indirect costs for contract research."[10] This recommendation was designed to assuage Hill's concerns that the previous "definition [of overhead charges was] too encompassing and so vague that almost any contract could be argued to require only minimal or no overhead charges."[11] Indirect costs were defined in such a way that private corporations could escape without paying the university for the contract research conducted on its premises, violating the Canadian Association of University Teachers' (CAUT) recommendation that "any element of subsidy for a particular firm should be public knowledge."[12] Even President Peter Mackinnon later admitted that "these indirect costs ... [are becoming] onerous and likely to grow as the innovation agenda unfolds."[13]

Nevertheless, the U of S continued to provide services that "add value" to the products of private corporations by increasing revenues and decreasing costs.[14] Dr Johnson's claim that, "in certain circumstances, the university places an overhead charge on all research contracts with the private sector"[15] gave rise to the following questions: "When was the policy changed, what rate is now being charged to corporations, is this sufficient to ensure the U of S is not losing money, and how much was recouped in 1996?"[16] In a subsequent newspaper article, several colleagues proposed that U of S charge a fair and business-like rate for the costs incurred for the use of its publicly funded facilities by private corporations.[17] There was no reply. Upon his retirement from U of S in 1998, Johnson was elected president of the Saskatoon Chamber of Commerce.[18]

When asked about subsidies for indirect costs, Dr Michael Corcoran, former vice-president of research, stated: "The university subsidizes all research, because all research comes with indirect costs attached to it ... [but] it's absolutely true that much of it is with the private sector, and in that sense there is a kind of subsidy if you want to call it that."[19] On this view, subsidies for the indirect costs of research for the business sector and for curiosity-based research are really no different since the U of S pays for both. But the distinction between the goals of the two kinds of research is crucial since the former is to maximize stockholder value, whereas the latter is to advance and disseminate shared knowledge.

The idea of subsidizing research with the private sector in order to maximize its market return is consistent with the Report of the Expert Panel on the Commercialization of University Research published by the federal government in 1999. The report states that the goal of contract research is to ensure that "the economic benefit from that research is more easily obtained [by] industrial partners [who] share in the funding of the work in the clear expectation of a significant economic return."[20] By partially funding contract research, private corporations ensure that the goal of private profit is foremost. In the case of U of S, industrial partners also make use of federal and provincial tax credits to write off the costs of any R&D with the university, an arrangement that Corcoran believed "really does make sense."[21] These "partners" can then contract work to university departments on a fee-for-service basis and still save money on overall research expenditures. As Gordon Hill had pointed out, public funds are directed towards market-oriented research and away from support for students and faculty engaged in teaching, learning, and the critical pursuit of knowledge.

This practice endangers the autonomy of university researchers in several ways:

1 Contract research takes the form of an agreement between individual faculty, research groups, or departments to undertake a project designed to increase "the economic benefit" of "industrial partners," whose value system is "wholly distinct and often opposed" to the university's own "logic[s] of value."[22]

2 The freedom to publish, for example, is "a fundamental academic value, and one in conflict with commercial values" since, as Conrad Russell has argued, "ideas and findings must be shared with fellow scholars, and become part of our professional stock-in-trade."[23] Yet, confidentiality clauses made by "contractors" can be used to prevent publication of research findings for months or years and threaten the livelihood of anyone who disobeys their prescriptions, as the case of Dr Nancy Olivieri makes clear.

3 Secrecy that prevents the dissemination of knowledge constitutes a threat to the goal of university education. Recognition of this fact prompted CAUT to advise that "the essential elements of all contracts signed by the university administration with the private sector for research and development should be public" and should

be reviewed annually to ensure they are "consistent with the academic values of the university."[24]

4 On the one hand, truth seeking, free and open communication, and self-direction in research have been defining characteristics of the university. On the other, the profit motive, corporate secrecy, and the matching of research to the market comprise the values of private corporations.[25]

5 Nevertheless, U of S still has considerable leverage to require companies wishing to conduct contract research to conform to its own distinctive principles. The private sector needs the mantle of impartiality conferred by university-based research to assure the public of the reliability of its products.[26] As an institution whose goal is to create knowledge for the common good, U of S is in a position to ensure that commercialization does not become an overriding concern.

6 Indeed, U of S did eventually enact a stricter policy on overhead or indirect costs on contract research. Since January 2005, businesses doing research at U of S have been charged 40 percent for these costs, a fee considerably higher than that for governments and other public agencies.

AUTONOMY OR DEPENDENCY?

Subsidies for applied research for business are but one example of an institutional sea-change that has taken place at U of S. An increasing dependency on the corporate market and the deep structural changes that this implies is the object of my analysis in this chapter. While previous chapters focus on the ways in which the academic freedom of individual faculty members has been violated, this case study shows how university research, at an institutional level, is subordinated to the market principle of monetary gain. A pattern of public financing for research capable of "adding value" to the products of the corporate market endangers both the university's autonomy and its distinctive functions. Not only is the intellectual independence of faculty at stake, but so is the university's own "collective autonomy." "[This is because] the time and financial security needed to carry on scholarly and scientific work"[27] is at risk if faculty are primarily engaged in research that provides goods and services to the market.

I begin by analyzing the shift from the "people's university" to the so-called "research intensive university."[28] Based on the imperative that faculty procure external funding from public and private sources, "research intensiveness" suppresses the goal of advancing and disseminating shared knowledge,[29] threatening university autonomy by tying research to its potential for commercialization. Research in biotechnology of benefit to the market is one example of the university's growing dependency, and, in order to demonstrate the extent to which commercialization has taken hold, I analyze the increasing emphasis placed on generating "spin-off" companies from the discoveries made by U of S researchers. This process of "innovation" shows the strategic importance of Innovation Place, the university's research park, and of U of S Technologies Inc (since renamed the Industry Liaison Office) in fostering the development of companies "spun out" from the university at public expense.

I turn next to the Canadian Light Source (CLS) synchrotron, the largest scientific installation in Canada in a generation, owned by U of S and paid for by the public purse for mostly private corporate benefit. Valuable curiosity-based and applied research undoubtedly takes place at the CLS. But much of it will dovetail with the demands of corporate clients, skewing research towards those "synchrotron-related areas [that] have been identified as a high priority"[30] by the university administration, whether in biotechnology, the health sciences, mining, or engineering. The actual workings of the synchrotron demonstrate its power both as a scientific instrument and as a tool for privatizing knowledge. Initial euphoria over the CLS gave way to pleas for greater public and corporate funds, and, more recently, to an acknowledgment that it can only function as a public facility. By tracking this ideological shift, I argue that the synchrotron constitutes a financial drain not only on governments but also on U of S itself. My criticism of the CLS does not mean that I am opposed to science and technology any more than the writings of a film critic mean that s/he dislikes going to films. Such simplistic dichotomies as "pro" or "anti-technology" are anathema to rational thought. As Professor David Noble argues, what is needed is the kind of "sober, serious, and sustained scrutiny and evaluation" that enables the "wise use" of science and technology in the public interest.[31]

In order to ensure that money is directed to high-priority synchrotron-based areas, the central administration has managed to channel funding its way and control those educational programs that do not relate directly to such research. These management strategies include a systematic program review, which provides "investment ...

[in] priority academic areas [and] program termination procedures
... [as] the divestment side,"[32] coupled with an integrated plan, the
goal of which is to restructure the university in ways that further
benefit the market.[33] The reforms, which have met with resistance,
are consistent with those advocated in a World Bank report of the
late 1990s, but the University of Alberta has commercialized research
to the point that U of S and others are falling behind. I conclude by
considering a counter argument to my overall thesis, which shows
why "substantive autonomy" is not fully protected by the University
of Saskatchewan Act.

FROM "PEOPLE'S UNIVERSITY" TO "RESEARCH INTENSIVE UNIVERSITY"

In the year 2000, a report of the Research Committee of Council
declared that the goal of U of S was to become "one of Canada's
leading research universities in the next decade." The need "to
increase research productivity ... [and enhance] our profile as
a research-intensive university ... [especially in areas utilizing]
synchrotron-related ... research and research training"[34] was central to this program. The phrases "research intensiveness" and
"research competitiveness" were repeated mantra-like in this and
other policy documents, announcing a new age in which the U of
S is "fully committed to the research enterprise ... [ensuring that]
prospects at this institution have never been brighter ... [because
it can truly] raise the profile of the research enterprise in general
[and] develop its unique role as this Province's research university."[35] A more recent report from the Corporate Administration
argues that the university should coordinate faculty consulting
activities since "the university is knowledge ... [and] we need to
ask ourselves if we should be marketing ourselves and this knowledge and not providing it for free."[36] Knowledge created at the
U of S was no longer to be publicly shared and disseminated but,
rather, sold for monetary gain.

The valorization of the research-intensive university as the only
way forward represents a clear departure from the institution's past,
when the "excellent reputation ... [that] the University did and does
have" was built primarily on its claim to be "the people's university."[37] This founding ideal was articulated by the first president,
Walter Murray, in 1909: "There should be ever present the consciousness that this is the university of the people, established by the people,

and devoted by the people to the advancement of learning and the promotion of happiness and virtue."[38] The advancement of learning at that time had as its goal the common good of the people of Saskatchewan. Murray's language may appear rhetorical, even archaic – would a university president today dare to make the claim that learning leads to virtue? – but its unequivocal message is that all knowledge advanced at U of S is to be shared with *the people of the province.*

In practice, this meant that a major goal of the university was to provide high-quality undergraduate education that was accessible to the sons and daughters of the people.[39] Of primary concern was the provision of opportunities for students to pursue knowledge, whether it was valued for its own sake or for the kind of employment they would obtain upon graduation. Faculty's involvement in research and graduate teaching was considered important, and some of it gained a national and international reputation, including two Nobel prizes in chemistry, a record surpassed only by McGill and the University of Toronto.[40] But the main responsibility of faculty was to educate the future citizens of Saskatchewan by means of a rich "tradition of concentration on teaching, preparation for that teaching by wide reading rather than original research, and, in the past, commitment to community service."[41]

A balance between teaching, research, and community service was at the core of the people's university. Service, both "intellectual and practical," was expected not only in the wide range of professional schools but also in the college of arts and science. In its early days, practical service required faculty members in agriculture to travel "around the province to provide short periods of training in improved methods of farming,"[42] attracting tens of thousands of people to events that related directly to their livelihood. Meanwhile, faculty in the humanities gave public lectures on history, philosophy, and economics in major centres. Both kinds of extension work continued until the 1960s. With advances in communications technology and the rising costs associated with extension work, these outreach activities diminished, but the overall "spirit of service" remained, at times giving the university the appearance of "a technical institute" potentially hostile to critical and creative thought. The tension between these "creative" and "practical" polarities never succeeded in expunging the former from the important place it occupied in "the people's university." As university historian Michael Hayden points out: "The trick is in maintaining a balance between creative intelligence and applied intelligence, between service and study ... The university must be free to offer criticism of the existing order, and it must be able to say we can do this but not that; to say that we can do only so much of this or we will cease to be a university."[43] Unless it enables the free expression of critical thought and makes independent decisions about internal policy, the university ceases to exist. The problem of balancing creative and practical intelligence, while hardly peculiar to U of S, has been central to its development since the earliest days of the people's university.

The research-intensive university, however, changes radically the meaning of both service and research, distorting them to suit corporate needs. This shift is apparent in a number of ways. The first of these is the familiar mantra of competitiveness. The president's report, entitled *Strategic Directions 2002*, declares that "this university must compete vigorously and effectively among [sic] the major research universities of the country."[44] Research competitiveness requires U of S to "exceed national norms for research intensive universities [outperforming other] leading research universities [by adapting to] a new reality,"[45] in which the advancement of shared knowledge is no longer its educational goal. This "new reality provides the impetus for change ... [and is] a fitting vision for a university created in a spirit of service," even though the university must now attain this goal by "compet[ing] in a global marketplace"[46] where "knowledge is the new currency,"[47] to be bought and sold at market price.

A second aspect of the research-intensive university is a greater concentration on postgraduate education. Graduate students are valued primarily as instruments in the competition for research grants: "Higher levels of research funding seem to be directly related to greater numbers of graduate students. Investing in graduate students may be the single most cost effective means to increased research intensiveness."[48] Graduate students, then, are a good investment strategy not because their education may have intrinsic value, or because they might contribute to the intellectual life of the university, but because they are the cheapest means for obtaining higher levels of research funding. By outperforming other leading research universities, U of S positions itself for "exploiting federal government and commercial funding opportunities."[49]

The third prong of "research intensiveness" is consistent with the other two. The "excellence," "productivity," and "quality" of research is now reduced to one single factor – namely, its monetary value: "Over the next five years the University of Saskatchewan faculty should increase the operating funding obtained from the federal granting councils (MRC/CIHR, NSERC and SSHRC) and increase total research funding from other sources so that both types of funding exceed the national average."[50] Faculty are urged to maximize the funding they obtain from federal Tri-Council agencies, which constitutes "the 'gold standard' for research performance across Canada."[51] They should also search for other sources, like provincial grants or targeted research conducted under contract for private corporations (the "commercial funding opportunities" referred to above) so that the total amount exceeds the national average. Faculty "must be encouraged to excel ... in attracting major research grants" from both corporate and public sources in order for U of S to become "one of Canada's leading research universities in the next decade."[52] This combined effort will "provide opportunities for collaborations [with] federally supported laboratories, [including Agriculture Canada and Agri-Food Canada] the maintenance and strengthening of partnerships ... [and ensure an] increase in research benefits made available to the private and public sectors through patents and technology transfer ... [as well as the number of spin-off companies] located at Innovation Place, including many in agricultural biotechnology."[53] Michael Hayden believes these proposals demean the work of many faculty: "The message is clear, research is what counts, bringing in big bucks is what counts and ... [this] sends a message that unless you are doing externally funded research, you're worthless."[54]

"RESEARCH INTENSIVENESS," BIOTECHNOLOGY, AND INTELLECTUAL PROPERTY RIGHTS

One example of the "high-priority" research that meets all the market criteria of "research intensiveness" is an $11 million research project in agricultural biotechnology. This multidisciplinary research partnership has involved faculty in the Department of Plant Sciences working with researchers from the National Research Council's Plant Biology Institute and Agriculture and Agri-Food Canada's Research Centre, all of whom are located on campus. Funded by Genome Canada, the partnership focuses on advanced genomics, "the science of deciphering and understanding the genetic code of life ... [so that knowledge of] how crops tolerate cold and other environmental stresses ... [can provide] the potential to improve agricultural productivity in Canada and around the world." Not surprisingly, the "U of S-owned Canadian Light Source synchrotron ... [will be used to] identify new genes and isolate, clone, and sequence them"[55] by observing the microstructures of life in ways I explain later in the chapter. While such research has the potential to advance public knowledge about how to improve genetic stocks of winter wheat, the "research benefits" to private corporations are enormous.

A major reason for the financial benefits of knowledge production in biotechnology accruing most efficiently to multinational corporations is the use of patents and intellectual property rights (IPRs). Richard Gold, BCE chair in e-governance in the Faculty of Law at McGill University, claims that IPRs, like all patents, benefit society as a whole and are not used for maximizing private wealth: "In our free market economy, we use patents to lure inventors to disclose their inventions to the public, we do not give – and never have – patent rights as a prize for having created something. A patent is no more than a tool to encourage those who have discovered something useful to make it available to the rest of us."[56] This statement begs the question of whether or not patents are generally used to disclose scientific inventions. Gold has in mind the "Harvard mouse case," in which the mouse's genes were patented for the purpose of cancer research. He suggests that IPRs that patent life in this way will be used for the public good because they are a tool for making such discoveries widely available. He ignores the considerable amount of counter-evidence, which indicates that human genetic material is being used by biotech companies for private monetary gain behind the veil of serving the common good.[57] In such cases, patents are claimed as "rights" to which private companies are entitled because they have the money to develop them into marketable products. The distinction between the private and public sectors is liquidated in order that "IPR interactions within and between the university, the public research sector, and the commercial sector"[58] become ever more permeable.

In contrast to Gold, Professor Claire Polster believes that IPRs undermine the public nature of knowledge creation in several ways as they "limit the content of knowledge academics produce, the access to the knowledge academics produce, and the ways in which this knowledge is disseminated in (and thus used by) the wider society. It actually impoverishes both the real and perceived value of the university to society."[59] The limitations placed on the content, accessibility, and dissemination of knowledge drastically reduce society's ability to resolve problems in a variety of fields. This, in turn, undermines the value of the university as an independent source of knowledge creation. For example, U of S's commitment to producing knowledge of use to biotechnology companies – a commitment that is enforced by IPRs – decreases opportunities for providing research support for alternative forms of agriculture. Unlike genetically modified winter wheat, organic farming provides natural products not subject to patent law, which could benefit immensely from university-created knowledge. But, as Professor Ann Clark of the Plant Agriculture Department at the University of Guelph has shown, the $700 million currently spent by the federal and provincial governments to support genetic engineering contrasts with the "*virtually undetectable* amounts allocated to support organic farming ... management intensive grazing ...or the design of *small-scale production cooperatives.*"[60] Where researchers are prevented from investigating these and other alternatives, their work hardly qualifies as scientific since they are unable to evaluate conflicting hypotheses. As a result, universities are likely to suffer from an erosion of public support as their work becomes no different in kind from that of corporations and private think tanks. U of S's "partnership" on advanced genomics disregards its own distinctive goal of sharing knowledge with all those who seek it by "skewing the whole process"[61] and subordinating it to the market goal of maximizing monetary profits.

INNOVATION, COMMERCIALIZATION, AND THE FEDERAL GOVERNMENT

The Report of the Expert Panel on the Commercialization of University Research, entitled *Public Investments in University Research: Reaping the Benefits*, explains quite clearly how the goal of "research intensiveness" is to benefit the private sector by tying funding for research and other core educational facilities to a university's ability to commercialize research.[62] The report, which was presented to the Prime Minister's Advisory Council on Science and Technology, adopted "innovation" as the new gold standard of university research, defining it as "the process of bringing new goods and services to market, or the result of that process." It recommended that "*innovation be included in the missions of the Federal Granting Councils and as a criterion for awarding research grants.*" This prescription would have imposed an exclusively market-driven approach on research at all Canadian "universities[, which] ... must recognize the importance of research-based innovation as a main-stream activity [either] by identifying 'innovation' as their fourth mission [or] by integrating it as an element of the three missions, teaching, research and community service ... universities ... must provide incentives to encourage faculty, staff and students engaged in research to create IP [by including] appropriate recognition of innovative researchers in tenure and promotion policies ... [and by offering students internships with business in order to] take the lead in building and upgrading Canada's skills base."[63] There were no alternatives to the prescriptions it made: universities *must* adopt "innovation" as an integral part of their mission, *must* make the creation of IP a criterion for tenure and promotion, and *must* upgrade Canada's skills base by offering students internships in the corporate world.

Nor were these prescriptions restricted to researchers in the natural and applied sciences; rather they were to apply across the university: "*The time has come to begin experimenting with models for identifying the element of social science that is capable of being commercialized, and* [sic] *mechanisms for achieving commercial outcomes.*"[64] Social science research was to be reduced to a single "element" capable of being commercialized, ensuring that it, too, would bring new goods and services to market. The totality of this regime would encompass every aspect of university research and teaching, from the natural and applied sciences to the social sciences and, eventually, to the fine arts and humanities.

Could universities that adopted this "innovation agenda" expect an increase in their operating budgets in line with current needs? Not according to the report: "Let us now be very clear in stating the main goal of the proposed actions. It is to increase wealth creation in Canada; it is not primarily to produce new revenue streams for universities."[65] This "new reality" of research intensiveness was already in place in the United States, where "revenues from commercializing research constitute a small addition to university budgets, generally well below 1%." The same approach to "innovation" would have a similar result here since "it would not be realistic to expect much more in Canada ... [and] could not be counted on to relieve the financial pressures that Canadian universities face today."[66] All of this raises the question of why any university would adopt such an agenda when its independence, financial security, educational integrity, and capacity for critical thought were being undermined.

A *Framework for Planning at the University of Saskatchewan* (1998) provides at least one answer to this question. The benefits to the people of Saskatchewan of adopting "research intensiveness" would, it seems, be far greater than would the benefits from the local knowledge produced by "the province's research university" and would form part of a global network for the commercialization of university research: "Bringing the world's work to our door and taking our work to the world is a fitting vision for a university created in a spirit of service and residing in a Province whose future, in large measure depends on how well it can compete in a global marketplace."[67] The notion of providing service to the community is now redefined as servicing the corporate market. What was once a public function, enabling the people of Saskatchewan to partake in the knowledge created at the university, becomes a private instrument, enabling business corporations to compete in a global marketplace. The history of a university created in the spirit of service is reinterpreted as one of adding value to corporate products, which, in turn, is seen as the new "touchstone for our academic and financial decision-making." While the university's mission statement still invokes the founding principle that "the University of Saskatchewan belongs to the people of Saskatchewan,"[68] this ideal is being rewritten in the language of "research intensiveness," whose overriding goal is to maximize stockholder value. Indeed, the very future of the province now depends on how well it can compete in the global marketplace, as though capital mobility across national economic boundaries were the only way forward. This strategy ignores the danger identified by economist Herman Daly, which is that it may "wound fatally the major unit of community capable of carrying out any policies for the common good."[69] In the case of U of S, a community of researchers engaged in advancing and sharing their knowledge for the common good was placed at risk.

SPIN-OFF COMPANIES AT INNOVATION PLACE

"Spin-Off" companies are an important vehicle for the commercialization of university research. Many of the spin-off companies at "the largest and most successful research park in the country, Innovation Place, [which] is located on the campus of the U of S,"[70] have been publicly subsidized at one time or another. Innovation Place itself received provincial grants worth $69 million over a period of ten years covering building costs alone,[71] and it is home to a variety of companies in the fields of agricultural biotechnology, pharmaceuticals, and information technology.

According to Glenn Mitchell, president of the Edmonton Research Park, research parks have become "a dynamic middle ground for both institutional collaboration between university and industry, and a refuge for mavericks and entrepreneurs from both cultures."[72] The goal of Innovation Place is to stimulate collaboration between university and industry, resulting in the growth of competitive private corporations from the fertile ground prepared by publicly funded research. One of the "success factors" contributing to the commercialization of research, Innovation Place is "the choice location for start-up companies, [which] house[] 2,200 people employed by 125 tenants which contribute over $217 million per year to the economy of Saskatoon and Saskatchewan." A report published in 2002 by University of Saskatchewan Technologies (UST) Inc, entitled *Creating Economic Activity: University of Saskatchewan Example*, repeats the mantra that Innovation Place is "Canada's most successful university-associated research park,"[73] even though its own data show that the University of British Columbia has three times as many spin-off companies employing almost twice as many people. U of S also lags behind UBC in each of the three sectors – life sciences, physical sciences, and information technology – and is inferior to the University of Alberta in all but the physical sciences.[74]

What, then, do the maverick entrepreneurs who find refuge at university research parks actually achieve? Mitchell describes their success in the following terms: "Successful parks have created, and actively encourage, a climate in which both university and industry can shed their organizational skins, and where they can develop new forms of collaboration for their mutual ends."[75] Mitchell envisages no less than the disbandment of the key differences between public universities and industry. Once they shed their organizational skins, knowledge can become an instrument for the corporate market, making universities indistinguishable from private corporations. In this new climate, which U of S initiated as early as 1972, the function of universities is to apply "sophisticated scientific and market knowledge"[76] by adding value to the ready-made products of private companies so that they can survive "in the highly competitive information-based society." In this way, university and industry come to share the same goal, which stems from the "motivation of self-interest."[77]

The forms of collaboration envisaged by Mitchell, and instantiated at Innovation Place, are founded on self-interest, which is seen as "the determining motivation of the market to satisfy the wants of whoever has the money to purchase the goods that are wanted." In order for want-satisfaction to be the "organizing principle of social exchange," potential customers must have enough money to purchase the products sold in the market. By way of contrast, "the determining motivation of education" is quite different for its goal is "to satisfy the desire for knowledge of anyone who seeks it, whether they have the money to pay for it or not."[78] Mitchell, however, does not acknowledge these opposing motivations, with their "wholly distinct and often opposed logics of value,"[79] because of his overriding desire to subordinate the university to the market.

Spin-off companies have become the preferred route of commercialization for UST Inc, recently renamed the Industrial Liaison Office (ILO), a wholly owned company of U of S, whose function is "to maximize the value of innovation at the University." UST's report defines a spin-off company as "an incorporated commercial entity, which would not have been formed had U of S not supported research and development work leading to the creation of intellectual property, know-how or other expertise on which the business is based."[80]

An early example of just such a spin-off company is SED Systems Inc. SED Systems developed from research conducted in the Space Engineering Division of the Department of Physics at U of S between 1965 and 1972. Funding during this period was provided "in the form of research and major installation grants"[81] by the National Research Council (NRC), a granting agency of the federal government. After seven years of intensive inquiry into the physics of the upper atmosphere, "a group of these researchers [Mitchell's mavericks] decided to take their knowledge and expertise and form their own company." U of S encouraged this process of commercialization, and, "in return for the provision of facilities and support, the university held equity in the company."[82] Such an early commitment to the commercialization of knowledge is striking since few universities

in Canada were involved in the process at the time, and U of S itself
had no technology commercialization office. In return for equity in
the company it provided laboratories, computer systems, and other
facilities and support, including graduate students. By doing so,
U of S embarked on a course that would erode the distinction
between a public institution advancing shared knowledge and a
private corporation maximizing stockholder value. The process of
"shedding its organizational skin" by "developing new forms of
collaboration" based on "the motivation of self-interest" definitive
of the market had begun. Indeed, the university anticipated some of
the policy recommendations of the Expert Panel on the Commercialization of University Research with regard to the need to "support
the creation of spin-off companies in commercializing publicly funded
research [and acting] as any other supportive shareholder whose
objective is to help maximize the value of their shares."[83] U of S did
both, supporting the growth of SED systems and maximizing its
market value by investing equity in the company.

So successful was this enterprise of commercializing publicly
funded research that SED systems was sold as a U of S spin-off in
1990 and became "a wholly owned subsidiary of Calian Technology
Ltd, [allowing] the university [that] sold [its] holdings to recover
[its] investment."[84] Still located at Innovation Place, SED Systems
now has annual revenues of $40 million, is wholly owned by its
shareholders, provides "ground-based systems and services to the
international satellite industry," and, according to a National Sciences
and Engineering Research Council (NSERC) report entitled *Research
Means Business* (2001), "employs 250 satellite industry professionals
and serves satellite operators and satellite communications service
providers around the world."[85]

SED Systems is able to compete in the global market only because
U of S and the NRC bore all of the initial costs for almost two decades
(laboratories, computer systems, salaries of graduate students, etc.)
and minimized the risks in the form of research and major installation grants. The familiar pattern in which "industrialists and their
campus counterparts [have] invented new ways to socialize the risks
and costs of creating this knowledge while privatizing the benefits"[86]
meant that SED Systems could be sold as a proven "winner" in the
market. Until that time, the company had been heavily subsidized
by the university in the form of equity invested. Calian Technology
now maximizes stockholder value with revenues of $40 million a

year. While SED Systems is referred to as a spin-off company, U of S has received nothing in return for its investment of public funds since 1990, when SED Systems became the property of Calian. This conforms to the expectations of the Expert Panel on the Commercialization of University Research, which holds that new revenue streams for universities will not be created since the main goal of spin-off companies is "to increase wealth creation"[87] for the private sector.

Not all companies spun out from U of S have been as successful as SED Systems. Of thirty-three companies surveyed by UST Inc, seven (more than 21 percent) were "inactive/closed."[88] Minerva Animal Health Corporation, once heralded as "a new shining star [with] limitless potential" by former U of S technology transfer officer Peter Wells, is a case in point. The company developed a line of more than forty animal-health products patented from natural and environmentally friendly ingredients, including shampoos and skin lotions drawn from "Saskatchewan agricultural products [whose] quality and value are supported by scientific studies conducted here by the Animal Biotechnology Group."[89] This experienced "network of university scientists who collaborate on projects from inception, through development and transfer processes, and into commercial products" seemed well placed to bring its products to market as it was connected to "the largest centre for biotechnology in Canada with about 30 per cent of the country's biotechnology companies based here." As one of a growing number of spin-off companies, whose goal was "to license the university's technology [through] control of a piece of intellectual property, or patent, usually in exchange for a percentage of the revenue arising from that property,"[90] Minerva seemed set "to become a major player in the international market."[91] When appearance finally gave way to reality, the university, which owned 100 percent of Minerva, received none of the promised "revenues for ownership [or] royalties for the use of its technology."[92] The risks of privatizing knowledge had again been socialized, the costs borne by U of S, and, in this case, the benefits proven to be illusory.

Minerva's market failure took place at a time when UST was fully operational in its "mission to spearhead the successful commercialization of inventions created by the researchers at the University of Saskatchewan." UST's own judgment about the failure of spin-off companies like Minerva is that "a 21% failure rate is much lower than one would expect in a normal high technology start-up business venture."[93] In order to counter this failure rate, UST (now ILO) offers training and development in the area of intellectual property management to faculty engaged in the commercialization of research so as to evaluate "inventions created at and controlled by the University of Saskatchewan for their commercial potential, patentability, and technical performance."[94] Consistent with the model prescribed by the Expert Panel on the Commercialization of University Research, UST/ILO assigns ownership of intellectual property to the university administration for purposes of commercialization, returning 50 percent of any royalties to individual faculty (less costs) and keeping the rest itself.[95] Alternatively, the company finds "partners" for inventions with commercial potential, who then patent the product and return a percentage of their profits to the university, which, in turn, pays the faculty member his/her share.

This latter approach is of particular benefit to multinational pharmaceutical companies, which are well placed to commercialize drugs by running clinical trials too expensive for universities or small companies. Despite the financial success of numerous "blockbuster drugs," some clinical trials result in market failure. A case in point is Alviva Biopharmaceuticals, a company spun out from the Department of Microbiology at U of S. Alviva had been investigating a cure for Parkinson's disease and sold the patent on a compound to an unnamed multinational. Subsequent clinical trials showed that there were serious side effects, preventing further development of the drug. None of the anticipated revenues accrued to the university, despite the fact that the company had received direct funding of $1.5 million from the provincial government.[96] Once again, the costs of developing the drug had been socialized with no benefits accruing either to the university, the government, or society.

Nevertheless, UST's report, *Creating Economic Activity*, states unequivocally that "it is imperative that the commercialization process continues to be supported at the U of S."[97] And the report goes on to claim that "University of Saskatchewan spin-off companies employ 1,383 people [with] combined revenues [of] approximately $190 million," with most of the benefits going to the local economy because "88% of the spin-off companies are located in Saskatchewan [and] 27 are located in Saskatoon."[98] These figures are contested by the 2001 NSERC report, *Research Means Business*, which states that the seven spin-off companies in Innovation Place have annual revenues of only $92.5 million.[99] The flawed methodology of the UST report may account for this discrepancy. The report maintains "the confidentiality of the data [from] private companies," reporting them "in an aggregate form only,"[100] ignoring the fact that open disclosure and communication of research findings are necessary conditions for the advancement of knowledge in any field.[101]

The UST report is consistent with the argument of the Expert Panel, which holds that all research must conform to the market's "high standards of excellence [by building] the foundation for future innovations [and by showing] that certain lines of industrial research and development (R&D) would be dead ends, thereby saving industry a great deal of time and money."[102] The panel's recommendation reduces the value of basic or curiosity-based research to the exclusively economic goal of bringing new goods and services to market ("future innovations"). By saving industry time and money in achieving this goal, university research meets the market's "high standards of excellence." Rather than enabling disinterested forms of understanding about the depth and breadth of problems, the market evaluates a line of products by how well they sell and how problem-free they remain for the customer.[103] Because of their desire to subordinate all inquiry to the dictates of the corporate market, neither the Expert Panel nor the UST report recognizes these two opposing standards of excellence.

It is worth taking note of how Innovation Place and UST are consistent with Mitchell's account of research parks as integral parts of the corporate program currently transforming the university by subverting the public nature of knowledge and turning it into an "engine of economic growth":[104]

1 Research parks, according to Mitchell, are "a dynamic middle ground" where "mavericks and entrepreneurs" from the university and business can "develop new forms of collaboration" and "shed their organizational skins" for "mutual ends" based on the "motivation of self-interest."

2 The commercialization of research is often effected through spin-off companies, which the UST report defined as "commercial entities" formed as a result of research and development carried out at the university, leading to "intellectual property, know-how or other expertise" designed for the market, where "the motivation of self-interest" predominates.

3 UST assigned IPRs to the university administration for the purposes of commercialization, returning 50 percent of any royalties to individual faculty. Alternatively, the company found "partners"

for inventions with commercial potential, who patented the product, returning a percentage of their profits to U of S and the individual. Both approaches are consistent with the recommendations of the Expert Panel on the Commercialization of Knowledge.

4 The UST report complied with the recommendations of the Expert Panel that research should conform to the market's "high standards of excellence" by enabling industry to know which R&D is likely to produce "future innovations," thereby saving companies time and money.

5 By holding equity in SED systems for several years, U of S sustained it as a spin-off company later sold to CALIAN Technology Ltd. The university "collaborated" with market agents in the pursuit of "mutual ends" by "shedding its organizational skin" and eroding the distinction between a public institution advancing shared knowledge and a private corporation maximizing stockholder value.

6 According to the UST report, 21 percent of the companies "spun out" from U of S were "inactive/closed." These included Minerva Animal Health Corporation, once declared "a new shining star," and Alviva Biopharmaceuticals, which received $1.5 million funding from the provincial government.

7 Neither Mitchell nor the UST acknowledge the "distinct and often opposed logics of value" of the market and education. The former is based on the satisfaction of wants for anyone who can afford to buy private goods, whereas in education the motivation is to satisfy the desire of anyone who seeks knowledge, regardless of their ability to pay.

8 The risks and costs involved in the creation of spin-off companies are borne by the public, whether through government funding or the university itself, while the benefits are privatized in the form of monetary profits. This well-established pattern shines through most brightly at the Canadian Light Source synchrotron, the apogee of research activities at U of S.

THE "VISIONARY LIGHT" OF THE CANADIAN LIGHT SOURCE (CLS) SYNCHROTRON

On 1 April 1999, the media announced that U of S had succeeded in securing the CLS, Canada's first synchrotron. The rhetoric that accompanied its advent knew no bounds. The CLS was heralded "as an economic saviour and a scientific beacon [capable of attracting] research money from around the globe."[105] The religious fervour for the largest public investment in a scientific facility in a generation was enhanced by then premier Roy Romanow, who extolled it as "a source of light, not only in the practical sense, but a visionary light in a philosophical sense." Faith in the power of the synchrotron to create private wealth for business corporations prompted Henry Dayday, then mayor of Saskatoon, to pronounce that "the CLS will add $122 million to Canada's gross domestic product (GDP) during construction and $12 million annually after that." Kent Smith-Windsor, executive director of the Saskatoon Chamber of Commerce, praised "the synchrotron [as] a potential cork in the brain drain," while Dennis Johnson, outgoing president of the chamber, added that it "will have the effect of doubling the activity level and size of Innovation Place," a theme taken up by Peter McCann, former president of AgWest Biotech, an agency located at Innovation Place, who declared that "the CLS will operate as a 'great magnet' for researchers." John Manley, then federal minister of industry, claimed that the synchrotron "is about economic development and coopera-tion [and] puts Saskatoon and Saskatchewan on the map as a centre of research for the world." Wilson Quail of the Department of Chemistry "attest[ed] to the amazing feats achieved by these massive scientific tools ... [which have] the potential to develop new drugs, reach medical break-throughs, even find a cure for cancer." And George Ivany, former president of U of S, pronounced the CLS "the light at the end of the tunnel."[106]

The magical powers of the CLS totally overshadowed any tempered claims about its scientific potential. Audacious statements about its ability to significantly increase the GDP, prevent the alleged brain drain of researchers in Canada, and perform amazing feats of science were matched by quips about the CLS as a light source and a magnet for researchers.[107] From medicine to economics, science to philoso-phy, the mystical power of the synchrotron's visionary beams was considered an elixir capable of curing all imaginable ills. Few of those making these pronouncements are still in office.

In the midst of the general euphoria, the chair of the Budget Committee of University Council, Professor Glen Beck, warned about the dangers accompanying the CLS: "The university's main mission is the pursuit of knowledge and excellence. To have a facility like this will change the complexion of the campus. Unless the resources are there to accommodate that, the rest of the institution will shrink like a prune."[108] For Beck, the threat to the university posed by the presence of the synchrotron struck at its very core. U of S was likely to "shrink like a prune" as scarce resources were channelled away from teaching, scholarship, and research unrelated to the CLS into its path, resulting in the destruction of the university's main mission. The autonomous pursuit of knowledge, posing "ever deeper and wider problems the higher the level of excellence it achieves,"[109] was being replaced by research whose goal is to produce new goods and services for the corporate market. Dazzled by the visionary light of the CLS, the university was systematically selecting against its own educational goals in favour of the market principle of monetary gain.

THE CLS CAPITAL COSTS: PUBLIC RISK FOR PRIVATE PROFIT

The CLS is a wholly owned not-for-profit company of U of S, but in a 2001 publication the facility's vision and mission statement declared that its goal is:

> To demonstrate global leadership in synchrotron research
> and development, and innovative multi-disciplinary industry
> partnerships ... To advance industrial competitiveness and
> support entrepreneurial commercialization opportunities
> thereby creating wealth and improving the quality of life
> for Canadian society.
> To provide a national venue for scholarly collaboration
> for academic, government and industry partners, and
> to facilitate cooperative fundamental and applied science
> and technology.
> To operate an industry friendly, not-for-profit facility, such
> that continuous investments and developments anticipate
> customer requirements and ensure international
> competitiveness.[110]

The need for Canada to compete in global markets drives the operations of the CLS. The not-for-profit facility *must* achieve this overriding goal through public funding and development that satisfies

Table 1
CLS Inc synchrotron declared capital funding for first phase (in $millions)

PUBLIC SECTOR	
Canada Foundation for Innovation:	$ 56.4
Federal departments of natural resources, western economic diversification, and National Research Council:	$ 28.3
Saskatchewan government (Sask. Economic and Cooperative Development):	$ 25.0
SaskPower:	$ 2.0
University of Saskatchewan	$ 7.3
University of Saskatchewan in-kind contribution of Linac	$ 32.6
City of Saskatoon:	$ 2.4
Universities of Alberta and Western Ontario:	$ .3
Alberta Innovation and Science and Alberta Heritage Foundation for Medical Research:	$ 9.6
Government of Ontario:	$ 9.6
TOTAL:	$173.5
PRIVATE SECTOR	
Boehringer Ingelheim	$ .5
TOTAL:	$ .5

Source: *www.lightsource.ca* and "Quick Facts," *StarPhoenix*, 1 April 1999, A1.

the demands of corporate customers, anticipating their wants, and adding value to their products through "innovation." Scholarly research is only mentioned as a means for strengthening links between curiosity-based research and applied science and technology. The value of research is thereby reduced to that of adding value to the corporate market through "innovation." The stated goals of the CLS ensure that costs and risks are socialized and monetary profits privatized – precisely the same pattern as that of spin-off companies in Innovation Place.

Yet the CLS (its full title is actually the Canadian Light Source Inc) was paid for almost entirely out of public funds from the federal and provincial governments, several universities, and a Saskatchewan Crown corporation.[111] The capital costs of $173.5 million were split into $140.9 million in cash and $32.6 million in in-kind contributions (see table 1).

The $7.3 million "donated" by U of S occurred despite the cuts to faculty positions and library holdings, raises to tuition fees, and depredations to university buildings already described. Moreover, this amount does not include the in-kind contribution of the university's Linear Accelerator, worth almost $33 million and previously used by researchers in theoretical physics, which would now act as a "gun" firing clusters of particles into the "booster ring" of the synchrotron.[112]

By far the largest amount of money came from the federal government – $56.4 million from the Canada Foundation for Innovation and $28.3 million from the Department of Natural Resources, the National Research Council, and the Department of Western Economic Diversification. As its name suggests, the Canada Foundation for Innovation, which was established in 1997, funds university research that produces innovation in the narrow sense of bringing new goods and services to market. It provides 40 percent of the funding, requiring universities to work in partnership with private corporations and governments from whom they must raise the remaining 60 percent. This gives "partners," whether from the private or public sectors, enormous leverage over what research gets done with public money.[113] In this instance, it was the public sector that contributed all of the remaining funds.

Dr Michael Bancroft of the University of Western Ontario (UWO), who was appointed interim director of the CLS, believed these contributions were crucial to U of S's obtaining the facility. In contrast to Ontario, where "the Harris government was in the process of slashing and burning ... Saskatchewan sources ponied up $36.7 million, including $25 million from the provincial government."[114] This process of "ponying up" consisted of raising $2.4 million from the city of Saskatoon, $2 million from SaskPower, $9.6 million from each of the governments of Alberta and Ontario, $300,000 from the universities of Alberta and Western Ontario, as well as the $7.3 million from U of S. Public money was being splashed around to build the CLS as a facility that would enable private corporations to maximize stockholder value. Moreover, the synchrotron's annual budget, estimated at that time to be $13 million, would require further financing from governments and universities, a point to which I shall return.[115] Bancroft's emphasis on the CLS's "strong commitment to industrial users and private/public partnerships, [with] designated Canadian and international mining companies as the top priority for industrial development"[116] was consistent with the facility's mission.

Only two private companies provided funding for the facility. The multinational pharmaceutical corporation, Boehringer Ingelheim, is alone in contributing $500,000 over a five-year period for the construction of part of a beamline, a sum matched by public funds from Saskatchewan Economic and Cooperative Development and, possibly, the Canadian Institutes of Health Research.[117] This "collaborative" funding formula, according to which the public sector bears most of the $6 million to $10 million cost, is to be adopted in each case of corporate involvement. In contrast, UWO, which had been the main competitor for the CLS, contributed three beamlines and $300,000 before construction started. This commitment underlines the importance of heavy subsidies from both universities and governments for the facility. The lack of corporate funding belies the "more than 40 letters of support from industry indicating that this [the CLS] is important for the sort of research that they do"[118] received by the synchrotron's first director.

GlaxoSmithKline contributed $500,000 towards a CLS research chair. As of October 2008, however, the chair had not materialized. No matching funds were forthcoming from government. The British parent company, Glaxo Wellcome PLC, had earlier tried to block access to less costly versions of its top-selling AIDS medicine in developing countries. In the year 2000, it warned Cipla Ltd of Bombay, India, that any generic versions of its drug Combivir would be illegal because they violated the company's patents. It also issued the same warning to a drug distributor in Ghana. Glaxo Wellcome was apparently concerned "that if a small country such as Ghana violates patent protection, that would open a Pandora's box of violations in larger markets, such as South Africa, Latin America and parts of southeast Asia where AIDS is also raging."[119] Combivir is a combination of two principal AIDS drugs – AZT and 3TC, and worldwide sales of the three drugs in the same year were "expected to top $1.1 billion, according to IMS Health, a drug marketing research firm in Westport, Connecticut."[120] All three drugs were beyond the reach of millions of people dying of AIDS and other diseases.[121] Fortunately, the Declaration on Trade in International Property and Public Health issued by the World Health Organization in November 2001 enabled countries to override patents such as that held by Glaxo Wellcome by licensing production to local companies in case of public health emergencies. But where countries lack domestic manufacturing capabilities and governments still do not have sufficient funds for purchasing drugs to fight AIDS and other diseases, the problem remains.[122]

Table 2
CLS Inc synchrotron declared funding for operating costs
(in $millions, for the period 1 January 2004 – 31 March 2009)

Natural Sciences and Engineering Research Council	$29.4
Government of Canada	$15.9
Western Economic Diversification	$ 3.0
National Research Council	$15.75
Canadian Institutes for Health Research	$10.5
University of Saskatchewan	$10.25
Fee for Service Revenue*	$ 5.0
TOTAL	$89.8

*The fee for service figure is a projection. All other line items represent committed funding.
Source: Sandra Ribeiro, Public Relations and Marketing Coordinator, Canadian Light Source Inc, e-mail message to author, 12 May 2004.

THE CLS OPERATING COSTS FOLLOW THE SAME PATTERN

As recently as 2004, ongoing funding for the CLS was still in doubt. Once the initial euphoria had subsided, there was a realization that, without support from the federal government for the synchrotron's operating costs, its future was in jeopardy.[123] No central funding agency existed that was capable of providing the kind of money that was needed. As a result, President Peter MacKinnon and the executive director of the CLS, Dr Bill Thomlinson, had to enlist the support of several of the same agencies that had funded the facility's capital costs.[124] By the spring of that year, their efforts had proven successful and funding was in place (see table 2).

The figures speak for themselves. For the first five years, the operating costs of the CLS were to be borne almost exclusively by the public, with the bulk of the funding ($74.55 million) coming from the federal government and its granting agencies. U of S "donated" $10.25 million, an amount that might otherwise have been used to hire faculty, provide more scholarships and bursaries to students, and generally improve teaching and learning. Unlike this public money, the fee for service charged only to private sector users was a projection ($5 million) based on the number of companies expected to use the facility.

Private corporations were to be allowed access to up to 25 percent of beamline use at the CLS, a far higher figure than at other synchrotrons. Moreover, "the results of contract research [conducted by private corporations] would not be made public [but] kept confidential."[125] The goal was to lure companies away from competitors in the United States and Europe by making the facility more attractive to the kind of "innovation" that generated private wealth. One of the ways of measuring the success of this policy involves looking at the number of private corporations that sign up to use the CLS. By the spring of 2005, there were just two. Synodon Inc, of Edmonton, manufacturers of an advanced airborne sensor system to detect leaks in natural gas pipelines, was the first paying customer.[126] Jacques-Whitford, an environmental consulting firm in Ontario, then signed a contract to study metals in air particulates for air quality standards.[127] The specific dollar figures for these contracts are not available, and the companies retain clear ownership of any intellectual property generated on the publicly owned facility.[128]

The tension between public ownership of the CLS and the need for private contracts highlights the opposing logics of value of education and the market. The educational goal to advance and disseminate shared knowledge from the synchrotron is contradicted in practice by policies that allow corporations to keep the results of their research confidential. When asked about this question, Dr Murray McLaughlin, director of business development at the CLS, replied: "I believe that those who pay can dictate confidentiality. In the case of industry contracts they are paying for the use of the facility and people time, therefore it is their choice. I do not see this as a contradiction but good management practices."[129] Put differently, he who pays the piper calls the tune. In this case, private corporations have the right to dictate the confidentiality of research results. McLaughlin does not recognize the contradiction since "good management practices," which facilitate the maximization of private profit, override any consideration of scientific knowledge as promoting the public interest.

The former federal economic diversification minister, Stephen Owen, questioned this logic when speaking in Saskatoon in February 2005: "This is the type of facility that needs to be in public hands to be able to do very deep research ... the synchrotron will allow researchers to do important and essential studies in environmental sciences and health and life sciences private industry alone won't look into because it's not profitable."[130] Owen recognized not only the necessity of public ownership if scientific research was to be conducted in the public interest but also that the market was incapable of conducting such research. But he failed to infer that, where the CLS itself engages in the practices of the market, the claim of independent scientific inquiry is undermined and its capacity to serve the common good radically compromised.

On the other hand, to what extent is the CLS fulfilling its stated mission to stimulate "innovation?" Is it significantly enlarging Canada's GDP and bringing vast amounts of wealth to Saskatoon and the Province of Saskatchewan, as promised by its promoters? Or is it too early to judge? After all, the facility only opened in October 2004 and beamlines only began operating in 2006. U of S emeritus professor John Conway believes the economic benefits of the synchrotron are proving largely illusory. In an article in the *StarPhoenix* in December 2006, he rehearsed an argument from an earlier editorial to the effect that annual revenues are only predicted to exceed costs by a few million by 2011. In the meantime, the promise of jobs and "scientific pilgrims" bringing money into the local economy should be weighed against the real public costs of more than $250 million, a figure that is likely to grow. Conway estimated that the provincial government's overall contribution (capital costs, matching grants for seven beamlines and for seven more under construction plus funding for individual faculty research projects) "now must exceed $100 million." This is only part of the story. In order to make the CLS a successful "big science" project, U of S, like the provincial government, is being drained of resources since "[the CLS] also must have priority in faculty hirings and course offerings and student recruitment."[131] The presence of the synchrotron was changing the nature of the university in precisely the way that Glen Beck had predicted. As a result, investment in curiosity-based research in the sciences, the social sciences, the humanities and fine arts, as well as in the undergraduate education of the large majority of students – "that is, those who will not do synchrotron science"[132] – was being cut.

Conway's concerns were soon confirmed by none other than the executive director of the CLS. In a speech to the Saskatoon Chamber of Commerce in March 2007, Bill Thomlinson concurred that "one of the biggest challenges for the synchrotron … is to get private users through the door." The goal of attracting 25 percent of users from the private sector was very far from the reality of "less than 10 per cent [who] do [use it] now." Moreover, "the synchrotron would be a 'world leader' in partnerships [only] if it could reap 10 per cent of its operating budget from private users." This was a particularly difficult problem because the annual costs of running the CLS would rise to $35 million a year by 2013, and with "the absence of guaranteed federal funds ... the CLS [was] waiting 'on pins and needles' for the federal government to release its science and technology strategy."[133] The new $64.5 million dollar expansion, for example, was only partially paid for. While seven hundred non-paying university and government scientists visited the CLS each year, private corporations were slow to fill the vacuum. This meant that a shortfall would probably occur in the synchrotron's five-year operating budget since the fee-for-service figure had been a projection.

Even Kent Smith-Windsor, executive director of the Saskatoon Chamber of Commerce, who in 1999 had claimed that the synchrotron was a potential cork in the brain drain, stated that "the Saskatoon business community believes the number of industrial users at the synchrotron is below where it expected it to be." Despite strong counter-evidence to his original judgment, he urged staying the course and "developing Saskatoon's science sector[, which] is key for the local economy."[134] The university's science community, as well as companies spun off at Innovation Place, required even more public funding in order to conduct synchrotron research capable of making money for private corporations. Smith-Windsor ignored the fact that corporations like Boehringer Ingelheim were already having doubts about using the CLS. More than two years earlier, Pierre Bonneau, director of research, admitted that, while Boehringer intended to use the CLS, the Brookhaven National Laboratory synchrotron in New York was closer to its Canadian head office in Montreal, and a synchrotron in Europe was located nearer to the company's head office in Germany.[135] Even though Boehringer had a financial stake in the CLS of $500,000, the company was not committed to using the facility. By 2007, the facility was "in talks with major corporations such as Cameco, IBM, General Electric, and [nuclear energy company] Areva [Resources Canada]."[136]

THE CLS: BRIGHT LIGHTS, BIG SCIENCE

Of the seventy-five synchrotrons either in operation or under construction throughout the world, the CLS is among the third generation, or most powerful. What, then, does it do? Described as a "cutting edge" facility, the synchrotron produces very high levels of electro-magnetic radiation by accelerating electrons to virtually the speed of light for as long as several hours, thereby "producing radiation a billion times brighter than that from the sun." The process of generating light begins with a linear accelerator equipped with an "electron gun," which fires clusters of particles into a "booster ring" capable of accelerating the particles to almost the speed of light. They are then "injected into the storage ring, [a] doughnut-shaped vacuum chamber" (the size of two football fields, housed in a building resembling a large railway station), where "focusing magnets" and "undulators" are used to bend or accelerate the particles. When the electrons are forced to bend by the powerful electromagnets, they lose energy that is encapsulated in photons, which then shoot off emitting a bright and highly focused beam of light over a spectrum from infrared to x-rays. This is known as "synchrotron light" because "it was first observed about 50 years ago in an electron synchrotron, a kind of particle accelerator."[137]

According to research scientist Dr T.K. Sham, synchrotron light has the following distinctive properties: "brightness," "tunability" (a broad spectrum from infra-red to gamma rays), "polarization" (operating on more than one plane), "time-structure" (nanosecond to sub-nanosecond pulses), and "coherence" (laser-like properties generated from undulators that "produce intense bright light at both hard X-ray and Ultra Violet range").[138] These characteristics enable scientists from a wide variety of disciplines to engage in research otherwise denied to them.

The CLS website declares that the facility will concentrate on three main areas: materials science, environmental sciences, and health sciences. Each area has at least two prongs: (1) curiosity-based research capable of providing the scientific community with new knowledge and (2) applied research of use to industry and the corporate market. Physicists and chemists in the field of materials science, for example, examine surfaces and materials by using photo-emission or photoelectron spectroscopy to study alloys, semi-conductors, nano-materials, superconductors, and non-conductors like polymers, minerals, and the surface reactions of these materials with gases and liquids. Their work can be used in the development of information technology and by the automobile industry, which is interested in the interaction between heavy oils and tribological films on automobile parts. Geoscientists in materials science study the chemistry of different minerals and their surface reactions, which may be of benefit to mining companies. Both academic and industrial environmental scientists conduct their investigations on any type of sample – gas, liquid, or solid – and are able to determine the chemistry of minerals and micro inclusions in minerals, soils, meteorites, particulates, glasses, coals, oils, mine tailings, and so on. Industrial researchers can focus on the chemistry of arsenic in mine tailings since "regulatory and mining companies need this information to predict the mobility and toxicity of the AS [arsenic]."[139]

Researchers in the health and biological sciences use the protein crystallography beamline to determine the atomic structures of biological macromolecules such as proteins by means of single crystal X-ray diffraction (a technique I describe in the next section). The crystal structures of proteins are critical to understanding basic physiological processes as well as the mechanisms of virus infections, which are important "for the design of antibiotics and other drugs, and all major pharmaceutical companies are using SR [synchrotron] sources to determine the structure of proteins with and without bound drug candidates."[140] Sequencing the complete genome of entire organisms and the study of the structure and function of proteins produced by those genes (known as structural genomics or structural proteomics) are also facilitated by the use of the synchrotron, as mentioned above. Researchers in biotechnology will also use the beamline to investigate the atomic structure of plant proteins related to the production of genetically modified organisms.

BRIGHT LIGHTS, BIG PROFITS

What, then, does this wide-ranging program of research at the CLS mean in concrete terms? To take one example, use of the protein crystallography beamline implies that "scientific mysteries [are open to] the most intimate look yet at the structure, composition, and chemical bonding of crystals and molecules, in materials ranging from semiconductors to proteins." The protein myoglobin, which is found in muscle tissue, for example, is responsible for the uptake and storage of oxygen. When subjected to synchrotron light, it reveals changes to its molecular structure that allow oxygen molecules to enter and leave what is known as "the heme site," or that part of the myoglobin molecule containing iron. This finding, made possible by a series of snapshots put together into a movie, shows "structural changes on a nanosecond-by-nanosecond timescale" that reveal "the time behavior of a dynamic molecular-biological process." This technique of macromolecular crystallography "opens the way to an understanding – in atomic detail – of the kinetics and dynamics of other important reactions involving proteins."[141] The very processes of life can now be scrutinized at the molecular level in ways that reveal the dynamic structural changes that enable healthy cells to grow and reproduce.

According to an article in *Scientific American*, the potential for "innovation" in the form of bringing new goods and services to market is fully recognized by pharmaceutical companies: "Biology researchers and the pharmaceutical industry are putting an ever-increasing demand on light sources, given the significance of proteins for the understanding of life and of disease and for the development of new drugs."[142] Increasingly, synchrotron light is used to investigate "protein molecules (which include enzymes, hormones, and antibodies) [as] ... fundamental building blocks of living beings" in order to commercialize "life ... disease and ... the development of new drugs." For pharmaceutical companies like Boehringer Ingelheim and GlaxoSmithKline, the "bright x-ray beams illuminating long-standing scientific mysteries"[143] open up a new frontier of knowledge, which serves their overriding goal of maximizing stockholder value. Once these and other companies do begin to use the CLS, the public will pay twice for the results of their research: first, for the capital and operating costs of the synchrotron and, second, for the expensive drug therapies they produce. The Canadian Institute for Health Information estimates that per capita costs for prescription drugs across Canada have grown by 15.4 percent, from $537 in 2001 to $620 in 2003. Bear in mind who is paying the bill for research and development facilities via higher education dollars. These laboratories now constitute the highest costs in health care and are increasing at a rate far above the rate of inflation. In British Columbia, pharmacare costs have jumped by 147 percent in the past decade and are projected to grow by almost 500 percent over the next twenty years.[144]

The patent laws already referred to enable private corporations like Glaxo to control their discoveries in the form of intellectual property, preventing others from developing cheaper, often healthier and more accessible, products, as happened with the generic form of Combivir. Even the genetic codes of microbes, plants, and animals, including human beings, have become the IPRs of private corporations and are often taken without their consent: "John Moore, a cancer patient, had his cell lines patented by his own doctor. In 1996, Myriad Pharmaceuticals, a US-based company, patented the breast cancer gene in women in order to get a monopoly on diagnostics and testing. The cell lines of the Hagahai of Papua New Guinea and the Guami of Panama are patented by the US commerce secretary."[145] These examples show how knowledge of the fundamental building blocks of living beings can be patented by individuals and business corporations for the purpose of private monetary gain, preventing its dissemination for the good of humankind.

Another such example is that of studies utilizing the bright X-ray beams of a synchrotron at the Lawrence Berkeley National Laboratory's Life Science Sciences Division in California to analyze the lifecycle of the protozoan carried by the female Anopheles mosquito. This research "could contribute to novel therapeutic approaches to the control of malaria,"[146] saving millions of lives throughout the developing world. However, the cost of a patented drug is often too prohibitive for "customers" in Africa, where the need is greatest. As a result, any company wanting to exploit this "limited market" is likely to withhold its development and distribution because the costs outweigh the benefits. Nor is this a fanciful example since pharmaceutical companies have, in the past, blocked access to known therapies for malaria, schistosomes (or bilharzia), sleeping sickness, and other tropical diseases.[147]

Multinational corporations that make use of the CLS now or in the future are not vehicles of innovation for the public good. Their goal in utilizing the synchrotron will be to maximize private profit. To think otherwise is to ignore the market's logic of value. Moreover, the distinction between academic and industrial research is blurred. Evidence from the facility's website shows that curiosity-based research conducted in any of the three main areas of concentration has clear industrial applications. The activities of the CLS embody the opposing logics of value of the market and of education. As a result, valuable knowledge created in the public interest will be compromised by the facility's stated goal of ensuring "international competitiveness" and providing "support [for] entrepreneurial commercialization."

CANADA RESEARCH CHAIRS, THE CLS, AND THE COMMERCIALIZATION OF KNOWLEDGE

The goal of U of S's Strategic Research Plan (2000) was to secure funding from the Canada Research Chairs (CRC) program by focusing on a handful of "research thrusts" and "mature research activities" that would use the CLS for the purpose of "innovation." The plan declared unequivocally that: "We intend to use the Chairs program to increase research intensiveness [by increasing] graduate enrollment and the recruitment of post-doctoral fellows, [maximizing] tri-council funding, [ensuring] the maintenance and strengthening [of] "partnerships" ... [with industry, and maximizing] patents and technology transfer [so as to ensure] an increase in research benefits made available to the private and public sectors."[148] Emphasis on this pattern of "research intensiveness" appeared to be precisely what the CRC program was looking for.

Two thousand research chairs were awarded to Canadian universities at a cost of $900 million to the federal government. Each chair was funded for a period of either five or seven years, after which time universities could possibly renew it for one further term. None of the money went to university operating budgets of universities, which had been starved for funds for more than two decades. As an integral part of the government's "innovation agenda," the program was heavily skewed in favour of the natural sciences, engineering, and the health sciences, which received 80 percent of the chairs, while the humanities and social sciences were allowed the remaining 20 percent, even though more than half of full-time Canadian academics teach in these areas.[149] The number of chairs awarded was based on each university's share of money from the three granting agencies (NSERC, MRC/CIHR, and SSHRC) over a period of three years, a formula that led to twelve universities getting two-thirds of the chairs, leaving the others (sixty or so) to compete for the rest. As Jim Turk, executive director of CAUT, pointed out, this "grossly inequitable distribution of the Canada Research Chairs helps undermine Canada's consistent quality, [propelling universities] in the direction of the American model of university education [with a few predominantly private] excellent giants at one end and a huge number of less than adequate institutions at the other."[150] U of S obtained thirty-one research chairs, or 1.65 percent of all those awarded. Three additional chairs were later awarded as a result of improved performance in obtaining federal grants, and the number increased to forty (2 percent) by 2007. Dr Michael Atkinson, former provost and vice-president academic, together with former vice-president research Michael Corcoran, assured faculty that "synchrotron-related areas have been identified as a high priority ... [and] a target of 50 percent of the chairs [are] to be allocated to Canadian Light Source users under appropriate research themes." The final figure is far higher. In biotechnology, for example, "all of these chairs are expected to utilize the synchrotron as an integral part of their research program."[151] Indeed, twenty-eight of the initial thirty-one research chairs were in materials science, environmental sciences, health sciences, biotechnology, and technology and change. Although the humanities and social sciences were entitled to 20 percent of the chairs, only three research chairs were awarded to the area of identity and diversity – this in a province that has the highest percentage of Aboriginal people per capita in the country.

President MacKinnon has claimed that the university will not be stood on its head by the presence of the synchrotron. The former vice-president of research was more blunt when he stated that "VIDO [Vaccine Infectious Diseases Organization] and CLS are what the University of Saskatchewan will be known for in the next decades." Powerful external forces may have shaped the path of "research intensiveness," in particular the federal government's CRC and Canada Foundation for Innovation (CFI) programs, but U of S did little to resist the threat to institutional autonomy. At no point did the central administration defend the autonomy of "the people's university" in the face of the federal government's "innovation agenda." They raised no objections to the design of the CRC program, "which gives an external government panel veto power over who is given a chair"[152] once candidates are selected by universities and then recommended by a college of reviewers. Even when the initial number of chairs was reduced from thirty-nine to thirty-one as a result of a change in the rules, MacKinnon announced that "at this time we have no plans to reduce the number of research thrusts we intend to develop."[153] Chairs in the humanities and social sciences were cut from five to three, allegedly because of a poor showing in SSHRC funding. A subsequent memorandum simply stated that "the

University welcomes the Canada Chairs Program and will adopt internal policies to support this initiative."[154] These policies are examined in the next section.

The narrow focus of the CRC program at the U of S, as well as some of its connections to the corporate market, is evident from the following list:[155]

1 Materials science (five chairs to use the CLS)
As we have seen, materials science incorporates research in physics, mathematics, chemistry, geology, and engineering and is capable of leading to faster computer chips, tougher plastics, and better lubricants. This "research thrust" makes use of two new laboratories in the Department of Geological Sciences, which were funded by CFI and are "available for collaboration with industries involved in prospecting for minerals, oil, and natural gas."[156]

2 Environmental sciences (six chairs to use the CLS)
These incorporate research in agriculture and bioresources, the natural sciences, and geography and focus on soil science, geochemistry, environmental engineering, and conservation and climate change. One of several "partnerships" with industry is with Cameco Ltd, a multinational uranium mining company, whose head office is in Saskatoon.

3 Health sciences (five chairs to use the CLS)
Health sciences, incorporating the colleges of medicine and veterinary medicine, as well as the Vaccine and Infectious Disease Organization (VIDO), will focus on neurosciences and reproductive biology. VIDO is a wholly owned U of S not-for-profit company specializing in the development of vaccines, which "has no long-term funding source and must rely on grants from supporters"[157] such as governments and U of S. In 2001, VIDO found two "corporate partners" in the biotechnology and pharmaceutical industries, and secured a $27 million grant from Genome Canada to study communicable diseases and the antibodies produced by animals and humans to combat them.[158] The impact of the federal grant was allegedly "bigger than the highest-profile attempt to stimulate economic growth in the city over the past twenty years,"[159] an apparent reference to the claims made about the CLS. In 2007, the International Vaccine Centre, a level-three biosafety facility connected with VIDO, received a total of $110 million from

the Canada Foundation for Innovation and the federal and provincial governments.[160]

4 Biotechnology (five chairs to use the CLS)

Structural biology, or the application of protein engineering to research in the life sciences, enables researchers to unlock the codes of life by using the techniques of genomics and the application of synchrotron light. In order to "strengthen the role of the University of Saskatchewan as an innovator, coordinator and a leader in the intellectual and economic development of the science of applying technology to living things,"[161] the Virtual College of Biotechnology (VCB) was established in 2000.

5 Technology and change (six chairs to use the CLS)

Technology and change also incorporated the VCB, computer science, and engineering, focusing on both information technology and biotechnology, and conducting research with various "industrial partners." A working relationship with industry is facilitated through the Saskatchewan Structural Sciences Centre, a $13 million facility funded exclusively by public money, whose "mandate is to be a support lab to the CLS synchrotron facility [and whose research for] industrial partners [will] be conducted under the strictest confidentiality agreements."[162]

6 Identity and diversity (three chairs, none of which are to use the CLS)

Identity and diversity has two main themes: Aboriginal experience, integrating research in the College of Law, sociology, and Native studies; and multiculturalism and citizenship, using expertise from the Prairie Centre of Excellence on Immigration and Integration, established in 1996.

The CRC program and the CLS provide the perfect platform for maximizing the value of "innovation." A prime example is the "industrial partnership" between U of S and Cameco. In 1993, the company awarded the university $1.5 million to establish a chair in environmental and aqueous geochemistry, known as the Cameco Chair. Professor Jim Hendry was appointed to the chair two years later to conduct research on "soils of low permeability [exploring] the processes of how pollutants move through these apparently impermeable materials."[163] More specifically, by examining the interaction between groundwater, surface rocks, and other materials,

Hendry studies the ways in which contaminants such as arsenic move through apparently impermeable materials.[164] The CLS is the perfect tool with which to conduct such research since its beamlines enable scientists to focus on the persistent environmental problem caused by uranium tailings at Cameco's mines in northern Saskatchewan. During the 1990s, the provincial government held a series of hearings, which resulted in Cameco's being required to deal with the problems of long-term waste from its mines at Key Lake and McClean Lake. In 2001, it became known that Brett Moldovan, a Cameco research chemist, would use the CLS to determine the stability of arsenic tailings at the company's Rabbit Lake mine.[165] Former director of the synchrotron, George Bancroft, had designated mining companies like Cameco as "the top priority for industrial development" and assured the research community that "the CLS has convinced a few mining companies that SL [synchrotron light] techniques give very valuable information for characterizing the chemistry of mine tailings."[166]

Hardly surprising, then, that Bernard Michel, former president of Cameco, was chair of a business consortium that lobbied the federal government to bring the synchrotron to Saskatoon in the first place.[167] Michel proclaimed the Cameco Chair "a new dimension of the company's cooperation between the university and industry"[168] and, as a sign of this growing cooperation, recommended the appointment of President George Ivany to Cameco's board of directors upon his retirement from U of S in July 1999. The company has since sponsored the Cameco MS Neuroscience Centre and, in September 2006, the Cameco Plaza, "a new landmark at the University of Saskatchewan ... being dedicated ... to recognize Cameco's generosity and community leadership in contributing $3 million to the University's *Thinking the World of Our Future* Campaign."[169] It should be pointed out that, according to its financial statements, Cameco paid $34.7 million in income taxes during the years 2004 to 2006 on pre-tax profits totalling $995 million.[170]

Cameco is just one example of "industrial partnerships" between U of S and private corporations. According to U of S's own statistics, one-fifth of all research conducted at the university in 1998–99 ($9.8 million) was in the form of grants and contracts with industry, much of it in the colleges of agriculture and pharmacy.[171] The actual amount may be considerably higher. A CAUT report calculated that corporate funding at both Saskatchewan universities for the same year reached $15.9 million, or 27.6 percent of research revenue, almost matching the provincial government's share of 29.4 percent.[172]

The Canada Research Chairs program, then, strengthens the commercialization of knowledge at U of S, tying research to the corporate market in the following ways:

1 The CRC program is reshaping Canadian universities, making them compete for chairs on the basis of funding received from the Tri-Councils, creating a strict hierarchy in which a few universities get the lion's share and ensuring that a disproportionate number of chairs are awarded to the health sciences, natural sciences, and engineering. U of S now has forty chairs out of a total of two thousand.[173]

2 U of S embraced the CRC program in order to "increase research intensiveness" and "ensure an increase in research benefits made available to the private and public sectors."

3 Five "research thrusts" based on synchrotron research were identified as "high priority areas." Thirty-one of the initial thirty-four chairs were assigned to these "thrusts," all of which have strong connections with the market.

4 One such connection is the "industrial partnership" with Cameco, a uranium mining company strategically positioned to use the CLS to analyze the environmental problem of tailings leeching arsenic into groundwater at its mines in northern Saskatchewan.

5 The central administration did little to protect the autonomy of U of S, preferring instead to welcome the CRC program and "adopt internal policies to support this initiative"[174] – policies that I now examine.

INTERNAL CONTROL MECHANISMS: ROUND ONE

In order to match the narrow market goals of the governments' programs, U of S devised its own mechanisms capable of "maximizing the value of innovation." Two documents, laced with the language of the market, comprised the ideological source for this scheme. *A framework for planning* prescribed the following measures: "The University needs a set of instruments, a toolkit ... [for]

the identification of priority academic areas into which the University will put its resources [in the form of] ... tenure track appointments, technical assistance, equipment, curriculum development, and support for graduate students ... four to six areas of academic priority ... [since] priority determination is the *investment part of the choice process.*"[175] The vice-president's *Strategic Research Plan* (2000) then identified the six "research thrusts" referred to above as beneficiaries of the "investment process" because they "build on our *comparative advantage* ... increase our research productivity and enhance our profile as *a research intensive university.*"[176] In order for the plan to take off, $1.5 million was reallocated through a 1 percent levy to all colleges, resulting in an annual "investment" of $250,000 to the following areas:

1 The Virtual College of Biotechnology (VCB) was to "coordinate teaching and research efforts" in the research thrust of biotechnology and was awarded four new faculty positions in anatomy and anatomy and cell biology, biochemistry, commerce, and sociology. This team of researchers represented the "*premium* ... placed on interdisciplinary and multidisciplinary programming [from which] new areas of *research innovation* would likely arise."[177] By 2008, however, the VCB was disbanded. Its "assets," including two of the faculty positions plus a named chair, and the trust established to fund it were transferred to the new School of Public Policy, whose overall theme was "*innovation policy*, including science, technology and society."[178]

2 The Saskatchewan Structural Sciences Centre, funded by the CFI and the Canada/Saskatchewan Western Economic Partnership Agreement, received money and resources for "four core scientists [whose] mandate [is] to be a support lab for the CLS synchrotron facility, to be an instrumentation facility for U of S, and to provide research services for industry organizations like those at Innovation Place."[179] In order to ensure "a storefront type of service [for industry], the fee for industrial users will be calculated at cost, [and] all research will be conducted under the strictest confidentiality agreements."[180]

3 The Teaching and Research Program in Biomolecular Structures, which complements synchrotron-based research in biochemistry and at VIDO, was also awarded new faculty, as was Northern Ecosystems and Toxicology.

The process of priority determination was extended in 2002 when a further levy was exacted on all colleges in order to further "maximize the value of innovation."

By way of contrast, *A Framework for Planning* recommended "program termination procedures [as] the *divestment side* [for] programs *for which demand is consistently low* and in which the quality of teaching, service or research has declined." This market-based criterion of customer demand drives "the divestment side" of the process, requiring the university to "systematically withdraw resources from programs that can no longer contribute satisfactorily to the mission of the institution [in order to meet] its own commitment to academic quality."[181] What is meant by "quality" is unclear since "there is no agreement on what 'excellent' means," but "*the principle test of quality lies in how well our work is appreciated outside of the institution.*"[182] Given the growing emphasis on the need to "increase the value of innovation," it is the corporate market's standards of quality that are likely to override all others. In place of education's ability to pose broader and deeper questions of reality, U of S's mission becomes one of producing "problem-free" research capable of bringing goods and services to market.[183]

The tool used to implement the twin processes of priority determination and program divestment was Systematic Program Review (SPR), which was described as "an evaluation opportunity, a chance to assess quality in a national and international context, a learning opportunity and a chance to improve and incorporate *innovations* ... [through] a thorough consideration, on a periodic basis, of the objectives of an academic program, the content of the curriculum, the qualifications of the faculty, and the outcomes of the teaching, learning and *service enterprises.*"[184] The measurement of inputs and outputs was designed to assess the still undefined "quality" of "*service enterprises*" and redirect resources towards those programs capable of maximizing "*innovations.*" The claim that SPR provided "open and transparent means"[185] in achieving its goals was belied by the fact that the two leadership units involved in its implementation – namely, "the Vice-President (Academic's) Office and the College of Graduate Studies and Research [-] are located outside the evaluative loop as far as a rating of their performance is concerned." Not only were the data from SPR kept secret, but "the inadequacy of its design, its top-down deployment, and its bias towards corporate imperatives,"[186] meant that SPR was far from being well designed, participatory, and non-standardized.[187]

The planning process also compromised academic freedom and university autonomy. *A Framework for Planning* acknowledged that "not only must individuals be able to work in an environment of open inquiry, but the University must also be autonomous in developing its own vision and setting its own academic priorities," thereby giving the appearance of protecting free inquiry. But the autonomy referred to (i.e., "setting its own priorities") was the very SPR-designed process whose purpose was to benefit programs tied to the market. Two seemingly strong assertions – "Governments cannot be allowed to censor scholarship; corporate sponsors cannot be permitted to stifle research" – were immediately qualified in the following terms: "this does not mean that the University of Saskatchewan should reject the pleas of government or the requests of the private sector."[188] This statement reduced university autonomy to a matter of deciding which of the demands made by governments and the corporate market should be adhered to. Given U of S's declared commitment in the *Strategic Research Plan* to "*an increase in research benefits made available to the private and public sectors,*"[189] a clear rationale emerged for making both university autonomy and academic freedom subservient to the goal of "bringing new goods and services to market."

INTERNAL CONTROL MECHANISMS: ROUND TWO

The planning cycle was spurred on by a series of documents emanating from the central administration. In 2002, President Mackinnon presented *Renewing the Dream: University of Saskatchewan Strategic Directions*, in which he set the tone for the entire process in the following terms: "This university *must compete* vigorously and effectively among the major research universities of the country ... [in a climate of] *intensity of competition, fiscal constraints,* and the *strong innovation agenda* ... [where] *knowledge is the new currency.*"[190] No attempt was made to conceal the market orientation of the "dream," as the familiar mantras of competition and innovation were supplemented by the neologism of knowledge as "the new currency."[191]

A series of foundational documents were then developed in several areas, as prescribed by the *Provost's White Paper on Integrated*

Planning (2002), and in the fall of the same year colleges and administrative units began developing their own plans. By November 2003, these plans were ready for evaluation, and University Council created the College Planning Review Committee, which also assisted in the development of the university-level plan. The major oversight committee for evaluating college plans as well as the architect of the university plan was the newly created Provost's Committee on Integrated Planning.

This flurry of activity culminated in the 2004 report, *A Framework for Action: University of Saskatchewan Integrated Plan 2003–07*, a document "inspired by an emphasis on change, community, and collaboration." A number of "core themes" were identified, particularly the need to adhere to the goals of *Renewing the Dream* by implementing the results of sPR and maximizing "innovation." From these, a series of "strategic directions" emerged, "areas such as biotechnology, synchrotron science, and computer science ... [which ensure that] the University of Saskatchewan joins those peer institutions as a top ten research university."[192] Proposals for new programs in the health sciences and an interdisciplinary environmental science centre also dovetailed with the emphasis on synchrotron-based research. In order to maximize the "research intensiveness" of faculty, the integrated plan declared that "the new Industry Liaison Office (ILO), will play a strategic role in facilitating the establishment of *research alliances* ... with external private and public organizations ... *Successful partnerships* with external organizations at the *front-end of the research enterprise* are more likely to yield *productive back-end outcomes* (e.g. *commercialization of research results, licensing agreements, spin-off companies*, etc.)."[193] The overriding need to produce knowledge of utility to the market would be met through partnerships with governments and private corporations at the so-called front-end of the research enterprise. "Research alliances" of this kind meant that the goals of the market (the commercialization of knowledge, development of patents, and formation of spin-off companies) were realized – goals that were referred to in scatological terms as "productive back-end outcomes."

Towards the end of *A Framework for Action*, several mechanisms emerged that were designed to "measure our success over this planning cycle in terms of the initiatives outlined in this Plan and against the goals of the *Strategic Directions*."[194] Performance indicators were prescribed as the appropriate means for developing a "'*Research*

Intensity Index' that captures the measurement of *changes in sponsored research and outputs* such as publications, performances, or presentations, and other scholarly and artistic activities." Armed with quantified data about outputs in research sponsored by private corporations and so on, the administration could compare "our progress on specific indicators with the position and progress of peer institutions ... [especially] the G10 universities, a self-selected group of research intensive universities" that excluded U of S. This process of "conscious comparison" with other universities, known as "benchmarking," was to ensure "the identification of a set of areas of academic pre-eminence for the University of Saskatchewan," even though these areas had already been identified and funds channelled in their direction. The full development of performance indicators and benchmarks required two further levels of bureaucracy. The first was "a Performance Measurement Task Force [that would] be established ... [to] report to the University community and update the Board of Governors on progress with development of these performance measures." The second was "the creation of an Office of Institutional Assessment ... [to] facilitate, consult, and provide leadership for institutional assessment activities."[195]

Management's use of performance indicators and benchmarks as conceptual tools is hardly new. There is a striking resemblance between the performance indicators prescribed in *A Framework for Action* and those enumerated in *Fostering Excellence: A Policy for Framework for Alberta's University Research System*, which appeared in the late 1990s.[196] Governments and university administrators in Canada increasingly define institutions of higher education in terms of narrowly defined, market-oriented outcomes. In doing so, they are merely following the example of their peers in Australia, New Zealand, the United Kingdom, and the United States.[197]

According to Professors Jan Currie and Janice Newson, "performance indicators make it possible to standardize aspects of work, such as teaching styles and formats, and through standardization, to classify institutions within national and international ranking systems."[198] Management thereby increases its control over faculty's research, teaching, and scholarly work in two ways. The first is through the process of standardized measurement of inputs and outputs of departments, faculties, and universities. This blunt instrument gives the appearance of capturing significant data about the "productivity" of faculty, for example, but in reality it offers far less.

As the Special Study Panel of the US National Centre for Education Statistics points out, "because we value education we should measure it. But the unintended effect is deceptive: We begin to value only what we can measure. Eventually, our hopes for what education can become are reduced to numbers, impressive in their apparent precision but silent on the essential meaning of learning in a free society."[199] The abstractions provided by performance indicators may seem precise, but they reveal little or nothing about how the process of learning at the core of education takes place. The second way in which control is wrested from the hands of faculty involves linking institutions together on a national and international grid. These networks contrive to increase competition among universities as each one tries to find a niche in which it can out-compete the others. This, after all, was the declared goal of "benchmarking" at U of S: to gain entry into the Canadian Ivy League of G10 universities by emphasizing areas of "academic pre-eminence" linked primarily to the synchrotron.

In sum, the conceptions of academic freedom and university autonomy undergirding the planning process at U of S were inadequate. Free and critical inquiry was undermined by a policy statement reducing the university's function to one of choosing which demands from governments and corporations should be followed. Independence, even of a relative kind, from these powerful forces was not considered; instead, the central administration took measures to create a "comparative advantage" with other universities by diverting money to the now familiar research thrusts by means of levies on all colleges. SPR, designed to "divest" programs not meeting market demand and "invest" in others capable of "increasing innovation," was a top-down process that omitted the units conducting it. The alleged need to compete in the global market meant that the university should build closer links with business through the ILO, assure new funding for "strategic directions" (identical to the six research thrusts), and adopt performance indicators and benchmarks, requiring more bureaucracy and control over the work of faculty.

RESISTANCE

As the effects of this pattern of commercialization were felt, different groups at U of S engaged in resistance. Five hundred students opposed to record increases in tuition fees joined a national day of protest in February 2002 in defiance of their student council, subsequently lobbying the provincial government, the Board of Governors, and the president to impose a freeze on fees.[200] A group of faculty, working in conjunction with the U of S Faculty Association, organized a series of fora on the issues of corporatization, tuition fees, academic freedom, university governance, and the elusive concept of "academic excellence."[201] In March 2006, an annual academic freedom week was instigated, featuring local and national speakers from among faculty, staff, and students.[202] In March 2007, four different unions, representing faculty, sessional lecturers, support staff, and other university workers, held a rally against delays in the university's approach to contract negotiations, resulting in settlements for the first two groups.[203] And a citizens' group, working in conjunction with faculty, staff, and students, established "a people's university community program to provide courses that meet the learning needs of the community and the university."[204] The result was the growth of the People's Free University of Saskatchewan, which I analyze in the final chapter.

Arguably the most spirited resistance came from students working in conjunction with faculty. In January 2005, a group calling itself Students Opposed to Liberal Arts Decline (SOLD) held two rallies to protest a hiring freeze affecting eighteen faculty positions in the fine arts and humanities. Students and faculty criticized the administration's refusal to fill the vacant positions with tenure stream appointments, and they expressed concern for the continuing viability of the Department of Languages and Linguistics (an amalgamation of the departments of Germanic and Slavic studies and modern languages). The teaching of Slavic languages in a province with a large Ukrainian population was a particular bone of contention since there was only one term appointment in this section of the department, which, in eleven years, had shrunk from six full-time members to one.[205] The lack of tenured professors meant that the department could only offer first- and second-year courses in languages with none in culture and literature.[206]

The central administration had already sent a hiring plan to all departments in the College of Arts and Science, which identified forty-two faculty positions as becoming vacant between 2005 and 2007. Only eighteen of these positions were to be filled in the first two years.[207] Faculty and students feared that the rest would be expunged. Students also felt these cuts were being imposed at the same time as they were being treated as "revenue units," whose only function was to fill the university's coffers.

There was opposition too to the implications of SPR and its rationalization in *A Framework for Action*. The Department of Languages and Linguistics had received a grade of D in SPR, according to which there were "deficiencies" in the program's resources. The Integrated Plan was clear about what would happen to such programs and why: "The University also needs fewer programs. We have to consolidate our efforts and resist the temptation to mount a myriad of small programs aimed at handfuls of students ... By the end of this planning cycle, we will have *shifted resources to areas of institutional commitment* ... [because] *we must change, innovate, economize, and invest in order to compete* in the post-secondary environment of the 21st century."[208] The mantra of the market – "compete" – emerges once again as an overriding obligation ("we must") and is used to justify the axing of small departments like languages and linguistics in order to fund programs capable of "innovation." Nevertheless, the report went on to assure the university community that "these and other themes have emerged in the journey that Integrated Planning has fostered," suggesting that a democratic consensus had been reached about "the clear direction for the institution."[209] A growing number of students and faculty believed that economic forces rather than academic priorities were steering the direction which U of S was now taking.

The opposing logics of value of the market and of education were being played out across the university. Professors whose research conformed to the market's standards of excellence had a higher status than did those whose teaching, scholarship, and research merely enhanced the intellectual quality of U of S. The activities of obtaining government or corporate research grants and the development of intellectual property or spin-off companies were deemed far more valuable than meeting old-fashioned standards of educational excellence. Donald G Stein writes of the situation in the United States in the following terms: "Faculty members whose research and expertise can generate substantial income are often treated very differently from their counterparts who focus on teaching and the pursuit of esoteric knowledge of no interest to the marketplace."[210] The knowledge created by professors in the departments of languages, anthropology, and classics is of little or no marketable value. Hardly surprising, therefore, that these departments at U of S continue to suffer from underfunding, gradual erosion, or assimilation with other departments. In contrast, faculty members with a history of successful patent generation or other forms of marketable prowess are paraded like superstars to the media and the public.

Following the second rally on 18 January, two representatives from SOLD met with the dean of the College of Arts and Science. They presented a list of twelve recommendations, which included the following: "An end to the faculty hiring freeze, especially in Languages and Linguistics; Adding a requirement that all liberal arts students must take six credits of a language other than English; Making deans subject to systematic program review [SPR]; Transparent election of college representatives to Academic Council [the equivalent of Senate]; Ensuring that every department has at least five tenured professors; and, Reducing the University's reliance on sessional lecturers to teach liberal arts."[211] The group recognized that cuts to languages and linguistics should be placed in the broad context of curriculum reform, systematic review of administrators, open election procedures to council, a critical mass of tenured faculty in every department, and an end to the hiring freeze. Unless these issues were addressed in their totality, collegiality would be replaced by corporate secrecy. Indeed, at the first SOLD rally, Glen Beck had stated that, at the budget committee of which he was chair, "there is no accountability and no access to what is going on ... [and the committee] is given very little detail on where exactly money is being spent ... [because of the] closed decision-making in place."[212]

In an article in the *StarPhoenix*, Provost Michael Atkinson then claimed that "positions are not being removed from the liberal arts and distributed elsewhere on campus, and operating funds are not being diverted to the Canadian Light Source synchrotron ... [and] students are not being treated as revenue streams."[213] The same theme was taken up by the associate dean of humanities and fine arts who, in an effort "to set the record straight," claimed that humanities programs were actually stronger than in the past since the "bachelor of circumpolar studies and Asian studies initiatives may revive former areas studied, and classics courses survive in programs too new for SPR."[214]

At a meeting of University Council on 27 January 2005, President MacKinnon criticized faculty and students for using several "corrosive" phrases when referring to administrators as "carpet baggers," "ambitious roving exploiters," and "worms of power."[215] The latter expression had actually been a "worm in the apple" and was described by English professor Terry Matheson as a "perfectly apt metaphor to describe a process whereby an institution's well-being may be damaged from within."[216]

MacKinnon then engaged in a "rebuttal" of the various claims made by SOLD. In keeping with the claims of the provost and associate dean, he asserted that the humanities had not been unfairly exposed to budget cuts since "106 or 35 percent [of] the tenure stream complement in the College of Arts and Science are assigned to the humanities and fine arts departments." Acknowledging that languages and linguistics had two vacancies, he stated that "this department has the third largest complement of tenure stream faculty in all of the Humanities departments" and that the administration was "strongly committed to liberal arts education."[217] These figures are difficult to verify. Examination of the 2004–05 *University of Saskatchewan Calendar* suggests that MacKinnon may have included term appointments as tenure stream faculty in his assessment of the size of the Department of Languages and Linguistics. He went on to deny that the CLS "exists for private corporate benefit and that the University is paying for its operation," but he acknowledged that "the University makes a contribution to the operating budget ... [and that] we increased our contribution"[218] to secure more government funding. The "contribution" amounted to $10.25 million between 2004 and 2009, as indicated in figure 2.

To the charge that the administration saw students as "revenue streams," MacKinnon appeared sympathetic to concerns about rising tuition. But he repeated the mantra that tuition rates were high because "*we must compete* [with other] Canadian medical-doctoral institutions ... in order to be successful [and] *manage the investments* [to] ensure ... [success by] *investment in the student experience* ... [including a] *multimillion dollar ... student information system* ... [furthermore] we have *leased land for real estate development* that will return rents for the exclusive purposes of student services and student aid."[219] In other words, U of S was behaving like a private corporation, leasing land to real estate companies, managing investments, and ploughing some of these into a computerized student information system in order to compete for students in the global marketplace. By meeting "national and international standards,"[220] the university would then attract more students from abroad. A document from the Corporate Administration at U of S was unequivocal in its support for this strategy: "there are opportunities to 'sell' education internationally ... There are *opportunities to better lever revenue from foreign students by targeting key markets*."[221] Provided that U of S targeted "key markets" in the developing world (China and India, for example), its education could be "sold" to international students who would increase "revenue streams."

Following the speech, there were several attempts to muzzle the free expression of ideas. The dean of St Thomas More College apologized during University Council for the comments of a non-tenured professor, who had criticized the administration at a SOLD rally. In an e-mail message sent to all faculty members at the federated college, he wrote: "I felt a need to distance STM [St Thomas More College] from any of the public comments as reported and assured the President that I would circulate his comments to our faculty," which he did. The dean urged professors in the college to be careful about making any "comment[s] in public about the situation faced by the Humanities" and to make sure that, if they did engage in the issue, "the tone be professional and reflect positively on the individuals making comments [since] our criticisms of our host institution may not be welcome."[222] The provost then reiterated the charge that critics' remarks were "divisive and corrosive ... completely undeserved, and I strongly suspect they do not represent the views of the vast majority of faculty, students, and staff."[223]

Despite these threats to their academic freedom, faculty and students continued to press for more funding to the liberal arts. The term appointment in Slavic languages, which had been under threat, was reinstated later in the spring of 2005. On 9 February, more than three hundred students held a rally, marching to the administration building in support of a tuition freeze that Gavin Gardiner, president of the student union, referred to as the first step in ensuring "affordable, accessible, post-secondary education in this province."[224] Saskatchewan still has the highest tuition fees in western Canada and the third highest in the country, while increases in undergraduate arts and undergraduate education between 1991–92 and 2006–07 were 172 percent, the third highest in Canada.[225] Calling on the provincial government to spend some of its $300 million surplus on a two-year freeze, Gardiner said the $14 million commitment was "a drop in the bucket for the province, but it's life and death for students."[226] He also called for "a public review of post-secondary funding and student financial aid, [since] it is only a full review of the system, not simply increasing operating grants to the universities, which will resolve these issues."[227] In the spring, the government implemented a tuition freeze as part of Saskatchewan's centennial celebrations and promised to study the affordability of postsecondary education.[228]

At the core of faculty support for the liberal arts was a recognition that the logic of the market had so penetrated the university that the humanities and fine arts were considered irrelevant. Professor Anthony Harding pointed out that A Framework for Action only referred to the liberal arts in "the sort of language that is used by a tobacco company when it donates a few thousand dollars to an opera production ... [This] trivialize[s] the primary professional commitment of Fine Arts and Humanities faculty ... reducing the content of their disciplines to banal catch-all phrases ... [and obscuring the fact that] humanists agree in considering education and critical method more central to university life than 'competitiveness, productivity and business innovation.'"[229]

The provost replied that, "unlike some commentators," Harding had read the Integrated Plan "closely enough to have found hidden messages that even its authors would be surprised to discover." He listed several projects as "opportunities for the humanities and the social sciences to take the lead in ... [including] international studies, the digital media lab, the Learning Centre and the Global Commons to name a few."[230] For Harding, this was further evidence that there was "no vision for the renewal of the humanities and fine arts." The provost's dismissal of the concerns of faculty was "disturbing" and only matched by his suggestion that they become involved in "vaguely-defined projects [and] technological set-ups ... that really amount to little more than elaborate ways of delivering information."[231]

The rejuvenation of faculty opposition to the market model of education was, nevertheless, significant. Their support for students striving for the recognition of the liberal arts made for a powerful alliance. A new group of faculty and students was formed to work in conjunction with SOLD in the planning of a one-day conference highlighting the importance of the humanities and fine arts to U of S. Another group of faculty working with the faculty association planned a series of panel discussions on the dangers of corporate values to the university, a series that ran from 2005 to 2006.

Eventually, the two groups combined their efforts. It was as though the winter of discontent had "let a thousand flowers bloom."

Nor were students satisfied with a one-year tuition freeze. U of S was planning to impose an increase of more than 5 percent in 2006–07, a rate based on the average increase at comparable universities across Canada. This rate compounded the increase that would have occurred in 2005–06 with that of the following year, meaning that "the university administration is going to get that money that is being rolled back into their operating grant." As Gardiner pointed out, "I don't think that's right and I don't think that's what the government intended ... we have a huge fight on our hands for next year,"[232] words reminiscent of the chants of Parisian students in 1968: "Ce n'est qu'un début, continuons le combat!" The provincial government extended the freeze for two more years.

ENTER THE WORLD BANK

Despite this wave of resistance, the central administration at U of S has continued to advance "the innovation agenda." Even when faced with temporary setbacks, the commercialization of research proceeds apace, and links with the corporate market become stronger.

One powerful source of the market model of education and university governance is the World Bank's privatization manifesto, presented at the UNESCO World Conference on Higher Education in Paris in October 1998. It demanded nothing less than "radical change, or restructuring ... which means altering who the faculty are, how they behave, the way they are organized, and the way they work and are compensated." At the same time, the report recognized that any such program of reform would result in widespread resistance: "In the case of public universities, the faculty have additional means with which to resist threats of radical change and job loss: *the idea of the university as a proper bastion of continuity and tradition*; *the tradition of academic freedom*; *and the army of students, former students, and would be students*, most of whom are *articulate, energetic, politically volatile*, and generally able to be enlisted [sic] in the cause of opposing the government's efforts to radically alter *their* university."[233] In other words, faculty, rooted in a tradition of knowledge as a public good, can appeal to academic freedom as a necessary condition for its advancement and dissemination. When buttressed by an "army" of articulate and politically active students and alumni/alumnae, they are capable of disrupting any program of "innovation" proposed by governments or the private sector. This description matches perfectly the actions of faculty and students engaged in resisting cuts to the liberal arts at U of S.

Not only did the World Bank warn administrators that political opposition to market reforms was likely, but it pointed to the dangers of such action on the part of faculty and students: "While public universities resist radical change, *they are not immune to the loss of large amounts of public revenue occasioned by the forces listed above* [i.e., faculty/student resistance]. In fact, the very short-term robustness of the university ... may be its worst enemy in *the competition for increasingly scarce public revenues* ... [for there may be a need] to *close down inefficient campuses, or lay off faculty no longer considered relevant* to the needs of students, the economy, or for· that matter the university."[234] The threat to universities is palpable and multifaceted. On the one hand, resistance to market reforms endangers continued public funding; on the other, the ability to absorb cuts undermines their capacity to compete for scarce government revenues. Faced with this dilemma, some "inefficient" campuses will have to be closed – namely, those that do not bring new goods and services to market – and faculty not engaged in such research will be laid off. This message is repeated in slightly different form in the planning documents at U of S. The dangers of government underfunding can only be avoided by following, in particular, the market imperative of "we must compete" for research dollars. This means that U of S *must* close down "inefficient" departments and lay off faculty not contributing to the process of "increasing the value of innovation."

The influence of the World Bank is neither surprising nor limited to U of S.[235] The 1998 report was one of many such instruments designed to impose market reforms on education, even when they proved unsuccessful.[236] Governments and universities have been keen to show themselves pliant to the bank's prescriptions. Only a few months later, in May 1999, the federal government's Expert Panel on the Commercialization of University Research produced its own report, which reinforced the World Bank's approach, setting the stage for the kinds of market reforms that have washed over U of S and other Canadian universities.[237]

A FAMILIAR PATTERN
AT THE UNIVERSITY OF ALBERTA

The "research intensiveness" dominant at U of S has generated what Professor Susan Haack calls "a preposterous environment" in which market imperatives drive "research in the sciences[, which] has become very expensive; a culture of grants-and-research-projects has grown up; and science has become, *inter alia*, big business. The consequences for science are not altogether healthy: think of ... the temptation to shade the truth about success or importance of one's project, of the cost to the progress of science when a condition of some body's supporting the research is that the results be withheld from the rest of the scientific community."[238] An overemphasis on research grants tied to the market distorts the culture of science, undermining its integrity to advance and disseminate shared knowledge.

The University of Alberta (U of A), as one of the leading research intensive universities in Canada, privileges research in the natural and applied sciences that meets the needs of the market. Its success rate in attracting hundreds of millions of dollars from government and corporate coffers is the envy of universities like U of S (whose "cumulative research performance" in 2007–08 amounted to $152 million, according to President MacKinnon).[239] Whereas the Canada Foundation for Innovation ($33.8 million), the Natural Sciences and Engineering Research Council ($39.8 million), and the Canadian Institutes for Health Research ($39.2 million) awarded a total of $112.8 million to U of A in 2006–07, the Social Sciences and Humanities Research Council provided only $9.5 million (with the SSHRC Indirect Costs Program providing an additional $17.2 million).[240] This bias in funding – more than ten-to-one in favour of research dollars to projects in the natural and applied sciences – reflects the national trend of a decade earlier, in which SSHRC funding was one-quarter that of NSERC, even though 40 percent of faculty teach and conduct research in the humanities and social sciences.[241]

Table 3 underlines this point even more graphically. The Faculty of Medicine and Oral Health Sciences received $224 million, almost half of the "total sponsored research revenue" at the U of A in the same year.[242] Research funding to the faculties of science, engineering, agriculture, forestry, and home economics ($142.9 million) totalled more than 50 percent of that awarded to Medicine. The Faculty of Arts, however, received $7.5 million. Combined CIHR,

Table 3
Research funding by faculty, University of Alberta, 2006–07*

AGRICULTURE, FORESTRY, AND HOME ECONOMICS   Total: 29.1 million
NSERC $3.8 million; CIHR $600,000; Other** $10.4 million;
Canadian business $9 million; Foreign business $440,000

ARTS   Total: 7.5 million
SSHRC $2.5 million; NSERC and CIHR $288,416; Other** 1.95 million;
Canadian business $47,000

ENGINEERING   Total: 42.1 million
NSERC $11.8 million; CIHR $377,000; Other** 19 million;
Canadian business $6.3 million; Foreign business $703,000

MEDICINE AND ORAL HEALTH SCIENCES   Total: 224.0 million
CIHR $31.4 million; NSERC $1.4 million; SSHRC $72,000; Other** $128.8 million;
Canadian business $11 million; Foreign business $2.5 million

SCIENCE   Total: $71.7 million
NSERC $17 million; CIHR 1.5 million; SSHRC $186,000; Other** $40.4 million;
Canadian business $4.4 million; Foreign business $1 million

TOTAL SPONSORED RESEARCH REVENUE (ALL SOURCES) $461.4 million

---

* Only government and corporate funding listed. Faculties not included are: business, education, law, Native studies, nursing, pharmacy and pharmaceutical sciences, physical education and recreation, public health, rehabilitation medicine, and extension.
** These are unspecified grants from both the federal and provincial governments.
Source: http://www.ualberta.ca/IDO/databook/index.html, 1–4, (viewed 16 July 2008)

NSERC, and SSHRC funding for Medicine, Science, Engineering, and Agriculture stood at $63.2 million, in marked contrast to the $2.8 million received by Arts.[243] Even more striking is the money obtained from "Other" federal and provincial grants. While medicine was awarded $128.8 million and Science, Engineering, and Forestry together received $69.8 million (making a total for the four faculties of $208.8 million), arts received only $1.95 million.

The *University of Alberta Data Book* also shows that corporate funding from Canadian companies amounted to $35.6 million, a figure greater than that from the Canada Foundation for Innovation. The Faculty of Arts received $46,000, whereas $11 million went to the Faculty of Medicine and Oral Health Sciences, including investments from multinational pharmaceutical companies amounting to $2.5 million.[244] Among these were Hoffmann La Roche ($593,000), Pfizer Canada ($358,000), Merck Frosst Canada ($343,000), GlaxoSmithKline ($318,000), and AstraZeneca ($164,000). Of the

$5 million from foreign multinationals, Philip Morris USA and US Smokeless Tobacco provided $924,000, though it is unclear if this money was for research in the medical sciences. Oil companies like Shell, Haliburton, and Imperial Oil were among the "donors," but Syncrude Canada ($1.3 million) and Suncor Energy ($752,000) were the largest investors, presumably for engineering research on the Alberta Oil Sands.[245]

Among the "perils of preposterism" identified by Haack is the corporate secrecy surrounding not only the results of research but also the grants obtained.[246] Approaching the Research Services Office at U of A, I made several attempts to find out the details regarding the five largest grants in the natural and applied sciences, on the one hand, and the five largest in the social sciences and humanities, on the other. This information would have enabled me to determine whether or not market imperatives were driving the largest research projects at the university. I was eventually told by the communications coordinator that "the information you requested about research grants given to the University of Alberta *cannot be released due to privacy regulations*. Typically, the only information we can release is what funding agencies publish on their websites and what is published on our website."[247] This despite the fact that public money from the federal and provincial governments had provided $420 million, or 91 percent, of the research grants to U of A in 2006–07.

THE LOSS OF SUBSTANTIVE AUTONOMY AT U OF S

I have argued that the autonomy of U of S is undermined by the commercialization of its research. The goal of advancing and disseminating shared knowledge can only be undertaken in an institution that enjoys a relative independence from powerful external influence. Where private corporations together with governments require the university to "to increase the value of innovation," the university's distinctive value system is at risk. As I argue in chapter one, the two value systems embody opposing goals, motivations, methods, and standards of excellence.[248] I have provided concrete evidence of how this process has taken hold at U of S, the manner in which educational values are systematically overriden by those of the corporate market, and the ways in which institutional autonomy is being eclipsed.

One counterargument to my position is that autonomy is guaranteed though the University of Saskatchewan Act, 1995. Since the act is based on "a more collegial decision-making process rather than a corporate model," Professors Jack Billinton and Xin Li argue that the university is well placed to resist the very forces I have analyzed. They believe that "the original *Act* setting up the University was developed to allow for this autonomy and for freedom from political and denominational interference. These principles still exist in the latest version of the *Act*, as does the concept of academic freedom."[249] From its inception, the autonomy of U of S has been protected and "there is no overt political pressure or interference that inhibits the president in the fulfilment of duties." This independence is strengthened within the university by "a consultation process [between] the vice president academic ... [and] various faculty committees and the university community as a whole." But the planning process now taking place, while nominally "collegial," is based on market imperatives. Nevertheless, Billinton and Li conclude that, "in relation to substantive autonomy, the University of Saskatchewan is clearly free from any external interference."[250]

The argument is sound only if the premises are true and the reasoning valid. The "substantive autonomy" referred to in the conclusion is defined as "the power of the university or college in its corporate form to determine its own goals and programs."[251] The claim that U of S is autonomous in this sense is based on its being "clearly free from any external interference," which is open to question. Michael Hayden has traced a pattern of overt political pressure back to 1974, when the NDP government of Alan Blakeney created the University of Regina as a separate institution against the will of both faculty and senior administrators at U of S. The Universities Commission Act reaffirmed the power of the Board of Governors, half of whom were government appointees (six in number), to "institute or abolish anything it wished, from a college to an individual course, without recourse to anyone unless spending new money was involved."[252] This power to institute or disband a course or college still rests very much in their hands, although any such measure has to be approved by University Council. Since the structure of the board has not changed, U of S's "substantive autonomy" from "political interference" is far from secure.[253]

More recent examples of government interference predicated on the market model of education are further eroding institutional autonomy. In 1996, *The Report of the Minister's Special Representative on University Revitalization* concluded that both the University of Regina and U of S must do more to make the provincial economy competitive in the global market: "Saskatchewan's present and future prosperity depends upon access to growing international markets. Saskatchewan is the most trade-dependent province of Canada ... Thus, on a conceptual level, the international orientation of Saskatchewan suggests that its universities should take the lead in fostering international educational exchange ... [and] expand the range of goods and services ... The marketing of high quality university education can be seen as such an endeavour."[254] The author of the report, Harold MacKay, QC, prescribed university research and education as an instrument to "expand the range of goods and services ... [for] growing international markets," arguing for "the marketing of high quality university education" as a private good. The logic of the market led MacKay to recommend "revitalization" primarily in those areas that feed the provincial economy.[255] This familiar pattern of overriding educational goals in favour of "innovation" was endorsed in a later report by the minister for postsecondary education, in which he claimed that "it is more than ever in the public interest for the universities to render 'service to the state.'"[256]

The notion of "service to the state" invoked by President Murray in 1909 as "the University's watchword,"[257] was being reinterpreted almost exclusively as service to the market. This was evident from a third report, which measured outputs from both universities and evaluated their success in achieving the process of revitalization prescribed by MacKay. The report was a parody of market logic, declaring that, in order to meet the "growing knowledge needs of the 21st century [and] the learning needs of the new global economy ... [universities must adopt] multimedia learning [and] multimedia technologies."[258] How, one wonders, can an economy have "learning needs?" Surely, it is people who learn, not machines. Or, is learning to be reduced to a mechanical rather than an organic process in the brave new world of "multimedia technologies?"

The report systematically ignored such questions, continuing in the same vein: "the Canadian Light Source will generate strong synergies with Innovation Place and is estimated to be capable of attracting $35 million annually in commercial research and development activity." It extolled the virtues of spin-off companies in "fields as diverse as medical imaging, pharmaceuticals, biotechnology, mining, semi-conductors, and miniaturized machine components [following the example of VIDO, which] is committed to applied research, vaccine development and the commercialization of products [with its] more than 30 patents worldwide, with 10 pending in the United States."[259] The same kinds of claims that were once made about the economic impact of the CLS are repeated with regard to VIDO. Moreover, the report's projection that the CLS will attract $35 million annually in commercial and development activity is belied by the lack of corporate investment to date as well as by the $90 million cost of its five-year operating budget. Despite this counter-evidence, the report concluded that "the two universities' impact on the Saskatchewan economy is well over $1 billion annually,"[260] and the NDP's minister of postsecondary education declared that, "to their credit, the universities have hunkered down and attended to these [economic] priorities."[261]

By reducing the value of research to its market value, U of S, aided and abetted by the federal and provincial governments, has abrogated its commitment to substantive autonomy. While Walter Murray may not have understood this principle,[262] his successors are willing to abandon it altogether, reducing university education to a private good to be bought and sold like any other. Any semblance of institutional autonomy is fast becoming servitude to the corporate market.

5

Going beyond the Market:
Evaluating Teaching by Evaluating Learning

Customers are not evaluated. The point is to sell them something and make them want it and like it so that they or their sisters will return for more. Customers are always right and cannot be failed.

Patricia Marchak[1]

AN INITIAL EXPERIENCE WITH STUDENT EVALUATIONS OF TEACHING

One of the ways in which university teaching exemplifies the market model of education is with regard to student evaluations of teaching (SETS). SETS tend to indicate "customer satisfaction" rather than the extent to which learning has taken place, and they are an inaccurate measure of the quality of a professor's teaching. Their systemic inaccuracy stems from their market orientation, at least so I argue in this chapter.

My first experience of student questionnaires as a tool for evaluating teaching occurred during the mid-1970s. I had been hired by the Department of Philosophy at the University of Western Ontario to teach several undergraduate courses, one of which consisted of a section of philosophy of education with almost two hundred students. The course attracted undergraduates from across the university, a few of whom hoped to become teachers, some with a general interest in the subject, and many who had learned of its reputation as a "bird course." I made it clear in the very first lecture that this would not be the case: the content of the course would be intellectually challenging and students would have to work hard in order to obtain a decent grade. These statements were greeted with something less than enthusiasm by the group of students wishing to "cruise or

snooze their way to an A." It would not be long before my authority
was challenged. James Coté and Anton Allahar explain this kind of
reaction in the following way: "The large numbers of students who
now want high grades for little effort exacerbates this frustration,
as does the adversarial relationship that develops when professors
do not kowtow to pressures for easy grades from students who are
accustomed to putting out little or no effort."[2] Resentment on the
part of some students coupled with a growing adversarial relationship
was the result of my emphasis on high standards.

Soon after the beginning of term, a student asked me what I
believed the school system did well. "I've been sitting here for some
time," he said, "and I haven't heard you say a good word about it."
I replied that, since school systems in Canada were controlled by the
provinces, they were more decentralized than most, more open to
adult learners wishing to continue their education, and that many
teachers were dedicated professionals who cared both about their
students and their subjects. This did not satisfy the student, whose
dissatisfaction clearly reflected the views of others in the class.
Following a meeting in my office, his attitude changed somewhat
and he occasionally raised questions during lectures that showed a
willingness to entertain the distinction between education and schooling. Many of the students, however, remained adamant that a
school's emphasis on competition was justified and should override
any move towards collaborative and cooperative learning. Why?
Because "that's the way things are."

As the academic year wore on, the views of this group hardened.
Unwilling to accommodate conceptions of education that were at
odds with their own experience, they refused to question their own
assumptions. As "products" of the school system, they could not
understand why others might have failed where they had succeeded.
Some of the students did recognize the need for critical questioning;
but, as they were a minority, they were often hesitant to express their
views, preferring to come and see me with questions after class or
during office hours.

As a relatively new faculty member – this was only my third year
of university teaching – I was discouraged by the attitudes of the
majority of students. Lacking any previous experience with such a
large class, I made limited use of teaching methods that I have since
learned to employ with students who resist ideas: small group discussions, posing questions throughout lectures, having students give

presentations on themes they consider important, larger group discussions of central ideas, and the use of humour.[3] At the time, I was struggling to incorporate these approaches into my repertoire.

Towards the end of the academic year, questionnaires were administered to the class for the purpose of evaluating my "teaching effectiveness." The questions took the familiar form of a five-point Likert scale, ranging from "strongly agree" to "strongly disagree," measuring such variables as whether or not "the professor relates well to students," "knows his/her subject matter," "is available to students outside of the classroom," and so on. At no point were students asked what they had learned from the course, how they had learned it, or how they might apply such knowledge to future life experience.

The results of the anonymous questionnaires were tabulated and published during the summer by the University of Western Ontario Student Council, together with those from other undergraduate courses across the university.[4] Not surprisingly, my section of philosophy of education received a significantly lower rating than did the other courses I taught that year. (The alternate section taught by a senior member of the department received the same rating.) I remember quite clearly a conversation with a senior administrator, who, knowing of my particular interest in philosophy of education, asked, "What went wrong?" He was not persuaded by my explanation that the nature and size of the class, as well as the kinds of students taking it (many of whom only took one philosophy course during their academic careers), were sound reasons for the lower rating. His belief in student questionnaires as accurate instruments for evaluating teaching was unshaken. The head of the department shared the same view.[5]

STUDENT EVALUATIONS OF TEACHING (SETS) TODAY

Since that time, the widespread use of SETS at universities in Canada and elsewhere has become a ritual. Faculty administer, and students routinely fill out, questionnaires towards the end of courses in the belief that they will improve teaching by providing accurate information about "teaching effectiveness." Students are largely unaware that SETS are used "for summative purposes" to provide "information used in decisions such as renewal of probation, tenure, promotion and right of first refusal." At some universities, standardized questionnaires have been adopted with the supposed goal of making teaching "more accountable to students and teachers alike."[6]

Even though they may appear desirable,[7] SETS are beset with problems. Any attempt to evaluate teaching that fails to take into account the different content, goals, methods, and context of each course does not reflect the complexities of the educational process.[8] Yet the use of standardized questionnaires presupposes that teaching and learning is the same in all disciplines and in every class. Strong advocates of SETS, like Herbert Marsh and Lawrence Roche, concede that "SETS are difficult to validate because *no single criterion of effective teaching is sufficient.*"[9] And advocate Peter Seldin states, "It is virtually impossible to design a single student questionnaire that is equally effective for a large lecture, a seminar, and a laboratory course."[10] All of which raises the following question: why have SETS become such an important part of the institutional landscape?

In this chapter I critically examine some of the evidence concerning SETS and the extent to which they embody market values.[11] In-depth interviews conducted with faculty and students in three different colleges at the University of Saskatchewan provide data on three main issues: the alleged validity of SETS as instruments for evaluating teaching and learning; the extent to which they reflect the view of "students as customers" seeking satisfaction in the market; and the ways in which they undermine the goals of education. The structure of this chapter differs from that of the others: first, I summarize the views of faculty and students with regard to each question, and then I reflect upon the emergent data by showing how they are mirrored in the literature. After re-emphasizing the conclusions reached on the basis of this evidence, I critically examine "the learning paradigm" as a flawed attempt to overcome the limitations of standardized questionnaires and the market model. I conclude by showing how teaching and learning could be evaluated along Whiteheadian lines in ways that avoid the pitfalls of the market.

DO SETS HELP US TO UNDERSTAND AND EVALUATE TEACHING AND LEARNING?

Professors' Views

The three faculty members I interviewed, all of whom had received awards for teaching, believed strongly that students should have the opportunity to evaluate their teaching. However, they recognized that SETS alone were inadequate as summative forms of evaluation because they did not provide reliable information about teaching and learning.

The professor of medicine was the most supportive of SETS based on a Likert scale. They helped her to improve her teaching by bringing "stuff out that you would never have thought to ask." At the same time, she acknowledged that "direct feedback from people in the classes ... is more helpful than all the Likert scales in the world." She regularly used formative evaluation of this kind to determine the strengths and weaknesses of her teaching, especially when trying something new in her classes. Similarly, the faculty member in arts and science used a formative evaluation process to ask about specific works used in a course or to "probe a dynamic in the class that [she was] unhappy about." The professor of education found that "open-ended questions [were] far more helpful" than standardized answers on a Likert scale because "they [gave] a more detailed account of how well [he was] presenting knowledge." Students' comments had led him to de-emphasize lectures in favour of an approach to learning that emphasized "ways in which to balance freedom and discipline in learning."

All three faculty members were sceptical of the introduction of a standardized evaluation that was being considered by university council. The professor from arts and science believed it would be skewed in favour of the natural sciences, while the faculty member from education thought it would "tend to measure the professor's popularity with students, not what they had learned." As a result, he did not believe such forms should be used in decisions about tenure and promotion. The professor of medicine disagreed because standardized forms would "certainly make the work easier" for committees making judgments about tenure and promotion. But she hoped that such forms would contain "unique" questions peculiar to each discipline in order to ensure that they were "comparing apples to apples" and did "not skew the way those scores happen."

Significantly, none of the faculty believed that SETS enabled her or him to understand what his/her students actually learned. The professor in arts and science thought that learning "takes place best when students are getting pleasure from what they are reading," but she balanced this approach with a conviction that there were some things students needed to learn. Required readings often elicited "a totally different appreciation by the time we have finished discussing them." It was not the use of SETS but, rather, "assignments and what [was] going on in the class that let [her] know what they [were] learning" – a point that I take up in the final section of the chapter. The faculty member in education went further, stating that SETS were flawed because they did not provide any evidence of what students learned but, rather, only their "attitudes towards teachers' observable behaviours," which are an "inadequate and unjust assessment of teaching and learning." While the professor of medicine believed in the reliability of SETS as a means of assessing "teaching effectiveness," she supplemented it with formative evaluations in the manner already described.

Students' Views

None of the students found SETS to be effective tools for improving the teaching of those professors most in need of it. This view was shared by students in both arts and science and education. One commented: "I wonder if those professors who just show up could really learn from the evaluations. Are they just hardwired to not care about teaching?" While another added, "I don't think that a lot of teachers take feedback seriously or look at it at all." Too often, "the only thing that mattered was their research," and professors made it clear that students were a hindrance to their "getting back to their laboratory." The students in medicine were also sceptical of the effectiveness of SETS because professors often introduced them as "a requirement of the department" rather than as a tool for becoming "proactive in terms of making changes based on student comments."

On the other hand, all of the students really appreciated faculty who used formative evaluations in an attempt to improve their teaching "because it was important to them." They also respected those who cared deeply about their subject and conveyed their enthusiasm to students. Professors of this kind took the time to find out about students' interests in order to incorporate them into their courses. One student gave the example of a literature course in which the faculty member built the curriculum around those plays with which students were less familiar, making the class "one of my best experiences." The ability to relate teaching and learning to the needs of students had little or nothing to do with SETS but, rather, stemmed from the ability of professors to engage in dialogue with students about matters of mutual concern.

The students in education did not believe that SETS reflected what they learned in courses or how they had learned it. This was because they were often constructed on the basis of three basic requests: (1) "Evaluate the content of the course"; (2) "Evaluate whether the professor has given you time to meet outside class time"; and (3) "Evaluate whether the professor has made the subject matter interesting." In the words of another student, "They do not allow you to put a comment in about what you learned. It's always just about the professor's methods." Another student pointed out that learning should be considered as an integral part of the process "and it should be valuable, something we can take with us ... we should be able to apply it, especially in a College of Education." The students in medicine were divided: one believed that SETS only reflected "teaching styles and course format," while another commented: "[they] make me reflect on how I learn as an individual ... certain teaching styles stand out that I know help me retain things better."

Only two of the students were initially aware that SETS were used in decisions about tenure and promotion. Both were in the College of Medicine, and one was "still skeptical that they make a difference." One student in arts and science went on to question the validity of SETS in this regard. She believed that they simply reflected "students' attitudes and work habits" and that they should not be taken as a serious guide to a professor's teaching ability. "If they *are* used to determine tenure," she explained, "I think that they are probably a little out of whack [and] should not necessarily have any weight."

Reflections on the Data

This general scepticism towards the validity of SETS reflects four central points in the literature. First, the use of a standardized questionnaire based on a Likert scale in no way guarantees scientific validity. The numerical tabulation of scores, which are then shown as means, standard deviations, or distributions is not a sufficient condition for validity. A prior question has to be asked; namely, are the students' judgments upon which these numbers are generated accurate? Some of the questions used to elicit them are unproblematical ("Was the professor on time?" or "Were course requirements clearly stated?"); however, as Stanley Coren argues, others, such as "Did the professor demonstrate a clear understanding of the material?" or "Was the material covered in the course appropriate?"

cannot always be validly answered by students. The reasons for this are clear: "Both [questions] presuppose prior knowledge and understanding of the substantive material from which the course was drawn as well as an understanding of how that content relates to other aspects of the discipline ... Remember that experts in any field often have different views about which course material is appropriate."[12] Coren's conclusions are based on a study of several hundred students in introductory courses at the University of British Columbia. My own qualitative research was conducted with final-year students in arts and science and education, and second-year medical students at U of S. While this group is more knowledgeable than their younger counterparts, one can still question whether or not their opinions provide an adequate basis for evaluating the content of a course. The professor of medicine was insistent on this point, even though she supported the idea of a standardized questionnaire.

Second, if it is true that the data upon which they are based are flawed, what *do* SETS measure? Evidence compiled by the Canadian Association of University Teachers (CAUT) suggests they simply reflect students' attitudes towards a course or a professor rather than what they have learned. The CAUT policy begins as follows: "It cannot be emphasized strongly enough that the evaluation questionnaires of the type we are discussing here measure only the attitudes of the students towards the class and the instructor. They do not measure the amount of learning which has taken place."[13] Ratings given by students on SETS tend to reflect their perceptions of their instructor's personality but are weak indications of what they have actually learned since SETS are "somewhat blunt instruments"[14] in this regard. A recent article analyzing a variety of SETS used at the University of Regina supports this view. Students were asked to comment on their "satisfaction in general with the course" as well as "instructor behaviors" but not on "the instructor's effectiveness in promoting student learning."[15] A questionnaire used by the Department of Psychology at U of S fares only slightly better, containing one question out of forty-eight that asks: "What one thing was done in the course that facilitated your learning?"[16] Even when the issue of student learning has been addressed, Marsh and Roche admit that "researchers have emphasized a narrow definition ... typically operationalized by performance on multiple-choice tests."[17]

Third, proponents of SETS respond to this criticism by arguing that they are primarily designed to measure "teaching effectiveness," not student learning. Teaching effectiveness is then defined in terms of "observable teacher behaviours," which are, in turn, related to student performance. A widely used model for SETS, known as the Teachers Behaviors Inventory, lists the following observable teacher behaviours as items for evaluation by students on a Likert scale: "Answer[s] students questions thoroughly," "Explain[s] subject matter in familiar colloquial language," "Encourage[s] students to ask questions," and "Incorporate[s] students' ideas into lecture."[18] So far, so good. But the inventory goes on to list the following: "Speaks in a dramatic or expressive way," "Gestures with hands or arms," and "Tells jokes and humorous anecdotes." By classifying these appealing "behaviors" as integral parts of teaching, the inventory suggests that they are *necessary conditions* for the dissemination of knowledge. The inclusion of "Stutters, mumbles, or slurs words," "Says 'um' or 'ah,'" and "Covers very little material in class sessions"[19] discriminates against professors who are nervous, foreign, thorough, demanding, or who present ideas students don't like.[20]

Fourth, another advocate of SETS believes that the interpretation of them for the purposes of tenure and promotion is "the major validity problem."[21] Bill McKeachie argues that tenure and promotion committees often do not understand how to interpret the data presented, especially when SETS are tabulated statistically and used in different contexts. McKeachie shows how mistaken it is to assume, as the *Framework for Student Evaluation of Teaching at the University of Saskatchewan* does, that a standardized questionnaire "with demonstrable reliability and validity in one academic setting can be assumed to have reliability and validity in similar settings for other academic units."[22] This point was made most forcefully by the student in arts and science, who believed that, while SETS should be included in decisions about tenure, they should not be weighted too heavily for fear of putting the whole process "out of whack."

DO SETS SUPPORT THE VIEW OF "STUDENTS AS CUSTOMERS"?

Professors' Views

All three faculty members believed that the conception of "students as customers" was mistaken because, unlike customers in the market, students lack the knowledge they are seeking. The professor of education found the view that "the customer is always right" misconceived because the job of teachers is to challenge students' beliefs, not to satisfy their wants as customers: "students do not always have the appropriate knowledge, and it is counterproductive to behave as though they do." This was reiterated by the faculty member in medicine, who commented: "The truth is, when you are a first-year medical student, you don't know what you need to know." Professors "have learned a thing or two" and "students need to trust our wisdom, and our judgment, and our experience." Moreover, since the goal of medical education is to improve the health of future patients, it necessarily involves the common good of society. Health care in Canada "is not truly a private enterprise but exists by virtue of society determining it's a common good that we will build together."

The professor in arts and science saw the view of "students as customers" as "a problematical model" because "it commodifies education and [she] definitely [didn't] think education should be a commodity." There is, she explained, "some form of contradiction between the market and education" because "if you are a customer and you don't like what you are getting, you should be able to return the product." This is far different in the case of education. Unlike the market, which deals exclusively with private goods, education, by its nature, involves "the public good," which means that "what society needs a student to hear, to learn, to be exposed to, are things that the student may not find at all comfortable, or make them happy." If education is to serve the common good, "some people's minds need to be opened and there must be classroom discourse" about controversial issues that "are challenging various kinds of hegemony."[23] As a result, "there is a real potential conflict between the idea of the 'student as customer' and the public good" because "sometimes what the individual may perceive to be in their best interest is not."

The professor of education also believed that once students are treated as customers, academic freedom is undermined. "Faculty who teach only what customers want," he said, "end up abandoning their own views if they run counter to those of students, or to those of society at large." The freedom to express well-researched opinions based on theories unpopular with those in power is thereby endangered. Even though SETS tended to reflect the view of "students as customers," he did not feel they inhibited his own academic freedom in the classroom. In contrast, the faculty member in arts and science recognized that, "if [she] started to get a lot of negative student evaluations," SETS would compromise her freedom to express views that challenged hegemony in its various forms.[24]

Students' Views

The three groups of students had different, sometimes contradictory, views about their being customers in an educational market. Students in education had, due to the growing cost of their education, reluctantly come to see themselves as customers buying a product. Escalating tuition fees and greater indebtedness had forced them to abandon their initial enthusiasm for learning as having a value in itself. "When I came to university," one student exclaimed, "I made myself a promise that I didn't come here to get a degree, or a job, or anything. I just came here to learn." But all that had changed "because I am so far in debt now" – a theme reiterated by another student, who commented: "Every class I take I want to be worth the money. This was never an issue before, and I thought everything I was taking was valuable." Without being prompted, the students criticized U of S for encouraging the view of students as customers: "Every which way you turn, [the university] pressures us to buy their merchandise – buy this, buy that ... I think it is really difficult not to feel like a consumer with the university being so corporate."

The students in medicine totally rejected the idea of being customers. They saw education as a different kind of activity from that of the market: "I don't think I've ever viewed myself as a customer. Regardless of whether you have a poor professor or a great one ... you need to take responsibility for your own learning." Another cautioned against the idea of "the customer always being right" because "education has to be focused on the learning abilities of the group as a whole," an idea taken up by a third student, who stated: "if the pressures are from an individual customer, then that might undermine education." A fourth student reemphasized this point: "When a small group of people that are the most vocal get what they want, it might not be in the best interest of the group as a whole."

However, some of the students in arts and science felt that being a customer not only enabled them to "shop around" for the best professors but was also actually conducive to their education. One student saw herself "as a customer out to purchase the best education possible." She did not believe this diminished the value of her education: "I have really high standards for myself. I rearrange courses to get the hard ones, because I want them to challenge me." As a result, she felt she could "share [in the] wealth of knowledge and come out a better person, one who feels really satisfied and well rounded, and has a new way of thinking, a deeper way of thinking. So that is what I am shopping for." A second student went much further in her support for a consumer approach, saying: "I think we should be viewing ourselves *more* as customers getting a service from our professors and paying them for it." The problem, she said, was that, "unlike customers, who have the power to demand things, students were afraid to return a crappy product." U of S should adopt "customer service just like at Future Shop."

This view of "students as customers" was directly related to tuition fees, which had doubled in a decade, making them the highest in western Canada.[25] Students in arts and science, like their colleagues in education, expressed a fear of debt. According to one, "when I think of the debt I am incurring, it's like a large cloud moving over my education." To which another added, "it makes me feel like I need to get certain things out of my education or I'll feel cheated." And another: "If we are to endure this debt for at least four years, it does add up, and even at the end we have no guarantee of getting a job, so we have to be consumers."

Reflections on the Data

In what ways, then, do SETS contribute to the view of "students as customers"? A connection between rising tuition fees and the need to provide greater "customer satisfaction" can be found in a policy document on the evaluation of teaching at U of S, which reads: "As students at the national and local level are experiencing rising tuition fees, they want to know that the evaluations they complete will improve the classroom experience."[26] The authors of the document assume that the adoption of a standardized questionnaire will persuade students they are getting their money's worth for the high costs of tuition. Faculty whose role becomes one of "customer service representative" persuade students to buy a product, and their customer satisfaction is quantified on a scale from 1 to 5. The statement is blind to the contradictory ways in which education and the market achieve their goals. On the one hand, "the better the education, the more its bearers become independent to think and do on their own," a belief expressed by a student in medicine as requiring her to take responsibility for her own learning. In contrast, "the better the market, the more its agents depend on others to provide their thinking and doing,"[27] an attitude that was reflected by a student in arts and science who wanted a "customer service" department that would give refunds on courses she did not like. In the former case, the student understood the importance of independent learning, whereas in the latter the student wanted the market to do her thinking for her.

While sceptical of the efficacy of SETS as instruments of assessment, the students in both education and arts and science had succumbed to the view of being "customers" precisely because they were so deeply in debt. The main difference between them was that those in education still resisted this approach, while some of those in arts and science accepted and even welcomed it. However, although one such student spoke of her "satisfaction" in "shopping around" for courses she made sure they were intellectually challenging and not just those in which she would get high marks with little or no effort. She was not seeking satisfaction of her wants through the purchase of a private good but,[28] rather, was seeking a deeper fulfillment that would enable her to "become a better person." This was very different from the student who wanted "a system of customer service" so that she could return "a crappy product ... just like at Future Shop."

The desire for "customer satisfaction" on the part of students is closely connected to the use of SETS. If SETS primarily measure students' attitudes towards their professors, they also reflect customer satisfaction. And customer satisfaction can work against the goal of education in the following manner, as described by Coté and Allahar. Professors seeking tenure and promotion may well begin to teach in ways that improve their scores on SETS. As a result, they become "as nice as possible, teach easy courses, give high grades, use the least possible amount of assessment, and do not require independent work. Of course, all of these options work against the ostensible mission of the university."[29] Both the goal of education to disseminate shared knowledge and its method of working autonomously to meet its requirements are undermined by the overriding demand to satisfy the expectations of students for high grades.

While customer satisfaction may be appropriate to the market, it is an inaccurate measure of what takes place in the classroom. It should be restricted in the context of university education as an inadequate criterion for determining whether or not effective teaching and learning have taken place. Dissatisfaction may well arise from students being asked to question their own presuppositions in ways that foster learning. If such dissatisfaction is excluded by considerations of customer satisfaction, the process of teaching and learning becomes distorted in a fundamental way, and the academic freedom of both faculty and students is threatened by market-oriented expectations.[30] An emphasis on customer satisfaction undermines a professor's capacity to pose questions critical of her students' preconceptions, as is indicated by the professor in arts and science.[31] Yet this problem does not register with some advocates of SETS, who have "seldom criticized [SETS] as measures of student satisfaction with instruction."[32]

Some of these limitations are now recognized by tenure and promotion committees, which often include teaching portfolios and peer evaluation in their decision making.[33] These approaches may provide a more comprehensive picture of classroom practice, but they also suffer from bias, are difficult to interpret, and require faculty to spend an inordinate amount of time in their preparation.[34]

DO SETS UNDERMINE THE GOALS OF EDUCATION?

Professors' Views

The professor of education believed that SETS were flawed because they only reflected students' attitudes towards professors, not what they actually learned. While some relevant information was available from SETS, they were an inadequate instrument for assessing teaching and learning, especially when based on a Likert scale. He believed they undermined the goals of education by blocking other flexible, open-ended, and inclusive forms of evaluation capable of providing an accurate picture of what took place in the classroom. The faculty member in arts and science agreed. A standardized questionnaire was inconsistent with the goals of education because "objective questions" ruled out the very "discipline-specific questions" required for any rigorous assessment of teaching and learning.[35] She designed her own instruments of summative evaluation, which provided her with ongoing feedback about her teaching. It was not the use of SETS but, rather, "students' assignments and what is going on in class that let [her] know what they [were] learning." The professor of medicine also recognized that "direct feedback from people in classes from a formative point of view is more helpful than all the Likert scales in the world." It enabled her to understand what students were learning, especially when used in conjunction with regular assignments such as essays and tests.

All three professors agreed that the goal of education was to serve the public interest. For the professor of medicine, the goal of medical education was to improve the health of future patients as part of the common good of society. As "health care providers," the status of physicians was based on "a covenantal relationship, which cannot be reduced to a contractual/customer one without distorting its distinctly public character." The professor in arts and science believed that the common good was best served when educators raised questions that challenged both the hegemony of those in power and the assumptions of students, precisely because "some peoples' minds need to be opened." Similarly, the professor of education criticized those educators who did not provide opportunities for students to question their own assumptions. Without this process of critical and reflective inquiry, the goal of education as a public good could not be served.

U of S's contribution to the public good, however, was being undermined. According to the professor in arts and science, "a more research intensive university" is one where "what really matters is getting research grants." As a result of this emphasis, teaching suffered, and whereas "teaching and research at the university should go hand-in-hand," the connection between the two was being severed in favour of grant maximization. The result, she argued, was a palpable decline in the quality of undergraduate education, which, combined with higher tuition fees, strengthened the view of "students as customers."

All three faculty members were sceptical of the university's declared goal of rejuvenating teaching in the form of the "Teacher-Scholar Model," an approach based on research conducted in the United States. The goal is a laudable one; namely, to enable students to learn in ways that connect their lived experience with the subject matter taught by faculty who engaged in "the scholarship of teaching"[36] – a point to which I return in the final section of this chapter. However, the professor of education believed the U of S's adoption of the "model" was "an attempt to make it seem as though teaching matters when the real emphasis is on 'research intensiveness,' which means getting more and larger grants." His colleague in arts and science felt that the university's emphasis on so-called "excellence" in research was not matched by "a corresponding discourse around the importance of teaching ... In theory, this university supports the 'Teacher-Scholar Model.' In theory. Does it do so in practice?" She had found little evidence of this. The professor of medicine believed that recognition of "the scholarship of teaching" was confined to "isolated examples of some of us who have been promoted largely on the strength of our teaching record." In general, however, "the mediocre teacher whom everybody acknowledges is a catastrophe, as long as they are a competent researcher, continues to rise through the ranks." The promise of the "Teacher-Scholar Model" to strengthen the role of teaching and learning was not being fulfilled.[37]

Students' Views

Many of the students found that SETS did not help them to understand what they had learned in a course and did little or nothing to further the goals of education. They recognized that the process of education was broader than vocational training, even though they had come to see themselves in the role of "customers." The students in education believed that the goals of education were undermined in the following ways: they were constantly thinking about how to pay for the high costs of their education; they tended to concentrate "mindlessly" on the marks needed for scholarships and bursaries; and they competed for grades rather than valuing what they learned. In the words of one student, "Marks and money play a huge role in our being programmed to think in this way." The students in arts and science were largely in agreement. They felt deprived of the opportunity to pursue a "broader-based liberal arts education" because of the costs involved, and one of them questioned the tendency of the university to "create employable people rather than better people. Is that the true aim of education?" The students in medicine saw the need for education to focus on the "abilities of the group as a whole" rather than to comply with "pressures from an individual customer," which "might undermine education." One of them felt that the use of SETS enabled him to reflect on those teaching styles that helped him to learn.

Reflections on the Data

If, indeed, the goal of education is to advance and disseminate shared knowledge, then freedom of inquiry is a precondition for this process.[38] Yet SETS are based on a behaviourist framework that undermines free inquiry. "Observable teacher behaviours" are, as I have shown, the main criteria for determining "teacher effectiveness."[39] These "behaviours" form part of "a scientific analysis and hence an effective technology ... of behavior," whose goal is the "reinforcement" of "operant behavior." According to B.F. Skinner, a repertoire of behaviours can be established through a process of rewards, or "reinforcers," in which "a bit of behavior is followed by a certain kind of consequence" so that "it is more likely to occur again."[40] For example, professors whose "observable behaviours" are reinforced on the basis of student preference are more likely to repeat them. Improvements to their teaching can then be made by adopting the behaviours that appeal to students and avoiding those that do not. This may involve professors inflating their grades in order to receive better student evaluations as a precondition for tenure and promotion.[41] Even those "personality types" who have greatest difficulty in adapting to the demands of "effective teaching" can improve their performance, which "is composed of learnable skills and behaviors."[42] The idea that teaching is reducible to a set of skills, which can then be measured, reinforced, and assessed as "observable behaviours," forms a common theme among those who advocate SETS.[43]

There is a certain irony in the fact that SETS are used as a "corrective mechanism" on professors when the behaviourist theory underlying them was first introduced as a means of controlling students. Skinner, after all, insists that a teacher should use "the most effective methods" to "improve his [sic] control of the student" by creating "behavioral processes" that result in "useful productive repertoires" and "successful work."[44] In other words, s/he must reinforce those behaviours that meet the well-defined, task-oriented objectives s/he devises in order to ensure control over her students. Skinner goes further, asserting that freedom, like dignity, is an antiquated notion to be expunged. By "dispossessing man [sic]" of the "particularly troublesome" view that "a person is free," he shifts "the credit as well as the blame to the environment" in the form of consequences that reinforce behaviours. "Sweeping changes" can then be made to the "traditional practices" of education so that "a certain amount of control can be tolerated."[45] Among these sweeping changes has been the introduction of a "technology of behaviour" capable of providing flawed data to administrators concerned with measuring and assessing "observable teacher behaviours." The "efficiency" of SETS in achieving this task depends upon how well students in the classroom environment elicit the operant behaviours required of faculty.

Some might argue that the validity of SETS is independent of behaviourism. However, the belief that teaching is reducible to "skills and behaviours" that are "learnable" as "observable teacher behaviours," in the manner suggested by the Teachers Behaviors Inventory, is an integral part of behaviourism. The theory excludes the interior lives of both teachers and students as part of the "black box" that is beyond scientific observation.[46] But this approach is inconsistent with the very notions of teaching and learning. Only where the pedagogical relationship enables students to think autonomously, critically, and imaginatively by examining commonly held presuppositions can it be truly educational. Without the opportunity to question knowledge claims on the basis of the broadest experiential evidence, teaching is reduced to indoctrination and learning becomes no more than the regurgitation of "inert ideas."[47]

Conclusions

The following conclusions are based on interviews with faculty and students as well as on an analysis of the literature. Throughout my inquiry I have searched conscientiously not only for evidence that would confirm them but also for evidence that would disconfirm them.[48]

1 SETS are poor instruments for evaluating professors' teaching because they primarily reflect students' attitudes towards teachers.[49] As a result, information gathered from SETS "is often biased and inaccurate."[50]
2 SETS are "difficult to validate because no single criterion of effective teaching is sufficient."[51] Standardized questionnaires such as those

used at many universities ignore the fact that "it is virtually impossible to design a single student questionnaire that is equally effective
for a large lecture, a seminar, and a laboratory course."[52]

3 SETS tell us very little about what or how students learn.[53]

4 SETS support the view of "students as customers" who know best
   and cannot be wrong,[54] and they reflect "the wider consumer
   mentality of contemporary society ... that encourages the perception that professors should satisfy students' expectations"[55] and
   fulfill the role of "customer service representatives."

5 SETS strengthen the view of "students as customers" by ignoring
   the opposing logics of achievement found in education and the
   market, respectively.[56]

6 SETS undermine the goal of education as the advancement and
   dissemination of shared knowledge by treating it as a private
   good.[57]

7 The "observable teacher behaviours" measured by SETS are an
   integral part of behaviourism, which precludes free and critical
   inquiry.[58]

8 SETS undermine academic freedom to the extent that faculty feel
   constrained not to challenge students' assumptions.[59]

If students know best and cannot be wrong, then "it is impossible
to find an easy way of reconciling [the] varying demands for teaching
excellence and academic freedom."[60] Fortunately, however, students
attend universities in order to learn what they often do not know.
All of the faculty and students I interviewed subscribed to this basic
idea. To think otherwise is to misunderstand the goal of education
as the creation and dissemination of knowledge to be shared as a
public good.

DANGERS OF THE "LEARNING PARADIGM"

Advocates of SETS have tried to address these issues by placing
greater emphasis on student learning. Their inability to break the
shackles of behaviourist theory, coupled with an unshaken belief in
standardized questionnaires, indicates an inability to recognize the
value of learning other than as "observable behaviours" seeking
customer satisfaction.

Herbert Marsh of the University of Western Sydney has devised a
questionnaire called the *Students' Evaluation of Educational Quality*

(SEEQ), which contains several questions on student learning and another section that can be adapted by faculty to suit their particular disciplines.[61] Marsh's influence in Canada has been considerable. At least two universities currently use SEEQ – the University of Manitoba and St Mary's University[62] – and U of S is currently following suit. The U of S report proposing its use was "based on the assumption that student learning is to be the goal of the teaching process," but in the absence of any account of what learning actually is, the default position becomes that of behaviourism. In other words, the measurement and evaluation of "observable learning behaviours" are likely to form the basis of SEEQ's approach, especially since Marsh himself is within the behaviourist camp. Moreover, the report's advocacy of a "common survey-instrument" designed to be "*summative* (i.e., to assist administrators in making informed and fair personnel decisions)"[63] ignores the problems involved in interpreting SETS, as reported by McKeachie[64] and the professors whom I interviewed.

An even clearer example of the use of behaviourist theory as a tool to steer both students and faculty towards the market is the so-called "Learning Paradigm." Its "primary drive," according to Robert Barr and John Tagg, "is to produce learning outcomes more efficiently" than the "Instruction Paradigm," which is currently "dominant" at universities. Their emphasis on "students' products ... outcomes [or] the effects of learning [that] can be measured"[65] means that evaluation of their work should be based on the following kinds of behaviours: "We could count the number of pages students write, the number of books they read, their number of hours at the computer, or the number of math problems they solve."[66] This, however, makes little sense. If students write poorly and without any appreciation of the books they have read, it hardly matters how long they spend at a computer. If they manage to solve a large number of math problems quite unrelated to a course on calculus, one would still want to question their knowledge of the subject matter.

The authors have little to say about the use of SETS, but it is likely that they would apply the same criteria to the assessment of observable teacher behaviours. The criteria of successful teaching would be uniformly quantitative: the number of students enrolled in a course, the number of As obtained, the number of dropouts from a course (the fewer the better), the number of hours spent in the classroom and courses taught, as well as the number of degrees held by the professor and so on. Once again, this makes little sense. Some of these criteria undermine the quality of teaching, falling foul of the overriding goal of ensuring "customer satisfaction," which I have already considered. Even advocates of SEEQ concede that "teaching effectiveness cannot be reduced to a single numerical value ... [because] teaching is a complex multidimensional activity,"[67] comprising a wide variety of factors. The subtleties of teaching and learning escape the crude model proposed by Barr and Tagg.

Their advocacy of "efficiency" in learning and their desire to achieve "a continuous improvement in [learning] productivity" is closely tied to an exclusively economic definition of productivity/ efficiency. "Under the Learning Paradigm," they write, "productivity is redefined as the cost per unit of learning per student ... Under this new definition ... it is possible to increase outcomes without increasing costs ... producing more with less ... because the more that is being produced [sic] is learning and not hours of instruction."[68] The goal of this "new" paradigm is to reconfigure universities so as to ensure the reduction of unit costs associated with teaching and learning. By emphasizing the learning pole of the pedagogical relationship, the authors aim to reduce the number of hours of instruction and, presumably, the number of faculty who teach – "producing more with less." But the market notion of efficiency/ productivity is "the enemy of scholarship in universities" because, as Conrad Russell has argued, it fails to take into account the "professional training, expertise and knowledge" of those qualified "to make an informed decision"[69] about teaching, learning, and research. "Efficiency" as a tool used by university administrators and governments to undermine collegial decision making weakens the autonomy of academics and replaces it with managerial techniques that are imported from the corporate market and that, at every level, are hostile to education.[70]

EVALUATING TEACHING
BY EVALUATING LEARNING

A real change in paradigm is needed if the evaluation of teaching is to become more than a market tool in which students are treated as customers seeking satisfaction and professors are no more than customer service representatives. This involves much more than just a shift in focus "from measuring teaching by what is taught (or other teacher behaviors) to measuring it by what is learned."[71] Learning, after all, is no more reducible to measurable behaviours than teaching. Students' thoughts and feelings, hopes and desires are essential to the process of learning and cannot be expunged without disconnecting what is learned from their own experience. Where students understand the connection between their lives and the ideas they encounter, they are likely to continue learning in creative ways.[72] As Ernest Boyer proposes, faculty engaged in "the scholarship of teaching" create "a common ground of intellectual commitment [through a] dynamic endeavour involving all the analogues, metaphors, and images that build bridges between the teacher's understanding and the student's learning."[73] Through the imaginative use of metaphor and example, faculty try to connect with students' experience. The goal is to nurture students' growth and connect them with others in a mutually enriching search for critical forms of understanding. Learning involves a living connection between faculty and students that cannot be reduced to the observable behaviours of either partner in the pedagogical relationship.

Within the behaviourist schema I have been criticizing, however, there is a clear distinction between the subjective attitudes of students and the observable behaviours of the professor. On the one hand, subjective preference is to be measured on a Likert scale; on the other, the professor's observable behaviours can be quantified and their "teaching effectiveness" assessed and measured in terms of how well they gesture, tell jokes, and avoid saying "um" or "ah" and so on.[74] Two aspects of this approach dehumanize the process of education. First, student and professor are both reduced to static bits of "stuff": the feelings and attitudes of students become points on a Likert scale rather than live, pulsating emotions and ideas that are entertained by real learners, while the knowledge and interpretative skill of the professor are mere "observable behaviours," an empty shell in which any passion s/he may feel about teaching becomes inert, part of "the black box" of a stimulus-response mechanism. Second, the radical split between the subject/student and the object/professor separates two aspects of teaching and learning that belong together. In order for education to be an active process in which students and faculty fully participate, both partners should be able to express their ideas freely and critically, while recognizing the other as a subject in a world that mediates their growing understanding.[75]

This latter point is crucial to a humanistic approach to education capable of breaking the behaviourist stranglehold of SETS. The

separation of the subjective awareness of students from the objective
"observable behaviours" of the professor precludes any possibility
of a unity of experience in which both partners share ideas in a
captivating moment that heightens their emotional commitment to
learning. This is often referred to as "the teachable moment." From
a Whiteheadian perspective, this momentary "concrescence" (literally, *a growing together*) occurs when teacher and learner engage in
a self-creative process, transforming their experience by uniting the
feelings at the base of their "subjective aim," or sense of purpose.
In order for their aim(s) to become objectified in a project and "clothe
the dry bones with the flesh of a real being, emotional, purposive,
appreciative," there is a need for what Whitehead calls "the lure for
feeling" as "the germ of mind."[76] Lured by feelings for the potency
and beauty of ideas, teacher/students now use conceptual understanding and meaning to determine which possibilities they wish to
select, interpret, and act upon.

For Whitehead, education is a process of growth in which three
"interweaving" cycles have an "alternating" rhythm of freedom-
discipline-freedom.[77] This rhythm provides the optimal conditions
for students to learn in ways that combine their own desire for
knowledge with the self-discipline required to fulfill its demands.
Why shouldn't the evaluation of teaching and learning also be a
process that roughly mirrors these same cycles? The following open-
ended, flexible schema is one that allows for this to take place.

When students are beginning a course, the professor can ask them
to answer in writing a series of questions germane to that course's
content. This enables her to know with which ideas they are familiar
and, just as important, with which they are not. It also enables her
to adjust the content accordingly. Some of the students I interviewed
in both the colleges of arts and science and medicine had had professors who administered detailed questionnaires in the first class,
asking questions about their knowledge of what was to be studied
and what they expected of the course. The goal of these pre-tests
varied from determining the different levels of fluency in language
courses to building the curriculum around plays they had not studied
to providing direction to particular courses and avoiding overlap
with other courses. Professors, *not* administrators, draw up the
questions since they are knowledgeable in the subject matter and
familiar with student needs. In cases where a course has multiple
sections, or faculty members are teaching it for the first time,

consultation with other colleagues may be encouraged. The process enables professors to understand quite clearly what they should teach in order to overcome the gaps in students' knowledge

During the course, professors can continue to use ongoing evaluations through essays, tests, class assignments, and so on in order to gain an understanding of how students are progressing. In order to overcome the constant competition for marks, faculty should try to develop a sense of community in the classroom, presenting it as a place where students learn to share knowledge. Professor Mary Elizabeth Mullino Moore suggests that a process of posing questions and engaging in dialogue should be encouraged as part of critical and creative inquiry. An emphasis on community might then replace the competitive search for meaning and grades, which now characterizes university classrooms. She proposes that, rather than evaluating students for the amount of technical information they have acquired, faculty should strive for something far more important, namely, the relational power of knowledge: "This definition of knowledge suggests an open process (questing) and an accent on communing (relating) with the world ... that probes below the surface of knowledge and evokes response from learners, including appreciation, critique, transformation, and construction of knowledge."[78] Knowledge viewed as an open vector to the world enables students to appreciate how different subjects relate to each other, to critique their shortcomings, and to move towards a process of transformation of self, other, and the world. These criteria provide a more adequate basis for evaluating students' understanding of complex issues than does testing for discrete bits of information. Moore believes they would also challenge "the inadequacy of the [current] evaluation process and instrument"[79] of SETS, which are a major stumbling block to achieving the goal of education.

At the end of the course, a final examination, or its equivalent, enables faculty to understand what students have learned. Their answers can be compared with what they knew at the beginning of the course. In this way, teaching can be evaluated in terms of what students have learned, how they have learned it, and, indeed, how well they have learned it. An examination, or its equivalent, could serve students and faculty alike as an indication of relational knowledge – knowledge that is useful for life and/or that encourages further study and action rather than being seen as the end point in learning.

As a method of evaluating teaching, this approach is distinctive and relatively accurate because it evaluates learning before, during, and at the end of any course. It would enable professors to improve their teaching and to avoid the market-orientation of SETS. It also provides faculty with greater control over their teaching, while, at the same time, enhancing students' ability to advance their learning. If these two points are established, it can be seen that the evaluation of teaching through the evaluation of learning has considerable potential to enhance the scope of academic freedom in the face of pressures from the market. Moreover, this practice would ensure true accountability by providing reliable criteria about the effectiveness of teaching based on what students actually learn. Until faculty can substitute direct evidence of student learning under their instruction, the administrative ease of producing numbers by means of SETS will continue to masquerade as accountability.[80] In the face of this reliance on "customer satisfaction," there is a growing need to strengthen institutional autonomy by enabling faculty and students to guide the university away from the market model of education towards a model in which the search for knowledge is a collegial activity.

6

The Value Program in Theory and Practice

The demands now being made on schools, colleges and universities are for vocational and professional training and cannot be described as education. A society that measures everything in terms of work done and money earned is not concerned with anything beyond the requisite number of persons duly trained and labeled with the correct diplomas and degrees and ready for use and service.

Dora Russell[1]

THE DOMINANT NARRATIVE

I have shown, through examples, how the market model of education threatens academic freedom in Canadian universities. Faculty who speak out in opposition to the goals and values of the market currently operating within universities run the risk of punishment and dismissal. The erosion of universities' institutional autonomy has made possible their capitulation to the demands of private corporations. Too often they have abrogated their social responsibility to question the presuppositions of the market model. The case studies I have presented also show that faculty and students have resisted the demands of the market, succeeding at times in pushing back the tide of corporate control and suggesting that the process of marketization is not inevitable. The goal of university education and research, after all, is to advance and disseminate knowledge by sharing it with others. In other words, knowledge as a public good shared among those who seek it is sustained by an institution whose goal is to ensure the public interest is served. The corporate market, on the other hand, is based on the principle of self-maximization, of consistently seeking to gain as much for oneself as possible.[2]

In this chapter, I take up a question raised in chapter 1 about the totalizing tendency of market advocates to expunge any counter-evidence that does not accord with their own presuppositions. The reason, I argue, is that they have adopted a value program that allows no thought beyond its own assumptions. As a result, the goals and motivations of education are reduced to those of the market. I provide several examples of market agents and university presidents who subscribe to the value program of the market and then contrast their statements with those of two presidents who critically examine its shortcomings. I follow this with an example of how the value program of the market works in practice; namely, York University's treatment of students protesting both the inauguration of George W. Bush and corporate links to the Board of Governors. The suppression of students' freedom of expression and the academic freedom of faculty shows how administrators imbued with the market program are unable to recognize the distinctive principles of university education. The program finds its fullest expression in the private for-profit universities and colleges that have blossomed in the United States and that have crossed the border into Canada. In the conclusion, I point to the possibility of an alternative direction to university education, one that I examine in the final chapter.

THE MARKET MODEL AS A VALUE PROGRAM

The market model of education has become the dominant narrative of the day, one that is proclaimed and adopted as though it were true a priori. "There Is No Alternative" (TINA) is a mantra we hear again and again – a position that contradicts rational and critical debate and the existence of universities as seats of learning. The market model is based on a system of values that rules out any thought that goes beyond that model's assumed structure of worth. Where a value system is closed in this manner it becomes a *value program*. Let me explain the distinction.

A value system is made up of a set of related goods, which are affirmed, and bads, which are repudiated in both thought and action. These related goods and bads may be more or less consciously arrived at, but those who hold them are capable of recognizing the worth represented by other systems. At times they may even modify their values on the basis of experience, judgment, intuition, evidence, and argument. A value system becomes a program, however, at the point at which its own assumptions about what constitutes worth rule out any thought that goes beyond it.[3]

For example, a value system based on a scientific materialist world view is one whose affirmed goods are the measurement, prediction, and control of a universe made up of lifeless matter. Scientific materialism released human beings from the limits to hubris that ancient world views had exerted on their actions, furnishing them with powerful methods with which to dominate an inert natural world.[4] Since its inception in the sixteenth and seventeenth centuries, scientific materialism was linked to the development of technologies that changed modern warfare and made possible greater "efficiencies" in the form of large-scale livestock farming, navigational astronomy, and so on.[5] While the disinterested nature of scientific inquiry may provide its raison d'être, the connection between the technical advances it spawns and the economic system that they serve cannot be overlooked.

Scientific materialism tends to exclude rational discussion about values because they are considered to be subjective and to lie outside the scope of scientific discourse. The most important questions about how best to live and what constitutes a just and equitable society are excluded from meaningful discussion. Where this happens, the system becomes a value program incapable of producing thought about the importance or worth of goods that are excluded from its narrow purview. Adherents to such a program fail to recognize it as such, precisely because their assumed structure of worth precludes them from thinking beyond its assumptions.

Consider, for example, the injunction to "stay near the customer" advocated more than two decades ago by William A.W. Cochrane, president and chief executive officer of Connaught Laboratories Ltd (now a division of Sanofi-Pasteur). Cochrane advanced this prescription as a "short and simple prerequisite of a successful business [that] should be at the forefront of any activity of universities." He assumed there was no difference between the motivations of education and those of the market. Both have "customers" whose wants must be satisfied as a necessary condition for success, and "the principal customers of the university are the general public, the business and industrial sector, and government."[6] Similarly, William Mackness (former senior vice-president of the Bank of Nova Scotia), during his tenure as dean of management at the University of Manitoba, asserted that the market must "dish out some very stern discipline to those [faculty] who aren't meeting [its demands]." The result was the disbandment of the Department of Public Policy, the attempted dismantlement of the Department of Actuarial and Management Services, and the transfer of resources from these programs, with their "low-demand courses[,to] high-demand mainline business disciplines – Finance, Marketing, Management and Accounting."[7] Neither of these market agents recognized the opposing values of education and the market.

Recent statements by two university presidents reflect the same value program. Robert Prichard, when president of the University of Toronto, acclaimed the corporate market as the ruling principle governing the university's every activity: "We need a more market-driven, deregulated, competitive and differentiated [i.e., product-mandated] system ... production of better services to customers. The market model give [sic] universities more freedom ... by allowing administrators to set fees higher and ... by aggressively courting private donors."[8] Prichard revealed the logic of the market in stark terms: universities *must* deregulate, and they *must* compete, bringing more products to market and providing better services to "customers." The *discipline* of the market is seen as a source of *freedom* that allows administrators to raise fees and seek funding from the private sector.

The same logic was at work when Peter MacKinnon, president of the University of Saskatchewan, prescribed a 15 percent raise in tuition fees across the board, 18 percent in medicine, and 28 percent in law in order "to prevent the erosion of quality at the institution." Gerry Klein quotes him in the *StarPhoenix*: "'We need to have a source of revenue that is reasonably consistent,' he said. Turning to the students to pay a greater share of the cost is the 'best way to sustain – or even advance – the reputation of the university,' he said."[9] By making tuition fees more "competitive" with those of other institutions, the "quality" of U of S is somehow improved and its "reputation" advanced as its market price increases. The fact that higher fees make undergraduate education less accessible to large numbers of students does not compute within this logic.

Both Prichard and MacKinnon's statements echo the privatization manifesto of the World Bank presented at the UNESCO World Conference on Higher Education in October 1998, according to which students as "consumers" should pay "the full cost" of their service and borrow at "market rates of interest." This prescription follows from the assertion that "higher education can not be treated as a public good ... [because it is] often available for a price" (a prime example of begging the question). Not content with urging the privatization of tuition fees, however, the manifesto demands "radical change, or restructuring ... [that calls for] radically altering who the faculty are, how they behave, the way they are organized, and the way they work and are compensated." At the same time, the Bank recognizes that any such program of reform will result in widespread resistance: "In the case of public universities, the faculty have additional means with which to resist threats of radical change and job loss: the idea of the university as a proper bastion of continuity and tradition; *the tradition of academic freedom*; and the army of students, former students, and would-be students, most of whom are articulate, energetic, politically volatile, and generally able to be enlisted [sic] in the cause of opposing the government's efforts to radically alter *their* university."[10] In other words, faculty are rooted in the tradition of knowledge as integral to the public good and of academic freedom as necessary for its advancement. When buttressed by an army of articulate and politically active students, they are capable of stemming any program of market reforms proposed by governments.

The manifesto goes on to warn against the folly of such an approach: "the very short-term robustness of the university ... may be its worst enemy in the competition for increasingly scarce revenues ... [since governments will then need] to close down inefficient campuses, or lay off faculty no longer relevant to the needs of students, the economy, or for that matter the university."[11] The threat is palpable. Unless the entire package of proposed reforms is accepted, universities face dissolution: tuition fees *must* be privatized, the work of faculty tailored to market demand, knowledge serve the interests of private corporations, academic freedom be disbanded, students conform to the will of governments, and the economy fully determine the operations of the university. The far-reaching nature of the World Bank's agenda demonstrates the intolerance of the value program of the market in expunging all alternatives.

The value judgments proclaimed by Cochrane, Mackness, Prichard, MacKinnon, and the World Bank go unquestioned because they are based on the idea that self-maximization is a universal principle of rationality. Where a value system is closed in this way to all but its own demands, it becomes hostile to education at every level. But the assumption on which it is based is counterintuitive: we normally consider someone to be rational if she/he is capable of thinking beyond the confines of her/his own self-interest and considers the interests of others to be as important as her/his own.[12]

ADMINISTRATORS BREAKING THE MOULD

Some university presidents are well aware of the dangers to education posed by the value program of the market model. They recognize the importance of interests other than their own, or those of business, and support the idea of universities sharing knowledge for the common good.

Colin Starnes, former president and vice-chancellor of University of King's College, has argued that underfunding by the federal government over a twenty-year period (amounting to 30 percent on a per student basis) combined with continually increasing student enrolment (more than 60 percent) has resulted in "a rising tide" that is engulfing universities. Two related currents in this tide particularly concern Starnes: "The indirect pressures and benefits of a vastly increased research agenda [has] created a new environment in which undergraduate education must now make its way ... [and] 'privatization' in the form of a dramatic increase in tuition at some institutions ... [is] creating a Canadian university system that would look and act much more like that in the US"[13] The twin prongs of "research intensiveness" and "privatization" of undergraduate education are producing "a more stratified system of universities ... like the American pattern," in which graduates, imbued with the idea that education is a private good, are expected to "support and improve the standing of their university in a context of competitive ranking." The assumption that government support at all levels will continue to decline, while individual and corporate "donations" will fill the growing void, is a threat to the distinctive features of the Canadian university system – its openness, accessibility, and quality.

According to Starnes, it is the federal government's emphasis on the Innovation Agenda that is producing "an irreversible sea change" towards research that serves the needs of the market. Because "matching funds" for such research must be "found from the provinces and the private sector ... [each] university [as well as] provincial governments and the private donors will have aligned themselves (*or been coopted*) *by the federal research agenda*."[14] While billions of dollars have been forthcoming for Millennium Scholarships, Canada Education Savings Grants, Canada Research Chairs (CRCs), and the Canada

Foundation for Innovation (CFI), none of these measures addresses the problem of privatized undergraduate education. The explicit goal of the CFI, CRCs, and the Innovation Agenda is "to have Canada move to fifth place in the world – from its position as 14th – in research support" and economic productivity. Among the many difficulties in this market-based agenda is the CFI's requirement that universities find sixty cents to add to every forty that the agency provides. "This amounts," Starnes continues, "to a demand to come up with more than $4.7 billion in new money, in addition to what the universities were already relying on from the private sector and provincial governments."[15] The overriding need to compete with one another in obtaining large sums of money for market-oriented research is driving universities to become "engines of economic growth," without the occurrence of a concomitant discussion of "the relationship between undergraduate education and big research." Undergraduate education is privatized at the same time as its importance is diminished by the scramble for research funding that feeds the economy.

More recently, James Downey, former president of the University of Waterloo, the University of New Brunswick, and Carleton University, gave a speech to the Association of Universities and Colleges of Canada in which he argued for a rejuvenation of the institution's currently muted role of social critic: "Through teaching and research the university must cultivate a spirit of intellectual dissent. Not for its own sake, but in the interests of a free, tolerant, enlightened, and improving society."[16] Research and teaching must encourage systematic questioning of the dominant images of the age in order to strengthen universities' active participation in a democratic society.

While Downey omits to mention that knowledge may have value in itself, he understands that universities today are out of balance. Like President Starnes, he is anxious for a public discussion to take place regarding the "quality and character of undergraduate teaching and learning, for it is there the broader and deeper values of life are shaped," particularly the ability to distinguish between fact and fiction, knowledge and opinion, which is so important for "effective citizenship." Unless universities carry out both their functions of social critic and educator, they "are in danger of being drawn too deeply into the economic functionalism of the age, of becoming too much the handmaiden of society, not enough its honest critic."[17]

Both Starnes and Downey recognize that "research intensiveness," interpreted narrowly as procuring more funds from granting agencies and the corporate sector, is a code word for the value program of the market. The federal government's Innovation Agenda, CRCs, and the CFI are drawn from the same lexicon. Universities seeking CFI funding, for example, must compete not only for awards from the agency but also for the extra 60 percent of "matching funds" from provincial coffers and the corporate sector. Since the latter amounts to more than $4.7 billion, the process ensures greater dependence upon the corporate market. The privatization of undergraduate education through dramatic increases in tuition fees is another aspect of the market's value program, convincing students and their parents that education is a private good. In contrast, Starnes and Downey recognize the public nature of an undergraduate education that is accessible, affordable, and of high quality, capable of enhancing students' capacity for critical and creative thought. And they advocate increased public funding for public universities so that education and research that is of benefit to the whole of society should thrive.

Furthermore, Starnes and Downey advance their case in ways quite different from those who advocate the value program of the market. They carefully analyze the counter-arguments in favour of "research intensiveness," privatization, and the Innovation Agenda. They then proceed to show the weaknesses in those arguments by considering alternatives and weighing the evidence as they go. This style of reasoned argument contrasts sharply with the proclamations of their presidential colleagues who conceive of rationality as self-maximization. Liberation from the value program of the market enables them to conceive of alternative possibilities consistent with the distinctive goals of higher education.

DISCIPLINING STUDENT DISSENT

If, as I have argued, the value program of the corporate market is hostile to education, then students, like faculty, who oppose its prescriptions are to be silenced, and senior administrators wedded to the program become instruments in silencing such dissent. The *discipline* of the market is then exposed as *antithetical* to *education, learning,* and the *freedom of expression* that lies at their core.

On 20 January 2005, a group of about forty students demonstrated in Vari Hall Rotunda at York University in Toronto. Their goal was twofold: to speak out against the inauguration of George W. Bush, which was taking place at the same time, and to voice concerns about "business interests among York's Board of Governors, which the demonstrators linked to American imperialism."[18] Toronto police eventually broke up the demonstration, using truncheons, wrestling students to the ground, dragging them away in handcuffs, and taking them to a locked room in an adjacent building. Five students were arrested. When their colleagues banged on the locked door, it opened and, according to eyewitness accounts, a student was grabbed, beaten, and had to be hospitalized.[19]

Among those observing the events was Professor Stanley Jeffers of the physics department who, in an e-mail message distributed to a faculty listserv shortly after the arrests, wrote: "In what appeared to be a coordinated strategy the police surrounded the central group and started to herd them ... [in order to] get their hands on the leaders of the group. One of these was pulled out and held down by two policemen while a third repeatedly punched the student. This took place within three feet of me."[20] Another faculty member sent an e-mail message with the web address on which were posted amateur videos and photographs taken during the demonstration.[21] These various pieces of evidence were consistent with one another, and none showed students acting violently towards the police.

A media release appeared almost immediately on the university administration's website that conflicted with the evidence of faculty and students: "Demonstrators carried on aggressively and disruptively, classes had to be cancelled, Toronto police were brought in to address the situation, some of the protestors became violent, and at least one officer was assaulted."[22] The following day, a similar story appeared in the *Toronto Star*.[23] Within a week, the administration published three additional versions of the 20 January rally, each significantly different and none consistent with eyewitness accounts or the photographic and video evidence on the internet.[24] When tapes of the demonstration recorded on university surveillance cameras were finally released, they did not support the administration's claims that students had been "aggressive" or "violent." The York University Faculty Association (YUFA) polled its members by e-mail to determine whether or not exams had been disrupted or classes cancelled and found no support for the administration's claims.[25] President Lorna Marsden then denied that the students were violent, asserting that the demonstration was merely "not peaceful."[26]

OPPOSING THE MARKET PROGRAM

Opposition to both the administration and the actions of the police grew. Daily gatherings in Vari Hall included "press conferences, appearances by social activists like Judy Rebick and a performance by the faculty-organized Megaphone Choir."[27] A joint statement issued by the executives of YUFA, the York Federation of Students, the York University Graduate Students, and CUPE Local 3903 (representing teaching assistants and contract staff) expressed concern with "the level of repression of student activity and political assembly on campus, [moreover] we were appalled by the York administration's response to this rally."[28] Open letters to President Marsden from several faculty associations and the Ontario Confederation of Faculty Associations were published, as was a letter of support from CAUT for freedom of expression and academic freedom.[29]

Amid this atmosphere, York's Senate passed two resolutions on 27 January. The first expressed "its disapproval of the administration's decision to invite police onto campus to deal with an otherwise peaceful demonstration"; the second that its "disapproval be communicated via a letter from the Chair to the Board of Governors and the Chief of the Toronto Police."[30] A special meeting was called for the following week to provide the executive of the Senate with direction on how to proceed. The following question was to be discussed: "how the University should balance the questions of academic integrity and the avoidance of disruption to academic activities with the principles of freedom of assembly and expression."[31] Senators also asked for four motions to be added to the agenda, and, despite opposition from senior administrators sitting as non-voting members of the executive, the motions were admitted. Three of the four were eventually passed: "That the Chair write a letter on Senate's behalf to the Toronto Police Services Board to request an inquiry into the allegations of police brutality during the January 20 protest; That Senate express its disapproval of the way the President used the University's communications surrounding the January 20 events; and That the Chair communicate these motions to the Board of Governors."[32]

In addition to their condemnation of police actions, senators raised concern over two regulations that showed just how far the market had compromised the university's independence. The first concerned restrictions on freedom of assembly and freedom of expression.

Freedom of assembly had been restricted at York since the introduction of the updated Temporary Use of University Space Policy, approved by the Board of Governors in August 2004. The policy included general principles relating to safety, security, damages, and compliance as well as the procedures and applications for sponsored events for groups and individuals using university space and facilities. Requests for venues had to be submitted at least thirty days in advance, and only those organizations that were officially recognized could apply. "Demonstration" is among the categories of events that the policy allows, but it forbids the use of candles in buildings, ruling out the possibility of a silent candlelight vigil.[33]

Professor Jay Rahn, YUFA's communications officer, asserted that a number of "large open spaces" were now "effectively excluded by the administration's claims concerning 'pedestrian traffic' and 'sound amplification,' particularly, 'the use of megaphones.'" Among the places excluded were the entrance and rotunda of Vari Hall, and bookings were only allowed at weekends during the regular school year, "when few passersby would witness a demonstration."[34]

A second source of conflict was the uneven implementation of the policy regarding the use of university space: "According to the regulations, if the Jan 20 demonstration was an instance of 'serious misconduct,' the vice-president (students) would have immediately convened the university discipline tribunal. Instead, the administration invited the police onto campus."[35] This heavy-handed action prompted the YUFA executive to call on the university administration to respect public, common space on campus and revoke the Temporary Use of University Space Policy. The executive also requested assistance from CAUT in promoting freedom of expression and academic freedom at York. CAUT established an ad hoc committee whose terms of reference were "to determine whether there were threats to, or breaches of, rights to free expression and academic freedom." The committee also had the responsibility of determining "whether there were inappropriate governance practices and to make recommendations to deal with any problems the investigators may find."[36]

What emerges from an analysis of the 20 January demonstration, according to Rahn, "is a conflict between a longstanding tradition of free expression and an administration's attempt to control communications in the service of good public relations and fundraising."[37] Students were considered a threat to York's relations with powerful business interests. In order to stem their opposition to the corporate agenda, the central administration bypassed established policy and "invited" police onto campus. Administrators then expunged students' twin freedoms of expression and assembly by invoking a "temporary" regulation designed to ensure safety, security, and the booking of university facilities – this, despite the regulation's allowing demonstrations as a legitimate use of public space. In order to ensure that the market's value program was obeyed, suspension of student freedoms was required.

BRANDING AS A THREAT
TO FREEDOM OF EXPRESSION

Senators at York were also opposed to the administration's increasing use of the Division of Communications and Marketing. The division's website includes a statement of purpose that incorporates another familiar mantra of the market: "To meet the specialized communications needs of the University in the highly competitive education marketplace by ensuring that all communications, throughout the university, consistently meet high standards, reflect our mission and are inline [sic] with *our brand strategy.*"[38]

The use of branding to ensure customer loyalty is a well established marketing strategy used by multinational corporations like Tommy Hilfiger, Coca-Cola, and McDonalds to maximize private profit. Customers come to identify with these corporations by wearing, drinking, eating, and consuming their products from an early age. The goal is to sell consumers a lifestyle that, in the words of Sir Richard Branson, CEO of Virgin Group, enables companies to "build brands not around products but around reputation," which, in turn, amounts to "a set of values."[39] The value system in question is "the way to live, the way to wear, the way to do anything" so that individuals not only consume products but also see themselves as "cool," "hot," or "trendy" when doing so.

Universities as seats of rational and critical thought should have been immune to branding. Nevertheless, name recognition has become a key to their successful marketing. In 1999, Howard Newby, vice-chancellor of the University of Southampton, declared that "branding is necessary for market credibility."[40] His sentiments are reflected in the branding policies of universities like Harvard, Oxford, Toronto, and Saskatchewan.[41] At York, the Division of Communication and Marketing's statement of purpose emphasizes the need for

"all communications ... [to] reflect our mission" and the treatment
of students as "customers" whose private wants must be satisfied.
The particular brand of market goods and services that York can
offer its customers is described in the following terms: "[As] part of
Toronto: we are dynamic, metropolitan and multi-cultural ... [as]
part of Canada: we encourage bilingual study, we value tolerance
and diversity. York University is open to the world: we explore global
concerns."[42] It is not the *content* of the mission statement that is
questionable – bilingualism, tolerance, and diversity are all worthwhile qualities – so much as the *manner* in which these goods are
packaged. They are part of an overall *strategy* to *capture* the minds
of student/customers and *brand* them as "dynamic, metropolitan,
and multicultural." Rather than encouraging students to experience
the diversity of disciplinary and interdisciplinary thought and to
think critically about their presuppositions, York has set itself a very
different goal: to satisfy its customers with a "dynamic" brand of
thinking that is both metropolitan and global. The ambiguity of
"global concerns" is such that customers can continue to study climate change, poverty, and desertification as long as they do not voice
their objections to corporate globalization too loudly. Being "open
to the world" means, among other things, that the university is now
open for business.

There is a related aspect to the process of branding at York that
has far-reaching implications. The Board of Governors' Communications Committee focuses primarily on public relations and alumni
through a process known as "advancement," a euphemism for fundraising from former students. The goal of the committee includes
the search for funds from private corporations willing to engage in
"the naming of buildings, faculties and space."[43] But an additional
function, which appeared among its priorities for the academic year
2004–05, is strikingly different. This new mandate for "fostering
peaceful campus relations"[44] was part of an earlier policy brought
forward to the Board of Governors, which stated that: "the introduction of community relations officers to Keele campus security
help[s] achieve the goal of balancing the rights and freedoms of
students and of [sic] fostering a safe and hospitable environment for
the York community."[45] Freedom of assembly and freedom of expression, which have characterized university life since the Middle Ages,
became threats to safety and hospitality and were to be dealt with
by "the introduction of community relations officers to Keele campus

security." This means that students who freely express their "global concerns" *outside* the classroom could be met by larger numbers of police. Whose safety are these officers protecting? Certainly not that of students, one of whom was severely injured by police on 20 January. And for whom was the university being guarded as a "hospitable environment"? For private corporations willing to donate money for buildings, faculties, and space as well as for the corporate interests represented by York's Board of Governors?

The central administration's invitation to police to come onto campus resulted in the use of force against students. When this failed, established policies and marketing strategies were used in order to excoriate students who threatened York's particular brand of goods and services. It was left to students and faculty to defend the university's distinctive principles of freedom of expression and academic freedom in their opposition to the value program of the corporate market. Administrators acted as they did because of an adherence to this program, which "has become pervasive and unquestioned, carried along like a religious crusade, with educationists and bureaucrats leaping to join the corporate propaganda apparatus, urging students, teachers, and professors to 'adapt to the new reality.'"[46]

PRIVATIZATION AT HOME AND ABROAD

The value program of the market finds its apotheosis in the private for-profit universities and colleges that have sprung up in the United States and, more recently, in Canada. These institutions exemplify the workings of the market model, competing for custom and providing a warning to public universities of what their own future might hold.

The logic of the market's value program is well captured in a suggestion made "only half in jest" by Professor Richard Chait of Harvard University's School of Education that "[the university] become a publicly held firm whose shares are traded on the New York Stock Exchange, its market value rising and falling with the 'knowledge products' it develops and the calibre of the 'knowledge workers' it recruits."[47] The proposal is a kind of reductio ad absurdum of the value program of the market. Given the premise that the goals and standards of excellence of education and the market are identical, the logical conclusion to privatize universities follows by making them for-profit companies in which "knowledge products" and "knowledge workers" maximize stockholder value.

Nor is this an imaginary scenario. The University of Phoenix is the best known example of an institution obligated by law to maximize private profit for its investors. Its primary function is to impart skills and knowledge to its "customers" in the most cost-effective manner, and for this purpose "programs and curricula are developed to serve not only the professional needs of the students, but also the needs of the secondary consumers – the companies that employ them."[48] Curricula developed by a team of faculty working with representatives from industry are pared down to the exclusive function of teaching business-related skills and are "'customized' to fit the needs of specific industries and organizations."[49] As the website of the Centre for Professional Education at the Sacramento Campus of the University of Phoenix states: "When you bring the Centre for Professional Education on site, you've entered into a partnership with an educational vendor that understands accountability. We work with you to create a customized curriculum with a measurable outcome in a specified time frame."[50]

Companies can hire this "educational vendor" to tailor a curriculum to produce "a measurable outcome," or increase in the marketable skills of their employees, in a time period that reflects the "accountability" of the market – namely, the reduction of unit costs. No pretence here of offering anything other than training for the corporate workplace since the goal is to meet the needs of universities' "down stream customers" (private corporations) in their competition for global market share. Indeed, Phoenix has unceremoniously replaced the idea of a university's serving the public good with "the idea of the university as a business serving other businesses ... dedicated only to the economic interest of its student-consumers, its industry employers, and its investors."[51]

The Devry Institute of Technology Inc provides another example of privatization that has direct implications for Canadian higher education. As a US-based private corporation with twenty-one campuses throughout North America, Devry was granted the right to grant academic degrees by the government of Alberta early in 2001. Under the North America Free Trade Agreement (NAFTA), Devry could then challenge government funding to postsecondary institutions, claiming that it gave public universities "a competitive advantage." Indeed, NAFTA requires the Alberta government to provide a "level playing field" for both public and private institutions, and opens up the postsecondary market to American and Mexican private corporations that meet the same conditions as Devry.[52] Recently, the company's share of the higher education market has slipped. In 2003, it closed its Toronto campus "because of falling enrollment and poor financial results," and announced that it would "assess Canadian operations and ... take further action to reduce losses."[53]

Private for-profit universities and colleges are prime examples of the value program of the corporate market. They openly espouse private profit maximization, measurable outcomes of "successful training" for the corporate market, curricula determined by the needs of private-sector "partners," and accountability in the narrow sense of reduction of unit costs. The threat to public university education that they pose is real. The federal government's apparent readiness to sign on to the General Agreement in Trades and Services has hastened their entrenchment in Canada since it could entitle foreign, for-profit providers to the same range of government supports as publicly funded universities.[54]

CONCLUSION: W(H)ITHER THE CORPORATE UNIVERSITY?

The value program of the market is hostile to the university's goal of advancing and disseminating shared knowledge. The program as a system of related goods and bads is unable to recognize anything beyond its own structure of worth, ruling out any knowledge that might lie beyond the closed patterns of thought that serve the market. The principle of self-maximization determines much of the knowledge now created by universities and used to increase stockholder value. Branding has become a familiar strategy with which to persuade "customers" – both students and corporations – that the values of the market provide the only conceivable goal of education and research. Students, like faculty, who oppose this regime are silenced, either by force, reprimand, the misuse of established university policies, or the techniques of branding.

University presidents who define education and research in terms of the objectives of the World Bank tie them to the value program of the corporate market. Their colleagues who argue against the privatization of undergraduate education and the commercialization of research provide hope for an alternative direction, one in which universities will be free from the overriding demands of the market's value program. In the final chapter, I consider an example of faculty, students, and staff working together to create just such an institution.

7

The People's Free University
as an Alternative Model

I mean that when we have reopened every question, every assumption
that underlies the going versions of education, it is this freedom to
explore which becomes our reason for being.

Dennis Lee[1]

BEYOND THE MARKET MODEL OF EDUCATION

Given everything I have written in previous chapters about the market
model of education and the ways in which it has invaded universities
in Canada, one might think that this trend cannot be resisted.
Nothing could be further from the truth. The marketization of university research and teaching contains within it the seeds of resistance,
precisely because it is opposed to the institution's own goals, motivations, methods, and standards of excellence. Each of the case studies
shows how faculty, staff, and students have refused to accept attacks
on academic freedom and the autonomy of universities as "natural,"
"inevitable," or "part of the new reality." Even though advocates of
the market model repeat these mantras ad nauseam, the endogenous
tradition of universities cannot easily be submerged. The advancement and dissemination of shared knowledge stands opposed to the
goal of the corporate market to maximize private monetary profits.
As long as citizens recognize this contradiction between the public
nature of knowledge and the private accumulation of money, they
can stem the tide of the corporate market.

Paul Axelrod, former dean of education at York University, argues
that universities can best resist the market by adopting approaches
to liberal education emancipated from past elitist practices. Education

of this kind has two main functions. On the one hand, it strengthens those aspects of universities that are currently under attack – namely, "intellectual autonomy, resilience, critical thinking" – by striving for "a balance of broad and specialized knowledge, tolerance, community participation, and effective communication." At the same time, it infuses applied, vocational, and professional education with a breadth and depth of vision that makes them "superior to practical training in which they are absent."[2] A robust and practically oriented liberal education at the centre of university education and research would create a counter-balance to the current expansion of the market. Liberal education would be fully integrated with vocational training so as to ensure that students graduating in professional faculties gain an understanding that transcends the narrow limitations of the market. Moreover, applied research for business conducted under contract with faculty and graduate students would have to conform to academic criteria pertaining to open disclosure of both their monetary value and the data that they uncover as well as the minimization of any delays in the publication of research results.[3]

The difficulties involved in bringing about these changes under current conditions lead Axelrod to imagine a scenario in which "those interested in exploring the world of ideas might have to set up new institutions (without public funding), perhaps like Plato's Academy, to enable intellectual life to thrive ... [and to] cultivate attitudes and skills that enhance individual and community life."[4] This strategy, he believes, is suitable for a future in which universities are completely regulated by government and business.

There have been several such institutions operating in Canada recently. One of these was the People's Free University of Saskatchewan (PFU). Between 2002 and 2004, the PFU was both a working model of lifelong learning capable of strengthening local communities and a reminder to universities of what they may be losing in their rush to privatize teaching and research. Scepticism towards the University of Saskatchewan's adoption of the market model, in particular, led advocates of the PFU to strike out in a different direction, one designed to benefit ordinary people rather than powerful corporate interests. At the same time, the PFU was capable of lighting the spark of a reform movement among Canadian universities, making the disjunction with institutional life less sharp than it appears. Many of those involved in the PFU worked and studied at U of S and saw no contradiction in bridging this divide. On the contrary, they considered it a healthy way of expanding their horizons by working in and with the community.

My own analysis of the PFU is based on two related insights. Together, they enable a broad conception of academic freedom, which acknowledges both intellectual and practical work as embodying free activity. The first insight, from Alfred North Whitehead, advances a conception of freedom that spans both theory and practice. "The essence of freedom," he writes, "is the practicability of purpose ... [since] freedom of action is a primary human need." Intellectuals have tended to stress the importance of freedom of thought and expression as well as freedom of the press while downplaying the significance of something more rudimentary. Only where a human being can effect "prevalent purposes" growing from those needs that "belong to the very definition of its species" can s/he be free. This kind of freedom has been denied "throughout the ages [to] the masses of mankind" while the free and open pursuit of ideas has been the prerogative of "the fortunate section of mankind whose basic human wants have been satisfied."[5] As a result, the importance of freedom of action for the majority of human beings has been systematically ignored.

This problem can be overcome, Whitehead argues, if the right balance between the abilities possessed by individuals and groups is found, so that their distinctive contributions enhance the growth of wide-ranging human purposes in the communities in which they live: "Indeed, one general aim is that these variously coordinated groups should contribute to the complex pattern of community life, each in virtue of its own peculiarity. In this way individuality gains the effectiveness which issues from coordination, and freedom obtains power necessary for its perfection."[6] Education is an important medium in which this balance of freedom and coordinated power can be achieved. Individuals only experience "perfection" in learning when they are in a situation in which their lives in community are the baseline of its operations. "Self-development" is best achieved where the learner's relationships with others are acknowledged: family, neighbourhood, region, nation, and the planet on which they live all form integral parts of the learning process. The "dry rot" of "inert ideas" can then be expunged in an ongoing "protest against dead knowledge," Whitehead continues, as teachers and learners come to use ideas in novel ways, connecting them with one another and testing their efficacy by relating them to "that stream, compounded of sense perceptions, feelings, hopes, desires, and of mental activities adjusting thought to thought which forms our life." Ideas come alive as they are related to the full emotional and intellectual life of each learner, while the process of learning itself becomes integrated with her life-in-community. The community, in turn, recognizes the importance of the following "sound rule," which encourages her freedom of action: "if you want to understand anything, make it yourself."[7] For learning requires not only the freedom to explore ideas but also the opportunity to put them into practice.

Advocates of the PFU concurred. Free collaboration on an alternative form of higher education in which knowledge is shared with the community achieves wide-ranging purposes that escape the narrow confines of the corporate market. The opportunity to put critical ideas into practice forms an integral part of people's lives as intellectuals. Faculty, staff, and students worked with members of the community to disseminate knowledge as a common good and strengthened the university's mission to promote the public interest. Their academic freedom was used to maximize the value of knowledge to society as a whole.

The second insight is taken from an article by John B. Cobb Jr, founding director of the Centre for Process Studies at Claremont Graduate School in California, in which he urged me and several colleagues "to go beyond essays to practical proposals ... informed by Whitehead's vision."[8] In addition to publishing articles in academic journals, we should look for practical and imaginative ways in which to apply Whitehead's ideas to educational contexts. Educational praxis could then enable the rich potentiality of the Whiteheadian vision to achieve concrete actuality. Cobb's emphasis on "practicability of purpose" reawakened my interest in becoming involved in just such an approach to education. While his focus was primarily on schools, his argument applies equally to universities in which knowledge has become a private good.

The question I examine in this chapter is whether or not the PFU provides a working model of free, open, and community-based education. Is this the kind of community that enables freedom of action to its learners in the manner advocated by Whitehead and Cobb? In order to answer this question, I give an account of how the PFU came into existence, the forces of commercialization to which it is opposed, and the particular ideals it espouses. I then turn to those aspects of Whitehead's educational thought most relevant to the PFU; namely, the growth in shared knowledge fostered by community-based education, the value of abstract and practical knowledge, and the power of the imagination to establish a community of learners capable of acting freely together. In order for the PFU to come to full fruition as a working model of education, I argue that the "civil commons," a network of institutions that sustains life in all its forms, should inform its practice. The goods of the civil commons are universally accessible and life-promoting and, because they match the ideals of the PFU, provide the basis for growth in ways that oppose the privatization of the corporate market.

In interpreting the PFU as a Whiteheadian project, I am not suggesting that those involved in establishing it were consciously applying his philosophical ideas. But a tacit understanding of their efficacy ran throughout their work, a kind of subterranean awareness of the value of working together in novel ways that ensured that knowledge remains a good to be shared by the community.

THE ECLIPSE OF "THE PEOPLE'S UNIVERSITY"

In order to understand the significance of the PFU, it is worth reemphasizing the ways in which U of S has moved away from its original vision as "the people's university." As Walter Murray, the first president, put it: "There should be ever present the consciousness that this is the university of the people, established by the people, and devoted by the people to the advancement of learning and the promotion of happiness and virtue."[9] Murray's vision charted a course in which the advancement of learning had as its goal the common good of the people of Saskatchewan. Affordable, accessible, quality undergraduate education was given the highest priority. Research in certain fields, notably the natural sciences, was excellent, and extension work provided training in improved methods of farming as well as instruction in the humanities. The overall "spirit of service" initiated by Murray underlined a tension between the university's "creative" and "practical" functions that produced a balance between these two polarities. Professor Michael Hayden points out that, in order for this "special tradition" to survive, however, "faculty ... must be prepared to devote themselves seriously to teaching at all levels and must be ready to share their knowledge with those in the province who need it, while also carrying on a private search for truth."[10] The public responsibility of faculty to teach, and to share their knowledge with citizens who need it, is balanced by a free and independent search for truth among the various disciplines. These two functions complement each other as long as institutional autonomy strongly supports their freedom of thought and action.[11]

Since the 1990s, this vision has rapidly given way to an opposing conception of knowledge as a private good, "the new currency" capable of adding value in the "knowledge-based economy."[12] U of S embraced the privatization of knowledge, attempting to couple the demands of the market with its own distinctive history. One of many documents advocating this new agenda claimed that research intensiveness provides "a fitting vision for a university created in a spirit of service" that will allow the province to "compete in a global marketplace."[13] A strategy of global competitiveness fast became a mantra among senior administrators and certain faculty, distorting the meaning of "service" to suit the needs of private corporations. According to the upside-down logic of "research intensiveness," quality of research is measured in terms of how much money accrues to faculty from public and private funding agencies. Not only is this reasoning fallacious, but its goal is in marked contrast to that of both "the people's university" and the PFU. In practice, "research-intensiveness" has resulted in U of S's mutating from the vision articulated by President Murray in a number of ways.

Less Emphasis on Undergraduate Education

The quality of undergraduate education has declined as a result of budget cuts and the loss of 130 faculty positions, with fewer professors teaching larger classes and little opportunity for dialogue or critical thought.[14] Undergraduate education is becoming a private good to be bought by those "customers" who can afford it, as the market model requires. An increase in tuition fees of more than 100 percent over the last decade has meant that affordable, accessible university education has become impossible for many students. Fees in the Province of Saskatchewan are now the highest in western Canada and the third highest in the country.[15] At the same time, an increase in student poverty resulted in the opening of a campus food bank in 2003 for those unable to afford the basic necessities to keep themselves alive. A "Generation of Debt" has emerged, with as many as 35 percent of students at U of S graduating with a debt load to private banks of more than $25,000.[16]

An Increase in Research Conducted for the Market

A rapid growth in strategic grants from federal and provincial funding agencies requires researchers to find "partners" from industry to provide matching funds. These partners exert considerable leverage over the nature and goals of research not only in the natural sciences but also, and increasingly, in the humanities and social sciences.[17] This shift is symbolized at U of S by the enthronement of the Canadian Light Source synchrotron. The largest scientific installation in Canada in a generation, it is owned by U of S and paid for by the public purse. The university has contributed more than $10 million over five years towards the total operating costs of $90 million, this in addition to more than $7 million and a contribution in kind towards capital costs.[18] Two drug company beneficiaries made a total contribution of $1 million – Boehringer Ingelheim (in partially funding a beamline) and GlaxoSmithKlein (in funding a research chair).[19] Meanwhile, the federal government's Innovation Agenda, defined in exclusively economic terms as "bringing new goods and services to market,"[20] continues to exert overriding pressure. Since U of S and other Canadian universities conduct most of the country's curiosity-based and applied research, they are required to increase its productivity by commercializing their "products" in order to take Canada into the top six nations in the global economy.[21]

The Centralization of University Governance

The central administration has undermined the collegial decision-making process through the mechanisms of Integrated Planning and Systematic Program Review, which limit the authority of University Council (the senior academic body). These measures pit one academic unit against another in the zero-sum game of resource allocation.[22] A prime example is the skewing of resources to those "high priority research thrusts" capable of using the synchrotron and "adding value" to private goods and services. These five areas of applied science, including biotechnology, health sciences, and technology and society, received twenty-eight of the first thirty-one Canada Research Chairs awarded to U of S. Departments in the humanities and social sciences are left either to redefine themselves or to face "divestment."[23]

It is not simply the push to privatization that is worrisome about these reforms, but the presumption that they tell the whole story about university education and research.[24] One can no longer question this "total" account of what universities are, and should be, without being considered "out of touch with the new reality." When raising questions about its validity, one often receives the response that "there is no alternative," which denies the very agency Whitehead considered a basic human capacity. At the same time, the needs of students and of ordinary citizens to share in the knowledge advanced by faculty are fast being forgotten.

THE EMERGENCE OF THE PEOPLE'S FREE UNIVERSITY

It was in this context that the PFU was founded. A series of public meetings organized on campus within the Department of Educational Foundations, entitled "U of S Ltd: W(h)ither the Corporate University?" were the first real opposition to research intensiveness and the Innovation Agenda. They were supported by the U of S Faculty Association and coincided with several student rallies opposed to the rise in tuition fees. Coupled with these fora on corporatization were meetings that took place off campus about the need for an alternative form of higher education, including a panel discussion at the public library that attracted 150 people.[25] This move was very much in the mediaeval tradition of secession, when bands of scholars freely decided to leave the University of Paris for Orléans to establish a new university on the river Loire. In similar fashion, Oxford came into existence in the late twelfth century, following secession by scholars from Paris, while Cambridge owed its existence to those in secession from Oxford somewhat later.[26] In the case of the PFU, it was simply a matter of moving across the South Saskatchewan River from the east to the west bank.

The PFU first opened its doors in the fall of 2002. Two hundred students between the ages of twelve and eighty-two from different social classes and ethnic backgrounds enrolled in six courses. Content

varied from Aboriginal spirituality to music and politics, Canadian
legal and political systems, psychology, human rights, and literature
for personal growth. So successful was this initial semester that
winter courses, ranging in length from four to twelve weeks, started
in March of 2003 and covered such topics as globalization, human
ecology, health care ethics, music, psychology, and community building. These drew fewer students than had the earlier semester as it
was a bitterly cold season. In the fall term, three courses were
offered – one on scientists questioning science, one on building global
consciousness, and one on public law in Canada – and there were
a series of café discussions on such topics as alternative budgets,
politics in the city, factory farming, the criminalization of dissent,
and agriculture in the global marketplace. In the winter of 2004,
courses on astronomy and Canadian law were given in addition to
café discussions on music, poetry, and civic politics.

The PFU provided learning experiences to anyone, regardless of
their ability to pay. Not only were courses offered free of charge,
but a philosophy of inclusiveness was embraced, which stated that
"everyone can learn, everyone can teach" – an approach first adopted
in slightly different form by the Free University Movement in the
United States.[27] In practice, this meant that qualified people from
the community as well as recognized university teachers provided
learning opportunities to many adults who could not otherwise
afford higher education. In the words of one such student, this
experience was "informal, informative, enjoyable, and educational."
Courses took place in a variety of accessible locations, and those
offered at St Thomas Wesley United Church in one of the poorest
core neighbourhoods of Saskatoon attracted the largest number of
students during the first semester. Public lectures and fora as well as
hands-on workshops on gardening, composting, success in the workplace, and putting together a resumé and learning portfolio were
scheduled in the spring and fall of 2003. A conscious effort to balance practical and theoretical subjects in ways that appeal to the
interests of students was a cornerstone of the PFU.

A COMMUNITY OF ADULT LEARNERS

Advocates of the PFU were determined to establish an institution
grounded in the history of both "the people's university" and the
province itself – a history characterized by social democracy, the

cooperative movement, and the struggle for social justice. The power of adult education to promote dialogue and enliven critical awareness among the general populace has been a central feature of all these movements. Although its goals have been ambiguous at times, adult education has been a distinctive feature of Saskatchewan's history. Farmers who formed the Wheat Pool in the 1930s went on to educate themselves about economics, politics, current affairs, literature, and philosophy, while many listened regularly to the Farm Radio Forum during the 1940s, discussing ideas and reading books so as to improve their education. In the mid-1940s, the newly elected Co-operative Commonwealth Federation government of Tommy Douglas launched a grassroots, radical, adult education program that, according to Professor Michael Welton, was "a massive campaign of study-action throughout the province – to begin the building of a new society." This society would be built on the concept of an "activated citizen," one who understood scientific and technological change, was aware of the causes of fascism and war, and was "committed to playing an intelligent role in the constructive life of the community." Although the goal envisaged by the campaign's leader, Watson Thomson, to create a province that could "boast it is truly possessed by its people"[28] was not fulfilled, a legacy of community-based education was firmly established.

Participants at an organizational meeting of the PFU in February 2002 drew upon this historical experience to articulate a distinctive value system, which they believed should guide the new institution:

1 The PFU should be a place for all citizens to have access to knowledge, education, and research, with classes located throughout the community.
2 University education should be a universal right, and it should be of the people and for the people, offering opportunities for self-directed learning.
3 The PFU should bring educators to work in the community together with citizens, meeting their needs, sharing knowledge, and enabling them to better understand their relationship with the world.
4 The principles of open access, equity, and participation must be respected; such practicalities as daycare and transportation costs should be covered in order for low-income women, in particular, to participate.

5 The PFU should be an institution inclusive of Aboriginal peoples and respectful of the marginalized; anti-racist education and sensitivity to issues of class, race, gender, disability, and inner-city communities should be stressed.

6 The curriculum should be both academic, stressing critical thought, and practical, enabling skills development in such areas as organic farming, traditional healing, indigenous arts and culture, and so on.

7 The curriculum should also be interdisciplinary in nature with an emphasis on people's economics, sense of place, community living, peace, environmental sustainability, people's history, and cooperative philosophy, using community resources and participatory research in an effort to include multiple perspectives.

8 The organizational structure should be autonomous and "bottom-up," with decisions made democratically through consensus; concerted efforts should be made to build links with labour, rural communities, and community groups engaged in broad approaches to education.

9 The PFU should provide an education for empowerment, an avenue for people to overcome their oppression, by providing services designed to narrow the gap between rich and poor.[29]

In sum, the vision was of an informal and flexible organization made up of a diverse group of people capable of linking their various communities and of recognizing the importance of class, race, and gender to education. As a place for sharing critical thought and community knowledge about a wide range of intellectual and practical matters, the PFU should strive to be accessible to all. By providing classes without walls that foster self-directed learning, the PFU should also encourage students and teachers to be responsible for the learning that takes place as well as for the research that is conducted.[30]

At the core of this ambitious program is the idea that education is an integral part of the community for, as John Cobb suggests, "we would want the boundaries between school and community to be fluid" in order to promote a "close interconnectedness with all the other educative activities in society."[31] In practice, this suggests a relationship between students' life experience and their learning, in which each is deeply affected by the other. The institutions of family, church, labour unions, women's organizations, Aboriginal bands,

Métis groups, and professional associations all have a role to play in the educative activities of the PFU.[32] Lifelong learning, "as a process of man's [sic] growth toward fulfilment as an individual as well as a member of many groups in societies,"[33] is a cornerstone of this approach. Students learn through a process of growth that is fully integrated with their lives. Relationships with others are important because they nurture their potential for learning not simply as future employees but also as citizens who participate in a variety of social contexts. By providing lifelong learning in this inclusive sense, the PFU sets itself apart from the market model of education, whose goal is to produce a workforce that will retrain whenever new skills are required "to compete in the global market." Like Whitehead, the PFU is opposed to "soul murder" of this kind, conceiving instead of education as an activity to "be transfused with intellectual and moral vision and thereby turned into a joy."[34] Students enjoy intellectual work when they understand its connection with both their own interests and those of others in a community of learners.

In order for the PFU to achieve this distinctive goal, the perspectives of each individual and group engaged in lifelong learning had to be respected. Their belief systems, especially their emotions, feelings, insights, and intuitions, formed the basis for a process of growth and understanding to be shared with others. Community-based knowledge of the public health care system, for example, enabled students to understand their rights as patients.[35] Since everyone will at some time during their lives require the services of this system, such knowledge is of great importance. Students learned to question the structure of the doctor-patient relationship, which can at times distort the full and frank disclosure of the nature of disease. Courage is often needed to begin this process of questioning the very medical expertise upon which one's health may depend. Sensitivity to the fears experienced by learners engaged in such questioning is also required if knowledge is to be disseminated about how best to cope in such situations. While this pedagogical approach is not unique to the PFU, the possibilities for using it were greater since students freely chose to pursue their studies without the need for summative evaluation, with few expectations of a job, and without paying any fees. These conditions increased the probability that they would consider education as a public rather than a private good, a lifelong activity in which knowledge could be shared with others through a process of dialogue and critical inquiry. The confidence to act in ways that incorporated this new-found understanding was enhanced as students learned to apply their knowledge to concrete situations.

Sharing community-based knowledge of this kind in an effective manner required educators to be aware of the limitations of their own value systems as well those of their students. A frank recognition of the ways in which teachers at the PFU were privileged by virtue of their own education and social status was necessary since this might separate them from some of their students. At the same time, their pedagogy enabled students to "transcend culturally imposed consciousness, allowing them to exit their circular, self-enclosed, and self-perpetuating 'uncritical immersion in the *status quo*.'"[36] A process of questioning emerged, in which teacher and student used their experience to critically examine collaborative ways in which to understand and interpret reality. Dissatisfaction with current modes of education and training, as well as valuable suggestions for reform, were brought to light. One of the dangers in this process was dichotomous thinking; namely, the tendency to divide reality into a simplistic us/them form in which the PFU was by definition good and the regular university system bad. The ambiguities and complexities of community based-education had to be acknowledged in order for the process of knowing to have real worth.[37] The goal throughout was to provide participants with opportunities to express their full range of thought, feeling, and action in order for learning to flourish.[38]

VALUING ABSTRACT AND PRACTICAL KNOWLEDGE

During the early days of the PFU there was considerable discussion about whether or not to issue diplomas to students. Were these merely trappings of a reward system to which the new institution was opposed by its very nature? The issue was resolved by giving students in "academically oriented" classes the option of submitting work for detailed feedback and conventional grading from instructors. Certificates were issued as part of a learner's portfolio on academic achievement in anticipation of a wider adoption by universities of a policy that allows credit for past experiences through prior learning assessment and recognition.[39] This approach avoided any binary opposition between the intrinsic and extrinsic value of knowledge, and it was an important step in enabling the community to create its own forms of understanding that were open to ongoing interpretation, discussion, and critique.[40]

The PFU's approach echoes Whitehead's belief in both kinds of knowledge as integral aspects of learning. Abstract ideas are important since "the really profound changes in human life all have their origin in knowledge pursued for its own sake." Whitehead gives a number of mathematical examples that illustrate their influence on intellectual and social development. One of these is of "conic sections [that] were studied for 1800 years merely as an abstract science without any thought of utility" before they were found to be "the necessary key with which to attain the knowledge of the most important laws of nature." At the same time, he recognizes that some abstract ideas have their origin in practical concerns. Trigonometry, for example, was invented as a means of pursuing astronomy and of understanding the movement of the spheres. Its importance both to the theory and practice of mathematics "is only one of innumerable instances of the fruitful ideas which the general science has gained from its practical applications."[41]

Whitehead emphasizes the need to base abstractions in any discipline on the fluidity of human experience in order to reflect the ways in which we actually learn. Our experience carries us through time like a stream or ongoing flux in which the various events making up our lives are interconnected. At the base of all experience are feelings that flow like energy through our bodies linking us to one another and to a natural world that is alive. This potency, or "causal efficacy," of nature is reflected in the human ability to effect change by putting ideas into practice, as Whitehead makes clear in his emphasis on freedom of action as a basic human need.[42]

In order for education to meet this need, it should, as Cobb points out, recognize the rhythmic cycles of growth constituting the natural process of human learning: "It would be guided by the interests gained in romance and geared towards ways of realizing visions of what might be. It would not subserve the progress of academic disciplines. It would, therefore, inherently call for generalization and testing in relation to what is known in other ways."[43] The joy of learning ("romance") provides insights into ways of bringing about new possibilities that enhance the growth of knowledge. The knowledge created in this manner is no less precise than strict disciplinary thought ("precision") because it includes insights gained from romantic understanding. By constantly relating theory to practical experience, one ensures that the entire process is grounded in "stubborn fact" and is unlikely to be abstracted from either ("generalization"). Rooted in the alternating rhythms of human experience, these abstractions enhance the freedom and discipline that constitute full self-development. Moving between the polarities of the aesthetic and the logical, students learn to integrate emotional and rational experience in ways that allow them to blend thought and action in ways that are too often absent from university classrooms. Even the least experienced learner is encouraged to exercise her potential because the answers she receives are provisional and open-ended. Participation in this process of growth enables renewed interpretation and critique of all knowledge claims and encourages imaginative speculation grounded in the full range of human experience.[44] While this approach may seem a daunting task for the very young, it is particularly suited to adult learners (such as those at the PFU, who brought a breadth of experience to the classroom).

An interdisciplinary study of "people's economics," for example, allows students to learn about market systems whose goal is to produce goods that enhance the range of individual and collective life rather than maximize private monetary profits. In many places, "money is redefined as a service to facilitate economic exchange," and its potential to become "more, not less, accessible to people with trading needs" ensured. Local employment and trading systems (LETS) enable citizens to exchange services in ways that substitute other tokens for the "convenient fiction" of money, freeing up their dependency on "central bankers, money traders and counterfeiters."[45] Such alternatives as neighbourhood currencies, LETS money, or the equivalent of average hourly wages have been used in promoting local economies in Europe, Australia, Toronto, Courtney (British Columbia), and Ithaca (New York). A growing understanding of how these systems work outside the money-code of value enabled students to consider their relevance to Saskatchewan. The study of people's economics developed a strong sense of place by situating the province in the context of a global economy capable of meeting human needs rather than seeking to expand their wants through the promise of "consumer choice."[46] Students learned how trading practices based on LETS could meet the needs of their community before any surplus value was extracted for use elsewhere. They recognized that economic exchange of this kind enhances citizens' productivity and is opposed to the market's "attempt to enlarge the geographic scope of its greed."[47] As such practices spread and local communities gain in strength, knowledge can be used to transcend greed and self-interest.

THE POWER OF THE IMAGINATION IN BUILDING COMMUNITIES

How, then, can local communities be constructed to meet the needs of their citizens? And what is the role of education in this process? Whitehead and Cobb have a good deal to say about this question. They both invoke the imagination's capacity for careful consideration of the realities of any situation and its power to combine a recognition of the possibilities for change with the potentialities for transforming reality. Community-based education has a key role to play because it appeals to the imagination of learners, particularly where it is, in Cobb's words, "guided by the interests gained in romance and geared toward ways of realizing visions of what might be." The various interests that grow out of students' love of learning embody a desire to transform themselves and the world. For both philosophers, this desire can be strengthened through a "primarily aesthetic" education capable of "increasing 'strength of beauty'" in the sense of "beauty of the soul rather than of art objects." Students are more likely to move from imaginative thought to practical action if they become aware of the kind of person it takes to achieve their goals. Imaginative expression provides a basis for "acting to realize what students have perceived as possible in their own lives or in the wider world."[48] Only where they recognize their lives as having greater potential for creative thought and action will students begin to transform themselves and the world. Aesthetic expression as the primary source of value sustains purposive activity by enabling students to grow in constructive ways. This can take many forms, from working collaboratively with others on a practical problem in the community, such as homelessness, to learning to paint, write, make pottery, or play basketball. But without a sense of beauty, students will continue to suffer from what Whitehead calls "a starvation of impulses, a denial of opportunity, a limitation of beneficial activity."[49]

In order to prevent the stultification of students' impulses, a university should be a place where there are "faculty whose learning is lighted up with imagination." Learning itself is not a marketable commodity, nor is its pursuit reducible to any exchange value because, in Whitehead's words, "the learned and imaginative life is a way of living, and is not an article of commerce." Ideas are to be freely and openly shared by faculty acting as "a band of imaginative scholars,"[50] working together on intellectual problems in collaborative ways that combine the vigour of youth with the experience of the more mature, so that students and professors can strengthen their inner beauty.

It is in this same spirit, I believe, that faculty at the PFU offered their services free of charge to students who themselves chose to attend courses out of a desire to learn. Together they shared knowledge in ways that strengthened a sense of what education might become. This was the ideal of the original system of free universities in the United States, as articulated by Bill Draves, one of its historians and founders. A diverse model of higher education provided "a new vision of what it means to learn" supported by "a 'community of scholars,'" in which "a feeling of learning with others" was sustained by "a new concept of learning – as a process that anyone can tackle at any point." By unlocking barriers to knowledge traditionally regarded as the domain of the privileged, "a deluge of possibilities for people to learn and act"[51] was established.

At the PFU, the same approach led to an imaginative conception of learning grounded in a sense of community outside of the money-code of value. In the words of Professor Michael Collins, education is conceived as "very much a public good in contrast to calculating market-driven 'knowledge economy' imperatives." The idea of "friends learning from friends ... prefigures a radical restructuring of educational systems for ordinary men, women, and children."[52] A community in which knowledge is shared as a public good among colleagues and friends serves the needs of ordinary people by providing an alternative model of education from that of the market. According to one instructor, freedom from an exclusive emphasis on job training enabled students at the PFU to engage in the pursuit of knowledge in imaginative and critical ways.

Nor is this surprising, since the imagination may be the most potent force in the construction of any community and, according to Professor Benjamin Barber, "the single most important mark of the effective citizen": "It is through imagination that private interests are stretched and enlarged to encompass the interests of others; that the wants and needs of others can be seen to resemble our own; that the welfare of the extended communities to which we belong is

recognized as the condition for the flourishing of our own interests."[53]
The imagination enables students and citizens alike to recognize a
connection between their own interests and those of others, fortified
by the various communities that make such "flourishing" possible.
Adult learners at the PFU came to understand their desire for knowledge as a process connecting them to one another as a band of
imaginative scholars. Learning shared as a public good strengthened
students' capacity to understand their many connections with reality – the local, the global, and the biotic community upon which we
all depend. At its base, the value system of the PFU, like that of all
cooperative and collaborative institutions, was based on life and
provided access for every member of the community "to grow and
express themselves as human."[54]

THE PFU, THE LIFE-CODE OF VALUE, AND THE CIVIL COMMONS

The PFU, then, grew into a community in which the interests and
imagination of learners were enhanced in a reflective space outside
the imperatives of the "calculating market-driven 'knowledge economy.'" A value system that does not reduce knowledge to a commodity to be bought and sold was at work in this fledgling institution.
Consciously or not, the PFU presupposed a different code of value
from the normative framework of the corporate marketplace. In this
section, I argue that the PFU is grounded in what Professor John
McMurtry calls the life-code of value and its "instituted bearer," the
"civil commons," which together sustain its activities in a manner
consistent with a Whiteheadian conception of life.

It is worth emphasizing that the life-code of value is primordial
in a way that the money-code is not. Life has value quite apart from
its utility in maximizing private monetary profits. Recognition of
life's intrinsic value makes possible an understanding that transcends
the limitations of the money-code in which life is simply a means to
making ever more money. From a renewed perspective based on life,
McMurtry argues, it makes little sense to ask "whether unpolluted
water to drink or freedom from hunger or having a place to sleep
is of value or disvalue" since these are preconditions for "the preservation and growth of our embodied being" and are recognized as
"universal values" by cultures that differ in many other ways. To
question whether freedom from hunger is good or bad is to disregard

the human condition in which food (as well as clean air, water, and shelter) makes life possible. At its base, life as "organic movement, sentience and feeling, and thought"[55] requires sustenance in order to reproduce itself. Only where basic survival needs are satisfied can questions about how to enhance life's range be addressed.

One of the ways in which this range can be maximized is by enhancing humanity's capacity for learning. Universal access to formal and informal education, with the goal of sharing knowledge among participants, makes possible a more comprehensive understanding of subject matter and the world. This potentiality can only be realized where institutions are in place that are capable of creating the conditions for human learning as a good for all participants. McMurtry argues that an institutional nexus of this kind is immanent in all human societies, despite the ravages of the corporate market. They comprise the most civilizing aspects of human achievement and are distinguished by an ability to offer universal access to services that ensure the survival and growth of all organic life. Public education and health care are two examples, but clean water supply systems, public transit structures, housing for the poor and resources for the handicapped, public libraries, public arts and broadcasting, parks and wilderness areas, and public spaces for interaction and enjoyment of shared life are part of this same network. This intricate web of institutions is, in other words, "what people ensure together as a society to protect and further life, as distinct from money aggregates."[56]

Unlike the goods of the market, which are only accessible to those who can pay, the goods of the civil commons are available to all. As I argue in chapter 3, universal accessibility is the key advantage of public-sector programs of health care, which provide life services needed by everybody at some time in their lives and from which people benefit in many ways. This inner logic of the civil commons, which leads it to provide services enabling a fuller realization of life, is a direct threat to the corporate market, which systematically denies access to such goods if "clients" are unable to pay.

The civil commons extends beyond the lives of human beings to the preservation of nature in general. Since the earth is the source of all life, and human beings are dependent upon it for their well-being, it is to be valued as "the life-ground" for our very existence. Human responsibilities in this regard stem from our interrelationship with all living organisms and from a preconscious recognition that they, too, constitute the future of the planet. This is expressed spontaneously as "a felt bond of being that crosses boundaries of membranes, classes, peoples, and even species"[57] when we experience other humans, animals, forests, or different life forms threatened with extinction.

The relationship between the civil commons and the PFU is an especially close one. As the creative link between mere survival and the full expression of human capacities in learning, the civil commons enables such life-enhancing activity. The potentiality for teaching and learning capable of enhancing life's range was actualized through a network of people working together at the PFU in concrete ways. United by a vision of an alternative form of higher education serving the needs of ordinary people, a web of students, community members, faculty, and staff made this a reality. A distinctive form of education based on structures and processes, which, in Professor Jennifer Sumner's words, "contribute to the civil commons …[through] teaching, learning, collaborating, and researching"[58] has come into being. The concept of universal accessibility enabling a fuller realization of life through education is a defining characteristic of both the PFU and the civil commons. Without this ideal and the educational praxis flowing from it as guide, the PFU's existence might not have been possible. The logic of value of the civil commons takes hold, McMurtry argues, in the form of "concepts and realities which are both material *and* spiritual in nature as humans themselves are." By striving to satisfy the material and spiritual needs of teachers and learners, the PFU enabled both partners to share knowledge of use to the community. While avoiding the reduction of education to job training, it also sustained the many living connections between knowing and its social context. A balance was constantly sought between "the internal and external as an integral unity of process in which their division breeds inertia."[59] Learning as a dynamic process integrating the internal and external lives of participants constituted both the ideal and the baseline for the PFU's ongoing educational practice.

The ideals concretized at the PFU enhanced life in ways currently frustrated by the market model of education. The PFU strove for an "integral unity of process" capable of satisfying the material and spiritual needs of ordinary people engaged in seeking and sharing knowledge among a community of learners. The internal impulse to pursue knowledge in conjunction with others is connected to a learning environment in which this potentiality becomes reality. For Whitehead, "this process of self-creation" involves an awareness of our internal life as "a unity of emotions, enjoyments, hopes, fears, regrets, valuations of alternatives, decisions" through which we shape a "welter of material into a consistent pattern of feelings" as the basis for understanding the world. At the same time, we can "shape the activities of the environment into a new creation" in the form of projects, which are part of "a continuation of the antecedent world" and of our participation in a community of learners. As individuals in such a community, we entertain "the conceptual anticipation of the future" in the form of an "ideal," or "teleological aim," which is also "an enjoyment in the present" because part of "the immediate self-creation of the new creature" we then become.[60]

Put differently, we achieve an internal unity by integrating our experience in order to understand the world; and on the basis of ideals enjoyed both in the present and as projections into the future, we can then act in order to change it. Throughout this process we are transformed by what Whitehead calls "a wider sweep of conscious interest" in which "the removal of the stress of acquisitive feeling arising from the soul's preoccupation with itself" makes possible the "deep metaphysical insight" that life is the founding principle for the "coordination of values."[61] Life, not the acquisition of money aggregates, becomes the goal of learning. Once emancipated from the demands of self-interest, this deep metaphysical insight becomes clear. On this central point, the PFU stood shoulder to shoulder with any "Whiteheadian [who] cannot support the marketization of the whole of society[,] including education that is now so far advanced."[62]

CONCLUSION

I have argued that the PFU embodied three main ideals of Whitehead's educational philosophy as explicated by John Cobb: a community-based approach to education in which there are permeable boundaries between learning and society; a respect for both abstract and practical knowledge; and a recognition of the imagination as a major factor in building a community of learners founded on a value system that enhances life. It is in this kind of community that freedom of action can be realized as individuality coupled with a coordination of purpose recognizes learning as a good that can be shared in the promotion of life. The civil commons, a concept articulated by McMurtry, is vital to the life-enhancing activities of the PFU, sustaining and promoting its Whiteheadian approach to learning.

The life of the PFU was sustained by its relationship with the broader community. The energy and vision with which it was infused provide a working model of what education might become. Much can be learned from the manner in which the PFU provided access to teaching, learning, scholarship, and research to the citizens of Saskatoon. It shows that alternative forms of university education can still be enacted in the face of the corporate Leviathan. Ironically, the PFU embodied some of the principles of the original "People's University" upon which U of S used to pride itself.

Notes

INTRODUCTION

1 George Orwell, *Why I Write* (London: Penguin Books 2004), 111.
2 There are many other cases I could have chosen, including those of Mary Brison at the University of British Columbia, *www.caut.ca/pages.asp?page=203&lang=1* (viewed 12 August 2007); David Noble at Simon Fraser University, *www.ianangus.ca/pub.htm* (viewed 14 June 2007). At York University, see "David Noble, CAUT Say Ruling a Victory for Academic Freedom," CAUT *Bulletin*, December 2007, A3. See also David Healy, "You Have No Right to Present this Research," in *Disciplining Dissent: The Curbing of Free Expression in Academia and the Media*, ed. William Bruneau and James L. Turk, 53–73 (Toronto: James Lorimer, 2004). On David Hitchcock, see William Bruneau, "Putting Clothes on the Emperor: University Governance and Academic Freedom (forthcoming). And on the First Nations University of Canada (FNUC), see Cory Wolfe, "FNUC Hit with Probation Order," *Saskatoon StarPhoenix*, 19 April 2007, A3, and "AFF Gives $100K to Aid FNUC Staff," CAUT *Bulletin*, June 2006, A1.
3 Jennifer Sumner, *Sustainability and the Civil Commons: Rural Communities in the Age of Globalization* (Toronto: University of Toronto Press, 2005), 5.
4 John McMurtry, *Unequal Freedoms: The Global Market as an Ethical System* (Toronto: Garamond Press, 1998), 188–9.
5 A.N. Whitehead, *The Aims of Education and Other Essays* (New York: The Free Press, 1957), 26.

6 David L. Kirp, *Shakespeare, Einstein, and the Bottom Line: The Marketing of Higher Education* (Cambridge, MA: Harvard University Press, 2003), 7.

7 Other works on Canadian universities using the case study approach include M. Patricia Marchak, *Racism, Sexism, and the University: The Political Science Affair at the University of British Columbia* (Montreal and Kingston: McGill-Queen's University Press, 1996); Kenneth Westhues, *Eliminating Professors: A Guide to the Dismissal Process* (Queenston, ON: Kempner Collegium Publications, 1998); Allen Fenichel and David Mandel, *The Academic Corporation: Justice, Freedom, and the University* (Montreal: Black Rose Books, 1987); David Bernans, *Con U Inc.: Privatization, Marketization and Globalization at Concordia (and Beyond)* (Montreal: Concordia Student Union, 2001); Marvin Brown, "Academic Freedom: The Troubling Present and Questionable Future," in *Pursuing Academic Freedom: "Free and Fearless"?* ed. Len M. Findlay and Paul M. Bidwell, 42–6 (Saskatoon: Purich Publishing, 2001); Arthur Schafer, "Biomedical Conflicts of Interest: A Defence of the Sequestration Thesis: Learning from the Cases of Nancy Olivieri and David Healy," *Journal of Medical Ethics* 30 (2004): 8–24; and Howard Woodhouse, "Killing Us Softly: How an Alternative Education Program Ceased to Be," *Orbit* 20, 2 (1989): 6–7. Recent American books using the same approach include Kirp, *Shakespeare, Einstein, and the Bottom Line*; Jennifer Washburn, *University Inc.: The Corporate Corruption of Higher Education* (New York: Basic Books, 2005); and Michael Parenti, *Contrary Notions: The Michael Parenti Reader* (San Francisco: City Lights Books, 2007), 40–60.

8 McMurtry, *Unequal Freedoms*, 188.

9 Perry W. Schulman, Q.C., *In the Matter of an Arbitration Award between University of Manitoba Faculty Association and University of Manitoba*, 11 February 1991, 63.

10 Nancy Olivieri, "When Money and Truth Collide," in *The Corporate Campus: Commercialization and the Dangers to Canada's Colleges and Universities*, ed. James L. Turk (Toronto: James Lorimer, 2000), 53–68. Apotex has been suing Dr Olivieri for millions of dollars worth of damages, while Dr Olivieri has been suing Apotex for defamation. See Schafer, "Biomedical Conflicts of Interest," 12.

11 The capital costs were made available at *http://www.lightsource.ca* (viewed 26 February 2003) and "Quick Facts," *Saskatoon StarPhoenix*, 1 April 1999, A1. The operating costs were sent by Sandra Ribiero, Public Relations and Marketing Coordinator, Canadian Light Source Inc., in an e-mail message to author, 12 May 2004.

12 Canadian Light Source, *Progress and Opportunity: Our National Synchrotron Facility* (Saskatoon: University of Saskatchewan, 2001), 2.

13 Marchak, *Racism, Sexism, and the University*, 31.

14 James E. Coté and Anton L. Allahar, *Ivory Tower Blues: A University System in Crisis* (Toronto: University of Toronto Press, 2007), 85.

15 For a satirical commentary on such an approach, see Thomas Cushman, "Hemlock Available in the Faculty Lounge," *The Chronicle of Higher Education*, 16 March 2007, available at *http://chronicle.com/temp/reprint.php* (viewed 20 May 2007).

16 Canadian Association of University Teachers, *Canadian Association of University Teachers Policy on the Use of Anonymous Questionnaires in the Evaluation of Teaching* (Ottawa, May 1998), 1–14, available at *www.caut.ca/english/about/policy/questionnaires. asp* (viewed 10 June 2007). See also Howard Woodhouse, "How Can We *Possibly* Evaluate University Teaching without Evaluating Student Learning?" panel presentation entitled "Issues in Post Secondary Teaching and Learning," Annual Conference of the Canadian Association of Foundations of Education, Congress of the Humanities and Social Sciences, University of Saskatchewan, 26–9 May 2007.

17 McMurtry, *Unequal Freedoms*, 15.

18 Jay Rahn, "Police Brutality Meets Communications and Marketing at a Public University," *Our Schools/Our Selves* 14, 3 (2005): 108.

19 Communications Home Page: *www.yorku.ca/ycom/* (viewed 15 May 2005).

20 McMurtry, *Unequal Freedoms*, 23–4; A.N. Whitehead, *Modes of Thought* (New York: The Free Press, 1966), 166.

21 David Ray Griffin, *The New Pearl Harbor: Disturbing Questions about the Bush Administration and 9/11* (Northampton, MA: Olive Branch Press, 2004), xxiv.

22 Canadian Association of University Teachers, *Handbook of Policy Statements, Guidelines and Model Clauses* (Ottawa: CAUT, 1979),

46. The wording of the more recent CAUT Policy Statement on Academic Freedom is slightly different and will be considered in chapter 1, notes 55–7. See *Canadian Association of University Teachers Policy Statement on Academic Freedom* (Approved by the CAUT Council, November 2005) *http://www,caut.ca/pages. asp?page=247&lang=1* (viewed 5 February 2006).

23 Robert Jensen, "September 11 and the Politics of University Teaching," CAUT *Bulletin*, February 2002, A14.

24 Janice Drakich, Marilyn Taylor, and Jennifer Bankier, "Academic Freedom *Is* the Inclusive University," in *Beyond Political Correctness*, ed. Stephen Richer and Lorna Weir, 120–7 (Toronto: University of Toronto Press, 1995). Fred Wilson, "In Defence of Speech Codes," *Interchange* 27, 2 (1996): 125–59, and Shadia B. Drury, "Political Correctness and the NeoConservative Reaction," *Interchange* 27, 2 (1996): 161–72, both provide different perspectives.

25 Marie Battiste, Lynne Bell, and L.M. Findlay, "Decolonizing Education in Canadian Universities: An Interdisciplinary, International, Indigenous Research Project," *Canadian Journal of Native Education* 26, 2 (2002): 82–95; Len Findlay, "Extraordinary Renditions: Translating the Humanities as Radical Processes Now," 6th Annual Lecture of the University of Saskatchewan Process Philosophy Research Unit, 23 January 2008; Howard Woodhouse, "Toward an Inclusive University: A Reply to Michael Kubara," *Interchange* 28, 4 (1997): 363–8.

26 See, for example, Westhues, *Eliminating Professors*, and Marchak, *Racism, Sexism and the University*.

27 Horn, *Academic Freedom in Canada*, 330; William Hare, *What Makes a Good Teacher: Reflections on Some Characteristics Central to the Educational Enterprise* (London, ON: The Althouse Press, 1993), 52.

28 Horn, *Academic Freedom in Canada*, 329. For a full analysis of the Cannizzo case, see Hare, *What Makes a Good Teacher*, 51–4, 174–7n.

29 A similar argument was used in a legal case against Professor Elizabeth Loftus of the University of Washington and was upheld on the basis of its *legality* (i.e., whether the appellant had a legal claim *if* the charge in question turned out to be true) rather than its *validity* (i.e., whether or not the claim was *actually* justified). See

Carol Tavris, "Whatever Happened to Jane Doe," *Skeptical Inquirer* 32, 1 (2008): 28–30.

30 John McMurtry, "Reclaiming the Teaching Profession: From Corporate Hierarchy to the Authority of Learning," Keynote Address, Ontario Teachers Federation and Ontario Association of Deans of Education Conference, 23 May 2003.

31 Bertrand Russell, *Sceptical Essays* (London: Routledge Classics, 2005), 128, 168–9.

CHAPTER ONE

1 A.N. Whitehead, *The Aims of Education and Other Essays* (New York: The Free Press, 1957), 97.

2 Glenn A. Mitchell, "Research Parks: Instrument, or Harbinger of a New University Paradigm?" *Interchange* 23, 1 & 2 (1992): 101–2 The international conference entitled "The University and Democracy" was held in Toronto at the Ontario Institute for Studies in Education, 18–19 October 1991, and the papers delivered there were published in a special issue of *Interchange*. Among the papers in this volume defending university autonomy and academic freedom are those by Torsten Husen, Frank Cunningham, Ruth Hayhoe, Ian Winchester, and myself.

3 Mitchell, "Research Parks," 101.

4 Ibid., 101–2.

5 Maude Barlow and Heather-Jane Robertson, *Class Warfare: The Assault on Canada's Schools* (Toronto: Key Porter Books, 1994), 106; John Harris, "Universities for Sale," *This Magazine* 25, 3 (1991): 14–18. In 2004, UBC released a report showing there had been "serious and 'indefensible' deficiencies with the university's clinical research ethics board ... that approved more than 500 research projects at UBC before mid-2001." The report stated that "UBC 'more or less' allowed investigators, whose research projects in some cases were worth hundreds of thousands of dollars, 'to do their own ethics review.'" Bear in mind that "UBC and its affiliates receive more than $130 million in medical research grants from federal agencies and private companies each year." See Margaret Munro, "Ethics Woes Detailed in UBC Report, Research Projects: University Decides to Release Data to End Provincial Inquiry," CanWest News Service, 5 November 2004, *http://www.canada.com/*

components/printstory/printstory4.aspx?id=2 (viewed 6 November 2004). UBC's administration also "created a Real Estate Development company so as to prepare 28 acres of park land, for lease to developers for luxury houses, condominiums and two 26–storey towers ... all arranged without any consultation or cooperation with the student tenants, whose territory they are invading, or with the local residents of the University Endowment Lands." See John R. Doheny, "The Industrialization of Education and the Intellectual," in *Anarcho-Modernism: Toward a New Critical Theory*, ed. Ian Angus (Vancouver, BC: Talonbooks, 2001), 51–2.

6 Corporate-Higher Education Forum, *Spending Smarter*, update, Montreal, May 1986. More recent approaches to intellectual property rights are analyzed by Christine Tausig Ford, "Ideas for Sale," *University Affairs*, January 1999, 18–19, and Michael Perelman, "The Political Economy of Intellectual Property," *Monthly Review* 54, 8 (2003): 29–37.

7 Mitchell, "Research Parks," 103.

8 D. Bruce Johnstone with Alka Arora and William Experton for the World Bank, *The Financing and Management of Higher Education: A Status Report on Worldwide Reforms* (Paris: UNESCO Conference on Higher Education, 5–9 October 1998), 23. I analyze this document in chapter 6.

9 Mitchell, "Research Parks," 100, 102, 101, 103.

10 For a critique of the "invisible hand" of the market, see Arran Gare, "Ecological Economics and Human Ecology," in *Handbook of Whiteheadian Process Thought*, vol. 1., ed. Michel Weber and Will Desmond (Frankfurt: Ontos Verlag, 2008), 163.

11 Cited in Julia Hinde, "Science Packed Off to Market" *Times Higher Education Supplement*, 18 December 1998, 1.

12 Mitchell, "Research Parks," 102, 101, 100, 103 (emphasis mine).

13 Ibid., 101.

14 John McMurtry, *The Cancer Stage of Capitalism* (London: Pluto Press, 1999), 40–1.

15 Janice Newson, "Preface," in *Universities and Globalization: Critical Perspectives*, ed. Jan Currie and Janice Newson (Thousand Oaks, CA: Sage, 1998), xii.

16 John McMurtry, *Unequal Freedoms: The Global Market as an Ethical System* (Toronto: Garamond Press, 1998), 188–9. Len Findlay claims that "McMurtry's ethical challenge to 'free'-market ideology needs buttressing by aesthetic and institutional traditions

whose histories and current implications are more conflicted and problematic than he would like." See Findlay, "All the World's a Stooge? Globalization as Aesthetic System," *Topia* 4 (2000): 42. McMurtry considers the importance of aesthetic value in his response to critics in "The Life Code of Value and the Civil Commons: A Reply to Three Educators," *Interchange* 32, 1 (2001): 261–70. He also looks at the implications of the struggles of the Zapatistas of Chiapas, the Innu of Labrador, and the people fighting for women's literacy in the state of Kerala, India. See McMurtry, *Unequal Freedoms*, 229–30, 386–7, 374–5.

17 Conrad Russell, *Academic Freedom* (London: Routledge, 1993), 59, 78–80, 80. For Russell's critical views of the Labour Party's approach to universities, see Huw Richards, "Whig Heir Shows Liberal Roots," *Times Higher Education Supplement*, 11 April 1997, 15. See also Howard Woodhouse, "Book Review of *Academic Freedom*," *Interchange* 27, 2 (1996): 213–16 for examples of the marketization of universities in both Britain and Canada.

18 Hinde, "Science Packed Off to Market," 1.

19 Matthew Taylor and Donald MacLeod, "Oxford Dons Rebel over Plan to Hand Powers to Business Leaders," *Guardian*, 26 April 2005, available at *www.guardian.co.uk* (viewed 26 April 2005); Matthew Taylor, "Dons Fear Betrayal as Oxford Looks to Business," *Guardian*, 30 April 2005, 13.

20 John McMurtry, "Education and the Market Model," *Paideusis* 5, 1 (1991): 38.

21 Janice Newson, "The Decline of Faculty Influence: Confronting the Effects of the Corporate Agenda," in *Fragile Truths: 25 Years of Sociology and Anthropology in Canada*, ed. W. Carroll, L. Christiansen-Rufman, R. Currie, and D. Harrison (Ottawa: Carleton University Press, 1992), 234.

22 McMurtry, *Unequal Freedoms*, 25.

23 McMurtry, "Education and the Market Model," 38.

24 Ibid.

25 Judith Maxwell and Stephanie Currie, *Partnership for Growth: Corporate-University Cooperation in Canada* (Montreal: The Corporate Higher Education Forum, 1984), 1–4.

26 Ibid., 14.

27 Mitchell, "Research Parks," 101.

28 Maxwell and Currie, *Partnership for Growth*, 3 (emphasis mine). For critical commentaries on *Partnership for Growth*, see Michiel

Horn, *Academic Freedom in Canada: A History* (Toronto:
University of Toronto Press, 1999), 334–5; Janice Newson and
Howard Buchbinder, "Corporation, Cooperation, Cooptation,"
Canadian Association of University Teachers Bulletin 32, 2 (1985):
5; Janice Newson and Howard Buchbinder, *The University Means
Business: Universities, Corporations and Academic Work* (Toronto:
Garamond Press, 1988), 59–61; Howard Woodhouse, "Legitimation
or Transformation: The Role of the State in University Education in
Readings in Canadian Higher Education," ed. Cicely Watson, 1–29
(Toronto: OISE Press, 1988).

29 Horn, *Academic Freedom in Canada*, 335.

30 Cited by William Graham, "From the President," *Ontario
Confederation of University Faculty Associations Bulletin* 6, 15
(1989): 3; and ibid., 6, 22 (1990): 3.

31 Expert Panel on the Commercialization of University Research,
Public Investments in University Research: Reaping the Benefits,
report presented to the Prime Minister's Advisory Council on
Science and Technology, 4 May 1999 (Ottawa: Government of
Canada, 4 May 1999). For criticism of the report, see Neil Tudiver,
"Growing Commercial Pressures Endanger Academic Freedom and
University Autonomy", *Canadian Association of University Teachers
Bulletin* 46, 6 (1999): 4; Canadian Association of University
Teachers, CAUT *Commentary on the Final Report of the Expert
Panel on the Commercialization of University Research* (Ottawa:
CAUT, 30 September 1999); and Letter to the Right Honourable
Jean Chretien, Ottawa, 8 March 2000, signed by university
researchers and scientists across Canada.

32 Conference Board of Canada, Corporate Council on Education,
Employability Skills Profile (Draft) (Ottawa: Conference Board of
Canada, 24 March 1992), 1–2. The quotation about "discrete
skills" is from Howard Woodhouse, "Robin Barrow, *Understanding
Skills: Thinking, Feeling and Caring*," *Paideusis* 4, 2 (1991): 33.

33 Conference Board of Canada, *Employability Skills Profile*, 2.

34 McMurtry, *Unequal Freedoms*, 7, 15.

35 McMurtry, "The Market Model of Education," 38. See also
Bertrand Russell, *Principles of Social Reconstruction* (London:
George Allen and Unwin, 1916).

36 McMurtry, *Unequal Freedoms*, 189; McMurtry, "Education and the
Market Model," 38–9.

37 William A. Cochrane, "Society's Expectations: Staying Near the Customer", in *Universities in Crisis: A Mediaeval Institution in the Twenty-first Century*, ed. William A. W. Neilson and Chad Gaffield (Montreal: The Institute for Research on Public Policy, 1986), 29–30.

38 McMurtry, "The Market Model of Education," 39. Richard Barrett points out that the market also provides goods that are not "consumed in passive or stultifying ways," like "tools, paint-brushes, hiking boots," which offer "endless possibilities of interest and challenge." See Barrett, "Comments on 'Education and the Market Model,'" *Paideusis* 5, 1 (1991): 46. Yet, he ignores the key question: Can the distinctive goods of education be produced by market principles?

39 "Students Pay More for Less," *Canadian Association of University Teachers Bulletin* 48, 6 (2001): 1.

40 Sir Geoffrey Holland, "Alma Matters," *Expression* (Spring 1999): 3. For Holland's views on the marketization of university teaching and research, see his "Under-exploited Assets," *Times Higher Education Supplement*, 4 November 1994, vi. For confirmation that high tuition fees in British universities exclude those "customers" unable to pay, see Alison Utley, "'I can only afford half the tuition fees,'" *Times Higher Education Supplement*, 28 May 1999, 60.

41 McMurtry, "The Market Model of Education," 39–40.

42 Ibid.; McMurtry, *Unequal Freedoms*, 167–90.

43 Michael R. Bloom, "Corporate Involvement in the Curriculum: Partnership Not Coercion," *The Struggle for Curriculum: Education, the State and the Corporate Sector*, ed. Marvin Wideen and Mary Clare Courtland (Burnaby, BC: Simon Fraser University, Institute for Studies in Teacher Education, 1996), 120.

44 Ibid.

45 McMurtry, *Unequal Freedoms*, 146.

46 Marc Renaud, *The Universities of the Future: From the Ivory Tower to the Market Square* (Saskatoon: University of Saskatchewan Press, 30th Annual Sorokin Lecture, 1999), 5.

47 Ibid, 10. Like Bloom, however, Renaud believes that "as nations increasingly compete on a world-wide scale, so too must universities" in order to give business a comparative advantage in the corporate market. See ibid., 12. Chad Gaffield, Renaud's successor as president of SSHRC, goes further and "proposes a new paradigm

for competitiveness in the 21st century," *A New Consensus for Building Canada's Competitiveness in the 21st Century*, Canadian Club of Toronto, 29 September 2008, *www.canadianclub.org/do/event;jsessionid=* (viewed 30 September 2008).

48 McMurtry, "The Market Model of Education," 40. Ian Winchester also emphasizes impartiality and disinterestedness as important characteristics of knowledge. See Winchester, "Government Power and University Principles: An Analysis of the Battle for Academic Freedom in Alberta," in *The Independence of the University and the Funding of the State: Essays on Academic Freedom in Canada*, ed. Ian Winchester (Toronto: OISE Press, 1983), 41–59.

49 McMurtry, "The Market Model of Education," 40, and *Unequal Freedoms*, 189. Some faculty find this condition "that all educators should force challenges on their charges ... excessive." See I.C. Jarvie and Joseph Agassi, "Education: Economic Enterprise or Intellectual Challenge?" *Canadian Association of University Teachers Bulletin* (December 1990): 28. Such criticism is at odds with the mission statement of at least one Canadian university, which states that "at the lowest level students are shown the possibilities of independent thinking by an instructor who ... challenges orthodoxies and criticizes received opinions." See *University of Guelph Learning Objectives* (December 1986), cited in *Collaborative Curriculum Planning at Universities: The Proceedings of an Invitational Conference*, ed. Chris Nash (Guelph: University of Guelph, 1989), 10.

50 Cochrane, "Society's Expectations," 35.

51 Ibid., 34–5. Nobel Laureate John Polanyi objects to business and government placing such pressures on science because they fail to recognize that "what, to the onlooker, appear to be worthless ends" actually embody the "creative effort" of discovery that embodies "a sense of direction sustained in the face of setbacks over a period of years." See Polanyi, "Understanding Discovery," in *Science and Society: The John C. Polanyi Nobel Laureates Lectures*, ed. Martin Moskovits (Toronto: Anansi, 1995), 8.

52 Cochrane, "Society's Expectations," 30, 34, 35, 43.

53 William Thorsell, "How to Encourage Universities to Play to Their Strengths," *Globe and Mail*, 25 April 1998.

54 See Horn, *Academic Freedom in Canada*, 349, who, on pages 348–9, also quotes Thorsell.

55 For the extent to which branding has been adopted by universities in Canada and Britain, see Howard Woodhouse, "No Logo," *Vox*, November 2005, 1; Paul Kingston, "Distance Learning: Britain Must Push the Pace," *Guardian Weekly*, 2 May 1999.

56 Cochrane, "Society's Expectations," 30, 43.

57 Michel Foucault, "Govenmentality," in *The Foucault Effect: Studies in Governmentality*, ed. G. Burchell, C. Gordon, and P. Miller (London: Harvester Wheatsheaf, 1991), cited by Jan Currie, "Introduction," in Currie and Newson, *Universities and Globalization*, 10. For an example of this totalizing trend, see Johnstone et al., *The Financing and Managing of Higher Education*, 4–26.

58 See, for example, George Grant, "The University Curriculum," in *Technology and Empire*, 113–33 (Toronto: Anansi Press, 1969); Amy Gutman, *Democratic Education* (Princeton: Princeton University Press, 1987), chap. 6; Horn, *Academic Freedom in Canada*, 280–354; Robert M. Hutchins, *The Learning Society* (New York: Mentor Books, 1968), 131–50; Ali A. Mazrui, *Political Values and the Educated Class in Africa* (Berkeley: University of California Press, 1978), ix-xiii, 285–319; Jacques Minot, *Histoire des Universités Françaises* (Paris: Presses Universitaires de France, 1991), 14–17; Newson and Buchbinder, *The University Means Business*, 60–1; Russell, *Academic Freedom*, 15–40.

59 Canadian Association of University Teachers, "Model Clause on Academic Freedom," in *Handbook of Policy Statements, Guidelines and Model Clauses*, (Ottawa: CAUT, 1979), 46. The CAUT Policy Statement on Academic Freedom asserts the connection between academic freedom and the public interest even more strongly: "Post-secondary educational institutions serve the common good of society through searching for, and disseminating, knowledge, truth, and understanding and through fostering independent thinking and expression in academic staff and students. Robust democracies require no less. These ends cannot be achieved without academic freedom." Available at *http://www.caut.ca/pages.asp?page=247& lang=1* (viewed 5 February 2008). The Supreme Court of Canada has declared unequivocally that: "Tenure provides the necessary academic freedom to allow free and fearless pursuit of knowledge and the propagation of ideas." See *McKinney v. University of Guelph, Supreme Court of Canada Reports Service*, ed. G. Sanagan

(Toronto: Butterworths, 1991), 9624. For international policies on academic freedom, see UNESCO, *Recommendations Concerning the Status of Higher Education Teaching Personnel* (Paris: UNESCO, 1997), chap. 6. UNESCO's policies have come under attack from a group led by the International Association of Universities, who conceive of academic freedom not as a right but as a duty "to uphold the balance" between "the spiraling demand for higher education on the one hand, and the globalization of economic, financial, and technical change on the other." See "UNESCO Declaration Puts Academic Freedom at Risk," *CAUT Bulletin*, January 1999, 5.

60 Canadian Association of University Teachers, "Model Clause," 46. The CAUT Policy Statement reads as follows: "Academic freedom includes the right, without restriction by prescribed doctrine, to freedom of teaching and discussion; freedom in carrying out research and disseminating and publishing the results thereof ... freedom to express freely one's opinion about the institution, its administration, or the system in which one works; freedom from institutional censorship [etc.]." Available at *http://www.caut.ca/pages.asp?page =247&lang=1* (viewed 5 February 2008).
For an analysis of critical thought and its ability to reveal underlying presuppositions, see John McMurtry, "The History of Inquiry and Social Reproduction: Educating for Critical Thought," *Interchange* 19, 1 (1988): 31–45.

61 Canadian Association of University Teachers, "Model Clause," 46. The CAUT Policy Statement on Academic Freedom omits any reference to the duty and scholarly obligation to base research and teaching on an honest search for knowledge. On the desirability of commitment and open-mindedness in teaching, see Dora and Bertrand Russell, *The Prospects of Industrial Civilization* (London: George Allen and Unwin, 1959), 242–8; and William Hare, *In Defence of Open-mindedness* (Montreal: McGill-Queen's University Press, 1985), 3–15.

62 See also Winchester, "Government Power and University Principles," 58.

63 Northrop Frye, for example, believed that "academic freedom is the key to all freedom ... [and] the university is the centre of all genuine social order." See Frye, *On Education* (Toronto: Fitzhenry and Whiteside, 1988), 3, 87. From a different perspective, see Howard Woodhouse, "Northrop Frye on Academic Freedom: A Critique,"

Interchange 23, Nos. 1&2 (1992): 71–90. The sense of scholarly community suggested here is developed by Herman Daly and John B. Cobb, Jr., *For the Common Good: Redirecting the Economy Toward Community, the Environment, and a Sustainable Future* (Boston: Beacon Press, 1994), 123–37.

64 Horn, *Academic Freedom in Canada*, 280. See also Russell, *Academic Freedom*, 2–3; Polanyi, "Understanding Discovery," 8; and A.N. Whitehead, *Adventures of Ideas* (New York: The Free Press, 1961), 58–62.

65 Horn, *Academic Freedom in Canada*, 154–65, 220–45, 276–8; William Christian, *George Grant: A Biography* (Toronto: University of Toronto Press, 1993), 199–204.

66 Winchester, "Government Power and University Principles," 45, 48–51.

67 Chris Arthur, "What Are Universities For?" *Contemporary Review* 285, 16664 (2004): 147; Hutchins argues that collegiality of this kind forms part of "the ancient ideal of a university." See Hutchins, *The Learning Society*, 138–9.

68 Ramsay Cook to Crowe, 15 December 1958, cited in Horn, *Academic Freedom in Canada*, 240. Crowe later resigned because of the board of regents' failure to guarantee academic freedom and its refusal to reinstate his colleagues Stewart Reid, Kenneth McNaught, and Richard Stingle. See ibid., 241.

69 Whitehead, *The Aims of Education*, 27. Whitehead's advocacy for "a balanced understanding" in education is expressed in *Science and the Modern World* (New York: The Free Press, 1953), 196–9.

70 Ibid., 3.

71 Edmund Sullivan, *Critical Psychology and Pedagogy: Interpretation of the Personal World* (Toronto: OISE Press, 1990), 18–19.

72 David Young, Grant Ingram, and Lise Swartz, *Cry of the Eagle: Encounters with a Cree Healer* (Toronto: University of Toronto Press, 1997), 3.

73 See Joseph Fashing and Steven E. Deutsch, *Academics in Retreat: The Politics of Educational Innovation* (Albuquerque: University of New Mexico Press, 1971), 289. "Triangulation" is often used to refer to the process of cross-checking. See Bill Gilham, *Case Study Research Methods* (London: Continuum, 2000), 13; and Gary Anderson, *Fundamentals of Educational Research* (London: The Falmer Press, 1990), 163. John Lofland and Lyn H. Lofland prefer the "interpenetration of data and analysis." See Lofland and

Lofland, *Understanding Social Situations* (Belmont, CA: Wadsworth, 1984), 146.

74 A.N. Whitehead, *Process and Reality: An Essay in Cosmology* (New York: The Free Press, 1957), ix.

75 Ian Angus, "Academic Freedom in the Corporate University," available at *www.ianangus.ca/corpu.wtm* (viewed 14 June 2007).

CHAPTER TWO

1 David T. Kearns and Denis P. Doyle, *Winning the Brain Race: A Bold Plan to Make Our Schools Competitive* (San Francisco, CA: ICS Press Institute for Contemporary Studies, 1988), 42.

2 Perry W. Schulman, QC, *In the Matter of an Arbitration Award between University of Manitoba Faculty Association and University of Manitoba*, Manitoba Labour Board, AA1991–02–03, 11 February 1991, 3. A summary of the arbitration award is also available in Canadian Labour Arbitration Summaries 21 C.L.A.S. 438. The letters AA, together with page numbers in brackets following quotations or paragraphs in the text, are used in the rest of the chapter to refer to this document.

3 Daniel Ish, "Committee of Inquiry Report: Inquiry into the University of Manitoba Faculty of Management," *Canadian Association of University Teachers Bulletin* (December 1992): 14.

4 Donald Benham, "William Mackness: Can He Work His Bay Street Magic at the U of M?" *Business People Magazine*, April/May 1989, 19.

5 Kevin Rollason, "Leading Tories Earn New Jobs," *Winnipeg Free Press*, 12 October 1991, B21.

6 Jerry Gray, "Vote on Motion," memo to all faculty members, Faculty of Management, University of Manitoba, 19 October 1993.

7 Benham, "Bay Street Magic," 19; *Leadership Record – Dean Mackness,* Dean's Office, Faculty of Management, University of Manitoba, January 1995, 2.

8 Faculty of Management Council, U of M, "No Confidence Motion," memo to the Faculty of Management, University of Manitoba, September 1993, 1.

9 The statements in this paragraph are a summary of the findings in Ish, "Committee of Inquiry Report," 13–15. The report saw nothing wrong with the hiring process of the dean.

10　John McMurtry, *Unequal Freedoms: The Global Market as an Ethical System* (Toronto: Garamond Press, 1998), 188.

11　Ish, "Committee of Inquiry Report," 13.

12　Conrad Russell, *Academic Freedom* (London: Routledge, 1993), 59–60; Janice Newson, "The Corporate-linked University: From Social Project to Market Force," *Canadian Journal of Communication* 23, 1 (1998): 115.

13　John McMurtry, "Definition of Economic Efficiency Is Insanity," *Kitchener-Waterloo Record*, 29 February 2000, 11.

14　Benham, "Bay Street Magic," 18.

15　Robert Kent, "A Dean's Views: University of Manitoba's Dean of Business, William Mackness, Offers Views on Business, Ethics and Education," *Manitoba Business* (October 1993): 11.

16　Benham, "Bay Street Magic," 19, 18.

17　Kent, "A Dean's Views," 11.

18　Ibid.

19　Ibid., 10, 9.

20　The preceding quotations from Mackness's development plan are taken from Ish, "Committee of Inquiry Report," 13 (my emphasis).

21　Benham, "Bay Street Magic," 19.

22　Ish, "Committee of Inquiry Report," 13.

23　CAUT, "Model Clause on Academic Freedom," *Handbook of Policy Statements, Guidelines and Model Clauses* (Ottawa: CAUT, 1979), 46.

24　Mel Myers, QC, the University of Manitoba Faculty Association lawyer, pointed out that the "prescribed doctrine" or "orthodoxy line" in the Faculty of Management was "positive relations with the business community" (AA 50). Professors Kenneth Osborne, President of UMFA, and Donald Savage, executive director of CAUT, who were both called as expert witnesses, agreed with Vedanand that Mackness's memo threatened his academic freedom in the classroom (AA, 39).

25　Kenneth Westhues, *Eliminating Professors: A Guide to the Dismissal Process* (Queenston, ON: Kempner Collegium, 1998), 57, 61.

26　McMurtry, *Unequal Freedoms*, 190.

27　Ish, "Committee of Inquiry Report," 14. As the report goes on to say, "it may be ... that in the business community one can manage an enterprise in a hierarchical fashion with very little consultation with the various stake-holders in the organization ... [but] such an approach ... is most certainly inappropriate within the university community" (ibid.).

28 Neil Tudiver, *Universities for Sale: Resisting Corporate Control over Canadian Higher Education* (Toronto: James Lorimer, 1999), 188.

29 Kent, "A Dean's Views," 10.

30 Arthur Schafer, *Medicine, Morals and Money* (Winnipeg: Centre for Professional and Applied Ethics, University of Manitoba, 1998), 7; William Graham, "Tainted Sick Kids Review Must be Shut Down," *Toronto Star*, 7 December 1998, A17.

31 Ish, "Committee of Inquiry Report," 13.

32 Ibid., 13. "Committees of inquiry are appointed to conduct objective investigations in cases where there are serious allegations involving violations of academic freedom or other professional rights, or involving discrimination." See "Committee of Inquiry Appointed in Olivieri Case," CAUT *Bulletin* 46, 9 (1999): 9.

33 Ish, "Committee of Inquiry Report," 15.

34 For an account of the attempt to dismiss Frank Underhill from the University of Toronto for his criticism of Canadian involvement in the British war effort during the late 1930s, see Michiel Horn, *Academic Freedom in Canada: A History* (Toronto: University of Toronto Press, 1999), 118–22. For a potted history of the same incident, quoting Professor Horn and referring to Underhill's defence of the right to take "unpopular" political stands as "an important victory for academic freedom," see AA 26.

35 In late November 1988, Vedanand sent a letter inviting James Lovie to speak to his class, as had been suggested at the end of the Xerox seminar on 28 September. Vedanand also made mention of "Mr Lovie's invitation" to him "to give some seminars to Xerox employees." A month later, "an employee of Xerox replied on behalf of Mr Lovie extending his apologies for not being able to be available to make a presentation to Dr Vedanand's class." However, "the letter ... omitted any reference to the subject of a presentation by Dr Vedanand to Xerox" (AA, 10).

36 CAUT, "Model Clause on Academic Freedom," 46.

37 Dr Gray, who later became dean of the Faculty of Management at U of M, refused to be interviewed in connection with this study because he "disagreed with its premises."

38 Despite Crispo's claims to be a maverick, Horn lists him as one of a number of academics whose views are sought by the media because

"whatever else may be said of them, [they] seem unlikely to offend many Canadians, and certainly not influential ones." See Horn, *Academic Freedom in Canada*, 330.

39 Irving M. Copi, *Introduction to Logic* (New York: MacMillan, 1982), 99–100.

40 McMurtry, *Unequal Freedoms*, 169–70.

41 *Reibl v. Hughes*, [1980] 114 D.L.R. (3d), 1980: 16. I am grateful to Viola Woodhouse for this reference. Schulman invoked a case from Scotland in 1943 (*Glasgow Corporation v. Muir*) as legal precedent to his flawed notion of a "reasonable man [sic]" (AA, 67n).

42 This pattern of unreason dovetails with the stock-in-trade of some university administrators, who, when faced with disagreement over a substantive question like the violation of academic freedom, insist that "the real issue may not be the academic content but the difficulty and the personal characteristics which precipitate it." See Westhues, *Eliminating Professors*, 16.

43 The inability to distinguish between appearance and reality typifies the market model of education, which tends to overlook the following questions: "Are the *representations* of the market system true to the world and their own claims? Or is their *reality* different from and opposed to their appearance?" See McMurtry, *Unequal Freedoms*, 36.

44 *The Concise Oxford Dictionary of Current English* (Oxford: Clarendon Press, 1964), 135.

45 Horn, *Academic Freedom in Canada*, 332.

46 Ibid., 338.

47 McMurtry, *Unequal Freedoms*, 25.

48 Ian Angus, "Academic Freedom in the Corporate University," available at *www.ianangus.ca/corpuhtm* (viewed 14 June 2007).

49 Benno Schmidt, former president of Yale University, quoted in Nat Hentoff, *Free Speech for Me – But Not for Thee: How the American Left and Right Relentlessly Censor Each Other* (Simon and Shuster: New York, 1992), 152. See Horn, *Academic Freedom in Canada*, 332–3.

50 McMurtry, *Unequal Freedoms*, 191; and McMurtry, "The Market Model of Education," *Paideusis* 5, 1 (1991): 42.

51 Kent, "A Dean's Views," 10.

52 William Mackness, *An Open Letter to Faculty*, 14 October 1993, 1–4.

53 Ibid., 2–5.

54 Ish, "Committee of Inquiry Report," 13. Most of the statements containing objectionable phrases were "softened, developed more fully and explained, or removed entirely" from the final version of Mackness's development plan.

55 Letter from Professor Yash Gupta to the President of UMFA, 8 September 1990, cited in Faculty of Management Council, "No Confidence Motion," September 1993, 5.

56 Ish, "Committee of Inquiry Report," 13–14.

57 Professors Chhajju Bector, Suresh Bhatt, and Earl Rosenbloom, "Dean Mackness' Proposal to Dismantle Our Department," memo to all faculty council members, Faculty of Management, 10 August 1993, 2–3. The authors point out that, in addition to Gupta, "established actuarial professors such as Elias Shiu, Eric Seah, and Ernie Vogt had either quit or retired" during the five years in which "Dean Mackness has been supporting a plan to dismantle the Department." See ibid., 1.

58 Ish, "Committee of Inquiry Report," 15.

59 Ibid.

60 "Statement of Dean's Meeting with Faculty Members," 6 September 1990, cited in Faculty of Management Council, "No Confidence Motion," September 1993, 4.

61 Ish, "Committee of Inquiry Report," 14.

62 Letter from Dean Mackness to Mr Paul Hayward, Managing Editor, *The Manitoban*, 10 September 1990, cited in Faculty of Management Council, "No Confidence Motion," 7.

63 Faculty of Management Council, "No Confidence Motion," 4.

64 Ish, "Committee of Inquiry Report," 14.

65 Professor R. Padmanabhan, "Third World/First Rate," *The Manitoban*, 4 October 1990, 9.

66 Ibid.

67 Ish, "Committee of Inquiry Report," 14

68 Maureen Houston, "Inquiry Probes U of M Faculty," *Winnipeg Free Press*, 26 April 1991.

69 Arnold Naimark, The President's Letter, 7 September 1990, 3.

70 Ish, "Committee of Inquiry Report," 14, 13.

71 Ibid., 15, 13.

72 This view was expressed by several faculty members at U of M whom I interviewed about the Vedanand case, especially Dennis Felbel (head librarian, Faculty of Management) and Professor Tom Booth (Department of Botany and former president of CAUT). Booth

was also critical of the "Committee of Inquiry Report" for not taking a stronger stand on Mackness's violation of the norms of university governance and his disrespect for academic freedom. A similar point was emphasized by UMFA in its response, "The Parties Respond, Committee of Inquiry Report," 15.

73 This inability to conceive of the pursuit of knowledge as having intrinsic value is analyzed in chapter 1 in relation to the views of Dr Tom Brzustowski, president of the Natural Sciences and Engineering Research Council of Canada; William A. Cochrane, president and chief executive officer of Connaught Laboratories; and Dr Michael R. Bloom, senior research associate, National Business and Education Centre, the Conference Board of Canada.

74 Faculty of Management Council, "No Confidence Motion," 1.

75 Bector, Bhatt, and Rosenbloom, "Dean Mackness' Proposal to Dismantle Our Department," 2. The lack of consultation with the regular faculty committees or department heads occurred, in the dean's own words, because "Dr. J. Gray [associate dean] and I are the principal authors of the two attached proposals." See William Mackness, memorandum to faculty council members, 10 August 1993.

76 These figures are taken from Faculty of Management Council, "No Confidence Motion," 8. Mackness conceded that six faculty positions were "lost to budget cuts," but he claimed that, as of October 1993, twenty positions were funded by his development plan. See Mackness, "An Open Letter," app. 2. This claim was later shown to be false by President Arnold Naimark, "The Faculty of Management, the Deanship and the University," *Notes for an Address to the Faculty of Management*, 24 March 1995, 4.

77 Faculty of Management Council, "No Confidence Motion," 4, 8.

78 Bob Raeburn, Secretary, Board of Governors, University of Manitoba, Letter to Professor E.A. Braid, Chair Designate, Faculty of Management Council, 13 October 1993, 1–2.

79 Mackness, "An Open Letter," 2–3.

80 William Mackness, "Appointment of the Dean," memorandum to associates, graduates and friends of the faculty, 22 February 1995.

81 Past Presidents' Group, "Advisory Committee Recommendation Against Reappointment of the Dean," to Board of Governors Chair Findlay, Chancellor Mauro, President Naimark, 23 February 1995. This powerful group included Jack Fraser, later chairman of Air Canada; Arni Thorsteinson, CEO of Cargill and subsequently

president of Petro Canada Ltd; and Kevin Kavanagh, president of Great-West Life.

82 Lawrie O. Pollard, President, Associates Board, letter to Mr Keith Findlay, Chair, Board of Governors, 6 March 1995. This letter, together with the memoranda from both the Past Presidents' Group and Del Crewson, were written on the Associates' University of Manitoba letterhead.

83 Del Crewson, Past Chairman, Associates Board, "The Reappointment of Dean Mackness," memorandum to all associates, 6 March 1995.

84 William W. Notz, letter to Mr Keith Findlay, Chair, Board of Governors, University of Manitoba, 13 March 1995.

85 E.S. Rosenbloom, letter to Mr Bob Raeburn, Secretary, Board of Governors, University of Manitoba, 2 June 1995.

86 William Mackness, letter to graduates of the Faculty of Management, 8 March 1995.

87 *Winnipeg Free Press*, 29 March 1995.

88 Mackness's remarks and the president's reply are quoted in Naimark, "The Faculty of Management, the Deanship and the University," 9.

89 Ibid., 4.

90 Mackness, "An Open Letter," 3, 6 (app. 2, tables 1 and 2); and *Faculty of Management, Statistical Performance Indicators*, Dean's Office, Faculty of Management, January 1995, table 2.

91 Naimark, "The Faculty of Management, the Deanship and the University," 3–4.

92 Ibid., 4.

93 Ibid., 12.

94 Ibid.

95 Ibid.

96 Ibid.

97 Ibid., 11, 10.

98 Martin Cash, "Business Faculty Leader Pledges Dedicated Term," *Winnipeg Free Press*, 8 July 1995, B12.

99 Naimark, "The Faculty of Management, the Deanship and the University," 13.

100 Ish, "Committee of Inquiry Report," 15.

101 Torsten Husén, "The Applicability of Democratic Principles and the Mission of the University," *Interchange* 23, 1&2 (1992): 11.

CHAPTER THREE

1 John le Carré, *The Constant Gardener* (Toronto: Viking, 2001), 507–8. Le Carré's reference is to Drs Nancy Olivieri, David Kern (formerly a professor of medicine at Brown University), and Betty Dong (a clinical researcher at the University of California, San Francisco), all of whom broke confidentiality clauses with private corporations in order to make public their research findings. See Jennifer Washburn, *University Inc.: The Corporate Corruption of Higher Education* (New York: Basic Books, 2005), 122–4, 76–81, 19–23.

2 Arthur Schafer, cited in U of T Faculty Association, *Nancy Olivieri and the Scandal at Sick Kids Hospital: Struggle for Academic Freedom – Not Yet Over* (Toronto: University of Toronto Faculty Association, n.d.), 1; Jon Thompson, Patricia Baird, and Jocelyn Downie, *The Olivieri Report: The Complete Text of the Report of the Independent Inquiry Commissioned by the Canadian Association of University Teachers* (Toronto: James Lorimer, 2001), 3 (hereafter *The Olivieri Report*); Derek Bok, *Universities in the Marketplace: The Commercialization of Higher Education* (Princeton: Princeton University Press, 2003), 74; Michiel Horn, *Academic Freedom in Canada: A History* (Toronto: University of Toronto Press, 1999), 344; Paul Axelrod, *Values in Conflict: The University, the Marketplace, and the Trials of Liberal Education* (Montreal and Kingston: McGill-Queen's University Press, 2002), 106.

3 *The Olivieri Report*, 17–20; Arthur Schafer, *Medicine, Morals, and Money* (Winnipeg: University of Manitoba Centre for Professional and Applied Ethics, December 1998), 1–2; Margaret Somerville, "A Postmodern Moral Tale: The Ethics of Research Relationships," *Perspectives* 1 (2002): 316–20; Margaret Somerville, *The Ethical Canary: Science, Society and the Human Spirit* (Toronto: Penguin, 2001), 256–7.

4 Arthur Schafer, "Biomedical Conflicts of Interest: A Defence of the Sequestration Thesis – Learning from the Cases of Nancy Olivieri and David Healy," *Journal of Medical Ethics* 30 (2004): 10.

5 Michael Valpy, "Science Friction," *Elm Street* (Summer 1998): 32.

6 Arnold Aberman, letter to Phillips, 1 October 1997, cited in *The Olivieri Report*, 390.

7 Nancy Olivieri, "When Money and Truth Collide," in *The Corporate Campus: Commercialization and the Dangers to Canada's Colleges and Universities*, ed. James L. Turk (Toronto: James Lorimer, 2000), 53; *The Olivieri Report*, 112–3.

8 Contract for LA-03 issued and signed by Apotex on 2 October 1995, by Dr Koren on 10 October 1995, and by Dr Olivieri on 12 October 1995. See *The Olivieri Report*, 115. Somerville ignores this legal point in her account, "A Postmodern Moral Tale," 316.

9 Personal interview with Dr Stanley Zlotkin, OC, professor, Department of Pediatrics and Nutritional Sciences, University of Toronto; senior scientist, Research Institute of the Hospital for Sick Children; medical director of Nutrition Support; and chief of the Division of Gastroenterology and Nutrition at the Hospital, 29 November 1999.

10 *The College of Physicians and Surgeons of Ontario: Complaints Committee Decision and Reasons – Complainant, Dr Laurence Becker; Respondent, Dr Nancy F. Olivieri*, Toronto, 19 December 2001, 17–18, available at *www.dal.ca/committeeofinquiry* (viewed 14 January 2002).

11 *The Olivieri Report*, 7.

12 Orna Diav-Citrin, Gordana Atanackovic, and Gideon Koren, "An Investigation into Variability of the Therapeutic Response to Deferiprone in Patients with Thalassemia Major," *Therapeutic Drug Monitoring* 21 (1999): 74–81.

13 *The Olivieri Report*, 404.

14 Manuel Buchwald and Hugh O'Brodovich, "HSC Clinical Trials Controversy Continues," *Nature Medicine* 5, 1 (1999): 2.

15 *The Olivieri Report*, 7, 5, 142, 404; Somerville, "A Postmodern Moral Tale," 316.

16 Board of Trustees, *Public Statement from the Board of Trustees, the Hospital for Sick Children*, Toronto, 9 December 1998, 2.

17 *The Olivieri Report*, 8; Somerville suggests that the HSC would have faced "a potential conflict of interest" had it undertaken Dr. Olivieri's legal defence. See Somerville, "A Postmodern Tale," 317. However, the hospital did eventually accept its responsibility "to pay her costs [for] any legal action brought by Apotex arising out of facts which occurred prior to 25 January 1999." See *Text of Olivieri/HSC Agreement – 25 January 1999*, clause no. 8, 2–3, available at *www.ufta.toronto.ca/html/press/html/olivieri.agreement* (viewed 20 June 1999).

18 *The Olivieri Report*, 8, 6, 13.

19 "Minutes from the University of Toronto's Executive Committee,"
    cited in Krista Foss and Nicola Luksic, "U of T Head Admits
    Lobbying Was Wrong," *Globe and Mail*, 16 September 1999, A5.

20 Ibid.

21 *The Olivieri Report*, 8, 211–16; N.F. Olivieri, G.M. Brittenham,
    C.E. McLaren, D.M. Templeton, R.G. Cameron, R.A. McClelland,
    A.D. Burt, and K.A. Fleming, "Long-Term Safety and Effectiveness
    of Iron-Chelation Therapy with Deferiprone for Thalassemia
    Major," *New England Journal of Medicine* 339, 7 (1998):
    417–23.

22 *The Olivieri Report*, 281.

23 Dr Nancy Olivieri, interview with author, 30 October 1999.

24 Arnold Naimark, Bartha Maria Knoppers, and Frederick H. Lowy,
    *On Selected Aspects of the Report of the Canadian Association of
    University Teachers Committee of Inquiry on the Case Involving
    Dr Nancy Olivieri, the Hospital for Sick Children, the University of
    Toronto and Apotex Inc*, Toronto, December 2001, 3n. The report
    is no longer available on HSC's website and was kindly sent to me
    by Jennifer Oxley.

25 Schafer, *Medicine, Morals, and Money*, 7.

26 Letter from Dr Olivieri and Colleagues to the Naimark Review,
    20 November 1998, cited in Arnold Naimark, Bartha Knoppers,
    and Frederick H. Lowy, *Clinical Trials of L1 (Deferiprone) at the
    Hospital for Sick Children in Toronto: A Review of Facts and
    Circumstances*, Toronto, 9 December 1998, 3, available at
    www.sickkids.ca/L1trials/revcontents.asp (viewed 8 August 2001)
    (hereafter *The Naimark Report*).

27 Ibid., 3; *The Olivieri Report*, 283–4.

28 *The Naimark Report*, 2, 144, 118, 119–24.

29 *Hospital for Sick Children, Policy Review Implementation
    Committee: Part 2 – Summary of Accomplishments*, Toronto,
    22 December 1999, 1–7, available at *www.sickkids.ca/policyreview/*
    (viewed 18 March 2005).

30 *The Olivieri Report*, 284.

31 *The Naimark Report*, 41, 43, 135, 139.

32 *The Olivieri Report*, 291.

33 *Public Statement from the Board of Trustees, The Hospital for Sick
    Children*, 1.

34 *The Naimark Report*, 41, 134, 42.

35 The Naimark Review Panel later claimed that "there is no discrepancy in these particular statements in so far as they refer to different proximate sources of the information, namely Apotex in the case of material received on February 8 and Dr. Olivieri on February 19." See *Commentary on Selected Aspects of the Report of the Canadian Association of University Teachers*, 8. *The Humphrey Report* shows that it was Dr Olivieri, through her counsel, who was the source of the 8 February information. See the quotation in the text to note 38.

36 Barbara Humphrey, *Re: Investigation of Harassment Complaint* (Toronto, Hospital for Sick Children, 20 December 1999), 195 (hereafter *The Humphrey Report*).

37 Naimark, Knoppers, and Lowy, *Commentary on selected aspects of the Report of the Canadian Association of University Teachers*, 8.

38 *The Humphrey Report*, 195.

39 *The Naimark Report*, 56, 136.

40 Letter from Dr Hugh O'Brodovich and Dr Blanchette, 6 January 1999, cited in *The Olivieri Report*, 233–4. Dr Olivieri had, in fact, provided reasons for not decentralizing the SCD program since 1995.

41 *The Olivieri Report*, 10.

42 U of T Faculty Association, *Nancy Olivieri and the Scandal at Sick Kids Hospital*, 3; for an excerpt from Dr Weatherall's 8 January letter to President Prichard, see *The Olivieri Report*, 235.

43 U of T Faculty Association, *Nancy Olivieri and the Scandal at Sick Kids Hospital*, 4; see also *The Olivieri Report*, 231–2, 260.

44 U of T Faculty Association, *Nancy Olivieri and the Scandal at Sick Kids Hospital*, 3, 4.

45 *The Olivieri Report*, 267–8.

46 *Text of Olivieri/HSC Agreement – 25 January 1999*, 2–3.

47 Krista Foss and Paul Taylor, "Olivieri Reinstated in Sick Kids Truce," *Globe and Mail*, 27 January 1999, A2.

48 UTFA and CAUT, *Joint UTFA and CAUT Press Release – 26 January 1999*, 2, as reported in N.A., "CAUT Brokers Settlement in Olivieri Case," *CAUT Bulletin*, February 1999, available at *www.cautbulletin.ca/en_article.asp?* (viewed 16 January 2000); *The Olivieri Report*, 266–7.

49 Anne McIlroy, "Olivieri, Supporters Win Settlement," *Globe and Mail*, 13 November 2002, A4.

50 HSC, *L1 Clinical Trials: Release and Publication of Research Information* (Toronto: Hospital for Sick Children, n.d.) available at *www.sickkids.ca/L1trials/* (viewed 1 January 2008). The statements in question are contained in Part V1, the "Summary" of the report: "By the end of 1996, Dr Olivieri had concluded that L1 caused liver fibrosis in some patients with thalassemia. Contrary to the requirements that adverse drug reactions be reported promptly, the Research Ethics Board was only informed of her findings in the latter part of February 1997 after Dr O'Brodovich learned indirectly of Dr Olivieri's finding of liver toxicity. Dr Olivieri indicated that she had been advised to delay reporting to the REB by legal counsel." Available at *www.sickkids.ca/L1trials/section.asp?sID= 7415+Clinical+TrialsssID=7455&ssPart+V1+*

51 *The Olivieri Report*, 346. Some of the supporting evidence is provided by Emanuele Angelucci, Donatella Baronciani, Guido Lucarelli, Massimo Baldassarri, Maria Galimberti, Claudio Giardini, Filiberto Martinelli, Paula Polchi, Vincenzo Polizzi, Marta Ripalti, and Pietro Muretto, "Analyses of Diagnostic Accuracy and Safety in 1184 Consecutive Cases," *British Journal of Haematology* 89 (1995): 761.

52 Report of the Ad Hoc Subcommittee to the MAC (n.d.), 7, cited in *The Olivieri Report*, 347.

53 Ibid., 348, 363.

54 Letters from Dr Becker to Complaints Committee of CPSO, 2 May 2000, and to Dr Phillipson (Chair, U of T Department of Medicine) 2 May 2000, cited in *The Olivieri Report*, 365.

55 College of Physicians and Surgeons of Ontario, *The College of Physicians and Surgeons of Ontario: Complaints Committee Decisions and Reasons*, 16–18.

56 Letter from Dr Naylor to Dr Olivieri, 7 January 2002, cited in *The Olivieri Report*, 549, 560.

57 Ibid., 97–8.

58 *The Naimark Report*, 16–17; Letter from Dr Koren to Dr Buchwald, 1 May 1998, cited in *The Olivieri Report*, 95.

59 Letter from Dr Spino to Dr Brittenham, 7 March 7 1997, cited in *The Olivieri Report*, 377.

60 Apotex Research Document entitled "Comprehensive Summary – Exferrum [an Apotex trade name for L1]," 30 January 1998, 46–7, cited in *The Olivieri Report*, 379.

61 Letter from Dr Spino to Dr O'Brodovich, 22 May 1998, cited in *The Olivieri Report*, 379–80.

62 Letter from Dr Spino to Dr Naimark, 24 November 1998, 3, 4, cited in *The Olivieri Report*, 380.

63 Letter from Dr Koren to Dr Roy (Chair, MAC ad hoc subcommittee), 18 December 1998, cited in *The Olivieri Report*, 381.

64 *The Naimark Report*, 41. Drs David Nathan and David Weatherall take a more critical view of the entire "debacle," arguing that it was "complicated by personal animosity, poor administrative judgment, and bad behaviour among colleagues." See Nathan and Weatherall, "Academic Freedom in Clinical Research," *New England Journal of Medicine* 347 (2002): 1368–70.

65 *The Olivieri Report*, 95, 107, 154–5.

66 Ibid., 396, 273, 393, citing *The Humphrey Report*, 227.

67 *The Olivieri Report*, 274–5.

68 Krista Ross, "Sick Kids Doctor Breaks His Silence," *Globe and Mail*, 7 January 2000, A2.

69 Naimark, Knoppers, and Lowy, *Commentary on Selected Aspects of the Report of the Canadian Association of University Teachers*, ii.

70 Ibid.

71 Letter from Presidents Prichard and Strofolino to Dr Koren, 11 April 2000, 6–7, cited in *The Olivieri Report*, 400–1.

72 Letter from Presidents Prichard and Strofolino to Dr Koren, 11 April 2000, 1, cited in *The Olivieri Report*, 406.

73 Letter from Presidents Prichard and Strofolino to Dr Koren, 11 April 2000, 6, cited in *The Olivieri Report*, 400.

74 Somerville, "A Postmodern Moral Tale," 317.

75 *The Olivieri Report*, 346.

76 Schafer, "Biomedical Conflicts of Interest," 12; Marcia Angell, "The Clinical Trials Business: Who Gains?" in *Buying In or Selling Out? The Commercialization of the American Research University*, ed. Donald G. Stein (New Brunswick, NJ: Rutgers University Press, 2004), 128, 131; Arthur Schafer, "The Drug Trial: Nancy Olivieri and the Science Scandal that Rocked the Hospital for Sick Children," *CAUT Bulletin*, June 2005, available at *www.caut.ca/en/bulletin/issues/2005_jun/bookshelf_drugtrial.asp* (viewed 3 November 2007); Elizabeth Church, "New Chapter in Apotex Legal Battle," *The Globe and Mail*, 2 December 2008, A11; N.A.,

"An Attack on Academic Freedom: Apotex vs. Olivieri," CAUT *Bulletin*, January 2009, A1.

77 *Webster's 3rd New International Dictionary* (Springfield, MA: Merriam Webster, 1961), 845.

78 John McMurtry, "Education and the Market Model," *Paideusis* 5, 1 (1991): 39.

79 Viola Nadia Woodhouse, "The Ethic of Informed Consent: Phronesis and Caring" (MA theses, University of Saskatchewan, 1996), 36–7n.

80 David J. Roy, John R. Williams, and Bernard M. Dickens, *Bioethics in Canada* (Scarborough, ON: Prentice-Hall, 1994), 115.

81 John McMurtry, *Unequal Freedoms: The Global Market as an Ethical System* (Toronto: Garamond Press, 1998), 24–5.

82 Eike-Henner W. Kluge, ed., *Readings in Biomedical Ethics: A Canadian Focus* (Toronto: Pearson, 2005), 51; Roy et al., *Bioethics in Canada*, 95–6.

83 Roy Romanow, *Building on Values: The Future of Health Care in Canada* (Ottawa: Final Report of the Royal Commission on the Future of Health Services, 2002), xx.

84 Dr Nancy Olivieri, interview with author, 30 October 1999.

85 Olivieri, "When Money and Truth Collide," 56.

86 Schafer, "Biomedical Conflicts of Interest," 10.

87 College of Physicians and Surgeons of Ontario, *College of Physicians and Surgeons of Ontario: Complaints Committee Decision and Reasons*, 16, 17.

88 Philip C. Hébert, *Doing Right: A Practical Guide for Medical Trainees and Physicians* (Toronto: Oxford University Press, 1996), 88–92; Woodhouse, *The Ethic of Informed Consent*, 37n.

89 Kluge, *Readings in Biomedical Ethics*, 146. For an analysis of the case of *Reibl v. Hughes*, see Roy et al., *Bioethics in Canada*, 78, 118–19; Hébert, *Doing Right*, 86–7; and Woodhouse, *The Ethic of Informed Consent*, 5–10, 102–19.

90 Roy, Williams, and Dickens, *Bioethics in Canada*, 119.

91 *Halushka v. University of Saskatchewan et al.*, in Kluge, *Readings in Biomedical Ethics*, 253–4. For a brief analysis of this case, which went before the Saskatchewan Court of Appeal, see *The Olivieri Report*, 69.

92 Benjamin Freedman, "A Moral Theory of Informed Consent," *Hastings Center Report* 5, 4 (1975): 34–5.

93 Lorne E. Rozovsky, *The Canadian Patient's Book of Rights* (Toronto: Butterworths, 1990), 3.

94 Medical Research Council of Canada, Natural Sciences and Engineering Research Council of Canada and Social Sciences and Humanities Research Council of Canada, *Tri-Council Policy Statement: Ethical Conduct for Research Involving Humans* (Ottawa: Public Works and Government Services Canada, 1998), at 2.10.

95 Françoise Baylis, Jocelyn Downie, and Nuala Kenny, "Children and Decision Making in Health Research," *Health Law Review* 8, 2 (1993): 6–7.

96 Schafer, *Medicine, Morals and Money*, 3.

97 Baylis, Downie, and Kenny, "Children and Decision Making in Health Research," 5.

98 *The Olivieri Report*, 510.

99 Ibid., 188–9, 208.

100 Somerville, "A Postmodern Moral Tale," 317.

101 *The Naimark Report*, 148.

102 *The Olivieri Report*, 413, 35.

103 Ibid., 86. At Brown Medical School, the university's affiliation agreement also failed to spell out the rights and responsibilities of faculty like Dr David Kern. See Washburn, *University Inc.*, 79.

104 CAUT, "Model Clause on Academic Freedom," *Handbook of Policy Statements, Guidelines and Model Clauses* (Ottawa: CAUT, 1979), 46. The clause on academic freedom at U of T is similar. See Memorandum of Agreement between the Governing Council of the University of Toronto and the University of Toronto Faculty Association, 16 June 1977 (consolidated with subsequent amendments 16 June 1998 and 31 December 2006), available at *www.governingcouncil.utoronto.ca/policies/memoagr.htm* (viewed 22 January 2009).

105 Somerville, "A Postmodern Tale," 319.

106 Olivieri, "When Money and Truth Collide," 56.

107 Philip Welch, Carol E. Cass, Gordon Guyatt, Alan C. Jackson, Derryck Smith, *Defending Medicine: Clinical Faculty and Academic Freedom* (Ottawa: CAUT, 2005), 15n. Clinical staff are now covered by the collective agreement at the University of Saskatchewan, *University of Saskatchewan Faculty Association: Collective Agreement 2002–2005*, Clause no. 36, 83–4.

108 Angell, "The Clinical Trials Business," 128.

109 Ibid., 131.

110 McMurtry, "Education and the Market Model," 38.

111 John McMurtry, "The Threat of Corporate Influence on University Campuses, Healthcare, Education: Introduction to Dr Nancy Olivieri Lecture," sponsored by University of Guelph Central Students Association, 1 November 2005, 7.

112 Olivieri, "When Money and Truth Collide," 55.

113 CAUT, "Model Clause on Academic Freedom," 46.

114 McMurtry, "Education and the Market Model," 38.

115 Somerville, "A Postmodern Tale,: 318; *The Olivieri Report*, 17–18, 41; Megan Easton, "High Degree of Compliance between U of T, Hospitals in Research Policies, Audit Shows," *News at U of T*, 8 March 2002.

116 Letter from Dr Spino to Dr Olivieri, 12 August 1996, cited in *The Olivieri Report*, 173.

117 Letter from Dr Spino to Drs Olivieri and Koren, 24 May 1996, cited in *The Olivieri Report*, 173.

118 Letter from Brown to Colangelo, 3 April 1997, cited in *The Olivieri Report*, 176.

119 Letter from Dr Spino to Dr Naimark, 24 November 1998, cited in *The Olivieri Report*, 177–8.

120 CBS News, *60 Minutes Transcript*, dated 10 December 1999, cited in *The Olivieri Report*, 178–9.

121 Transcription of voice-mail message from Dr Spino to Dr Olivieri, 24 May 1996, cited in *The Olivieri Report*, 144.

122 McMurtry, *Unequal Freedoms*, 181.

123 Schafer, "Biomedical Conflicts of Interest," 10–11.

124 *The Olivieri Report*, 37.

125 E-mail message from Dr Aberman to Dr Naimark, 8 October 1998, cited in *The Olivieri Report*, 242.

126 Ibid., 243.

127 Letter from Dr Monroe-Blum to Dr Olivieri, 24 September 1997, cited in *The Olivieri Report*, 245. Since becoming principal of McGill University, Dr Munroe-Blum has written that, "as an institution, the university is an active and influential leader in society … whose responsibility is to encourage, support and protect the independence and freedom of the individuals who comprise the immediate university family." See James Downey, Yvon Fontaine, Heather

Munroe-Blum, and Harvey Weingarten, *The Consenting University and the Dissenting Academy* (Ottawa: Association of Universities and Colleges of Canada, 2003), 26.

128 *The Olivieri Report*, 248–55.

129 Letters from Dr Gooch to Dr Olivieri, 27 November 1997 and 2 December 1997, cited in *The Olivieri Report*, 245.

130 Letter from Dr Olivieri to Dr Monroe-Blum, 1 August 1998, cited in *The Olivieri Report*, 245.

131 Ibid.

132 Letters between Dr Olivieri and Dr Monroe-Blum, 1 August 1998 and 6 August 1998, cited in *The Olivieri Report*, 246.

133 Letter from Dr Sedra to Dr Olivieri, 12 August 1998, cited in *The Olivieri Report*, 246.

134 E-mail message from Dr Olivieri to Dr Aberman, 18 August 1998, cited in *The Olivieri Report*, 246.

135 Letter from Dr Aberman to Dr Olivieri, 20 August 1998, cited in *The Olivieri Report*, 246.

136 Memorandum of Agreement between the Governing Council of the University of Toronto and University of Toronto Faculty Association, 28 June 1977 (consolidated with subsequent amendments 16 June 1998 and updated 31 December 2006), available at *www.governingcouncil.utoronto.ca/policies/memoagr.htm* (viewed 22 January 2009).

137 Memorandum from Mason (McCarthy Tetrault) to Gertner (same firm), 19 July 1996, cited in *The Olivieri Report*, 168.

138 Letter from Colangelo to Kay, 19 August 1996, cited in *The Olivieri Report*, 168.

139 Letter from Spino to Dr Olivieri, 22 August 1996, cited in *The Olivieri Report*, 169.

140 Letter from Dr Olivieri to Spino, 23 August 1996, cited in *The Olivieri Report*, 169.

141 Letter from Kay to Colangelo, 23 August 1996, cited in *The Olivieri Report*, 169.

142 Public statement by President Prichard on the Olivieri case, 9 December 1998, cited in *The Olivieri Report*, 82.

143 Cited by Alison Azer, "Industry Dollars and the Pursuit of Truth," *Alberta Views* (Parkland Institute), October-November 2005, 37.

144 McMurtry, "The Threat of Corporate Influence on University Campuses," 5.

145 Schafer, "Biomedical Conflicts of Interest," 12.

146 James L. Turk, "Introduction: What Commercialization Means for Education," in Turk, *The Corporate Campus*, 10–11.

147 Welch et al., *Defending Medicine*, 5–7.

148 Helke Ferrie, "Big Pharma Unhappy with Measly $638 Billion in Sales," CCPA *Monitor* 11, 3 (2004): 14.

149 Available at *www.apotex.ca/En/AboutApotex/ApotexFacts/Default. htm* (viewed 23 March 2005); *www.apotex.ca/En/AboutApotex/ Philanthropy/ChairsMessage.htm* (viewed 25 March 2005); and *www.apotex.ca/En/AboutApotex/Philanthropy/Default.htm* (viewed 25 March 2005).

150 Ibid.

151 "Gifts to the Heart: A Philanthropic Culture," *University of Toronto Campaign Quarterly*, Fall 2004, available at *www.apotex. ca/En/AboutApotex/PressReleases/20041214-01.asp* (viewed 29 March 2005).

152 University of Manitoba, "$3 Million Gift to Help Establish Cutting Edge Facility for Faculty of Pharmacy," available at *www.apotex.ca/ En/AboutApotex/PressReleases/20050221-01.asp* (viewed 27 March 2005).

153 Anne McIlroy, "Toronto Doctor Loses Round in Drug Battle," *Globe and Mail*, 19 December 2003, A10.

154 Apotex Inc, "Executive Summary of Background Information Re: *Nancy Fern Olivieri vs. Commission of the European Communities*," available at *www.apotex.ca/En/AboutApotex/ PressReleases/20031218-01.asp* (viewed 27 March 2005).

155 *The Olivieri Report*, 248–9.

156 University of Manitoba, "$3 Million Gift to Help Establish Cutting Edge Facility for Faculty of Pharmacy," available at *www.apotex.ca/ En/AboutApotex/PressReleases/20050221-01.asp* (viewed 26 March 2005).

157 Apotex Inc., "Executive Summary," available at *www.apotex.ca/En/ AboutApotex/PressReleases/20031218-01.asp* (viewed 27 March 2005).

158 A. Victor Hoffbrand, Faris AL-Refaie, Bernard Davis, Noppadol Siritanakatkul, Beverly F.A. Jackson, John Cochrane, Emma Prescott, and Beatrix Wonke, "Long-Term Trial of Deferiprone in 51 Transmission-Dependent Iron Overloaded Patients," *Blood* 91, 1 (1998): 295–300. See *The Olivieri Report*, 187, and section 5K, notes 2–4.

159 Ibid., 164, 207.

160 Final written report by Dr Callea, 24 May 1997, cited in
The Olivieri Report, 207.

161 Ibid., 188–9.

162 Testimony of Drs Olivieri, Dick, and Nathan to the Independent
Committee of Inquiry, cited in *The Olivieri Report*, 208.

163 Ibid.

164 Ibid, 383–4. Petrign Tondury, Arthur Zimmermann, Peter Nielsen,
and Andreas Hirt, "Liver Iron and Fibrosis during Long-term
Treatment with Deferiprone (L1) in Swiss Thalassaemic Patients,"
British Journal of Haemetology 101 (1998): 415.

165 McMurtry, "Education and the Market Model," 40; McMurtry,
Unequal Freedoms, 189.

166 *The Olivieri Report*, 94.

167 "Apotex Announce Largest Pharmaceutical Investment in Canadian
History: $627 Million Expansion Has Created 1,500 Jobs,"
available at *www.apotex.ca/En/AboutApotex/Pressreleases/
20041109-01.asp* (viewed 21 March 2005).

168 "Donation and Charitable Trust Agreement, 6 December 1996,
between the Joseph Louis Rotman Charitable Foundation and the
Governing Council of the University of Toronto." Cited in Bill
Graham, "Academic Freedom or Commercial Licence?" in Turk,
The Corporate Campus, 210n. See also Bill Graham, "Corporatism
and the University Part 2: Donor Agreements and Academic
Freedom," UTFA *Newsletter*, 25 February 1998; Bill Graham,
memorandum to the Academic Board, University of Toronto,
12 December 1996 and 19 December 1996; and *The Varsity*,
27 January 1997.

169 Bill Graham, "Academic Freedom or Commercial Licence?" in Turk,
The Corporate Campus, 23.

170 Memorandum from the Acting Vice-President and Provost Carolyn
Tuohy to the University of Toronto Policy and Budget Committee,
Academic Board, Business Board, and Governing Council,
5 December 1996. Cited in Bill Graham, "Academic Freedom or
Commercial Licence?" in Turk, *The Corporate Campus*, 211n.

171 Graham, "Academic Freedom or Commercial Licence?" 24.

172 "Donation and Charitable Trust Agreement, made as of the
27th day of September, 1996 among Horsham Corporation, Barrick
Gold Corporation, and Peter Munk, and Peter Munk Charitable
Foundation, and the Governing Council of the University of

Toronto," cited in Graham, "Academic Freedom or Commercial Licence?" 24.

173 Ibid.

174 "Agreement between Bell Northern Research Ltd. and the Governing Council of the University of Toronto, February 1997," cited in Graham, "Academic Freedom or Commercial Licence?" 23–4.

175 Stephen Petrina and Lorraine Weir, "Transferring Academic Freedom and Intellectual Property," *Faculty Focus: UBC Faculty Association Newsletter* 2 (n.d.). For a critique of AUTM's corporatist views, see McMurtry, "The Threat of Corporate Influence on University Campuses," 7.

176 McMurtry, *Unequal Freedoms*, 188.

177 Steven Lewis, Patricia Baird, Robert G. Evans, William A. Ghali, Charles J. Wright, Elaine Gibson, and Françoise Baylis, "Dancing with the Porcupine: Rules for Governing the University-Industry Relationship," *Canadian Medical Association Journal* 165, 6 (2001): 784–5.

178 Ibid., 784.

179 Ibid.

180 David Healy, *Let Them Eat Prozac* (Toronto: James Lorimer, 2003), 312.

181 Ibid., 312, 313.

182 Lewis et al., "Dancing with the Porcupine," 784.

183 Schafer, "Biomedical Conflicts of Interest," 13. In light of the conflicting evidence, it is wise to remain sceptical towards knowledge claims by "experts" supporting the status quo. See William Hare, "Bertrand Russell on Critical Thinking," *Journal of Thought* 36, 1 (2001): 12–13.

184 Healy, *Let Them Eat Prozac*, 386.

185 Ibid., 307.

186 Michelle Brill-Edwards, "Private Interest and Public Peril at the Health Protection Branch," Turk, *The Corporate Campus*, 66. See also Mark Nichols, "Money and Influence," *Maclean's*, 28 September 1998, 58–9.

187 Lewis et al., "Dancing with the Porcupine," 783, 785.

188 Claire Polster, "Academic Freedom and the Special Challenges for the Sciences," presentation at conference entitled "Understanding Excellence," organized by a concerned group of faculty with

support from the University of Saskatchewan Faculty Association, Saskatoon, 22–3 March 2002.

189 Ibid. See also Conrad Russell, *Academic Freedom* (London: Routledge, 1993), 1–3, 18; and Robert Paul Wolff, *The Ideal of the University* (Boston: Beacon Press, 1969), 129–31.

190 Lewis et al., "Dancing with the Porcupine," 785. See also Canadian Association of University Teachers, *Information Paper: University/ Business Relationships in Research and Development – A Guide for Universities and Researchers* (Ottawa: CAUT, July 1990).

191 James L. Turk, Remarks at conference entitled "Academic Freedom and the Public Interest," organized by the Simon Fraser Student Society (Canadian Federation of Students Local 23) and the Canadian Association of University Teachers, Simon Fraser University, Burnaby, 25–6 April 2003.

192 Lewis et al., "Dancing with the Porcupine," 783. See also Barbara Mintzes, "University Research and the Pharmaceutical Industry," paper delivered at conference entitled "Academic Freedom and the Public Interest," organized by the Simon Fraser Student Society (Canadian Federation of Students Local 23) and the Canadian Association of University Teachers, Simon Fraser University, Burnaby, 25–6 April 2003.

193 Arthur Schafer, "Bad Rx: Big Pharma and Medical Research," CAUT *Bulletin*, October 2003 available at *www.caut.ca/en/bulletin/ issues/2004_jan/commentary.asp* (viewed 13 September 2005).

194 Schafer, "Biomedical Conflicts of Interest," 8, 22–4.

195 Schafer, "Bad Rx." In the United Kingdom, "drug companies spend twice as much on marketing as on research – $60 bn last year (33bn pounds sterling) – but do not publish information on their drug promotion practices." See Sarah Boseley, "Drug Firms a Danger to Health," *Guardian*, 26 June 2006. See also "New Drugs, Big Dollars," *ConsumerReports.org*, available at *http://www.consumerreports.org/cro/health-fitness/health-care/ medical-ripoffs-11-07/new* (viewed 15 October 2007).

196 Healy, *Let Them Eat Prozac*, 12, 104–8, 205, 255–6, 308, 314, 352–5.

197 Neil Tudiver, *Universities for Sale: Resisting Corporate Control over Canadian Higher Education* (Toronto: James Lorimer, 1999), 180.

198 Schafer, "Biomedical Conflicts of Interest," 24.

199 Schafer, "Bad Rx." Scandals over the suppression of adverse data regarding the painkiller Vioxx have become more common recently.

See Carolyn Abraham, "'Deletions' Alleged in Vioxx Study," *Globe and Mail*, 9 December 2005, A1, A21.

200 Healy, *Let Them Eat Prozac*, 350–1. See also Jeff Blackner, "Professionalism and the Medical Association," *World Medical Journal* 53, 3 (2007): 58–72.

201 Jeanne Whalen, "Medical Journals Support Database on Drug Trials," *Wall Street Journal*, 8 September 2004; André Picard, "Top Medical Journals Get Tough on Drug Firms," *Globe and Mail*, 9 September 2004, A1, A12; Laurie Barclay, "Call for Mandatory Clinical Trial Registration, Open Access to Results," *Medscape Medical News*, 14 September 2004, available at *www.medcsape. com/viewarticle/489219* (viewed 21 October 2004).

202 Picard, "Top Medical Journals Get Tough on Drug Firms," A1.

203 Ian Steele, "Bush Can Banish Killer Parasite," *Globe and Mail*, 22 November 1986, D4; Howard Woodhouse, "Tradition or Modernity? The Fallacy of Misplaced Concreteness among Women Science Educators in Cameroon," *Interchange* 28, 2&3 (1997): 254–5, 257–9.

204 Mark Schoofs, "Glaxo Attempts to Block Access to Generic AIDS Drugs in Ghana," *Wall Street Journal*, 1 December 2000.

205 James R. Brown, "The Community of Science®," presentation to the Department of Philosophy, University of Saskatchewan, 29 January 2004.

206 Ibid. There are those who disapprove of socialized medicine because they claim it would lead to "an unaccountable and self-serving bureaucracy [of the kind in] command-and-control regimes like the Soviet Union." See Hymie Rubenstein, "Cure Worse than Disease," *CAUT Bulletin*, November 2003, available at *www.caut.ca/en/ bulletin/issues/2003_nov/letters.asp* (viewed 5 April 2004). For a similar perspective, see Sidney Taurel, "Hands Off My Industry," *Wall Street Journal*, 3 November 2003, available at online.wsj.com/ article_print/0,,SB106782096631988000,00.html (viewed 14 November 2003). This argument commits the informal fallacy of "the straw man argument." See Gregory Pence, *A Dictionary of Common Philosophical Terms* (New York: McGraw Hill, 2000), 50. It also commits the fallacy of the "argumentum ad adversarium." See John McMurtry, "Argumentum ad Adversarium," *Informal Logic* 8, 1 (1986): 27–36.

207 Healy, *Let Them Eat Prozac*, 350, 352.

208 Brown, "The Community of Science®."

209 McMurtry, "Education and the Market Model," 38–40; McMurtry, *Unequal Freedoms*, 188–9.
210 Jon Thompson, "Abstract: The Olivieri Case: Medical Ethics, Academic Freedom, and Scientific Integrity," presentation at conference entitled "Understanding Excellence," organized by a concerned group of faculty with support from the University of Saskatchewan Faculty Association, Saskatoon, 22–3 March 2002.

CHAPTER FOUR

1 Peter MacKinnon, "State of the University Address to the Saskatoon Chamber of Commerce," 30 March 2005, 1, available at *www.usask. ca/president/pdf/cc_address2005.pdf* (viewed 18 May 2005).
2 Jens Nielsen, "Charge Set Rate for Research, U of S Panel Told," *StarPhoenix*, 15 May 1995, A8. For details of the 1995 federal cut of $25.3 billion from all expenditures, including health, education, and social services, see Murray Dobbin, "What Can We Expect from Paul Martin? Read His Budget Speeches," CCPA *Monitor* 10, 7 (2004): 8.
3 Mark Flynn, Robert Regnier, Edward Thompson, and Howard Woodhouse, "Imbalance Exists in Applied Research at U of S," *StarPhoenix*, 17 April 1997, A9.
4 John Conway, *Whose University? Theirs or Ours: A Critical Look at the U of S* (Saskatoon: Peoples Free University, 11 April 2002). The phrase "the people's university" was first used in September 1909 by President Walter Murray to describe U of S's original mission, cited in Michael Hayden, *Seeking a Balance: The University of Saskatchewan, 1907–1982* (Vancouver: UBC Press, 1983), 295. Peter MacKinnon has shown that tuition fees increased from 13 percent to 29 percent of operating costs between 1990 and 2000, while government funding shrank from 77 percent to 64 percent of revenues in the same time period. See MacKinnon, "Strategic Directions: A Presentation to the University of Saskatchewan Community," 9 February 2002, available at *www.usask.ca/vpacademic/integrated-planning/key_planning_planning_* (viewed 18 January 2009).
5 The 1996 U of S operating budget was $158 million, according to *University of Saskatchewan Statistics*, vol. 22 (Saskatoon: University of Saskatchewan, 1996). By 2007–08 the operating budget had risen to $208 million. See "University of Saskatchewan Approves 2007–08 Operating Budget," *University News*, 8 May 2007. The global

budget for the same year was $294 million. See Lori Collican, "U of S Budget Freezes Tuition," *StarPhoenix*, 9 May 2007, A3. In 2009–10 the annual operating budget was $246.5 million. See Colleen MacPherson, "Operations Forecast," *On Campus News*, 9 January 2009, 1.

6 Nielsen, "Charge Set Rate for Research," A8.

7 University of Saskatchewan Archives, University Secretary's Office (2009), Minutes of University Council, University of Saskatchewan, 7 April 1995, 5.

8 Professor Gordon Hill, cited in Nielsen, "Charge Set Rate for Research," A8.

9 Dennis Johnson, "Research Provides Return," *StarPhoenix*, 14 March 1997, A5. Johnson also claimed that, "in 1996, university faculty members received about $5.5 million from industry to support their research activities." Ibid.

10 University of Saskatchewan Archives, University Secretary's Office, Minutes of University Council, University of Saskatchewan, 7 April 1995, 5.

11 University of Saskatchewan Archives, University Secretary's Office, Memorandum from G.A. Hill, Chair, Research Committee of Council, to Dr M.N., Esmail, Chair, Coordinating Committee of Council, 5 February 1995, 2.

12 Canadian Association of University Teachers (hereafter CAUT), *Information Paper: University/Business Relationships in Research and Development – A Guide for Universities and Researchers* (Ottawa: CAUT, July 1990), 32–11.

13 Peter MacKinnon, cited in "Universities Get $5.6 Million Grant," *Saskatoon Sun*, 7 April 2002, 15.

14 A "value added" creation is the "'difference between the value society derives from the product, the price consumers are prepared to pay for it at the margin' *and* 'what this product costs society to produce, measured by the price of labour, capital and other inputs,'" John McMurtry, *The Cancer Stage of Capitalism* (London: Pluto Press, 1999), 167.

15 Johnson, "Research Provides Return," A5.

16 Mark Flynn, Robert Regnier, Ed Thompson, and Howard Woodhouse, "Who Pays for Research?" *StarPhoenix*, 31 March 1997, A6.

17 Flynn, Regnier, Thompson, and Woodhouse, "Imbalance Exists in Applied Research at U of S," A9.

18 Dwight Percy, "Synchrotron Finding Good News for Economy,"
   Star Phoenix, 6 June 1998, B1; Howard Woodhouse, "The
   Seduction of the Market: Whitehead, Hutchins, and the Harvard
   Business School," *Interchange* 31, 2&3 (2000): 155n.

19 Michael Corcoran, former vice-president research, University of
   Saskatchewan, interview with author, 4 October 2000. For figures
   regarding corporate funding of research at U of S, see notes 171–2.

20 Expert Panel on the Commercialization of University Research,
   Public Investments in University Research: Reaping the Benefits,
   report presented to the Prime Minister's Advisory Council on
   Science and Technology, 4 May 1999 (Ottawa: Government of
   Canada, 1999), ii.

21 Joanne Paulson, "High Tech Firms Applaud New Research Tax
   Credit," *StarPhoenix*, 20 March 1998, D10.

22 John McMurtry, *Unequal Freedoms: The Global Market as an
   Ethical System* (Toronto: Garamond Press, 1998), 25.

23 Conrad Russell, *Academic Freedom* (Routledge: London, 1993),
   80.

24 CAUT, *Information Paper*, 32–12.

25 Howard Woodhouse, "Legitimation or Transformation: The Role of
   the State in University Education," in *Readings in Canadian Higher
   Education*, ed. Cicely Watson (Toronto: Higher Education Group,
   the Ontario Institute for Studies in Education, 1988), 17.

26 For different strategies of resistance to corporate control of research,
   see Claire Polster, "From Public Resource to Industry's Instrument:
   Reshaping the Production of Knowledge in Canada's Universities,"
   Canadian Journal of Communication 23, 1 (1998): 102–3.

27 Michiel Horn, *Academic Freedom in Canada: A History* (Toronto:
   University of Toronto Press, 1999), 280.

28 Research Committee of Council, *Increasing Research Intensiveness
   at the University of Saskatchewan* (Saskatoon: University of
   Saskatchewan, January 2000), *passim*; and University of
   Saskatchewan Council, *A Framework for Planning at the University
   of Saskatchewan* (Saskatoon: University of Saskatchewan, March
   1998), 6. The concept of "research intensiveness" seems to have
   originated in California. See Richard C. Atkinson, "The Role of
   Research in the University of the Future," paper presented at the
   United Nations University, Tokyo, Japan, 4 November 1997, cited
   in Masao Miyoshi, "Ivory Tower in Escrow," *boundary 2*, 27, 2
   (2000): 8.

29 The tension between the ideals of service to the province and university autonomy is analyzed by Hayden, *Seeking a Balance*, xvi, 291–4. This tension is analyzed in the final section of the chapter.

30 University of Saskatchewan Archives, University Secretary's Office, Offices of the Vice-President (Academic) and Provost and Vice-President (Research), memorandum to University of Saskatchewan Campus Community, 6 July 2001, 1–2.

31 David F. Noble, *Digital Diploma Mills: The Automation of Higher Education* (Toronto: Between the Lines, 2002), xii.

32 University of Saskatchewan Council, *A Framework for Planning*, 7–8.

33 University of Saskatchewan, *A Framework for Action: University of Saskatchewan Integrated Plan 2003–07*, Saskatoon, 14 May 2004, 8, available at *www.usask.ca/vpacademic/integrated-planning/key_planning_docs/plandocs/May2004/Integrated_Plan_May2004.pdf* (viewed 21 March 2005).

34 Research Committee of Council, *Increasing Research Intensiveness*, 2; Office of the Vice-President (Academic), *Strategic Research Plan*, 1, 11.

35 Research Committee of Council, *Increasing Research Intensiveness*, 4, 7; University of Saskatchewan Archives, University Secretary's Office, Offices of the Vice-President and Provost and Vice-President Research, memorandum to the University of Saskatchewan Campus Community, 1; Office of the Vice-President (Academic), *Strategic Research Plan*, 11; University of Saskatchewan Council, *A Framework for Planning*, 9.

36 Corporate Administration, *Business Opportunities: Strategic Directions, Interview Program Summary* (Saskatoon: University of Saskatchewan, 4 February 2005), 5.

37 Hayden, *Seeking a Balance*, 305.

38 Senate minutes, University of Saskatchewan, September 1909, cited in Hayden, *Seeking a Balance*, 295.

39 Women were represented at the "people's university" from its inception, their numbers growing to match those of men in certain colleges, but Aboriginal people were excluded until the opening of the Indian and Northern Education Program, the Indian Teacher Education Program, and the Native Law Centre in the 1960s and 1970s. See Hayden, *Seeking a Balance*, 62, 142, 301.

40 MacKinnon, "University of Saskatchewan Strategic Directions: Renewing the Dream," 9 February 2002. This was a speech

designed to "renew the dream" of U of S "in the context of the knowledge-based economy of the twenty-first century." Available at *www.usask.ca/vpacademic/integratedplanning/key_planning_* (viewed 18 January 2009). On 6 February 2006, President MacKinnon spoke of "Renewing the Dream: Reflecting on Progress" in similar terms. See *www.usask.ca/president/pdf/ renewingthedream.pdf* (viewed 18 January 2009).

41 Hayden, *Seeking a Balance*, 305. Three studies conducted in the United States during the 1950s ranked U of S among "the very best universities not only in Canada but in North America in terms of the number of eminent graduates" in physics, botany, and the natural sciences in general. Ibid., 297.

42 Ibid., 67.

43 Ibid., 292.

44 MacKinnon, "University of Saskatchewan Strategic Directions," available at *www.usask.ca/vpacademic/integratedplanning/key_ planning_* (viewed 18 January 2009).

45 Research Committee of Council, *Increasing Research Intensiveness*, 8, 1. For a critical analysis of this view, see Claire Polster, "Dismantling the Liberal University: The State's New Approach to Academic Research," in *The University in the Liberal State*, ed. Bob Brecher, Otakar Fleischmann, and Jo Halliday (Aldershot, UK: Avebury Press, 1996), 113–15.

46 University of Saskatchewan Council, *A Framework for Planning*, 9, 3.

47 MacKinnon, *Renewing the Dream*.

48 Research Committee of Council, *Increasing Research Intensiveness*, 10.

49 Ibid. The declared goal is to increase graduate enrollment from its current rate of "about nine percent" to "about 15 percent of total enrollment." Ibid., 5.

50 Ibid., 7–8.

51 Michael Corcoran, cited in Kathryn Warden, "Research Gains Could Boost *Maclean's* Ranking More," *On Campus News*, 16 November 2001, 7.

52 Research Committee of Council, *Increasing Research Intensiveness*, 7, 2.

53 Office of the Vice President (Academic), *Strategic Research Plan*, 1, 10. Kathryn Warden, who is communications officer for the

vice-president (research), claimed that, in order to "bring us up to the mean level of NSERC/CIHR performance nationally," researchers at U of S needed to acquire "304 additional grants totaling $21.4 million," while in the SSHRC area "we'd need another 65 grants totaling $1.9 million." See Warden, "Research Gains Could Boost *Maclean's* Ranking More," 7.

54 Michael Hayden, interview with author, 19 June 2000.

55 Kathryn Warden, "Campus Gets $11m Boost for Advanced Genomics Research," *On Campus News*, 20 April 2001, 7.

56 E. Richard Gold, "Building a Better Patent Law," *Globe and Mail*, 17 May 2002, A13. Among advocates of IPRS, see W. Park and J. Ginarte, "Intellectual Property Rights in a North-South Economic Context," *Science Communication* 17, 3 (1996): 379–87.

57 Vanessa Williams, "Biotech Firm Buys Tonga's Gene Pool," *Adelaide Advertiser*, 22 November 2000, 2. For a critique of the ways in which IPRS preclude the dissemination of scientific knowledge, see Paul A. David, *A Tragedy of the Public Knowledge "Commons"? Global Science, Intellectual Property and the Digital Technology Boomerang* (Stanford, CA: Stanford Institute for Economic Policy Research, October 2000).

58 Gregory Graff, Alan Bennett, Brian Wright, and David Zilberman, *An Industry-Academia-International Development Roundtable Workshop: Intellectual Property Clearinghouse Mechanisms for Agriculture – A Summary of Workshop Proceedings* (Berkeley: University of California, 16 February 2001), 2, available at *www.cnr.berkeley.edu/csrd/technology/ipcmech/Summary-Berkeley-2-16-2001-Agbio-IP-Clearinghouse-Workshop.pdf* (viewed 18 January 2009).

59 Claire Polster, "The Future of the Liberal University in the Era of the Global Knowledge Grab," *Higher Education* 39, 1 (2000): 34. See also Janice Newson, "To Not Intend, or to Intend not … That is the Question," in *The Corporate Campus: Commercialization and the Dangers to Canada's Colleges and Universities*, ed. James L. Turk (Toronto: James Lorimer, 2000), 186; and Sheila Slaughter, "National Higher Education Policies in a Global Economy," in *Universities and Globalization: Critical Perspectives*, ed. Jan Currie and Janice Newson (Thousand Oaks, CA: Sage, 1998), 57.

60 E. Ann Clark, "Academia in the Service of Industry: The Ag Biotech Model," in Turk, *The Corporate Campus*, 74 (emphasis in original).

For ways in which IPRS limit the scope of knowledge and how they could be overcome, see Polster, "The Future of the Liberal University," 34–7; and Horn, *Academic Freedom in Canada*, 344.

61 Hayden, interview with author, 19 June 2000.

62 Michael Conlon, "Betrayal of the Public Trust: Corporate Governance of Canadian Universities," in Turk, *The Corporate Campus*, 147.

63 Expert Panel, *Public Investments in University Research*, 49, 31, v, vi, 36 (emphasis in original).

64 Ibid., 34 (emphasis in original). Corcoran believed the federal government made "a huge mistake" because the Expert Panel "neglected to make it clear that what they are talking about is the commercialization of research that is funded by the Tri-Council." See Corcoran, interview with author, 4 October 2000.

65 Expert Panel, *Public Investments in University Research*, iii.

66 Ibid.

67 University of Saskatchewan Council, *A Framework for Planning*, 9, 3, 1.

68 Ibid., 3, 1.

69 Herman E. Daly, *Beyond Growth: The Economics of Sustainable Development* (Boston: Beacon Press, 1996), 93.

70 Office of Vice-President (Academic), *Strategic Research Plan*, 10.

71 N.A., "Innovation Place, Leading Saskatoon onto World Stage," *StarPhoenix*, 22 February 1997, A7. A more recent article claimed that "Innovation Place in Saskatoon contributed $195 million to the economy of Saskatoon and $259 million to the provincial GDP," See N.A., "Innovation Place Creates $259 million for GDP," *StarPhoenix*, 31 March 2007, C1.

72 Glenn Mitchell, "Research Parks: Instrument, or Harbinger of a New University Paradigm?" *Interchange* 23, 1&2 (1992): 103.

73 Diane Harms, Rachelle Girard, and Branko F. Peterman, *Creating Economic Activity: University of Saskatchewan Example* (Saskatoon: University of Saskatchewan Technologies Inc, 2002), 6–7.

74 Ibid., 6.

75 Mitchell, "Research Parks," 103.

76 Newson, "To not Intend, or to Intend not," 185.

77 Mitchell, "Research Parks," 101, 103. Private spin-off companies throughout Canada "employ more than 7,500 Canadians and

generate close to $1.3 billion in annual sales/revenue." See National Science and Engineering Research Council (hereafter NSERC), *Research Means Business* (Ottawa: National Science and Engineering Research Council, March 2001), xi.

78 John McMurtry, "Education and the Market Model," *Paideusis* 5, 1 (1991): 39; and McMurtry, *Unequal Freedoms*, 189.

79 Ibid., 25.

80 Harms, Girard, and Peterman, *Creating Economic Activity*, 2.

81 NSERC, *Research Means Business*, 91.

82 Michelle Hudon, "U of S Buying into Commercial Ventures," *On Campus News*, 9 September 1994, 7.

83 Expert Panel, *Public Investments in University Research*, vi, 51. UST practised the same supportive role: "The University's senior administration ... have created an environment that facilitates ... the commercialization of ... technologies [resulting in nine] start-ups [during] the last four years." See Harms, Girard, and Peterman, *Creating Economic Activity*, 7.

84 Hudon, "U of S Buying into Commercial Ventures," 7. In June 2007, the former US ambassador Paul Cellucci joined the Board of Directors of Calian Technologies Ltd. Cellucci was "the first ambassador to Canada by US president George W. Bush ... [and] Calian provides information services and IT personnel on an outsourcing basis to other companies and government agencies." See N.A., "Cellucci Joins Board," *StarPhoenix*, 19 June 2007, C7.

85 NSERC, *Research Means Business*, 91; and Hudon, "U of S Buying into Commercial Ventures," 7. In toto, the seven spin-off companies in Innovation Place had annual revenues of $92.5 million in 2001. See NSERC, *Research Means Business*, xi.

86 Noble, *Digital Diploma Mills*, 27.

87 Report of the Expert Panel, *Public Investments in University Research*, iii.

88 Harms, Girard, and Peterman, *Creating Economic Activity*, app. 1.

89 N.A., "U of S Launches Animal Health Products Corporation with 'Almost Limitless Potential,'" *Green and White: University of Saskatchewan Alumni Association Magazine*, Spring 1995, 28.

90 Hudon, "U of S Buying into Commercial Ventures," 7.

91 N.A., "U of S Launches Animal Health Products Corporation," 28.

92 Hudon, "U of S Buying into Commercial Ventures," 7.

93 Harms, Girard, and Peterman, *Creating Economic Activity*, 4.

94 Ibid., 2.
95 CAUT, CAUT *Commentary on the Final Report of the Expert Panel on the Commercialization of University Research* (Ottawa: CAUT, 30 September 1999), 3.
96 Murray Lyons, "Gov't Pumps Up Science Projects," *StarPhoenix*, 21 August 2001, D5.
97 Harms, Girard, and Peterman, *Creating Economic Activity*, 1.
98 Ibid., 4–5.
99 NSERC, *Research Means Business*, xi.
100 Harms, Girard, and Peterman, *Creating Economic Activity*, 4–5, 3.
101 John Keeves, "The Unity of Educational Research," *Interchange* 19, 1 (1988): 14–30.
102 Report of the Expert Panel, *Public Investments in University Research*, ii.
103 Howard Woodhouse, "Contradicting the Market," *Paideusis* 5, 1 (1991): 50.
104 A phrase used by Peter Mandelson, Britain's former secretary of state for trade and industry, cited in Julia Hinde, "Science Packed Off to Market," *Times Higher Education Supplement*, 18 December 1998, 1.
105 Randy Burton, "This Time, Canada Works the Way It Should," *StarPhoenix*, 1 April 1999, A2. The same kind of rhetoric is now being used to describe universities in Alberta. See Elizabeth Church, "Will Alberta's Energy Boom Revolutionize Higher Education?" *The Globe and Mail*, 2 January 2008. This despite the fact that only 61 percent of students graduate from the University of Calgary and that morale among faculty is lower than "during the 23% cuts over 4 years in the early 1990s." See Alan Smart, "The Ripple Effects of the Global Fossil Fuel Boom: A View from Inside the University of Calgary," *GlobalHigherEd*, 29 January 2008, available at *http://globalhighered.wordpress.com/2008/01/29/the-ripple-effects-of-the-global-fossil-fuel-* (viewed 3 February 2008).
106 These comments are drawn from several articles: Burton, "This Time, Canada Works the Way It Should," A2; Gerry Klein, "Field of Beams," *StarPhoenix*, 1 April 1999, A1; Joanne Paulson, "Light Source Accelerates City's Economic Prospects," *Star Phoenix*, 1 April 1999, A1, A12; Percy, "Synchrotron Funding Good News for Economy," B1; and Gerry Klein, "Benefits Huge, Says Chemist," *Star Phoenix*, 1 April 1999, D4.

107 Rhetoric about the CLS's ability to find a cure for cancer contrasts with the dispassionate claims of Dr Cathleen Magowan, whose synchrotron-based research on the malaria parasite at the Advanced Light Source at Lawrence Berkeley National Laboratory's Life Sciences Division *"could contribute* to novel therapeutic approaches to the control of malaria." See Massimo Altarelli, Fred Schlachter, and Jane Cross, "Making Ultrabright X-rays," *Scientific American* 279, 6 (1998): 70 (my emphasis).

108 Glen Beck, cited in G. McNairn, "Some Fear Synchrotron May Drain University Resources," *StarPhoenix*, 1 April 1999, D5.

109 McMurtry, "The Market Model of Education," 40.

110 Canadian Light Source Inc, *Progress and Opportunity*: Our National Synchrotron Facility (Saskatoon: University of Saskatchewan 2001), 2. Industrial research as the primary goal of the CLS is even clearer in a recent publication: "The CLS is globally unique with its focus on private-public partnerships and service to industrial researchers. CLS targets set for industrial participation, and resulting revenue, are the most aggressive of any synchrotron facility and the CLS is committed to being the world leader in synchrotron industrial utilization." *www.lightsource.ca/brochures/pdf/CLS_General_Brochure.pdf* (viewed 22 January 2009).

111 The in-kind contributions were from a consortium of nineteen universities and six support groups across Canada. See Canadian Light Source Inc, *Progress and Opportunity*, 11.

112 N.A., "Retooled 'Linac' Passes Early Synchrotron Test," *On Campus News*, 21 September 2001, 3; Gerry Klein, "Idle Beam Revived for Use," *StarPhoenix*, 14 September 2001, A8; "Council Approves Subatomic Physics Research Institute," N.A., *On Campus News*, 10 August 2001: 19; Michael Smith, "Lights on in Saskatoon: Canada's Newest Piece of Big Science Prepares to Probe Deeply into Just about Anything," *University Affairs*, January 2004, 12.

113 James L. Turk, "Feds Redesigning Universities," *CAUT Bulletin* 47, 9 (2000): 3.

114 Brian Bergman, "The Powerhouse," *Maclean's*, 21 January 2002, 37.

115 Ibid.

116 G.M. Bancroft and E.L. Hallin, "The Canadian Light Source: Progress and Opportunities for Earth, Environmental and Materials

Science Applications," in *Synchrotron Radiation: Earth, Environmental and Material Sciences Applications*, ed. Grant S. Henderson and Don R. Baker (Ottawa: Mineralogical Association of Canada, 2002), 26.

117 Gerry Klein, "Another Ray of Light for Synchrotron," *Star Phoenix*, 27 February 2001, A1.

118 Paulson, "Light Source Accelerates City's Economic Prospects," A12.

119 Mark Schoofs, "Glaxo Attempts to Block Access to Generic AIDS Drugs in Ghana," *Wall Street Journal*, 1 December 2000.

120 Ibid.

121 Adetokunbo Lucas, "Public-Private Partnerships: Illustrative Examples," in *Public-Private Partnerships for Public Health*, ed. Michael R. Reich (Cambridge, MA: Harvard University Press, 2002).

122 Marc Lee, "Africa Shortchanged: The Global Fund and the G8 Agenda," *Behind the Numbers: Economic Facts, Figures and Analysis* (Ottawa: Canadian Centre for Policy Alternatives, 20 June 2002), 2.

123 Smith, "Lights on in Saskatoon": 13.

124 Ibid.

125 Klein, "Another Ray of Light for Synchrotron," A1, A4.

126 *On Campus News*, 13 May 2005, 12.

127 Canadian Light Source Inc, CLS *Industrial Science Program Highlights – 2005*, (Saskatoon: Canadian Light Source Inc, 31 May 2005).

128 In an e-mail message to Sandra Ribeiro of 25 January 2006, I asked for these figures without success. In an earlier message of 10 January 2006, Ms Ribeiro provided me with details of the two-part fee structure for purchased beamtime access "that is competitive with other facilities" for the period from May 2005 to March 2006: $1.00 fee per eight-hour shift access fee; $400 per one hour of beamtime (including set-up and data collection so long as the beam is available).

129 Murray McLaughlin, e-mail message to author, 11 May 2007.

130 Janet French, "Synchrotron Funding Safe: Owen," *StarPhoenix*, 28 February 2005, A3.

131 John Conway, "Synchrotron Economic Boons Oversold," *StarPhoenix*, 1 December 2006, A14. The phrase "scientific pilgrims" is taken from Smith, "Lights on in Saskatoon," 13,

who foresaw two thousand such transients trekking to Saskatoon annually.

132 Conway, "Synchrotron Economic Boons Oversold," A14.

133 Janet French, "Synchrotron Boom: CLS Boss Beaming with Optimism," *StarPhoenix*, 28 March 2007, A1, A2.

134 Ibid., A2.

135 Chantal Srivastava, "Le synchrotron de Saskatoon," *Les Années lumière*, Radio Canada, 28 November 2004.

136 French, "Synchrotron Boom," A1. McLaughlin stated that the CLS had an agreement with IBM to develop data-managing software for the facility; that MOSAIC, INCO, Imperial Oil, and Rockwell Collins were all "working with" the synchrotron; and that "several discussions and contracts [were] being developed but we [were] working under confidential situations or not in a position to disclose yet." See Murray McLaughlin, e-mail message to author, 11 May 2007. A list of the CLS's "capital funding partners" contains only Boehringer Ingelheim and Rockwell Collins Canada from the private sector in a list of twenty-six partners. *www.lightsource.ca/partners/index.php* (viewed 22 January 2009).

137 The quotations in this paragraph are from Altarelli, Schlachter, and Cross, "Making Ultrabright X-rays," 67–68. See also Bancroft and Hallin, "The Canadian Light Source," 25–42; and Smith, "Lights on in Saskatoon," 11–12. The figure of seventy-five synchrotrons is from "Storage Ring Synchrotron Radiation Sources," available at *http://wwwssrl.slac.stanford.edu/sr_sources.html* (viewed 3 March 2004).

138 T.K. Sham, "Synchrotron Radiation: An Overview," in Grant and Baker, *Synchrotron Radiation*, 9, 6.

139 *http//: www.lightsource.ca/science/* (viewed on 4 April 2007).

140 Ibid.

141 Altarelli, Schlachter, and Cross, "Making Ultrabright X-rays," 67–73.

142 Ibid., 72.

143 Ibid., 71–2.

144 John Ibbotson, "The Pharmacare Grenade," *Globe and Mail*, 5 August 2004, A4. In 2002, pharmaceutical companies had worldwide sales in excess of US$638 billion, making them the second largest industry after armaments. See Helke Ferrie, "Big Pharma Unhappy with Measly $638 billion in Sales," *CCPA Monitor* 10, 3

(2004): 14. See also Howard Woodhouse, "Privatization Threatens University Autonomy," *CAUT Bulletin*, November 2004, A3, A7.

145 Vandana Shiva, *Biopiracy: The Plunder of Nature and Knowledge* (Toronto: Between the Lines, 1997), 3–4. See also Sheryl Gay Stolberg, "Patent Laws May Determine Shape of Stem Cell Research," *New York Times*, 17 August 2001.

146 Altarelli, Schlacter, and Cross, "Making Ultrabright X-rays," 70.

147 Lucas, "Public-Private Partnerships"; Ian Steele, "Bush Can Banish Killer Parasite," *Globe and Mail*, 22 November 1986, D4; and Howard Woodhouse, "Tradition or Modernity: The Fallacy of Misplaced Concreteness among Women Science Educators in Cameroon," *Interchange* 28, 2&3 (1997): 259–60.

148 Office of Vice-President (Academic) and Provost, *Strategic Research Plan Summary for the Canada Research Chairs Program* (Saskatoon: University of Saskatchewan, 2001), 1.

149 Turk, "Feds Redesigning Universities," 3.

150 Ibid.

151 Offices of the Vice-President Academic and Provost and Vice-President Research, memorandum, 1–2.

152 Turk, "Feds Redesigning Universities," 3. See also Claire Polster, "Universities, Academics Forced to Compete for Federal Funds," *CCPA Monitor* 9, 1 (2002): 34–5.

153 Peter MacKinnon, memorandum re: Canada Research Chairs Program, 7 November 2000, 1. See also Warden, "Research Gains Could Boost *Maclean's* Ranking More," 7.

154 Office of Vice-President (Academic), *Strategic Research Plan*, 5.

155 All the information about the six high-priority areas of research is taken from Office of Vice-President (Academic), *Strategic Research Plan*, 3–9, unless otherwise stated.

156 Ibid., 10.

157 Dan Zakreski, "VIDO Studying Streptococcal Bacteria," *StarPhoenix*, 27 May 1995, B1.

158 Kathryn Warden, "Campus Leads Research to Help Unlock the Genetic Code," *StarPhoenix*, 13 June 2002, E7.

159 N.A., "VIDO Shows U of S Impact on Community," *StarPhoenix*, 8 April 2002, A8.

160 Colleen MacPherson, "InterVac Funds Now in Place," *On Campus News*, 23 March 2007, 1, 8. In 2005, the cost of InterVac was cited as only $61.8 million. See French, "Synchrotron Funding Safe," A3.

161 Proposal for a Virtual College of Biotechnology (January 2000), available at *http://biotechnology.usask.ca* (viewed 7 September 2000).

162 Dr Ramaswami Sammynaiken, Manager of the Saskatchewan Structural Sciences Centre, cited in N.A., "Saskatchewan Structural Science Centre Offers Tours, Presentations," *Innovation Place Newsletter*, March 2001, 3.

163 Professor Jim Hendry, cited in N.A., "Cameco Chair Researcher Named," *Green and White* (Spring 1995): 30.

164 Jens Nielsen, "Hydrology Researcher Awarded Cameco Chair in U of S Geology Dept.," *StarPhoenix*, 20 January 1995, A9.

165 Kathryn Warden, "Synchrotron Can Combat Ills of Anthrax and Arsenic," *On Campus News*, 2 November 2001, 7.

166 Bancroft and Hallin, "The Canadian Light Source," 26. In June 2007, David Wilkins, the US ambassador to Canada, toured the CLS and, in a speech to the Greater Saskatoon Chamber of Commerce, stated that "there's a renewed interest in nuclear energy in America ... and the uranium mines in this province could help feed the demand." See Cassandra Kyle, "Fuelling the US Economy: Canada Has Resources that America Needs, US Ambassador Says," *StarPhoenix*, 22 June 2007, C10.

167 Burton, "This Time," A2.

168 Nielsen, "Hydrology Researcher Awarded Cameco Chair," A9.

169 University of Saskatchewan, "Help Us Celebrate the Dedication of Cameco Plaza," *StarPhoenix*, 22 September 2006, A16. The same homily is repeated in University of Saskatchewan, *Annual Report on Giving: 1 May 2005, 30 April 2006* (Saskatoon: University of Saskatchewan, 2006), 16.

170 *Cameco Corp., 2006 Annual Financial Review*, 94, available at *http://www.cameco.com/investor_relations/annual/2006/* (viewed 27 October 2008).

171 *University of Saskatchewan Statistics*, vol. 25 (Saskatoon: University of Saskatchewan, 1999), 9.8, 9.11.

172 Canadian Association of University Teachers, *Creeping Privatization, CAUT Education Review* 3, 1 (2001): 3–4; and Darren Bernhardt, "Surge in Private Funding for Research at Sask. Universities Concerns Group," *StarPhoenix*, 12 February 2001, A6.

173 Colleen MacPherson, "Report, Question Highlight GAA Meeting," *On Campus News*, 20 April 2007, 11. Canadian universities are currently "much more aggressive in the hunt for ... name-brand

academics," providing them with "academic star treatment" in order to promote their "globalized and international rankings." See John Allemang, "We Will Rock U," *Globe and Mail*, 2 February 2008, F1, F6.

174 University of Saskatchewan, *Strategic Research Plan Summary for the Canada Research Chairs Program*, 5.

175 University of Saskatchewan Council, *A Framework for Planning*, 7–8 (my emphasis).

176 Office of the Vice-President (Academic), *Strategic Research Plan*, 2, 1 (my emphasis). The concept of comparative advantage is taken from Adam Smith, who claimed that, for nations, the act of producing what is most cost-effective and importing the rest was always advantageous. See Smith, *An Inquiry into the Nature and Understanding of the Wealth of Nations* (New York: P.F. Collier and Son, 1909), 353–4.

177 Office of the Vice-President (Academic), *Strategic Research Plan*, 3 (my emphasis).

178 Prepared by Kyla Shea on behalf of the Virtual College of Biotechnology Executive Committee, *A Proposal to Discontinue the Virtual College of Biotechnology*, Virtual College of Biotechnology, submitted to the Provost's Committee on Integrated Planning, University of Saskatchewan, 26 September 2007, 4, available at *www.usask.ca/university_secretary/council/committees/planning_priorities/report_files/pdf/Planning_Report_07_10_17_Discontinue_Virtual_College_Biotechnology.pdf* (viewed 22 January 2009). The report admits that, "despite the very significant combined investment (several thousand dollars in laboratory equipment, nine faculty members and one Visiting Chair), there is little evidence of synergy or coordination between these three major initiatives." Ibid, 3.

179 N.A., "Saskatchewan Structural Sciences Centre Offers Tours," 3.

180 Dr Ramaswami Sammynaiken, cited in Ibid. The phrase "one-stop shopping" is also used of Surface Science Western, a laboratory at UWO from which Dr Sammynaiken came to U of S and that will use the CLS. See Jim Anderson, "Surface Science Western: 'A Model for Blending Entrepreneurship and Academic Priorities,'" *Western Alumni Gazette* 78, 2 (2002): 17.

181 University of Saskatchewan Council, *A Framework for Planning*, 8 (my emphasis).

182 Ibid., 2, 4 (my emphasis).

183 McMurtry, *Unequal Freedoms*, 189.

184 University of Saskatchewan Council, *A Framework for Planning*, 8. For a critique of "performance indicators [as] technologies for managing and controlling academic activities," see Claire Polster and Janice Newson, "Don't Count Your Blessings: The Social Accomplishments of Performance Indicators," in Currie and Newson, *Universities and Globalization*, 173–91.

185 University of Saskatchewan Council, *A Framework for Planning*, 8.

186 Michael Collins and Howard Woodhouse, "Professors Argue It's Time to Reassess Value of SPR," *On Campus News*, 19 October 2001, 4.

187 Michael Collins, "Critical Perspectives on Educational Evaluation," *Canadian Journal of Program Evaluation* 15 (2000): 116, 131.

188 University of Saskatchewan Council, *A Framework for Planning*, 4.

189 Office of Vice-President (Academic), *Strategic Research Plan*, 1 (my emphasis).

190 MacKinnon, *Renewing the Dream*.

191 However, "there is one fatal flaw to this global vision ... no criterion of truth has ever emerged in the new knowledge order. It is enough to declare 'knowledge' and 'information' as self-certifying slogans." See McMurtry, *Unequal Freedoms*, 179.

192 University of Saskatchewan, *A Framework for Action*, 1, 2–3, 5.

193 Ibid., 13 (my emphasis).

194 Ibid., 2.

195 Ibid., 22 (my emphasis).

196 See William Bruneau and Donald C. Savage, *Counting Out the Scholars: How Performance Indicators Undermine Universities and Colleges* (Toronto: James Lorimer, 2002), 197.

197 Ibid., 73–170.

198 Jan Currie and Janice Newson, "Globalizing Practices: Corporate Managerialism, Accountability, and Privatization," in Currie and Newson, *Universities and Globalization*, 146.

199 Special Study Panel on Education Indicators, *Education Counts: An Indicator System to Monitor the Nation's Educational Health*, US Department of Education, National Center for Education Statistics: Washington, DC), 5.

200 Gerry Klein, "Students Rally over Burden in Tuition," *StarPhoenix*, 7 February 2002, A3; N.A., "Tuition Issue Sparks Campus Debate," *On Campus News*, 8 February 2002, 8; Mark Ferguson, "Students Protest Tuition Hike," *The Sheaf*, 14 February 2002, A1–A4.

201 U of S Faculty Association-sponsored fora, *W(h)ither the Corporate University? Parts One and Two*, University of Saskatchewan, 21 November 2001, and 23 January 2002; "Forum Blasts 'Corporate Ideology' at U of S," *On Campus News*, 30 November 2001, 2; Gerry Klein, "Synchrotron Draws Too Much Energy: Faculty Members," *StarPhoenix*, 25 January 2002, A3; U of S Faculty Association-sponsored fora, *Understanding Excellence: A Discussion Series*, 1–2 March and 22–3 March 2002; U of S Faculty Association-sponsored forum, *University of Saskatchewan Ltd.: W(h)ither the Corporate University? Part 3*, University of Saskatchewan, 29 October 2003; U of S Faculty Association sponsored forum, *W(h)ither the Corporate University? No PAWS for Thought*, University of Saskatchewan, 1 February 2006.

202 In March 2006, speakers included Jim Turk, executive director of CAUT; Maude Barlow of the Council of Canadians; Angela Regnier of the Canadian Federation of Students; Larry Hubich, president of the Saskatchewan Federation of Labour; Gavin Gardiner, president of the U of S Students Union; and the president of the Graduate Students Association. In March 2007, William Bruneau, former president of CAUT, was the main speaker, in April 2008, Jim Turk was the keynote speaker, and in April 2009, John McMartry.

203 N.A., "Labour Unrest Escalating at University of Saskatchewan," *CAUT Bulletin*, March 2007, A5.

204 Lois Dumbovic, *A People's University Community Program*, February 2002, 1, People's Free University Archives, Department of Educational Foundations, University of Saskatchewan.

205 Terry Matheson, "Administration Reaction Sign Funding Critics Have Hit Mark," *StarPhoenix*, 28 January 2005, A11. Matheson was acting head of the former Department of Modern Languages for three years during the 1990s.

206 Darren Bernhardt, "U of S Profs Protest Liberal Arts Decline," *StarPhoenix*, 26 October 2004, A4. See also Karen Hepp, "Healthy Languages Program Vital," *StarPhoenix*, 19 November 2004, A11.

207 Bernhardt, "U of S Profs Protest Liberal Arts Decline," A4.

208 University of Saskatchewan, *A Framework for Action*, 3 (my emphasis).

209 Ibid. On 25 January, following the second SOLD rally, the provost and the chair of University Council issued "A Message to the University Community," in which they assured everyone that

Integrated Planning would continue to "be developed in broad consultation with the campus community."

210 Donald G. Stein, "A Personal Perspective on the Selling of Academia" in *Buying In or Selling Out?*, ed. Donald G. Stein (New Brunswick, NJ: Rutgers University Press, 2004), 5.

211 N.A., "Critics and Admin Exchange Barbs on Liberal Arts," *On Campus News*, 21 January 2005, 2.

212 David Hutton, "Profs Slam Administration at Discussion Forum," *The Sheaf*, 13 January 2005, A3; N.A., "Critics and Admin. Exchange Barbs on Liberal Arts," 2.

213 Michael Atkinson, "Attacks on U of S Administration, Planning Unfair," *StarPhoenix*, 21 January 2005, A9.

214 Judith Rice Henderson, "Stories, SOLD Unfairly Denigrate U of S Liberal Arts Programs," *StarPhoenix*, 21 January 2005, A9.

215 Peter MacKinnon, *President' [sic] Report to University Council*, 27 January 2005, 1, University of Saskatchewan, University Secretary's Office.

216 Matheson, "Administration Reaction Sign Funding Critics Have Hit Mark," A11.

217 MacKinnon, *President' Report to University Council*, 1.

218 Ibid., 2.

219 Ibid., 2–3 (my emphasis).

220 Ibid.

221 Corporate Administration at the University of Saskatchewan, *Business Opportunities – Strategic Directions*, 7.

222 E-mail message from Wilfred Denis to Faculty, St Thomas More College, 8 February 2005.

223 Atkinson, "Attacks on U of S Administration," A9.

224 N.A., "Rally Supports Tuition Freeze," *On Campus News*, 18 February 2005, 2; Jamie Komarnicki, "Rally Targets Tuition Hikes," *StarPhoenix*, 10 February 2005, A8.

225 CAUT, *CAUT Almanac of Post-Secondary Education 2007*, 37; the source of the figures is Statistics Canada.

226 N.A., "Rally Supports Tuition Freeze," 2.

227 Gavin Gardiner, "Tuition Freeze First Step to Fixing Larger Problems," *StarPhoenix*, 4 February 2005, A11.

228 Lana Haight, "U of S Announces Tuition Freeze," *StarPhoenix*, 7 May 2005, A11.

229 Anthony Harding, "Central Role of Humanities and Fine Arts Not Appreciated, Says Departing Prof," *On Campus News*, 4 February

2005, 4. Harding's views on the importance of the critical method are shared by Paul Axelrod, *Values in Conflict: The University, the Marketplace, and the Trials of Liberal Education* (Montreal and Kingston: McGill-Queen's University Press 2002), 34–5.

230 Atkinson, "Provost Rebuts Integrated Plan Criticism and Defends University's New Direction," *On Campus News*, 18 February 2005, 4.

231 Anthony Harding, "Professor Reiterates His Concern Over Role of Humanities at U of S," *On Campus News*, 4 March 2005, 4.

232 Haight, "U of S Announces Budget Cuts," A11. At a meeting of the General Academic Assembly in April 2007, President Mackinnon opposed governments' freezing tuition as "bad public policy. You can't freeze one area of funding without discussion of enriching others." See MacPherson, "Report," 11.

233 D. Bruce Johnstone with Alka Arora and William Experton for the World Bank, *The Financing and Management of Higher Education: A Status Report on Worldwide Reforms* (Paris: UNESCO Conference on Higher Education, 5–9 October 1998), 22 (my emphasis).

234 Ibid., 23 (my emphasis).

235 David Bernans, *Con U Inc: Privatization, Marketization and Globalization at Concordia University (and beyond)* (Montreal: Concordia Student Union, 2001), 22–3, 64–5.

236 For the disastrous effects of World Bank reforms on primary education in Malawi and elsewhere, see Katarina Tomasevski, *Education Denied: Costs and Remedies* (London: Zed Books, 2003), 69–82.

237 Yves Jalbert, "Innover dans le sens des mots?" *CAUT Bulletin*, October 2001, A3.

238 Susan Haack, "Preposterism and Its Consequences," *Social Philosophy and Policy* 13, 2 (1996): 301–2.

239 Peter MacKinnon, "State of the University Address," General Academic Assembly, University of Saskatchewan, 8 April 2008. Since 2000, eighty-three capital programs worth $1 billion were initiated at U of S.

240 *http://www.ualberta.ca/IDO/databook/index.html*, Schedule 4B (viewed 16 July 2008).

241 Axelrod, *Values in Conflict*, 100.

242 *http://www.ualberta.ca/IDO/databook/index.html*, Schedule 4B (viewed 16 July 2008)

243 In addition, SSHRC funding to the faculties of business, education, Native studies, nursing, and physical education at U of A amounted

to $2.4 million. See *http://www.ualberta.ca/IDO/databook/index. html*, Schedule 4B (viewed 16 July 2008). The $15 million from the Canada Research Chairs program is likely to reflect the national pattern in favour of the natural and social sciences. See Axelrod, *Values in Conflict*, 94.

244 The Faculty of Pharmacy and Pharmaceutical Sciences received only $295,000 from Canadian business. See *http://www.ualberta.ca/IDO/ databook/index.html*, Schedule 4B (viewed 16 July 2008).

245 Ibid.

246 Haack, "Preposterism and Its Consequences," 302, 309.

247 E-Mail to author from Cindy Lieu, Communications Coordinator, Research Services Office, University of Alberta, 21 July 2008 (my emphasis).

248 McMurtry, "The Market Model of Education," 38–41; Howard Woodhouse, "The Market Model of Education and the Threat to Canadian Universities," *Encounters on Education* 2 (2001): 105–22.

249 Jack Billinton and Xin Li, "An Analysis of University Autonomy and Governance in Three Universities: Canada, Britain, and China," *International Education* 30, 1 (2000): 59, 63. See Government of Saskatchewan, *The University of Saskatchewan Act, 1995* (Regina, Saskatchewan: The Queen's Printer 2006).

250 Billinton and Li, "An Analysis of University Autonomy and Governance in Three Universities": 65. For a critical discussion of this issue, see L.M. Findlay, "Academic Freedom, Autonomy, Theory, Duty," in *Pursuing Academic Freedom: "Free and Fearless?"*, ed. Len M. Findlay and Paul M. Bidwell (Saskatoon: Purich Publishers, 2001), 224–36.

251 Robert Berdahl, "Academic Freedom, Autonomy and Accountability in British Universities," *Studies in Higher Education* 15, 2 (1990): 171. See also Robert Berdahl, "Universities and Society: Mutual Obligations," in *Ontario Universities: Access, Operations and Funding*, ed. David Conklin and Thomas Courchene (Toronto: Ontario Economic Council, 1983), 7. Berdahl became chancellor of the University of California, Berkeley, where commercial links between Novartis, the Swiss multinational pharmaceutical and bio-technology corporation, and the Department of Plant and Microbial Biology caused concern over the university's autonomy. See Eyal Press and Jennifer Washburn, "The Kept University," *Atlantic Monthly* 285, 3 (2000): 39–54; and Jennifer Washburn, *University, Inc: The Corporate Corruption of American Higher Education* (New York: Basic Books, 2005), 3–24.

252 Hayden, *Seeking a Balance*, 286.

253 John G. McConnell, "Council – Voting Away Our Autonomy," *Vox* 25 (1998): 2–3.

254 Harold H. MacKay, *The Report of the Minister's Special Representative on University Revitalization* (Regina: Department of Postsecondary Education and Skills Training, 1996), 70.

255 Gerry Klein, "Sask. Universities Get a Glowing Review from Province," *StarPhoenix*, 16 November 2001, A7.

256 Department of Postsecondary Education, Government of Saskatchewan, *Public Interest and Revitalization of Saskatchewan's Universities* (Regina: Department of Postsecondary Education and Skills Training, 1997), 3.

257 Murray, senate minutes, University of Saskatchewan, September 1909, cited in Hayden, *Seeking a Balance*, 295.

258 Department of Postsecondary Education, Government of Saskatchewan, *A Progress Report on University Revitalization* (Regina: Department of Postsecondary Education and Skills Training, 2001), 4, 10, 20. The same technical approach to teaching and learning can be found in University of Saskatchewan Council, *A Framework for Planning*, 5–6, and University of Saskatchewan, *A Framework for Action*, 14. For a critique, see Noble, *Digital Diploma Mills*, 29–30.

259 Department of Postsecondary Education, Government of Saskatchewan, *A Progress Report on University Revitalization*, 18, 12, 13.

260 Ibid., 18.

261 Pat Lorje, former minister of Postsecondary education and skills training, cited in Klein, "Sask. Universities Get Glowing Review from Province," A7.

262 Nor did Murray show much respect for the academic freedom of dissenting faculty. See Horn, *Academic Freedom in Canada*, 54–61, 285–6.

CHAPTER FIVE

1 M. Patricia Marchak, *Racism, Sexism, and the University: The Political Science Affair at the University of British Columbia* (Montreal and Kingston: McGill-Queen's University Press, 1996), 31.

2 James E. Coté and Anton L. Allahar, *Ivory Tower Blues: A University System in Crisis* (Toronto: University of Toronto Press, 2007), 10.

3 Allan J. Gedalof, *Teaching Large Classes* (Halifax: Society for Teaching and Learning in Higher Education, 1998), 31–40.

4 The practice of publishing anonymous student questionnaires is criticized as a threat to academic freedom in *Canadian Association of University Teachers Policy on the Use of Anonymous Student Questionnaires in the Evaluation of Teaching* (Ottawa: May 1998), especially sections 2.1 and 4.6 (hereafter referred to as *CAUT Policy*), available at *www.caut.ca/english/about/policy/questionnaires.asp* (viewed 10 June 2000).

5 *CAUT Policy*, sections 3.2 and 3.4, contests these views. Howard C. Clark, who was a senior member of the Department of Chemistry at Western, claims that some departments in the natural sciences "were forerunners in the use of teaching evaluation questionnaires in all courses. We used a standard questionnaire, the results were readily available to all ... By 1970–71, the same questionnaire was being employed throughout the Faculty of Science, well in advance of the rest of the university." See Clark, *Growth and Governance of Canadian Universities: An Insider's View* (Vancouver: UBC Press, 2004), 68–9.

6 University of Saskatchewan, *Framework for Student Evaluation of Teaching at the University of Saskatchewan* (Saskatoon: University of Saskatchewan, 2004), 3, 4, 1. *CAUT Policy* advises that the results of student questionnaires in personnel decisions "should be treated with extreme caution" (6).

7 Professor Harry G. Murray, author of the "Teachers Behaviors Inventory" (see footnote 18), claims that "some three-quarters of professors surveyed across North America feel that student evaluations provide useful feedback on their teaching ... [but he] admits that there is evidence they contribute to grade inflation and lower standards." See Coté and Allahar, *Ivory Tower Blues*, 217n.

8 William J. McKeachie, "Student Ratings: The Validity of Use," *American Psychologist* 52, 11 (1997): 1,222.

9 Herbert W. Marsh and Lawrence A. Roche, "Making Students' Evaluations of Teaching Effectiveness Effective: The Critical Uses of Validity, Bias, and Utility," *American Psychologist* 52, 11 (1997): 1,189 (my emphasis).

10 Peter Seldin, "Using Student Feedback to Improve Teaching," in *To Improve the Academy*, ed. D. Zezure (Stillwater, OK: New Forums Press, 1997), 336.

11 These points are reiterated by Michiel Horn, *Academic Freedom in Canada: A History* (Toronto: University of Toronto Press, 1999),

322–3; Stanley Coren, "Are Course Evaluations a Threat to Academic Freedom?" in *Academic Freedom and the Inclusive University*, ed. Sharon E. Kahn and Dennis Pavlich (Vancouver: UBC Press, 2000), 106–7; Lesley Vidovich and Jan Currie, "Changing Accountability and Autonomy at the 'Coalface' of Academic Work in Australia," in *Universities and Globalization: Critical Perspectives*, ed. Jan Currie and Janice Newson (Thousand Oaks, CA: Sage, 1998), 201; John McMurtry, "Education and the Market Model," *Paideusis* 5, 1 (1991): 39; *CAUT Policy*, 2.1.

12 Coren, "Are Course Evaluations a Threat to Academic Freedom?" 105.

13 *CAUT Policy*, 1.

14 David Campbell, *A Guide to Student Evaluation of Teaching: A Sesquicentennial Project of the Queen's University Alma Mater Society* (Kingston, ON: Queen's University, 1991).

15 Christopher Fries and James McNinch, "Signed versus Unsigned Evaluations of Teaching: An Example of How Research Informs Teaching and Teaching Informs Research," in *What Is a Teacher-Scholar?* ed. Gwenna Moss Teaching and Learning Centre (Saskatoon: Gwenna Moss Teaching and Learning Centre, University of Saskatchewan, 2002), 75.

16 University of Saskatchewan, *Framework for Student Evaluation of Teaching at the University of Saskatchewan*, 18.

17 Marsh and Roche, "Making Students' Evaluations of Teaching Effectiveness Effective," 1,189.

18 Harry G. Murray, "Teachers Behaviors Inventory," in *How Am I Teaching? Forms and Activities for Acquiring Instructional Input*, ed. M. Weimer, J. Parrett, and M. Kerns (Madison, WI: Magna Publications, 1988), 97–8.

19 Ibid., 98–100.

20 Coren, "Are Course Evaluations a Threat to Academic Freedom?" 117.

21 McKeachie, "Student Ratings," 1,222.

22 University of Saskatchewan, *Framework for Student Evaluation of Teaching at the University of Saskatchewan*, 7.

23 See Coté and Allahar, *Ivory Tower Blues*, 157–8.

24 Howard Woodhouse, "Evaluating University Teaching and Learning: Taking a Whiteheadian Turn," in *Alfred North Whitehead on Learning and Education*, ed. Franz G. Riffert (Newcastle: Cambridge Scholars Press, 2005), 396.

25 Anna Rosenbluth, "Provincial Support for PSE in Saskatchewan," in *An Alternative Guide to Canadian Post-Secondary Education*, ed. Denise Doherty-Delorme and Erika Shaker (Ottawa: Canadian Centre for Policy Alternatives, 2004), 49–50.

26 University of Saskatchewan, *Framework for Student Evaluation of Teaching at the University of Saskatchewan*, 2.

27 McMurtry, "Education and the Market Model," 40.

28 John McMurtry, *Unequal Freedoms: The Global Market as an Ethical System* (Toronto: Garamond Press, 1998), 189.

29 Coté and Allahar, *Ivory Tower Blues*, 86.

30 McMurtry, "Education and the Market Model," 39; Howard Woodhouse, "Contradicting the Market," *Paideusis* 5, 1 (1991): 50; Howard Woodhouse, "The Market Model of Education and the Threat to Canadian Universities," *Encounters on Education* 2, (2001): 111–13.

31 Marchak, *Racism, Sexism, and the University*, 31.

32 Philip C. Abrami, R.P. Perry, and L. Leventhal, "The Relationship between Student Personality Characteristics, Teacher Ratings, and Student Achievement," *Journal of Educational Psychology* 74, 1 (1982): 119.

33 Lewis Elton, "Dimensions of Excellence in University Teaching," *International Journal for Academic Development* 3, 1 (1998): 8.

34 William J. McKeachie and Matthew Kaplan, "Persistent Problems in Evaluating College Teaching," *National Teaching and Learning Forum* (1999): 6, available at *http://ntlf.com/html/lib/faq/at-umiss.htm* (viewed 21 January 2001).

35 A similar point is made by Tom Pocklington and Allan Tupper, *No Place to Learn: Why Universities Aren't Working* (Vancouver: UBC Press, 2002), 76–7.

36 Ernest L. Boyer, *Scholarship Reconsidered: Priorities of the Professoriate* (Princeton, NJ: The Carnegie Foundation for the Advancement of Learning, 1990), 17–24.

37 Mark Flynn, "Learning in the Process of Teaching," in Gwenna Moss Teaching and Learning Centre, *What Is a Teacher-Scholar?*, 1; Adam Scarfe, "An Historical Overview of Instructional Development in Canadian Higher Education," *Bridges* 2, 4 (2004): 6; Howard Woodhouse, "The False Promise of the 'Teacher-Scholar Model,'" in Gwenna Moss Teaching and Learning Centre, *What Is a Teacher-Scholar?* 17–20.

38 McMurtry, *Unequal Freedoms*, 188–9.

39 Harry G. Murray, "Student Evaluation of College and University Teaching: A 25–year Retrospective," paper presented at the annual meeting of the Canadian Society for the Study of Higher Education, Calgary, Alberta,, 1994.

40 B.F. Skinner, *Beyond Freedom and Dignity* (New York: Alfred A. Knopf, 1972), 4, 5, 147–8, 27.

41 Valen Johnson found that, in the United States, professors can "double their odds of getting high evaluations from students simply by awarding As rather than Bs or Cs." See Johnson, *Grade Inflation: A Crisis in College Education* (New York: Springer, 2003), 83.

42 M.L. Lawall, *Students Rating Teaching: How Student Feedback Can Inform Your Teaching* (Winnipeg: University of Manitoba Press, 1998), 6.

43 Harry G. Murray, J. Philippe Rushton, and Sampo V. Paunonen, "Teacher Personality Traits and Student Instructional Ratings in Six Types of University Course," *Journal of Educational Psychology* 82, 2 (1990): 250–1.

44 B.F. Skinner, "The Free and Happy Student," *New York University Educational Quarterly* 4, 2 (1973): 6.

45 Skinner, *Beyond Freedom and Dignity*, 19–21.

46 For a critique of behaviourist approaches, see Mark Flynn, "Process Philosophy of Education as an Antidote to Some Systemic Inhibitors of Learning: Rethinking the Concept of 'Learning Disabilities,'" in *Process, Epistemology and Education: Recent Work in Educational Process Philosophy*, ed. Bryant Griffith and Garth Benson (Toronto: Canadian Scholars Press, 1996), 125–43.

47 A.N. Whitehead, *Process and Reality: An Essay on Cosmology* (New York: The Free Press, 1957), 5–6, 399; A.N. Whitehead, *The Aims of Education and Other Essays* (New York: The Free Press 1957), v, 1–5.

48 In contrast, the *Framework for Student Evaluation of Teaching at the University of Saskatchewan* systematically ignores any counter-evidence to the validity of standardized questionnaires.

49 Fries and McNinch, "Signed versus Unsigned Evaluations of Teaching," 75.

50 Coren, "Are Course Evaluations a Threat to Academic Freedom?" 117. See also Scarfe, "An Historical Overview of Instructional Development in Canadian Higher Education," 4–5; Barbara Bulman-Fleming, "Evaluation of Your Teaching: Don't Leave it Entirely in the Hands of Your Students," *TRACE Teaching Matters*

13 (2003): 1, 4, available at *www.adm.uwaterloo.ca/infotrac*
   (viewed 14 December 2003).
51 Marsh and Roche, "Making Students' Evaluations of Teaching
   Effectiveness Effective," 1,189.
52 Seldin, "Using Student Feedback to Improve Teaching," 336.
53 Fries and McNinch, "Signed versus Unsigned Evaluations of
   Teaching," 73.
54 Marchak, *Racism, Sexism, and the University*, 31.
55 Coté and Allahar, *Ivory Tower Blues*, 85. See also Thomas
   Cushman, "Hemlock Available in the Faculty Lounge," *Chronicle of
   Higher Education*, 16 March 2007.
56 McMurtry, "Education and the Market Model," 40.
57 Woodhouse, "The Market Model of Education and the Threat to
   Canadian Universities," 107–8.
58 Woodhouse, "Evaluating University Teaching and Learning,"
   397–9.
59 Horn, *Academic Freedom in Canada*, 323.
60 Christopher K. Knapper, "Teaching Evaluation and Academic
   Freedom," in *If Teaching Is Important: The Evaluation of
   Instruction in Higher Education*, ed. Christopher K. Knapper,
   George L. Geis, Charles E. Pascal, and Bruce M. Shore (Toronto:
   Clarke Irwin, 1977), 200.
61 Herbert Marsh, *Students' Evaluation of Educational Quality:* SEEQ
   (Sydney, AU: University of Western Sydney, Educational
   Development Centre, 2002). Universities in Australia, Ireland, and
   the United States have also adopted SEEQ.
62 University of Manitoba, *A Brief Description of the Students'
   Evaluations of Educational Quality (SEEQ)* (Winnipeg: University
   Teaching Services, 2005); Thomas Murphy, "Saint Mary's Senate
   Approves New Student Evaluation of Teaching Instrument,"
   Teaching and Learning at St Mary's 15, 2 (2005): 1–2.
63 Bob Tyler and Edwin Ralph, *University of Saskatchewan Student
   Survey of Teaching* (Saskatoon: Instructional Development
   Committee of Council, University of Saskatchewan, November
   2005), 3, 2, 3. Worthwhile aspects of the report include statements
   to the effect that SEEQ should be only one of several sources for the
   evaluation of teaching.
64 McKeachie, "Student Ratings of Faculty," 1,222.
65 Robert Barr and John Tagg, "From Teaching to Learning: A New
   Paradigm for Undergraduate Education," *Change* (November/

December 1995) available at *http://critical.tamucc.edu/~blalock/ readings/tch2learn.htm* (viewed 14 May 2000).

66 Ibid., 5.

67 Tyler and Ralph, *University of Saskatchewan Student Survey of Teaching*, 3.

68 Barr and Tagg, "From Teaching to Learning," 4, 10–11.

69 Conrad Russell, *Academic Freedom* (London: Routledge, 1993), 60, 61.

70 Barr and Tagg wax eloquent about the work of market "guru" Peter Senge. See Barr and Tagg, "From Teaching to Learning," 5–6.

71 Craig E. Nelson, "Student Diversity Requires Different Approaches to College Teaching, Even in Math and Science," *American Behavioral Scientist* 40, 2 (1996): 172.

72 Whitehead, *The Aims of Education*, 3.

73 Boyer, *Scholarship Reconsidered*, 23–4.

74 Murray, "Teachers Behaviors Inventory," 97–100.

75 Paulo Freire, *Pedagogy of the Oppressed* (New York: Continuum, 2000), 79–80.

76 Whitehead, *Process and Reality*, 30, 103.

77 Whitehead, *The Aims of Education*, 27–8.

78 Mary Elizabeth Mullino Moore, "The Relational Power of Education: The Immeasurability of Knowledge, Value, and Meaning," *Interchange* 36, 1 and 2 (2005): 29.

79 Ibid., 35.

80 Frank Furedi, "The New Chief Inquisitor on Campus," *Spiked*, 16 February 2005, 1–4, available at *www.spiked-online.com/articles* (viewed 21 April 2005).

CHAPTER SIX

1 Dora Russell, *The Tamarisk Tree 2: My School and the Years of War* (London: Virago, 1981), 204.

2 John McMurtry, *Unequal Freedoms: The Global Market as an Ethical System* (Toronto: Garamond Press, 1998), 128.

3 *Ibid.*, 7, 15.

4 A.N. Whitehead, *Modes of Thought* (New York: The Free Press, 1938), 134–5; George Grant, *Technology and Empire: Perspectives on North America* (Toronto: Anansi Press, 1969) 19–25; Bruce Morito, *Thinking Ecologically: Environmental Thought, Values and Policy* (Halifax: Fernwood, 2003), 45–51.

5 John McMurtry, *Value Wars: The Global Market Versus the Life Economy* (London: Pluto Press, 2002), 248–9n; Whitehead, *Modes of Thought*, 130.

6 William A.W. Cochrane, "Society's Expectations: Staying Near the Customer," in *Universities in Crisis: A Mediaeval Institution in the Twenty-first Century*, ed. William A.W. Neilson and Chad Gaffield (Montreal: The Institute for Research on Public Policy, 1986), 29, 30.

7 Robert Kent, "A Dean's Views: University of Manitoba's Dean of Business, William Mackness, Offers Views on Business, Ethics, and Education," *Manitoba Business* (October 1993): 10; William Mackness, "Development Plan for the Faculty of Management," cited in Daniel Ish, "Committee of Inquiry Report: Inquiry into the University of Manitoba Faculty of Management," CAUT *Bulletin*, December 1992, 13.

8 Robert Prichard, cited in "Congress News," CAUT *Bulletin*, June 2001, A50.

9 Gerry Klein, "U of S Tuition Hike Straps Students: University Cornered by Years of Underfunding, Officials Say in Announcing 15 Per Cent Increase," *StarPhoenix*, 12 May 2001, A3.

10 D. Bruce Johnstone with Alka Arora and William Experton for the World Bank, *The Financing and Management of Higher Education: A Status Report on Worldwide Reforms* (Paris: UNESCO Conference on Higher Education, 5–9 October 1998), 3, 12, 3, 22.

11 Ibid., 23. For a critique of the World Bank Report, see David Bernans, *Con U Inc.: Privatization, Marketization and Globalization at Concordia University (and beyond)* (Montreal: Concordia Student Union, 2001), 22–3, 64–5.

12 McMurtry, *Unequal Freedoms*, 128–9.

13 Colin Starnes, "Core Funding Lost in the Struggle," CAUT *Bulletin*, November 2002, A12.

14 Ibid. (my emphasis).

15 Ibid.

16 James Downey, *The Consenting University and the Dissenting Academy: Binary Friction* (Ottawa: Association of Universities and Colleges of Canada, 2003), 16.

17 Ibid., 17, 16. Howard C. Clark, president and vice-chancellor emeritus of Dalhousie University, also raises concerns about corporate funding to universities as "their pressures for accountability and often confidentiality can be a serious risk to academic freedom."

See Clark, *Growth and Governance of Canadian Universities: An Insider's View* (Vancouver: UBC Press, 2004), 223.

18 Jay Rahn, "Police Brutality Meets Communications and Marketing at a Public University," *Our Schools/Our Selves* 14, 3 (2005): 105.

19 N.A., "York Condemned for Use of Police Force at Rally," *CAUT Bulletin*, February 2005, A11, A1.

20 Subsequently published as Stanley Jeffers, "Misleading Statements," *Critical Times* 2, 4 (2005): 3.

21 Rahn, "Police Brutality," 105–6. The original photographic and video evidence were made available at *http://auto_sol.tao.ca/node/view/1119* (viewed 21 February 2005).

22 N.A., "York U Says No to Violent Protest, Condemns Disruption of Classes," York University Media Relations, 20 January 2005, available at *www.yorku/mediar/archive/Release.asp?Release=782* (viewed 15 March 2005).

23 Neil Raposo, "Three Officers Hurt in York U Protest," *Toronto Star*, 21 January 2005.

24 Rahn, "Police Brutality," 106.

25 N.A., "Were Classes Cancelled and Exams Disrupted at Vari Hall on Jan 20? YUFA Members Respond," York University Faculty Association, 2 March 2005, available at *www.yufa.org/news/cancelled_classes.html* (viewed 15 March 2007).

26 N.A., "York Condemned for Use of Police Force at Rally," A1.

27 Ibid., A11.

28 Ibid., A1.

29 N.A., "From Sea to Sea Canadian Faculty Associations Condemn York Administration's Response to the Anti-Bush Demonstration," York University Faculty Association, 2 March 2005, available at *www.yufa.org/news/freespeechsupport.html* (viewed 16 March 2007); James L. Turk, "Extreme Admin," *Critical Times* 2, 4 (2005): 3. Michiel Horn distinguishes between academic freedom and freedom of expression as follows: "The corresponding freedom of students from administrative control in the learning process, *Lernfreiheit*, has had little or no influence in North America." See Horn, "Academic Freedom in Canada: Past, Present, and Future," in *Pursuing Academic Freedom: "Free and Fearless"?* ed. Len M. Findlay and Paul M. Bidwell (Saskatoon: Purich Publishing, 2001), 22.

30 "[Item] 7.1 New Motions," minutes, York University Senate, 27 January 2005, available at *www.yorku.ca/secretariat/senate/minutes/2004-2005/050127.htm* (viewed 20 March 2005).

31 "Notice of a Special Meeting," meetings, York University Senate, 3 February 2005, *www.yorku.ca/secretariat/senate/agenda/050203.htm* (viewed 17 May 2005).

32 Rahn, "Police Brutality," 108, available at *www.yorku.ca/secretariat/senate/agenda/05203.htm* (viewed 20 March 2005).

33 N.A., "York Condemned For Use of Police Force at Rally," A11.

34 Ibid.

35 Ibid.

36 N.A., "CAUT Committee to Investigate Allegations at York," *CAUT Bulletin*, April 2005, A1.

37 Rahn, "Police Brutality," 105.

38 Communications Home Page: *www.yorku.ca/ycom/* (emphasis mine) (viewed 12 June 2005).

39 *Report on Business Magazine, World in 1997*, cited in Naomi Klein, *No Logo: Taking Aim at the Brand Bullies* (Toronto: Vintage, 2000), 24.

40 Paul Kingston, "Distance Learning: Britain Must Push the Pace," *Guardian Weekly*, 2 May 1999.

41 Howard Woodhouse, "No Logo," *Vox*, University of Saskatchewan Faculty Association, November 2005, 1. Ron Marken, "A Modest Proposal: For Preventing the Post-Secondary Children of Saskatchewan from Being a Burden to their Parents, and for Making them and the University Beneficial to the Public," *Vox*, University of Saskatchewan Faculty Association, November 2005, 2–6.

42 "York University Mission Statement," York University Senate, 28 January 1999, and York University Board of Governors, 22 February 1999, available at *www.yorku.ca/calendars/2003-2004/ug/mission/english.htm* (viewed 17 June 2005). The mission statement also describes York as a "community of faculty, students and staff committed to academic freedom, social justice, accessible education, and collegial self-governance."

43 York University Board of Governors, Communications Committee, Terms of Reference, available at *www.yorku.ca/secretariat/board/committees/univadv/terms.htm* (viewed 17 June 2005).

44 "[Item] 3. Priorities for 2004–05," York University Board of Governors, Communications Committee, *Report to Board*, 21 June 2004, available at *www.yorku.ca/secretariat/board/committees/univadv/reports/2003-2004/040621.htm* (viewed 21 June 2005).

45 "[Item] 3. Looking Ahead," York University Board of Governors, Communications Committee, *Report to Board*, 24 October 2003,

available at *www.yorku.ca/secretariat/board/committees/univadv/ reports/2003-2004/031024.htm* (viewed 23 June 2005).

46 McMurtry, *Unequal Freedoms*, 187.

47 David L. Kirp, *Shakespeare, Einstein, and the Bottom Line* (Cambridge, MA: Harvard University Press, 2003), 314n.

48 John Sperling and Robert W. Tucker, *For-Profit Higher Education: Developing a World-Class Workforce* (New Brunswick, NJ: Transaction Publishers, 1997), 93

49 Marcus Peter Ford, *Beyond the Modern University: Toward a Constructive Postmodern University* (Westport, CT: Praeger, 2002), 32.

50 *www.phoenix.edu* (viewed 25 July 2005).

51 Ford, *Beyond the Modern University*, 34.

52 N.A., "Devry Given Degree Granting Privileges," CAUT *Bulletin* (March 2001): A1, A9.

53 Karen Howlett and Paul Waldie, "Colleges in Turmoil," *Globe and Mail*, 27 September 2003, A4

54 Loretta Czernis, "Higher Education Not for Trade," CAUT *Bulletin*, December 2005, A3; Marjorie Griffin Cohen, "Trading Away the Public Systems: The WTO and Post-Secondary Education," in *The Corporate Campus: Commercialization and the Dangers to Canada's Colleges and Universities*, ed. James L. Turk (Toronto: James Lorimer, 2000), 123–41.

CHAPTER SEVEN

1 Dennis Lee, "Getting to Rochdale," in *The University Game*, ed. Howard Adelman and Dennis Lee (Toronto: Anansi, 1968), 80–1. Lee was one of the founders of Rochdale College, "an experiment in higher education and urban living which opened in Toronto in the fall of 1967" based on the principles of participatory democracy, which he describes as "both old co-op and new left" (Ibid., 77–8). In addition to Lee, Howard Adelman, a professor from York University, and renowned philosopher George Grant were among the faculty. The college closed during the 1970s when its eighteen-storey building became filled with tenants who were more interested in exploring drugs than ideas. Nevertheless, a recent article admitted that "Rochdale nourished the beginnings of such cultural forces as Théatre Passe Muraille, Nishnawbe Institute and Coach House Press." See Margaret Webb, "The Age of Dissent," *University of Toronto Magazine* 29, 3 (2002): 29.

2 Paul Axelrod, *Values in Conflict: The University, the Marketplace, and the Trials of Liberal Education* (Montreal and Kingston: McGill-Queen's University Press, 2002), 148.

3 Ibid., 103–5. These proposals are consistent with the Canadian Association of University Teachers' *Information Paper: University/Business Relationships in Research and Development: A Guide for Universities and Researchers* (Ottawa: CAUT, 1987), 32–11.

4 Axelrod, *Values in Conflict*, 4, 148.

5 A.N. Whitehead, *Adventures of Ideas* (New York: The Free Press, 1961), 66.

6 Ibid., 67.

7 A.N. Whitehead, *The Aims of Education and Other Essays* (New York: The Free Press, 1957), v, 1–2, 3, 53.

8 John Cobb, "Beyond Essays," *Interchange* 29, 1 (1998): 110, 105. Cobb's article was one of several responding to Howard Woodhouse, Mark Flynn, and Robert Regnier," "A Symposium on Process Philosophy and Education," *Interchange* 26, 4 (1995): 341–415.

9 Senate Meetings, U of S, September 1909, cited in Michael Hayden, *Seeking a Balance: The University of Saskatchewan, 1907–1982* (Vancouver: UBC Press, 1983), 295.

10 Ibid., 306–7. Hayden's use of the term "private" with regard to faculty research is misleading. I have interpreted it as meaning "free and independent."

11 However enlightened Murray's vision for the U of S may have been, he was not always respectful of the academic freedom of faculty when they expressed divergent views. See Michiel Horn, *Academic Freedom in Canada* (Toronto: University of Toronto Press, 1999), 54–61, 285–6.

12 Peter MacKinnon, "Strategic Directions: A Presentation to the University of Saskatchewan Community," 9 February 2002, available at *www.usask.ca/vpacademic/integratedplanning/key_planning_planning_* (viewed 18 January 2009).

13 University of Saskatchewan Council, *A Framework for Planning at the University of Saskatchewan* (Saskatoon: University of Saskatchewan, March 1998), 3.

14 Len Findlay, "Out of Step with the University 'On the Move,'" *Vox*, March 2003, 1–3.

15 Janet French, "Sask. Students Pay Third-Highest Tuition," *StarPhoenix*, 18 November 2004, A10.

16 Craig Stehr, "The Future of University Education," *Vox*,
   March 2003, 4. For figures on national debt loads of students,
   see James E. Coté and Anton L. Allahar, *Ivory Tower Blues:
   A University System in Crisis* (Toronto: University of Toronto Press,
   2007), 132, 226n.

17 Michel Groulx, "Marc Renaud: Restoring the Value of Humanities
   Research," *University Affairs*, February 1998, 14–15.

18 See figures 1 and 2 in chapter four.

19 Howard Woodhouse, "Commercializing Research at the University
   of Saskatchewan," *Saskatchewan Notes: Canadian Society for
   Policy Alternatives* 2, 8 (2003): 1–4. The Glaxo Smith Klein chair
   has not materialized.

20 Report of the Expert Panel on the Commercialization of University
   Research, *Public Investments in University Research: Reaping the
   Benefits,* presented to the Prime Minister's Advisory Council on
   Science and Technology (Ottawa: Government of Canada, May
   1999), vi.

21 Government of Canada with the Conference Board of Canada,
   National Summit on Innovation and Learning: Summary (Ottawa:
   The Government of Canada with the Conference Board of Canada
   2002), 24–30.

22 Tim Quigley, "A Study in Top-Down Mismanagement," *CAUT
   Bulletin*, January 2003, A13.

23 Woodhouse, "Commercializing Research at the University of
   Saskatchewan," 1–4; University of Saskatchewan Council,
   A Framework for Planning at the University of Saskatchewan, 8

24 Ted Hamilton, "Academic Freedom and the Culture of Innovation:
   Technology, Innovation and Responsibility in the Contemporary
   University," paper presented at a conference entitled Academic
   Freedom and the Public Interest, organized by the Simon Fraser
   University Student Society and the Canadian Association of
   University Teachers, Simon Fraser University, 24–5 April 2003.

25 Michael Collins, "The People's Free University: Counteracting the
   Innovation Agenda on Campus and Model for Lifelong Learning,"
   Saskatchewan Notes: Canadian Centre for Policy Alternatives 2, 9
   (2003): 1–2.

26 Ian Winchester, "The Future of a Mediaeval Institution: The
   University in the Twenty-first Century," in *Universities in Crisis:
   A Mediaeval Institution in the Twenty-first Century*, ed. William A.
   W. Neilson and Chad Gaffield (Montreal: The Institute for Research
   on Public Policy, 1986), 275.

27 Bill Draves, *The Free University: A Model for Lifelong Learning* (Chicago: Association Press, 1980), 16, 122.

28 Michael R. Welton, "Mobilizing the People for Socialism: The Politics of Adult Education in Saskatchewan, 1944–45," in *Knowledge for the People: The Struggle for Adult Learning in English-Speaking Canada*, ed. Michael R. Welton (Toronto: Ontario Institute for Studies in Education, 1987), 154–9.

29 N.A., *Comments on a People's University – From February 4 2002, Organizing Meeting* (Saskatoon: People's Free University, 2002), 1–5.

30 These goals are similar to those of the free universities described in Draves, *The Free University*, 138.

31 Cobb, "Beyond Essays," 105–6.

32 Howard Woodhouse, "Building Saskatchewan Communities through Education," *Saskatchewan Notes, Canadian Centre for Policy Alternatives* 2, 3 (2003): 4.

33 *Alberta Educational Planning Commission's Reform Policy*, cited in Edgar Faure, *Learning To Be: The World of Education Today and Tomorrow* (Toronto: Ontario Institute for Studies in Education, 1973), 184.

34 Whitehead, *The Aims of Education*, 57, 44.

35 My understanding of health care issues owes a great deal to Viola Woodhouse, whose course "Knowledge Is the Best Medicine: Health Care Ethics and the Public" was offered by the PFU in the winter semester of 2003.

36 Charles Paine, "Relativism, Radical Pedagogy and the Ideology of Paralysis," *College English* 50, 6 (1989): 558.

37 Sherene H. Razack, *Looking White People in the Eye: Gender, Race, and Culture in Courtrooms and Classrooms* (Toronto: University of Toronto Press, 1998), 43–6, 54–5.

38 John McMurtry, "Reclaiming the Teaching Profession: From Corporate Hierarchy to the Authority of Learning," keynote address, Ontario Teachers Federation and Ontario Association of Deans of Education Conference, 23 May 2003.

39 Collins, "The People's Free University," 2.

40 Michael Collins, "Critical Commentaries on Citizenship, Civil Society and Adult Education," *Journal of Adult and Continuing Education* 4 (2001): 45–7.

41 A.N. Whitehead, *An Introduction to Mathematics* (New York: Oxford University Press, 1958), 100, 128–9. Brian Hendley provided some of the insights in this paragraph. See Hendley, *Dewey,*

Russell, Whitehead: Philosophers as Educators (Carbondale and Edwardsville: University of Southern Illinois Press, 1986), 82.

42 Whitehead, *The Aims of Education*, 2; Whitehead, *Adventures of Ideas*, 67, 186–9.

43 Cobb, "Beyond Essays," 110. For Whitehead's analysis of the alternating rhythms of education, see Whitehead, *The Aims of Education*, chaps 2 and 3.

44 A.N. Whitehead, *Process and Reality: An Essay in Cosmology* (New York: The Free Press, 1957), ix, 20–21.

45 Wayne Roberts and Susan Brandum, *Get a Life! How to Make A Good Buck and Dance around the Dinosaurs and Save the World While You're At It* (Toronto: Get A Life Publishing, 1995), 313, 311.

46 John McMurtry, *Unequal Freedoms: The Global Market as an Ethical System* (Toronto: Garamond Press, 1998), 165–6.

47 Wendell Berry, "Here's Why a Local Economy Is Preferable to a Globalized One," CCPA *Monitor* 9, 3 (2002): 16.

48 Cobb, "Beyond Essays," 106–8.

49 A.N. Whitehead, "The Study of the Past: Its Uses and Its Dangers," in *Whitehead's American Essays in Social Philosophy*, ed. A.H. Johnson (New York: Harper and Brothers, 1959), 76.

50 Whitehead, *The Aims of Education*, 97–100.

51 Draves, *The Free University*, 21. The tendency of free universities in the United States to become market-oriented since the 1980s was already signalled by Draves, ibid., 276–7.

52 Collins, "The People's Free University," 1–3; Michael Collins, "Back to the Future in Community Education: The People's Free University," in *Learning for Life: A Compendium of Papers on Lifelong Learning*, ed. Michael Collins (Saskatoon: Department of Educational Foundations, University of Saskatchewan, 2003), 45–54.

53 Benjamin R. Barber, "The Discourse of Civility," in *Citizen Competence and Democratic Institutions*, ed. Stephen L. Elkin and Karol Edward Soltan (University Park, PA: Pennsylvania State University Press, 1999), 44–5.

54 Jennifer Sumner, *Sustainability and the Civil Commons: Rural Communities in the Age of Globalization* (Toronto: University of Toronto Press, 2005), 12.

55 McMurtry, *Unequal Freedoms*, 19, 298.

56 Ibid., 24.

57 Ibid., 23.

58 Sumner, *Sustainability and the Civil Commons*, 113–14.

59 John McMurtry, "The Life Code of Value and the Civil Commons: A Reply to Three Educators," *Interchange* 32, 3 (2001): 264–5.

60 A.N. Whitehead, *Modes of Thought* (New York: The Free Press, 1966), 166.

61 Whitehead, *Adventures of Ideas*, 285.

62 Cobb, "Beyond Essays," 106.

Index

Aberman, Arnold, 122–3
aboriginal, 252
above all, do no harm
  (*primum non nocere*),
  115
academic freedom: and
  administrators, 6; of
  author, 3; in Britain,
  20; in Canadian Asso-
  ciation of University
  Teachers (CAUT), 55;
  in Canadian organi-
  zations, 39; in clinical
  context, 117–19; and
  commercial values,
  21; contracting of, 20;
  for critical understanding, 38, 40–1, 57;
  as defined by Horn,
  73; as defined by
  Somerville, 118; defi-
  nition of, 135; defini-
  tive of, 73; of Dr
  Olivieri, 100–3, 105,
  108, 117, 132, 141;
  of Dr Olivieri, Gallie,
  Durie, and Chan, 100–
  3, 108; importance
  of, 38–9; and inclusive

university, 11; and
  individual liberty, 42;
  as integral part of
  university, 11; for learning, 43; and market,
  119–25; and market
  model, 39; and politi-
  cal correctness, 11; as
  related to institutional
  autonomy, 4; and
  Renaud, 33, 38; social
  limits to, 71; of stu-
  dents undermined, 211;
  threats to, 10–11, 42–
  3, 215; weakening of,
  12. *See also* market
  model; universities
academic freedom week,
  188
academic skills, 25, 26
ACE, 140
Agriculture Canada, 151
Agri-Food Canada, 151
AgWest Biotech, 163
Allahar, Anton, 9, 203,
  214
American Association
  for the Advancement
  of Science, 101

American Society of
  Hematology (ASH),
  124
Angell, Marcia, 118
Angus, Ian, 45, 76
Animal Biotechnology
  Group, 159
anonymous, 106–7
Apotex Inc: articles on
  Website, 127; dispute
  with Dr Olivieri, 91;
  donation to Univer-
  sity of Manitoba, 126;
  history of, 125–31;
  investment in Univer-
  sity of Toronto's Fac-
  ulty of Pharmacy, 129;
  letters, 120–1; relationship with Naimark,
  57; statement on liver
  biopsy, 105
Areva, 171
*argumentum ad hominem
  (fallacy)*, 67
Arthur, Chris, 43
ASH (American Society
  of Hematology),
  124
Associates program, 48